LITERARY KNOWING AND THE MAKING OF ENGLISH TEACHERS

At a time when knowledge is being 're-valued' as central to curriculum concerns, subject English is being called to account. *Literary Knowing and the Making of English Teachers* puts long-standing debates about knowledge and knowing in English in dialogue with an investigation of how English teachers are made in the 21st century.

This book explores, for the first time, the role of literature in shaping English teachers' professional knowledge and identities by examining the impacts, in particular, of their own school teaching in their 'making'. The voices of early career English teachers feature throughout the work, in a series of vignettes providing reflective accounts of their professional learning. The authors bring a range of disciplinary expertise and standpoints to explore the complexity of knowledge and knowing in English. They ask: How do English teachers negotiate competing curriculum demands? How do they understand literary knowledge in a neoliberal context? What is core English knowledge for students, and what role should literature play in the contemporary curriculum? Drawing on a major longitudinal research project, they bring to light what English teachers see as central to their work, the ways they connect teaching with their disciplinary training, and how their understandings of literary practice are contested and reimagined in the classroom.

This innovative work is essential reading for scholars and postgraduate students in the fields of teacher education, English education, literary studies and curriculum studies.

Larissa McLean Davies is Professor of Teacher Education in the Melbourne Graduate School of Education, at the University of Melbourne. Larissa's research is concerned with the way teachers' knowledge is developed across the career span, and specifically with how disciplinary knowledge is understood in the context of decolonising curricula imperatives. To this end, she leads substantive priority projects in partnership with Australian Federal, State and Territory Governments which support the development of teacher knowledge and practice in diverse social, geographical and disciplinary contexts. She has published widely in the areas of teacher education and English curriculum and is known for her work at the intersection of literary studies and English education. She was the Lead CI of the Australian Research Council funded project *Investigating Literary Knowledge in the Making of English Teachers*, is a former editor of *English in Australia*, and is co-founder of the Literary Education Lab: https://literaryeducationlab.org/.

Brenton Doecke is Emeritus Professor in the Faculty of Arts and Education at Deakin University. He has published widely in the fields of English education, teacher education and literary studies. He is a former editor of *English in Australia*, the journal of the Australian Association for the Teaching of English (AATE) and is currently a co-editor of *Changing English*. He played a leading role, with Margaret Gill, in developing the Standards for Teachers of English Language and Literature in Australia (STELLA), a joint project involving both the AATE and the Australian Literacy Educators' Association (ALEA). His books include *Literary Praxis: A Conversational Inquiry into the Teaching of Literature* (Springer, 2011), co-edited with Piet-Hein van de Ven; *Confronting Practice: Classroom Investigations into Language and Learning* (Phoenix Education, 2011), co-authored with Douglas McClenaghan; and *Becoming a Teacher of Language and Literacy* (Cambridge University Press, 2014), co-edited with Glenn Auld and Muriel Wells. Brenton is a life member of the Australian Association for the Teaching of English and the Victorian Association for the Teaching of English.

Philip Mead was inaugural Chair of Australian Literature at the University of Western Australia (2009–2018). He is currently Emeritus Chair in Australian Literature, University of Western Australia, and Honorary Professorial Fellow in the Melbourne Graduate School of Education, University of Melbourne. From 2009–2010 Philip was Ludwig Hirschfeld-Mack Visiting Chair of Interdisciplinary Australian Studies, at the Free University, Berlin and in 2015–2016 was Gough Whitlam and Malcolm Fraser Visiting Professor of Australian Studies at Harvard University. Philip has published in the areas of national and transnational literary studies, Indigenous literatures, cultural history and theory, poetics, literary education, and digital humanities. In 2018 Philip published *Antipodal Shakespeare: Remembering and Forgetting in Britain, Australia and New Zealand, 1916–2016* with Gordon McMullan (Arden/Bloomsbury, 2018) and *The Social Work of Narrative: Human Rights and the Cultural Imaginary*, co-edited with Gareth Griffiths (Columbia University Press, 2018). He is currently editing, with Professor Ann Vickery of Deakin University, the *Cambridge History of Australian Poetry*.

Wayne Sawyer is Emeritus Professor in the School of Education at Western Sydney University. Before joining WSU, Wayne was a secondary school Head of English. He is a past President of the New South Wales (NSW) English Teachers Association (ETA) and past Chair of the NSW Board of Studies English

Curriculum Committee. He is an Honorary Life Member of both the NSW ETA and the Australian Association for the Teaching of English, and a former editor of *English in Australia*. Wayne's doctoral research was on English curriculum history in NSW and he currently researches in the areas of secondary English curriculum, curriculum history, literacy policy, literary knowledge, and pedagogy in low SES schools. His most recent books include *Charged with Meaning: Becoming an English Teacher* (Phoenix Education, 2019) and the co-edited, *The Future of English Teaching Worldwide: Celebrating 50 Years from the Dartmouth Conference* (Routledge, 2018). He is currently co-editing a book on teacher education in English for Routledge.

Lyn Yates' long-standing research interests have been in the possibilities and constraints of institutional education, both schooling and post-school education. Her work has included a range of research on curriculum and the schooling experience as shapers of identity, and of gender- and class-based inequalities and opportunities within this. It has also included many essays and analyses of changing education policies, both in Australia and internationally, with particular attention to knowledge and social change, and to the longer-term implications of how the roles of schools and universities are being understood and enacted. Lyn is now Redmond Barry Distinguished Professor Emeritus at the University of Melbourne. Her major books include *Making Modern Lives* (with Julie McLeod) (Suny Press, 2006), *What Does Good Education Research Look Like?* (McGraw-Hill Education, 2004), *Curriculum in Today's World* (with Madeleine Grumet) (Routledge, 2011) and *Knowledge at the Crossroads?* (with Peter Woelert, Victoria Millar and Kate O'Connor) (Springer, 2017).

LITERARY KNOWING AND THE MAKING OF ENGLISH TEACHERS

The Role of Literature in Shaping English Teachers' Professional Knowledge and Identities

Larissa McLean Davies, Brenton Doecke, Philip Mead, Wayne Sawyer and Lyn Yates

Routledge
Taylor & Francis Group

LONDON AND NEW YORK

Cover image: © oxygen/Getty Images

First published 2023
by Routledge
4 Park Square, Milton Park, Abingdon, Oxon OX14 4RN

and by Routledge
605 Third Avenue, New York, NY 10158

Routledge is an imprint of the Taylor & Francis Group, an informa business

British Library Cataloguing-in-Publication Data
A catalogue record for this book is available from the British Library

ISBN: 978-0-367-61863-6 (hbk)
ISBN: 978-0-367-61868-1 (pbk)
ISBN: 978-1-003-10689-0 (ebk)

DOI: 10.4324/9781003106890

Typeset in Bembo
by Taylor & Francis Books

CONTENTS

ACKNOWLEDGEMENTS

The research project that inspired this book was supported by an Australian Research Council Discovery Project (**DP160101084**) funded by the Australian Government. The views expressed herein are those of the authors and are not necessarily those of the Australian Research Council.

The voices and perspectives of early career English teachers are at the heart of this project. We would like to sincerely thank the teachers who were part of our study for three years, who allowed us to walk alongside them in their first years of practice, and generously shared their insights on issues of knowledge, literature and professional identity. Beyond this core group, we are also grateful for the many English teachers who were part of our study through focus groups, the survey and interviews, and acknowledge the literary studies academics, teacher educators, curriculum authority, and teacher accreditation authority, representatives and members of professional English teaching associations who offered important perspectives on questions of literature and knowledge, and enabled us to explore the complex network contributing to the 'making' of English teachers.

A project of this nature is not completed without an excellent team. The authors would like to thank Dr Lucy Buzacott, who was an outstanding, intellectually involved Research and Project Manager over the course of the study and assisted with initial drafts of Chapters and Vignettes. We also acknowledge the significant contribution of Prue Adams (Lead Research Assistant) and thank Dr Trish Dowsett and Claire Jones for valued research support. We extend our gratitude to Professor Bill Green for his critical engagement with 'the knowledge question' and our work, and Dr Michele Hinton Herrington for her patient and professional assistance with the preparation of this book for publication. We would also like to thank each of our universities for their ongoing support of the project: the University of Melbourne, Western Sydney University, Deakin University and the University of Western Australia. Our thanks go to the Melbourne Graduate School of Education for housing the project, for funding an associated post-doctoral position, and for assisting with public events and meetings.

This book was written during the COVID-19 pandemic under sometimes extensive lockdowns. We would like to acknowledge the support of our families and friends during this period of isolated writing, and the value of regular online team meetings in providing stimulating and productive conversation over the many months of confinement.

GLOSSARY OF KEY TERMS / ABBREVIATIONS

ACARA: Australian Curriculum, Assessment and Reporting Authority: the national authority in Australia which oversees the *Australian Curriculum*, national standardised testing through NAPLAN and the *My School* website, which gives an overview of each school in Australia, including its NAPLAN results.

AC:E: Australian Curriculum: English

AITSL: Australian Institute for Teaching and School Leadership: the national body responsible for accreditation standards for teachers and accreditation of pre-service teacher education.

ATAR: Australian Tertiary Admissions Rank: a ranking given to Australian students based on their end-of-schooling credential which ranks them for university entrance requirements by indicating their position relative to all the students completing their final year of schooling in the same year..

Australian Curriculum, Assessment and Reporting Authority: see **ACARA**

EALD: English as an Additional Language or Dialect

Higher School Certificate: see **HSC**

HSC: Higher School Certificate: the two-year, end-of-schooling credential in the State of New South Wales, Australia.

NAPLAN: National Assessment Program: Literacy and Numeracy: the national standardised testing instrument in Australia for literacy and numeracy.

NESA: New South Wales Education Standards Authority: the body that sets curriculum in the State of NSW. NESA also accredits PSTE courses, oversees initial teacher accreditation, approves teacher professional development courses and oversees professional standards for teachers. Overseeing both curriculum and teacher accreditation and training has previously been unusual.

NSW: New South Wales

PSTE: Pre-service Teacher Education

VCE: Victorian Certificate of Education: the two-year, end-of-schooling credential in the State of Victoria, Australia.

Victorian Certificate of Education: see **VCE**

WACE: Western Australian Certificate of Education: the two-year, end-of-schooling credential in the State of Western Australia, Australia.

Western Australian Certificate of Education: see **WACE**

1

KNOWLEDGE, MAKING AND ENGLISH TEACHERS

Larissa McLean Davies and Wayne Sawyer

Prologue

When we commenced this book, we could not have imagined that most of the book's authors, like its readers, would eventually experience extended times in lockdown due to the COVID-19 pandemic. Much has been said about teachers' work and student learning as a result of the pandemic, and English teaching journals and professional associations led the way both in supporting the profession to make sense of the experience, and resourcing English teachers in the day-to-day, as they took their classrooms online (Marstaller, 2020; Yandell, 2020). It is not our purpose to focus on this specifically, but it is worth drawing attention to one of the many insights that the COVID period has offered us. At a time when standardised tests, in countries such as Australia, were temporarily paused, curriculum content was reduced, and assessment expectations more generally scaled back (for general discussion, see Hughes, 2020), many people – children, adults and families – undoubtedly took to reading. In part, this was because there was more discretionary time available, no commutes, or other regularly scheduled activities outside the house. However, there was another aspect to the turn to text. Boucher et al. reported that in the early months of the pandemic, 'Books about (literal and metaphorical) isolation, like Sylvia Plath's *The Bell Jar* and Gabriel García Marquez's novels *One Hundred Years of Solitude* and *Love in the Time of Cholera* saw an increased uptake in sales' (Boucher et al., 2020).

As individuals across the world attempted to understand their situation, a (so far) once-in-a-hundred-year phenomenon that saw restriction of movement, curfews, masks, 'checking in' via QR codes and limited contact with others, literary texts offered a way of taking us outside our immediate contexts. Indeed, for some people, literature came into its own, as a means of knowing, or understanding, that could be sustaining and transformative, and at the same time make sense of an

DOI: 10.4324/9781003106890-1

experience that had no lived reference points. This was the case for the senior secondary students in English teacher Dan Forstner's class in Minneapolis, and indeed for Forstner himself. Faced with an International Baccalaureate class he could only see as boxes on a screen, Forstner decided to set a reading assignment around Albert Camus' *The Plague* (Heim, 2020). Ironically, amidst the now-familiar weight of neoliberalism and its attendant accountability cultures (Power, 1997; Rose, 1999), the conditions of the pandemic disrupted the curriculum and assessment routine and enabled Forstner to offer a different type of reading experience.

Speaking to the *Washington Post*, Forstner noted that the choice was a 'leap of faith' (Heim, 2020), but that he had engaged with the text in college, and his interest had been renewed by an essay recently written about the book by philosopher Alain de Botton (de Botton, 2020), linking it to the COVID-19 pandemic. Forstner and a colleague ran discussions about the book throughout the online learning period. Initially, the Washburn High School students were unimpressed with the weighty philosophical text and feared it would make their experience of isolation more acute. However, through conversation, both in the online class, and outside with locked-down family members, they came to some shared, and some different, understandings of the text and its relevance. For one student it was inspirational; for another, it reflected humanity's inability to learn from history; and for another, it made clear that hope and despair are at once ever-present in the day to day business of living.

We refer to this story at the start of this book because it gestures to the potential and importance of literary knowing and meaning-making, for both students and teachers in our current moment, which are core to our concerns and interests. It also raises key questions that are central to our inquiry here, about the nature of the knowledge that students and their teachers are creating in English classrooms; about the sociable nature of literary knowing and the institutional and curricula conditions that create or limit this; and importantly for our focus, about ways in which teachers and their literary knowledges and experiences are shaped. This book is prompted by a desire to take up these questions, and in this chapter, we briefly outline the background, context and intentions of the book, the study on which it is based, and the ways readers might approach it.

English, literature, and knowledge – outlining the tensions

As a secondary school subject, English is considered fundamental to an individual's personal, cultural and literate development, and literary studies has been viewed, historically, as a core component of the subject (Goodwyn, 2012; Peel & Hargraves, 1995). Indeed, it is literature, and the opportunity to read it and teach it, that has usually been seen as the key motivator for those wishing to become English teachers (Doecke & McKnight, 2003; Patterson, 2000; Peel, 2000a). Yet, although literature in the school curriculum is valued both by English teachers and their students (and also governments and regulators), the knowledge that provides its foundations, as well as that of the broader subject, 'English', sits within a history of contestation.

Part of this contestation seems inherent in the nature of the English subject itself. As has been well discussed since its inception, English has held a paradoxical role in the curriculum (Yates et al., 2019). It is at once the only subject mandated throughout the years of schooling and charged with preparing students 'for life' (Protherough & Atkinson, 1991, p.1), but at the same time is a curriculum area that has been difficult to define in terms of purpose and content. At the Dartmouth conference, James Britton famously characterised English as 'what is left' after other parts of the 'curriculum tart' such as geography, history and science have been 'cut out' (Britton, 1966, p.12). His contemporary Harold Rosen referred to English as 'the least subject-like of subjects, the least susceptible to the definition by reference to the accumulation of wisdom within a single academic discipline… No one can confidently map its frontiers' (Rosen, 1981, p.5). Protherough and Atkinson were still arguing in the 1990s that 'the boundaries of the subject are notoriously unclear and cannot be neatly defined' (Protherough & Atkinson, 1991, p.16) and in the early 21st century Peel could still assert that '(f)rom its earliest days as a school and university subject English has been concerned with attempts to define itself' (Peel, 2000c, p.1). What might follow from this are issues picked up further in this chapter and, indeed, throughout the book.

This historical difficulty of defining school English can be traced to its often uneasy relationship with the tertiary discipline of literary studies, which is constantly in a state of flux – a position which may be characterised as 'unstable', or rather seen as a state of continual renewal. In more recent decades, English departments are, like the humanities more generally, fighting for survival in a context which prioritises tertiary study that appears to support clearer pathways to employment (Duffy, 2020). Indeed, such departments in many universities no longer have the title 'English'. Somewhat ironically, in this context, governments and teacher education regulators in Australia demand that those aspiring to become English teachers have had a strong disciplinary grounding in literature to meet the entry requirement of postgraduate Initial Teacher Education Programs (AITSL, 2018; NESA, 2018; VIT, 2013), and for employment. Yet, the nature of this disciplinary experience is not consistent, nor do the grounds of the education it provides immediately transfer to specific *knowledge*, especially in the more junior years of secondary school.

The challenge of defining school English means that questions of knowledge in this school subject can play out differently from other subjects, as the statements from Britton and Rosen above have suggested. The Bullock Report, *A Language for Life*, argued in 1975 that subject English in general 'does not hold together as a body of knowledge which can be identified, quantified, then transmitted' (DES, 1975, p.5). In 1980, Medway argued that English constituted 'nothing less than a different model of education' that included 'educational processes to be embarked on with outcomes unpredictable' and 'students' perceptions, experiences and unsystematically acquired knowledge admitted as legitimate curricular content' (Medway, 1980, p.10).

Is English in general, and literary study in particular, then, 'without' knowledge? In fact, there are many examples of the different ways literature specifically might be understood epistemologically (for a brief survey, see Sawyer & McLean Davies,

2021) and constructed as a form of knowledge, or as a form of 'knowing' – yet most such discussions depend on broader, and not necessarily shared, definitions of what constitutes 'knowledge'. In recent times, we have seen increased attention to the role and nature of 'knowledge' in the curriculum, resulting in further contestation over the curriculum generally (for discussion see Doecke et al., 2021; Yandell, 2017; Yates et al., 2019). This has come about through government attention, particularly in the UK (United Kingdom), to notions of 'powerful knowledge' presented by Michael Young and colleagues, which have sought to redress a curriculum that has been said to focus more on transferable skills, rather than on subject epistemologies. Young and his collaborators argue knowledge transmission is the primary purpose of schooling and are concerned with the kind of knowledge which schooling offers – concerns that go to the purposes of education. They have made particular claims that certain forms of knowledge, derived from the academic disciplines, are the most 'powerful' (Moore & Muller, 1999; Muller & Young, 2019; Young & Muller, 2010). Much has been said about the limitations of their initial thinking for disciplines other than science (Barrett et al., 2018; Yates et al., 2017; Yates, 2018) and particularly about English (Doecke & Mead, 2017; Yates et al., 2019). These critiques are partly to do with the privileging of propositional knowledge, and a lack of recognition that knowledge may be necessarily constituted in other forms. However, Young's ideas have been taken up strongly in the UK and have been connected, in terms of school English, with conservative educators such as E. D. Hirsch, who seeks to position English within a project of knowledge about cultural touchstones, such as 'great works' (Hirsch, 1989).

While there is reason to question whether Young's model of the relationship between subject and discipline is adequate to explain the connections between English and literary studies – or, indeed, to question such notions of 'powerful' knowledge, this book nonetheless recognises the importance of conversations about knowledge, and ways of knowing, and recognises a value in engaging with these, despite, and perhaps because of, the inherent challenges of the subject as outlined above. This is particularly the case in settler contexts, such as Australia, from where we are writing – where imperatives to decolonise curriculum (McLean Davies & Buzacott, 2021) challenge us to think anew about the purposes, structures and knowledges being experienced by students in a subject such as English, the understandings teachers are bringing to their classrooms, and how these develop and are mobilised.

Making teachers, making English – an ongoing inquiry

If we make an argument about English as a subject that is partly locally contextualised, and epistemologically constituted largely through texts and conversations, then the role and positioning of teachers are fundamentally important. This focus on English teachers, and how they are made, has often been at the heart of discussions about the English curriculum area. It was a major concern in the Newbolt Report (Newbolt, 1921) and has been taken up by several scholarly studies which pre-date this book. Margaret Mathieson's well-known (1975) study, *The Preachers of Culture*, explored this terrain and argued that English teachers had often been positioned as moral and social missionaries in the classroom, with their role as shaping the sensibilities of future citizens. Being charged with core responsibilities for the moral and ethical, as well as with the creative, critical and aesthetic development of students places a similarly strong focus on the role of teachers. Within a British context, Protherough and Atkinson explored pre-service teacher education in *The Making of English Teachers* (1991), and Peel, Patterson and Gerlach also took up this theme with respect to England, Australia and America, in *Questions of English* (2000). Taken together, these books offer insight into the 'making' of English teachers' practice, knowledge and identities, particularly throughout the 20th century. Most interestingly, a set of questions posed by Protherough and Atkinson at the beginning of their book remain centrally relevant to our concerns here:

> What does it … mean to be an English teacher; what does such a person know and do? What qualifies one for such a role? How do English teachers come to be? … what forces help to shape them? … How do they actually view the nature of the ill-defined subject and the work they do in it? What gives them a sense of identity?
> *(Protherough & Atkinson, 1991, p.1)*

Yet, having noted the ongoing relevance of these questions we argue that there is a particular need to open these conversations in light of the global policy imperatives in which we are currently operating, and which continue to shape the work of teachers and the nature of subject English in contemporary classrooms.

The global and local policy contexts

While Protherough and Atkinson give an account of a subject that is focused on 'the individual and personal' (Protherough & Atkinson, 1991, p.15), they characterise the 1980s in the UK as a time when 'the language of morality and the imagination with concern for human values was squeezed out in favour of balance-sheet economics' (p.30). Similarly, ten years later Peel particularly highlights the individual at the centre of subject English as being 'the individual as consumer, not the individual as conceived by Romantic theory', with their 'transferable skills' as 'the cultural capital which society demands' (Peel, 2000b, p.109). In this third decade of the 21st century, the policy and ideological landscapes shaping the studies of Protherough and Atkinson, and Peel et al have shifted again. We live in a period in which the Global Education Reform Movement ('GERM': Sahlberg, 2011) has become well-established, and dominates especially the majority-English-speaking cultures. For Sahlberg (2011), GERM is characterised, among other things, by: standardisation; increased focus on core subjects, especially literacy and numeracy; international standardised testing; centrally prescribed curricula; corporate models of change management and high-stakes accountability. All of this, of course, is part of wider social policy shifts within what has been termed the global 'audit culture' (Power, 1997), the 'technology of performativity' (Ball, 2003, p.216) and 'policy as numbers' (Rose, 1999).

Though relevant States such as the US (United States), UK and Australia strongly subscribe to this policy environment in general terms, and often very similarly in terms of detail, not all take-up is identical. Though not unique, one particularly dominant feature of GERM in Australia is universal standardised testing, with the media publishing 'league tables' based on schools' results – with consequences for schools' reputations and demand around enrolments. Results in PISA (Programme for International Student Assessment) and similar international testing promote a media feeding frenzy, as do results in national testing. For some time now, Australia has epitomised the marketisation of education with a flight from public schools leading to 'greater socioeconomic segregation (in education)… in which the average socioeconomic status of advantaged schools (was) increasing' (Erebus International, 2005, p.13; see also Bonnor & Caro, 2007, p.116; Firth & Huntley, 2014; Lawrence, 2012). The relevance of that testing and its consequences for this book is particularly in the area of literacy.

Just as it has this GERM-related focus on literacy and its testing, so too has Australia developed its first national centralised curriculum, the relevant aspect of which here is the *Australian Curriculum: English* (AC:E) (ACARA, 2016a, 2016b). It is worth noting that in Australia this national curriculum was developed after the implementation of national literacy testing (Doecke et al., 2018). Though individual States in Australia's federal system can make decisions on how the Australian Curriculum is implemented, all its Outcomes need to be accounted for in those State curricula. As might be expected, the development of the *Australian Curriculum: English* in a federalised system was particularly fraught (Doecke et al., 2018). One of the key dimensions of the debate was around the so-called 'return' of literature as a key organising principle of the subject, alongside literacy and language, but specific references to knowledge in the curriculum tend to focus on knowledge about language underpinning literacy, with the association of knowledge with literature being less directly articulated (McLean Davies & Sawyer, 2018).

Pre-service teacher education (PSTE) has also come under significant constraint, strongly reflecting the bureaucratised discourse of GERM. In Australia, AITSL (the Australian Institute for Teaching and School Leadership) oversees 'Professional Standards for Teachers', divided into career levels. For 'Graduate Level', these are attached to 'Accreditation Standards and Procedures' for pre-service teacher education programs. These latter have morphed into 'Program Standards', which mandate 'Program outcomes', 'Program development, design and delivery', 'Program entry', 'Professional experience' and 'Program evaluation, reporting and improvement'. Between these centrally mandated Standards and those aspects of teacher education that are intended to reflect local syllabus content or local policy imperatives, a major proportion of the content of PSTE is mandated outside the institution which delivers it. In the last decade alone, there have been more than 15 new and revised policies, frameworks, and regulatory and compliance requirements for PSTE across Australia.

Arguments for the principles of professional teaching standards and regulatory frameworks around PSTE have partly emphasised the elevation of the status of teaching and PSTE programs, to which such standards may contribute.

Nevertheless, what is contestable is the wholesale standardisation of the complex, heterogeneous and context-contingent nature of teachers' work (see Mills & Goos, 2017). The Australian Professional Standards for Teachers (AITSL, 2018), like the standardisation of PTSE programs, reflects a universal formula for producing a kind of 'ideal' teacher, defined in terms of measurable performance indicators that take no account of the rich diversity of teachers' and students' contexts and resources, or the discipline-specific knowledge, skills and pedagogies of each curriculum area. The reforms can be understood in the context of a pervasive political 'hyper narrative of declining standards of student achievement and teacher quality' (Kennedy, 2014, p.691). In Australia, just as in the UK, and the US, aspects of literacy teaching are weaponised in media and political attacks on teacher education (see, for example, Baker, 2020; Gannon & Sawyer, 2015; Urban, 2021). The issue for this book is how we might conceptualise the making of English teachers within this overall policy environment.

The research informing the book

The research informing this book was generated through a four-year Australian Research Council funded project entitled *Investigating literary knowledge in the making of English teachers*. The overall project's key research questions were specifically concerned with the role of literary knowledge (however that might be understood) within secondary English curriculum and pedagogy, and the ways that institutional and social contexts, such as tertiary study and teaching experience, shape early career English teachers' literary knowledge.

To address these aims and questions, our research approach had several components. Central to the research was a longitudinal study of 24 early career English teachers[1] in the Australian States of Victoria, New South Wales, and Western Australia. These States were chosen because of the strong (but different) history each has had regarding a focus on the teaching of literature. In the end-of-schooling credentials in Victoria and Western Australia, for example, 'Literature' exists as a separate study and is able to be undertaken as well as 'English' and in New South Wales, all such senior 'English' courses are literature focused. We interviewed these teachers at first in their second or third years of teaching, and then in each of the following two years.

So that we might better understand the institutional forces that shape and 'make' English teachers' sense of literary knowledge and professional identity, we also interviewed professors of literary studies, prominent academics in English Education, officers of teacher accreditation authorities, officers from national and State-based curriculum authorities, representatives of English teacher professional associations and Heads of literary studies associations, along with cohorts of teachers in mid-career. Interviews with this latter group also enabled us to further explore and add nuance to our interpretation of the accounts of practice that were emerging through the longitudinal study. All interviews were transcribed and coded using NVivo software, as an aid to later interpretive work. In this book, pseudonyms are used for all interviewees. In addition to the interviews, we administered a national survey of English teachers, the first of its size in Australia, with over 700 respondents.

The notion of teachers' literary knowledge, or 'knowing' (Doecke et al., 2021) as being 'made' (Reid, 1984) rather than 'received', evident in our methodological approach, was also reflected in our decision to investigate the potential of literary sociability to explain the kinds of meaning-making that takes place in English classrooms. This concept was first developed in the field of literary studies (Kasprisin, 1987; Kirkpatrick & Dixon, 2012), where it gained traction because it opened ways of understanding diverse relations between texts and readers. 'Literary sociability' positions the nature of reading and the uses of literature in interpersonal, social, historically situated and institutionally mediated practice (Guillory, 1993), and supports analysis which is concerned with both the particular properties of literary texts that enable meanings to be made sociably and the activities and practices which animate these meanings. Some of the book's authors had adapted literary sociability in earlier research (McLean Davies et al., 2013), and the possibilities of this framework have been further explored throughout the course of the research project itself (Doecke, 2019; Mead et al., 2020; Mello et al., 2019) and are consequently taken up and debated in various chapters throughout the book.

This book has its boundaries. In it, we focus on the longitudinal study and the early career English teachers. It is the stories shared by these teachers that inspire the substantive discussions throughout the book's mainstream chapters. The survey and interviews with those other groups influencing, and/or invested in, the teaching of English are referred to in different parts of the book to illuminate the discussion of those teachers participating in the longitudinal study. Additionally, we are primarily concerned with the 'making' of English teachers as that 'making' occurs and changes in the early career phase – rather than being centrally focused on pre-service teacher education (as in the case of the earlier work of, say, Protherough & Atkinson, 1991; Peel et al., 2000) and with the place of literary knowledge in that early experience.

Multivocality and the book's structure and approach

It is important to emphasise that the project, and this book, ranged across a number of fields, working at the intersections of subject English, teacher education, literary and curriculum studies. We speak about the different perspectives that each author brought to the project in Chapter 2 and again at the conclusion. This means that while the book has been jointly planned around key ideas, themes and concerns regarding literary knowledge and the making of English teachers, individual authors have taken up these concepts and tensions in small teams, or individually, in the following chapters in ways which reflect the disciplinary backgrounds, questions and/or theoretical perspectives which have informed their research interests and positions. This approach resonates with Bakhtin's idea that language exists within a polyphonic, many-voiced network, a heteroglossia, which recognises that individual utterances (Bakhtin, 1981, 1993) must be taken together for meaning to be made.

Interleaved throughout the chapters are vignettes depicting various ways in which the early career English teachers who took part in our study have experienced their entry into the profession. The vignettes, like others created through our research (Truman et al., 2020, 2021), are pen portraits, rendered in an 'expressive realist' mode. Sitting apart from the themes and concerns which characterise the mainstream chapters, these vignettes give a unique perspective on the work of these teachers as told to us over a series of interviews. It is the series that is important here: the vignettes give the reader access to a longer-term account of these teachers' work by presenting those stories more directly in terms of what they said and emphasised over that total set of interviews. Any large claim we might make about a literary education emerges through an interplay between the interpretive frameworks we have brought to our inquiry and the particularities of these teachers' experiences.

What principles of selection informed our choice of interviewees for these vignettes? All the early career English teachers who took part in our study provided reflective accounts of their professional learning, and the stories they each told us might form the basis for further pen portraits that would convey an even richer sense of the diversity of their experiences. The emphasis in the selection we have made has been on acknowledging diversity in terms of motivation to become an English teacher and in terms of pathways to the profession. The vignettes should in no way be taken as 'representative' of particular points of view, but, at best, as reflective of this diversity. Taken together, their stories register difference rather than sameness, generating a different impression of the making of English teachers from what has underpinned some earlier studies, such as Mathieson's *Preachers of Culture*.

While the book is designed in such a way as to reflect diverse perspectives and multivocality, the chapters also unfold in a way that moves from consideration of the debates and issues informing the book, towards a close analysis of the perspectives of participants in our study, to what this means for our understanding of a literary education and the teaching of English in current times. Specifically:

- Chapter 2, as we have said, introduces the different perspectives that each author brought to the project.
- Chapters 3–5 offer historical and theoretical perspectives on some of the key issues that are informing and being extended through this book. Chapter 3 explores debates about knowledge and school English; Chapter 4 follows with an analysis of the way curriculum questions about knowledge intersect with our inquiry, and Chapter 5 offers a historical perspective on the discipline of English in Australia, and how this has informed the teaching of the school subject.
- Chapters 6–7 look at the ways understandings of literary knowledge were expressed by participants in our research. Chapter 6 explores the tensions and synergies between understandings of literary knowledge as articulated by literary studies academics, teacher educators and English education bureaucrats, and Chapter 7 turns to the ways the early career English teachers in our study responded to, and conceptualised, literary knowledge in their practice over the period of our study.

- Chapters 8–10 then take up the ways literary knowledge or knowing might be understood in the context of the 'making' of English teachers. Chapter 8 explores how literary sociability can offer us new ways of framing literary knowing in school English; Chapter 9 takes up the ways in which assessment and text selection serve as substitutes for literary knowledge in English; and Chapter 10 looks at the tensions between literature and literacy, and the implication for 'knowing' in English.
- Chapters 11 and 12 turn to questions of curriculum and English teachers' identity. Chapter 11 brings together questions of knowledge and making central to our study by examining early career English teachers' negotiation of the curriculum in the context of classroom practice, and Chapter 12 examines the way teachers cross institutional boundaries to negotiate their identity as English teachers.
- The final chapter again brings together each of the authors to consider how their initial conceptualisations have changed through the course of the project, the writing of the book and other publications from this research – and what this might mean for the fields of English teaching and literary studies going forward.

Note

1 This study interviewed 24 early career English teachers over three years of the project. A further 16 teachers were interviewed once in the first year of the project and this group was known as 'Cohort 2' and were included to supplement the longitudinal study and to allow for attrition in the longitudinal group.

References

Australian Curriculum, Assessment & Reporting Authority (ACARA). (2016a). *Australian Curriculum: English*. Available: www.acara.edu.au/_resources/English_-_Sequence_of_content.pdf. Accessed 20 April 2022.

Australian Curriculum, Assessment & Reporting Authority (ACARA). (2016b). *Australian Curriculum: English*. Available: www.australiancurriculum.edu.au/english/structure. Accessed 20 April 2022.

Australian Institute for Teaching and School Leadership (AITSL). (2018). *Australian Professional Standards for Teachers*. Carlton South: Education Services Australia. Available: www.aitsl.edu.au/docs/default-source/national-policy-framework/australian-professional-standards-for-teachers.pdf. Accessed 27 May 2021.

Baker, J. (2020). Phonics check to be compulsory as minister declares reading wars won. *Sydney Morning Herald*, 30 November. Available: www.smh.com.au/national/phonics-check-to-be-compulsory-as-minister-declares-reading-wars-won-20201127-p56iol.html. Accessed 21 September 2021.

Bakhtin, M. M. (1981). *The Dialogic Imagination: Four Essays*. M. Holquist (Ed.). Austin: University of Texas Press.

Bakhtin, M. M. (1993). *Speech Genres, and Other Late Essays*. C. Emerson and M. Holquist (Eds.). Austin: University of Texas Press.

Ball, S. J. (2003). The teacher's soul and the terrors of performativity. *Journal of Education Policy*, 18(2), 215–228. https://doi.org/10.1080/0268093022000043065.

Barrett, B., Hoadley, U., & Morgan, J. (2018). *Knowledge, Curriculum and Equity: Social Realist Perspectives*. London: Routledge.

Bonnor, C., & Caro, J. (2007). *The Stupid Country: How Australia is Dismantling Public Education*. Sydney: University of New South Wales Press.

Boucher, A., Harrison, C., & Giovanelli, M. (2020). How reading habits have changed during the COVID-19 lockdown. *The Conversation*. Available: https://theconversation.com/how-reading-habits-have-changed-during-the-covid-19-lockdown-146894. Accessed November 22 202.

Britton, J. (1966). Response to Working Party Paper I: 'What is English?' In A. R. Kitzhaber et al., *Working Party Paper No1; Response, Report to the Seminar, and Supporting Papers One through Six*, ERIC document number ED082201. Available: http://files.eric.ed.gov/fulltext/ED082201.pdf. Accessed 21 November 2021.

de Botton, A. (2020). Camus on the coronavirus. *The New York Times*, 19 March. Available: www.nytimes.com/2020/03/19/opinion/sunday/coronavirus-camus-plague.html. Accessed 20 April 2022.

Department for Education (DFE). (2013). *The National Curriculum in England Framework Document*. London: Department for Education. Available: www.gov.uk/government/uploads/system/uploads/attachment_data/file/210969/NC_framework_document_-_FINAL.pdf. Accessed 20 April 2022.

Department of Education and Science (DES). (1975). *A Language for Life: Report of the Committee of Inquiry appointed by the Secretary of State for Education and Science under the Chairmanship of Sir Allan Bullock F.B.A.* London: Her Majesty's Stationery Office.

Doecke, B. (2019). Rewriting the history of subject English through the lens of "literary sociability". *Changing English*, 26(4), 339–356. https://doi.org/10.1080/1358684X.2019.1649116.

Doecke, B., & McKnight, L. (2003). Handling irony: Forming a professional identity as an English teacher. In B. Doecke, D. Homer, & H. Nixon (Eds.), *English Teachers at Work: Narratives, Counter Narratives and Arguments*. Kent Town: Wakefield Press: 291–311.

Doecke, B., McLean Davies, L., & Sawyer, W. (2018). Blowing and blundering in space: English in the Australian Curriculum. In A. Reid & D. Price (Eds.), *The Australian Curriculum: Promises, Problems and Possibilities*. Deakin West: Australian Curriculum Studies Association: 33–42.

Doecke, B., & Mead, P. (2017). English and the knowledge question. *Pedagogy, Culture & Society*, 26(2), 249–264. https://doi.org/10.1080/14681366.2017.1380691.

Doecke, B., Parr, G., & Yandell, J. (2021). Knowing in English. *Changing English*, 28(1), 1–4. https://doi.org/10.1080/1358684X.2021.1864931.

Duffy, C. (2020). University fees to be overhauled, some course costs to double as domestic student places boosted. *ABC News*, 19 June. Available: www.abc.net.au/news/2020-06-19/university-fees-tertiary-education-overhaul-course-costs/12367742. Accessed 20 April 2022.

Erebus International. (2005). *Review of the Literature on Socio-Economic Status and Learning: Report to the NSW Department of Education and Training*. Darlinghurst: NSW Department of Education and Training.

Firth, V., & Huntley, R. (2014). *Who's Afraid of a Public School? Public Perceptions of Education in Australia*. Per Capita. Available: https://percapita.org.au/wp-content/uploads/2018/05/Whos-Afraid-of-a-Public-School.pdf. Accessed 21 September 2021.

Gannon, S., & Sawyer, W. (2015). Literacy, literature, and moral panic in Australia. In M. Yunus & B. Bertram (Eds.), *The International Handbook of Progressive Education*. New York: Peter Lang: 309–324.

Goodwyn, A. (2012). The status of literature: English teaching and the condition of literature teaching in schools. *English in Education*, 46(3), 212–227.

Guillory, J. (1993). *Cultural Capital: The Problem of Literary Canon Formation*. Chicago: Chicago University Press.

Heim, J. (2020). For locked-down high-schoolers, reading *The Plague* is daunting, and then comforting. *The Washington Post*. 19 June 2020. Available: www.washingtonpost.com/local/education/the-plague-high-school-reading-coronavirus/2020/04/30/6e5fe8f6-8635-11ea-878a-86477a724bdb_story. Accessed 22 November 2021.

Hirsch, E. D. (1989). *Cultural Literacy: What Every American Needs to Know*. Australian ed. Melbourne: Schwartz Publishing

Hughes, C. (2020). COVID-19 and the opportunity to design a more mindful approach to learning. *Prospects*, 49, 69–72. https://doi.org/10.1007/s11125-020-09492-z.

Kasprisin, L. (1987). Literature as a way of knowing: An epistemological justification for literary studies. *Journal of Aesthetic Education*, 21(3), 17–27. https://doi.org/10.2307/3332867.

Kennedy, A. (2014). Understanding continuing professional development: The need for theory to impact on policy and practice. *Professional Development in Education*, 40(5), 688–697. https://doi.org/10.1080/19415257.2014.955122.

Kirkpatrick, P., & Dixon, R. (Eds.) (2012). *Republic of Letters: Literary Communities in Australia*. Sydney: Sydney University Press.

Lawrence, C. (2012). Mind the gap: Why the rising inequality of our schools is dangerous. *The Monthly*, 32–37. Available: www.themonthly.com.au/issue/2012/july/1344475666/carmen-lawrence/mind-gap. Accessed 21 September 2021.

Marstaller, M. (2020). Student experiences of the Covid-19 lockdown. *Changing English*, 27 (3), 231–234. https://doi.org/10.1080/1358684X.2020.1777533.

Mathieson, M. (1975). *The Preachers of Culture: A Study of English and its Teachers*. London: Allen & Unwin.

McLean Davies, L., & Buzacott, L. (2021). Rethinking literature, knowledge and justice: Selecting "difficult" stories for study in school English. *Pedagogy, Culture & Society*, 1–15. https://doi.org/10.1080/14681366.2021.1977981.

McLean Davies, L., Doecke, B., & Mead, P. (2013). Reading the local and global: Teaching literature in secondary schools in Australia. *Changing English: Studies in Culture and Education*, 20(3), 224–240. https://doi.org/10.1080/1358684X.2013.816529.

McLean Davies, L., & Sawyer, W. (2018). (K)now you see it, (k)now you don't: Literary knowledge in the Australian Curriculum: English. *Journal of Curriculum Studies*, 50(6), 836–849. https://doi.org/10.1080/00220272.2018.1499807.

Mead, P., Doecke, B., & McLean Davies, L. (2020). Contingencies of meaning-making: English teaching and literary sociability. *Australian Literary Studies*, 35(2), 1-19https://doi.org/10.20314/als.00225a9681.

Medway, P. (1980). *Finding a Language: Autonomy and Learning in School*. London: Writers and Readers Publishing Cooperative.

Mello, C., Doecke, B., McLean Davies, L., & Buzacott, L. (2019). Literary sociability: A transnational perspective. *English in Education*, 53(2), 175–189. https://doi.org/10.1080/04250494.2018.1561149.

Mills, M., & Goos, M. (2017). The place of research in teacher education? An analysis of the Australian Teacher Education Ministerial Advisory Group Report. "Action Now: Classroom Ready Teachers." In M. A. Peters, B. Cowie, & I. Menter (Eds.), *A Companion to Research in Teacher Education*. Singapore: Springer: 637–650. https://doi.org/10.1007/978-981-10-4075-7_43.

Moore, R., & Muller, J. (1999). The discourse of 'voice" and the problem of knowledge and identity in the sociology of education. *British Journal of Sociology of Education*, 20(2), 189–206. https://doi.org/10.1080/01425699995407.

Muller, J., & Young, M. (2019). Knowledge, power and powerful knowledge re-visited. *The Curriculum Journal*, 30(2), 196–214. https://doi.org/10.1080/09585176.2019.1570292.

Newbolt, H. (Chair), The Departmental Committee appointed by the President of the Board of Education to inquire into the position of English in the educational system of England (1921). *The Teaching of English in England*. London: His Majesty's Stationery Office.

NSW Education Standards Authority (2018). *NSW Supplementary Documentation: Subject Content Knowledge Requirements*. Available: https://www.educationstandards.nsw.edu.au/wps/wcm/connect/1bea4323-19a6-4af6-b657-95ae4cea954b/subject-content-knowl-edge-requirements-policy.pdf?MOD=AJPERES&CVID=. Accessed 29 June 2022.

Patterson, A. (2000). Shaping the English specialist in Australia. In R. Peel, A. Patterson, & J. Gerlach,, *Questions of English: Ethics, Aesthetics, Rhetoric and the Formation of the Subject in England, Australia and the United States*. London and New York: Routledge Falmer: 283–300.

Peel, R. (2000a). Beliefs about English in England. In R. Peel, A. Patterson, & J. Gerlach, *Questions of English: Ethics, Aesthetics, Rhetoric and the Formation of the Subject in England, Australia and the United States*. London and New York: Routledge Falmer: 166–188.

Peel, R. (2000b). "English" in England: Its history and transformations. In R. Peel, A. Patterson, & J. Gerlach, *Questions of English: Ethics, Aesthetics, Rhetoric and the Formation of the Subject in England, Australia and the United States*. London and New York: Routledge Falmer: 39–115.

Peel, R. (2000c). Introduction. In R. Peel, A. Patterson, & J. Gerlach, *Questions of English: Ethics, Aesthetics, Rhetoric and the Formation of the Subject in England, Australia and the United States*. London and New York: Routledge Falmer: 1–35.

Peel, R., & Hargraves, S. (1995). Beliefs about English: Trends in Australia, England and the United States. *English in Education*, 29(3), 38–50.

Peel, R., Patterson, A., & Gerlach, J. (2000). *Questions of English: Ethics, Aesthetics, Rhetoric and the Formation of the Subject in England, Australia and the United States*. London and New York: Routledge Falmer.

Power, M. (1997). *The Audit Society: Rituals of Verification*. Oxford: Oxford University Press.

Protherough, R., & Atkinson, J. (1991). *The Making of English Teachers*. Milton Keynes and Philadelphia: Open University Press.

Reid, I. (1984). *The Making of Literature: Texts, Contexts and Classroom Practices*. Norwood: Australian Association for the Teaching of English.

Rose, N. (1999). *Powers of Freedom: Reframing Political Thought*. Cambridge: Cambridge University Press.

Rosen, H. (1981). *Neither Bleak House Nor Liberty Hall: English in the Curriculum*. London: University of London Institute of Education.

Sahlberg, P. (2011). *Finnish Lessons What Can the World Learn from Educational Change in Finland?* New York: Teachers College Press.

Sawyer, W., & McLean Davies, L. (2021). What do we want students to know from being taught a poem? *Changing English: Studies in Culture and Education*, 28(1), 103–117. https://doi.org/10.1080/1358684X.2020.1842174.

Truman, S. E., Hackett, A., Pahl, K., McLean Davies, L., & Escott, H. (2020). The capaciousness of no: Affective refusals as literacy practices. *Reading Research Quarterly*, 56(2), 223–236. https://doi.org/10.1002/rrq.306.

Truman, S. E., McLean Davies, L., & Buzacott, L. (2021). Disrupting intertextual power networks: Challenging literature in schools. *Discourse: Studies in the Cultural Politics of Education*. https://doi.org/10.1080/01596306.2021.1910929.

Urban, R. (2021). Phonics makes a comeback as a sound foundation of learning. *The Australian*, 22 January. Available: www.theaustralian.com.au/inquirer/phonics-makes-a-comeback-as-a

-sound-foundation-of-learning/news-story/618073c28809bcaacb842de4886fd0db. Accessed 21 September 2021.

Victorian Institute of Teaching (VIT) (2013). *Specialist Area Guidelines*. Available: www.vit.vic.edu.au/SiteCollectionDocuments/PDF/specialist_Area_Guidelines_2013.pdf. Accessed 20 April 2022.

Yandell, J. (2017). Culture, knowledge and power: What the Conservatives have learnt from E.D. Hirsch. *Changing English*, 24(3), 246–252. https://doi.org/10.1080/1358684X.2017.1351231.

Yandell, J. (2020). Learning under lockdown: English teaching in the time of Covid-19. *Changing English*, 27(3), 262–269. https://doi.org/10.1080/1358684X.2020.1779029.

Yates, L. (2018). History as knowledge: Humanities challenges for a knowledge-based curriculum. In B. Barrett, U. Hoadley & J. Morgan (Eds.), *Knowledge, Curriculum and Equity: Social Realist Perspectives*. London: Routledge: 45–60.

Yates, L., McLean Davies, L., Buzacott, L., Doecke, B., Mead, P., & Sawyer, W. (2019). School English, literature and the knowledge-base question. *The Curriculum Journal*, 30(1), 51–68. https://doi.org/10.1080/09585176.2018.1543603.

Yates, L., Woelert, P., Millar, V., & O'Connor, K. (2017). *Knowledge at the Crossroads? Physics and History in the Changing World of Schools and Universities*. Singapore: Springer.

Young, M., & Muller, J. (2010). Three educational scenarios for the future: Lessons from the sociology of knowledge. *European Journal of Education*, 45(1), 11–27. https://doi.org/10.1111/j.1465-3435.2009.01413.x.

2

AUTOBIOGRAPHIES OF THE QUESTION

*Brenton Doecke, Larissa McLean Davies, Philip Mead,
Wayne Sawyer and Lyn Yates*

The title of this chapter derives from an essay that Jane Miller wrote a few years ago where she describes a strategy she used with students about to embark on research for a higher degree. Students typically arrive at their first meeting with their supervisor with a topic or question they would like to investigate, but rather than sending them off to begin reading the literature of the field in which they wanted to work, Miller would ask them to start by telling a story about why they had become interested in the topic they wished to explore. She calls this writing 'the autobiography of the question' (Miller, 1995, p.23). The strategy was partly directed at a preconception commonly held by her students – mainly teachers or people 'in the process of becoming tea-chers' – that as researchers they should achieve the 'detachment', 'disinterestedness' and 'impartiality' they felt characterised 'scientific' inquiry (p.23). She aimed to affirm the potential of the stories they might tell about their classrooms to yield insights that elude 'abstractions that are deaf to questions of "Who?" "When?" "Where?"' (p.23). And this was more than an attempt to allow teachers' voices to be heard within a research community whose fundamental principles of scientific 'objectivity' would otherwise go unchallenged. By investigating the autobiographical impulse behind their work, Miller's students began to recognise the values and beliefs that shaped it. The 'autobiography of the question' was not something that, once written, constituted a mere pretext for the research, but a means for cultivating a reflexive awareness that they sustained throughout their inquiries (p.26).

This chapter comprises attempts by each of us to write an 'autobiography of the question' in which we explore how we each came to engage in the question of the role that a literary education might play in the professional learning of early career English teachers. At an obvious level, this is to highlight the interdisciplinary character of our inquiry. A strength of our inquiry has been the way it arises out of the diverse knowledges that we have each brought to it, spanning the fields of curriculum theory, teacher education, literary studies and English curriculum and

DOI: 10.4324/9781003106890-2

pedagogy. The project has not, in short, consisted simply of English educators speaking to other English educators. Lyn's standpoint as an educational sociologist has been crucial in moving us beyond the complacency that can set in when you talk to likeminded people, prompting the team as a whole to identify and interrogate assumptions about English curriculum and pedagogy in a way that we might not otherwise have done. Equally important has been the part that Philip has played as a Professor of Literature in reminding us of how debates about the status of literary studies as a field of inquiry get played out differently from the way the 'knowledge' question has been posed in connection with the secondary English curriculum. And although Larissa, Wayne and Brenton all see their work as being located within the field of English curriculum and pedagogy, they each bring different knowledge and experience to their teaching and research. Their standpoints have also undoubtedly been shaped by the contrastive policy settings in which they operate (Australia is a federation comprising States and territories, all with distinctive histories, cultures and education systems).

But by foregrounding the autobiographical character of this inquiry, we are before all else accentuating its dialogical character as arising out of the conversations we had with early career teachers. The early career teachers who have participated in this study brought their own purposes to the interviews we conducted with them (cf. Mishler [1986] 1991). They used the questions we posed to engage in a deeper level of questioning relating to their emerging identities as English teachers. The interviews were a vehicle for them to participate in a wider professional discourse community based on the experiences and knowledge they had acquired as early career English teachers. A key purpose of this chapter is to highlight the way as interlocutors our values and beliefs might have shaped those conversations.

Autobiography in this sense is not simply the story of an individual's life. The subjective dimensions that inhere within the 'I' of an autobiographical narrative have meaning as a response to the social conditions that have produced 'me', including my education and upbringing and my place within society. These latter dimensions have an 'objective' character, requiring the use of analytical categories that might produce an understanding of larger social structures that are not visible to me in my everyday life. But my everyday experiences are not therefore to be diminished as simply 'personal'. Part of the aim of writing an 'autobiography of the question' is to explore how my interest in a question intersects with these larger public dimensions, enhancing my self-awareness with respect to why the question should matter to 'me' personally, as well as mapping out – as Miller puts it – the question's interest within 'the history of more public kinds of attention to it' (Miller, 1995, p.23). This is to bring the 'personal' and the 'public' together in a dialectical relationship, each generating insights into the other.

Larissa

Before I went to school, my grandfather taught me to read. My mother, a teacher, returned to work relatively soon after I was born and so my days were spent at the local Presbyterian church manse, where my grandparents were in ministry. For the most part, I was in the kitchen, or at meetings in the hall with my grandmother. But for a short time in the afternoon, I would sit in front of the old colonial window in my grandfather's study, overlooking the garden, and read under his watch. His study was lined with books, including many works of fiction that had been donated to him as he moved across Australian States. Apparently, this was a cultural phenomenon in the 1960s and 70s: ministers were known to be poor and thought to be keen on reading, and so when someone with a large library died, their books found a natural home with the clergy. The nature of the books was not important, though, which meant that my grandfather's library was diverse, as were his reading habits.

At some time, during my early years in secondary school, he shared with me a book innocuously covered in brown paper. This was *Lady Chatterley's Lover*, he explained, and it had been banned but had made its way to Australia chapter-by-chapter, to be assembled with string. Although by then it was the 1980s, we spoke quietly, conscious of the status of this illegal text. This was my first insight into the cultural power of fiction, to the idea that texts could be so liberating or dangerous that they needed to be controlled.

Later, when my grandfather died, I inherited his smorgasbord of a library, and among this a slim volume of the Gospels he kept next to his bed. I found it full of marginalia, questions he wanted answering and cross-references that needed explanation – the markings of a dialogue carried out over a long adult life. Here was evidence of deep and close textual engagement, of wrestling with language, of not accepting dominant institutional reading practices at face value. I interpret his reading practices in this way, of course, because this is what has become important to me, the tussle with language, the reaching of words beyond the page, and a concern with institutions that are both shaped by and shape textual experiences. In different ways, and in different contexts, as a student, an English teacher and a teacher educator, this dialectic between knowing, literature and power – and the forms of reading and writing that support the nexus between them – has occupied my attention.

In Year 4, at about age 10, a classmate and I, both keen readers, decided to write a class play. Inspired by our individual experiences with the adolescent detective genre from the UK and the US (for him, the Hardy Boys, and me, Trixie Belden), we wrote 'The Royal Murderers', a mystery to be performed by the class. What seems incredible, now, in these days of high-stakes testing in the primary years, and the primacy of certain genres, is the freedom we were given to read and write, the permission to negotiate the curriculum (Boomer, 1982). There were many things I took away from this experience – the way a text could stop and redirect the routines of the classrooms, the interest of my classmates when they had a part to play, and perhaps more than anything, the confidence of our teacher, freshly out of college, that students could write a text and bring it to life.

While I continued to read and write during my teenage years, I increasingly saw this as something that belonged to my home life, not school, where set texts were forgettable, and where teachers and students seemed primarily occupied with the language and practices of survival. It wasn't until Year 11, having moved from my local secondary school to one for music students that, amidst increased hours dedicated to practice, I was once again captivated by texts and their meanings. My English literature teacher, Toni Glasson, introduced the class to Sylvia Plath, John Donne and Shakespeare. I understood for the first time that form, image and context enabled new understandings, new ways of knowing, and I felt like I'd been reading on the surface, half-asleep, until that time.

Although my senior high school years had prepared me for a future with the piano, I could not let go of language and commenced a double degree in Music and Arts. Focusing entirely on literature in my Arts degree, I sought out diverse genres, periods and paradigms: I wanted to read and know everything. Yet English at university was nothing like the text work I had encountered at school; it moved quickly: a book a week across several subjects, with accompanying literary criticism. I recall the feeling of great frustration when, encountering the university library in my first year, I realised that thousands of people – critics – had written about the texts I had studied in Year 12. I wondered why I had laboured to make meanings as if I was the text's first reader when I could have built on the opinions and ideas of others. However, it was not enough to simply be able to cite these opinions, I learnt from Peter Otto, who took the first-year survey course in 21st-century literature. The task, it became clear, was to think originally about texts, synthesising the ideas of others, to create new paratextual networks. Knowledge didn't lie with the text, with the readings, or with me as the reader, but somewhere, often elusively it seemed, in between.

As the years progressed, this notion that texts could, and should, be read alongside other texts took a different turn. I encountered post-structuralist theory, particularly Marxism and feminism, and the readings of 19th-century women's fiction by critics Gilbert and Gubar (1984), among others, changed my reading practices and priorities irrevocably. Discovering Australian literature for the first time, and particularly colonial women's writing, I felt reading most keenly as a justice issue. I realised how little I had read of Australian women's writing, but how important it should be in the society in which I was living and planned to teach. This became a focus which I took into Honours, and this concern, now directed towards marginalised voices, particularly Aboriginal and Torres Strait Islander authors in the context of decolonising the curriculum, frames much of my scholarly work.

By the time I graduated, it was the mid-1990s and Jeff Kennett, the Liberal Premier for Victoria, had closed schools in the service of expediency, privatisation and a budget surplus. Many teachers were made 'in excess' and the State would not employ any new graduates for government school jobs. I was fortunate to find a teaching position in a small, independent semi-rural Christian school where I was loaded with English and senior literature classes (and where, with a nod to my music degree, I conducted the choir). As a new teacher, feeling somewhat isolated, I joined the Victorian Association for the Teaching of English (VATE) and soon became involved in delivering professional learning in workshops for other English teachers. The literary theory I had learnt at university was being introduced into the curriculum as critical literacy, and I was keen to contribute to this work.

As I visited different schools for VATE, it seemed that for many experienced English teachers, particularly those whose expertise was in literature, critical literacy was destabilising. The text could no longer be relied on to offer a consistent reading; what was known, say, about *Macbeth*, was open to contestation and what students should take away from literature was unclear. The feminist agenda I had become committed to was often not welcome – and rather than being a subject constantly evolving, English seemed stuck. At my school, parents contested contemporary works for inclusion, and Australian writing remained para-curricular. I felt that in order to contribute to change, I needed to know more.

After a year of teaching, I commenced a PhD in second-wave Australian women's writing. The thesis became my companion as I changed schools and had two children. In each new school, my PhD aspirations were met with a mixture of interest and suspicion. Why was I doing it when I was already a senior teacher? Did it impact my classroom practice? How long *had* I been doing the thesis? Were there enough women writers from the 1970s to sustain a PhD? For some colleagues, as I've written elsewhere (McLean Davies, 2011), my focus on Australian women's literature was inconceivable, as it bore so little resemblance to the canon of literature being taught in the curriculum we were enacting.

As a teacher educator, these questions of connections and dissonances between tertiary study and secondary teaching, the discipline and subject of English, have become important to my scholarship and practice. Underpinning these questions is an abiding interest in the dynamics of power, between texts, readers and institutions, and the role of teachers, in shaping literary experiences and knowledges. As a mid-career academic leading this inquiry I am grateful that this project has enabled me to engage in sustained dialogue about these questions, both with my esteemed colleagues across English education, curriculum studies and literary studies, and with the early career English teachers who have been central to our work.

Lyn

One way I might describe my own research interests in school and university education is that I want to keep alive both what these open up and the harms they encompass. This, of course, is deeply autobiographical in its grounding. I am someone who has had a long and reasonably successful career courtesy of education and even more has appreciated the joy of working with ideas and the dialogues and seminars and writing with students and colleagues in many different places that were part of this. But I am also someone who experienced first-hand what it meant to be an outsider and to lack cultural capital, long before I heard of that term, when I came on a teaching scholarship as a first-in-family working-class young woman from the provinces to a university full of private school educated 'sophisticates'. Later, when I had my daughters, I had the uncomfortable experience of constantly noticing their educationally relevant privilege growing up in a two-PhD family, relative to my childhood and to the educational inequalities that occupy a good deal of my research interest.

I came to university in the late 1960s intending to make English my main study. Like Wayne and Brenton, I was the beneficiary of a demographic boom and need for teachers that had led to generous scholarships for would-be teachers. This enabled many young people from working-class families with no previous university experiences to go to university.

Since discovering the local library as a young child, I had been a voracious reader and enjoyed novels and plays in particular. At school, English had generally been my favourite subject. But in first-year university, although I loved many of the books we were assigned, I found I couldn't crack the code of what the lecturers seemed to be looking for in responses and essays. (I also remember deeply resenting T. S. Eliot and the cultural allusions that were a mystery to me.) By contrast, the kinds of analytic questions favoured in history and philosophy seemed more congenial and I continued to make the 16th-century history of ideas the focus for my Honours thesis and then my MA. I was bonded to teach and assigned to a teachers' college to teach history, but this sparked my interest in studying education more seriously rather than continuing with history, and I went on to do an M Ed in the UK in the 1970s. In that degree, my thesis looked at the different assumptions being made by teacher unions, government and others about the appropriate knowledge base for teaching, in particular the weight that should be given to disciplinary studies compared with 'education' studies. Later again, while working as a lecturer back in Melbourne, I embarked on a PhD on 'curriculum theory and non-sexist education', inspired by the new questions and challenges for education being raised by the women's movement.

From my initial pre-service education studies, I remember being interested in some of the analytic philosophy questions (now deeply unfashionable), in particular, what distinguishes education from indoctrination; and later being introduced to the 'new' sociology of education and its interest in power and knowledge as a social construction. Both interests continue to seep into the current project. And of course, the rise of second-wave feminism generated so many things to notice and question and write about: What is different and similar about gendered and class inequalities and experiences in education? Whose questions and interests are credited and whose are demeaned or silenced? Why is rationality valued over emotion; quantitative measures and studies over qualitative ones; and 'objective' research over 'situated' research? (see Yates, 2013). As with Brenton's comments in this chapter, I was interested in the ways some of the major feminist theorists and Marxist theorists either had little other than critique to say about education or seemed to have an over-simplistic view that deep differences and inequalities (e.g. gendered career choice) would be easily overturned by education if it simply taught a different 'message'. For those of us whose research focus was education, it is clear its relationship with identity formation is much more complex than that, and in the 1990s I undertook an eight-year qualitative longitudinal project, somewhat inspired by the 7 Up series, to look more closely at different lives in different school contexts as they developed over the course of the high school years (McLeod & Yates, 2006).

For the decade or so before I became involved in the current project, I was working more generally on the changes in curriculum frameworks around the world. I led a research project investigating how two school and university subjects, history and physics, were faring in, and responding to, these new contexts, and how those who worked in these fields understood the forms of knowledge and the value each subject offered (Yates et al., 2016). In Australia, a country often known (politically at least) for its anti-intellectualism, there is considerable pressure to see both school and university education in terms of a skills-oriented vocationalism. And the 21st century has been marked by a ramped-up concern with testing and measurement as the prime means of accountability of individual schools and teachers. With my project on history and physics, I was able to look at some of the curriculum arguments about the power of 'disciplinary' knowledge and the challenges to it from other ways of thinking about what matters in education. I examined the pressures to subordinate these traditional subjects to new external purposes. I was also interested in what was similar and what was different between a classic science discipline and a classic humanistic or social science one.

When I was invited to be part of the current project I was delighted. Not only would it enable me to continue to explore those questions about the value and harms of education that have been constants for me, and to further test the issues about knowledge I had seen with the previous study, but it would allow me to work in the field of literature, a field I had continued to pursue from outside my working life, via book groups, writers' festivals and a constant diet of novels, films and plays. And it might allow me to see more about why, in my first encounters with it at university, I had found it so difficult to crack the codes of what the study of literature is about.

Wayne

Literature brought me to the study of English. If I'm honest, up until what is now termed Year 9 in Australian schools (usually 14–15 year-olds), I hated the subject. From (the then) 'Grade' 3 (usually 8–9 year-olds), it had been a seemingly endless collection of comprehension exercises, grammar work (especially parsing and analysis in primary/elementary school) and occasional bursts of 'story' writing. I remember reading *Treasure Island* in Year 7 and *Silas Marner* in Year 8, but I can recall no discussion or activities around them. Two highlights from my school life were the teacher who read *Enoch Arden* to us in serial form, and a friend and I writing a short episodic comedy-drama set in outer space to the amusement at least of ourselves. But in Year 9, a new teacher arrived – let's call him Mr Blair. Mr Blair was very blokey in a middle-aged, scruffy way, and he thought poetry was something worth spending one's time talking about. We read a bunch of variously engaging novels – but a bunch of them, nevertheless, which were rotated around the class every couple of weeks. That was new. We wrote essays because next year was the School Certificate – that felt a bit grown-up. But more importantly, English became about the resonances that words contained or set up. And it became about ideas. Above all, we read Shakespeare. *Julius Caesar* seemed to take the resonances of words into new realms. The next year Mr Blair took us through *Macbeth* and Orwell – *Animal Farm* as well as Orwell's essays – as set texts for the School Certificate (Year 10). I did enough to achieve the right results at the levels I sat in all other subjects but focused my real thought and energy on English and Maths. Maths was engaging, logical, satisfying. English was words and big ideas and that seemed to sit well in the late 1960s. I changed schools for the Higher School Certificate (Years 11 and 12) and was lucky enough to have again two brilliant teachers for English and Maths. I enjoyed the challenge and beautiful logic of calculus and induction, while *Antony and Cleopatra, The Spire* and T. S. Eliot continued to supply the words and the big ideas that adolescents can be so grabbed by. Art's role in both reflecting and challenging worldviews and values, the ways in which symbols can reverberate with suggestion– these again were ideas that seemed to speak to that age and to my age. What Felski (2008) theorises as recognition, enchantment and knowledge might each come in and out of play at different times and places in our lives. At that time and place, they all seemed to be playing out for me.

It was pretty well inevitable, then, that going to university to study English was the immediate future. 1972–1975 witnessed a reforming national Labor Government under Prime Minister Gough Whitlam, after 23 years of conservative rule, and one of its reforms was the abolition of university fees. My undergraduate career was almost all encompassed by these years, but I have to forego gratitude to Whitlam for my undergraduate education. Like many other students at that time, I was able to access a university education because I had received a State Government Teacher's Scholarship. My own State of New South Wales (NSW) in those days paid students' fees, as well as providing a living allowance while studying, in return for a period of being 'bonded' to the state school system after graduation. So, I enrolled in English and History – and Maths, not wanting to let it go. Maths lasted a week – television lectures to thousands of students as well as being thrown onto my own resources to keep up was enough to see me walking away. I needed, of course, good teaching. I largely received that in English and History, where I followed the Honours courses in English Literature and Modern History – from the second year, as one did in those days. In English, we studied mostly 20th century in the first year, Renaissance to Neo-Augustans in the second year, Romantics and the 19th century in the third year. Shakespeare was ubiquitous. I completed the fourth year in English Literature by studying the Renaissance, Romantic poetry, and 19th-century Literature and Thought, with a thesis on Wordsworth. I had great teachers in the Sydney English Department (Gerry Wilkes, Andrew Riemer, Michael Wilding, Adrian Coleman, Stephen Knight, Margaret Harris and Simon Petch), with some of these the most famous names of its immediate post-Goldberg era.

I've dwelt on a level of detail here to mark out the particularity of an education in English that at least seems to be very different from those pursued by many of the teachers you'll meet in this book. This was the literary education of a particular time and place. And this isn't just because the texture of the discipline has changed. It's true that literary theory hadn't yet become 'Theory', and creative writing and media didn't have many footholds. But the socio-political world was different too. Baby boomers were moving into new suburbs with babies of their own; migration was strong; school enrolments were expanding, and new schools were being built in those suburbs. The NSW Education Department largely staffed those schools with those scholarship holders it had funded; teaching positions were guaranteed and there seemed to be no shortage of takers. Among most of my friends, teaching was the option that made us the first in our families to gain a university education. There were enough English students for Sydney University to have separate – and big – Departments of Literature and Old English Literature and Language (with an additional Chair in Australian Literature). For their first two years, students took courses from both departments: Chaucer, Icelandic sagas, the history of English, semantics and the language of literature were some of mine from Old English Literature and Language. Departments of that size and that extent of course offerings, as well as that particular structuring of courses, are rare in Australia now, partly because of the social conditions discussed elsewhere in this book. These days, State Departments of Education – at least in my State – offer few scholarships and these are finely targeted at subjects with dwindling numbers of teachers (such as Maths). At the time of writing, a conservative Australian Government has just increased fees for arts courses and reduced them for STEM courses. During the COVID pandemic, when this government, formerly obsessed with budget surpluses, took a major shift in a Keynesian direction and spent huge amounts of money to keep the economy alive and people in jobs, universities were specifically excluded from emergency budget support.

Public universities in general in Australia (i.e. almost all universities in Australia) are suffering from reduced real public funding. Big departments with full-time tenured staff have everywhere been replaced by big classes run by a sea of sessional staff. These are the materialities that drive what students experience as their educational reality as much as the big conceptual debates in the field – if only because they determine the extent to which students are exposed to those big conceptual debates.

I said earlier that it was inevitable that I would study English Literature at university. Undoubtedly that sounds like I was treating a Teacher's Scholarship as a means to an end that didn't have much to do with a burning passion to teach. Though I thought teaching would always be interesting, that judgement probably isn't wrong. Universities weren't free when I began; I felt neither my parents nor I could afford the fees and, while other scholarships were on offer, the 'Teacher's' was the most attractive by far. However, any lukewarm commitment towards the teaching profession changed very quickly when I entered the Diploma of Education that followed my Literature degree. My DipEd was in the Sydney University Teacher Development Program, which was still fairly new, and in which Ken Watson and Roslyn Arnold introduced me to the major influences of the age: John Dixon, James Britton, Douglas Barnes. James Moffett was to come later. Literature at schools was being taught through imaginative recreation; research was problematising the relationship between knowledge of grammar and writing development; speaking was central in the English classroom; language was important across all of the curricula, and young adult literature was a still relatively new burgeoning field. As well as the central English Method, I studied courses on educational drama, teaching reading, film study, language-in-education, aspects of the history and philosophy of education, and a year-long specialism in small group teaching in the regular classroom. It was stimulating, engaging and quite quickly made me glad I'd opted for that Teacher's Scholarship. The sheer plethora of what was available meant enrolling in as much as I could over and above the minimum course requirements.

Again, this was the education of a particular age: I'd be reasonably sure that every student in the DipEd was on a Teacher's Scholarship; many of the academic staff were on four-year rotating positions from the NSW Department of Education (as I was later to be), but there was also a solid majority of tenured staff at the core of the program. This period was the heyday of 'growth' and 'experience' in English, and of language-across-the-curriculum (the 'textbook' for the specialist course in small group teaching was not something on simply organising classroom groupings, but Barnes, Britton and Rosen, *Language, the Learner and the School* [1971]). One reason I could enrol in as many courses as I liked over the minimum requirements was that these were the days when one didn't pay a fee-per-subject. Though the Education Department dictated minimum subject-content requirements for its future teachers, centralised, systemic standards-setting bodies were not yet effectively dictating the curricula of teacher education courses to reflect centralised teacher standards, local syllabuses, and little else.

My first appointment was to a school in Sydney's Western suburbs, in what was itself an older suburb, but on the fringes of the new growth areas. About ten of us were first-year-out in that school in that year. I joined the local branch of the English Teachers' Association (every Department of Education region had such a branch – a link that has been long lost). Every Head of English in the region was in their first Head position and most held office in the ETA branch. It was a highly energising group of people to become part of, especially as they were led by the then English Inspectors, who saw themselves primarily as resources for professional development in their subjects and their regions – a very different role for the Inspectorate from, say, the current Ofsted model in the UK. When the Third International Conference on the Teaching of English came to Sydney in 1980, many of that group attended, many supported by the system to spend a week with people such as James Britton, Harold Rosen, James Moffett, John Dixon, Leslie Stratta, Margaret Meek and others. That conference was part of what eventually led to the formalising of the International Federation for the Teaching of English (IFTE) and cemented for me the importance of professional association in the culture of teaching.

This is not just an exercise in nostalgia. While I continue to value all of these formative experiences, they were, as I've said, the experiences of a different time – and a different place: after all, the past is a foreign country and they *do* do things differently there. I can see, though, that I am still presenting one age as a time of constraint, the other as liberating. Maybe that's a subjectivity I can't slough off. In fact, much was wrong in those days. Classes were invariably streamed, and first-year-out teachers were routinely assigned the toughest classes because they weren't around when the timetable was being 'done' in the previous year. There was a sink-or-swim attitude that was quite blatant. Even if the kind of mentoring and support of beginning teachers available these days can become merely lip-service in some schools, at least that's more than was usually available then. But none of us can act as if we suddenly exist in a different time and place. We all have to negotiate the contingencies of our here and now. And, on balance, I do believe that systemic practices were less constraining and fairer in those times – to everybody: teachers and schools and, above all, to students. This book gives an account of how early career teachers negotiate conditions that are quite different from those I encountered.

On a related issue, my background also reflects my straddling of different fields. This is not unique. My straddling of fields reflects the transition – or perhaps the back and forth – that others involved in the writing team for this book have done between the fields of literature and English education. In my case, this played itself out in my later pursuing Master's degrees in both English Literature and English Education. (Here's where I can be more directly grateful to the Whitlam legacy: as long as the university was free, that was too good an opportunity not to take advantage of.) High school English teaching can be a bit of a tug-of-love world between curriculum and peda-gogy. For my generation, 'language' and 'experience' demanded a kind of pedagogical allegiance, if only because our mandated syllabuses reflected those ideas (though in far more nuanced ways than is usually recognised [Sawyer, 2016]). Young adult literature was seen as important, as a growing field with its own 'classics', with texts that engaged adolescents while manifesting a complexity that demanded serious attention. On the other hand, our very qualifications for employment meant a focus by the system (as it still usually does), not on our pedagogical education, but the content of our under-graduate degree – and, in the case of English teaching in NSW, on how much (then, invariably canonical) literature was in that degree. In classroom teaching, our educa-tion in that area more often came to the fore in our senior exam classes, while in junior (Years 7–10) classes, our work in English education was far more central. Eventually, my doctoral work was in English education. But fields of interest do bleed into each other. Even senior literature teaching benefitted from those pedagogies that were usually more prevalent in the junior school, and careful thought about pedagogy even in the most senior/exam-focused/canon-as-content classes is a given. Similarly, I think a literary orientation gives one a particular perspective on areas of the school curricu-lum such as writing which is quite different from orientations influenced by, say, genre approaches (Sawyer, 1995, 2005). As with the other authors, it's the way that different fields of interest talk to each other that I'm bringing into this work.

Brenton

One of my favourite mottoes comes from the Bullock Report:

> It is characteristic of English that it does not hold together as a body of knowledge which can be identified, quantified, then transmitted. Literary studies lead constantly outside themselves…
>
> *(DES, 1975, p.5)*

But for me, the 'outside' is not firstly history or society and those fields of inquiry directed towards producing a historical or sociological knowledge. The 'outside', rather, is the world around me whenever I read a novel or a poem or watch a play. The 'outside' is the social relationships that I negotiate from day to day as I try to make sense of my life. I cannot account for the books I've read without connecting them with the moment when I first read them and the person I was at that time.

This perhaps applies especially to the books I read at school. An English teacher who looms large in my memory is one who challenged my small-town conservatism (I was the product of my parents' upbringing) by asking: 'What evidence is there for an absolute condemnation of Communism?' This was in response to an essay I'd written on *Animal Farm* in which I'd trotted out all the clichés that were circulating in Australia at that time. Harold Holt had just won a sweeping electoral victory with the slogan: 'All the way with LBJ!' Posters used during the election campaign showed a map of Asia illustrating the domino effect if the NLF were to gain victory in South Vietnam. Next, it would be Singapore, then Indonesia and Papua New Guinea. And finally, the Red Menace would be at our doorstep! A few more years were necessary before the tide of opinion turned against Australia's involvement in the war and the Moratoriums were held across the capital cities.

After all these years I still find myself wondering how I could have been open to Monsieur Patrick's provocation, which, in addition to the question I've just posed, included a summary comment at the bottom of the page: 'A vitriolic tirade!' I have published an account of Monsieur Patrick's teaching elsewhere (see Parr & Doecke, 2012), and so I won't dwell any further on the impact he had on me, except to say that the insights he made available to me as we read novels like *Animal Farm, Down and Out in Paris in London* and *The Catcher in the Rye* hardly coalesced in a new version of myself that miraculously transcended the values and beliefs of a Lutheran upbringing and the culture of the sleepy country town where I grew up. What I experienced, instead, was a conflict within myself between those values and beliefs and glimpses of possibilities that pointed beyond the world as I knew it. I remained mired in that world, and the books I read then remain bound up with my memories of the people and scenes around me at that time, even as they offered me insights into the nature of human experience that challenged the prejudices instilled in me by my upbringing. Those people and scenes still formed the ineluctable backdrop for my attempts to make meaning from what I was reading.

The contradictory nature of my personal growth was played out even more starkly when I began a degree in English at Flinders University. By that time everyone seemed to be affected by the wave of public protest against the Vietnam War, giving rise to conflict between friends and within families. Several of my contemporaries became draft resisters, one was sentenced to prison for refusing to register for national service, while others found themselves as conscripts fighting in Vietnam. There was an inevitability about my decision to do an Honours degree in English, but I was equally drawn to Marxism (Flinders University had just introduced a new subject, Marxism-Leninism, in which I was permitted to enrol as part of my Honours degree). This involved not only reading texts like Lenin's *The State and Revolution* and Marx's *18th Brumaire of Louis Bonaparte* but participating in demonstrations against the war (as a kind of unofficial extra-curricular activity!). Our weekly seminars would begin with students swapping advice about how best to defend their cases and planning for the next demo. If I struggled to bring the reading I was required to do in 'Marxism-Leninism' together with the reading prescribed for my English subjects (which included texts like T. S. Eliot's 'The Wasteland', William Wordsworth's *The Prelude*, Matthew Arnold's *Culture and Anarchy*, Walter Pater's *The Renaissance*), the need to defend myself against a charge of hindering a police officer at a demonstration proved to be an abiding preoccupation in the final year of my Honours program that heightened the conflict I was experiencing. I only completed my degree by the skin of my teeth, writing all my overdue essays over the summer break, whereupon I immediately took up a job as a fettler in Chrysler's engine foundry at Lonsdale in a bid to rid myself of the traces of the bourgeois class consciousness that inhered in being an English Honours graduate.

Yet the contradictions I was experiencing were nonetheless intellectually generative ones, motivating me to resume my university studies to grapple with the question of the value of a literary education within a Marxist philosophical framework. This was after my stint at Chrysler's foundry: my naïve attempt to join the working class was compromised from the start by the fact that I always had a means of escaping from the drudgery of the production line by returning to university and immersing myself in reading the works of major Marxist literary theorists. Lukács, Benjamin, Williams, Jameson, Eagleton, Macherey (to stop with just those names) – the intellectual resources these names signify in their various attempts to explore the significance of a literary imagination in the struggle for social reform were to become a vital frame of reference for me in my work as an educator.

But I am getting ahead of myself in saying this. For it is not as though the insights offered by these theorists into language and literature have translated directly into my teaching. My decision to become a teacher might paradoxically be explained as resulting from an emerging dissatisfaction with the fact that none of these theorists (except for the educational writings of Benjamin and Williams, which I was only to read much later) showed any abiding interest in education. For all the complexity of their understandings of the epistemological and ontological status of the literary text vis-à-vis history, they have generally neglected to engage with the question of how people make meaning from literary texts within classrooms and other social settings. I don't want to be misinterpreted. Taken together the work of these theorists reflects a remarkably sophisticated understanding of the formal complexities of literary works, including in Jameson's case a powerful argument about the way any reading of a literary text is mediated by previous interpretations and the reading habits and categories associated with the interpretive traditions in which people operate (Jameson, 1981, p.9). Critical activity as Jameson envisages it opens up the possibility of exploring how successive generations have read and appropriated literary texts for their own purposes, engaging in a dialogue with the work as it emerges out of their sense of their needs and desires (cf.

Doecke, 2004, 2020, 2021). Yet if this gives due emphasis to literary interpretation as an active process, it is not one that Marxist literary theorists have generally applied to an analysis of how students engage with texts in classroom settings, though as I have just said few have even bothered to consider the role that schools play in the socialisation of young people and specifically in supporting them to make meaning from the texts chosen for study.

How do these reflections provide a perspective on my engagement in this project?

The discrepant nature of the people and scenes that I have just recounted is meant to dispel any impression that they can be interpreted as moments in a continuous unfolding of my identity as an English educator that might be charted against the books I've read. The false starts and byways I've followed hardly reflect an abiding belief in the humanising potential of a literary imagination often ascribed to English teachers. On the contrary, I've become convinced that at the heart of any literary education worthy of the name should be a radical doubt about its value (Doecke, 2021). Only in this way can you jettison all that old baggage about a literary canon ('a charnel house of long dead interiorities' as the young Lukács expressed it) and begin anew. But that is precisely why I became an English teacher. My decision to become an English teacher after completing postgraduate studies was driven by my perception that while Marxist literary theorists have said a lot about the place of literature within history, including its role in the class struggle, they have failed to grapple specifically with the question of the significance of a *literary education* for social reform. English classrooms seemed to me to open up the possibility of appreciating the role that reading and writing might play in the formation of people as they engage in their relationships with one another and participate in a culture *in the making*.

Yet I am obviously not suggesting that the literary scholarship in which I have engaged has been a complete waste of time. It all gets back to what might be meant by the word 'outside' as it is used in the Bullock Report. As I remarked at the start of these reflections, the 'outside' is more than the knowledges that have been produced to understand history or society The place that English ought to occupy within the education of young people cannot properly be determined by arguing its location within a field of inquiry alongside the other fields of inquiry that provide the foundations of subjects like Science or Mathematics within the school curriculum. That would be to suppose that English requires exactly the same kind of warrant as subjects that are based on propositional knowledge. So many dimensions of reading are lost when English is understood in these terms. English is about the identity work in which students engage and the social relationships they negotiate when they talk about the books that have been chosen for study. It is about their efforts to make meaning out of their experiences by reflecting on the books they have read.

'Knowledge' is still at the heart of what I do as an English educator, but it is a knowledge directed towards an ever more refined appreciation of the meaning-making that occurs when students talk about the books they have read or are in the process of reading. I feel that I can better understand their conversations because of the knowledge on which I am able to draw, and there have certainly been moments when I have been able to encourage them to be more self-aware with respect to their interpretive practices, but at the same time, I am also conscious that the complexity of their exchanges always exceeds what I 'know', in the same way that I would step back from any conceit to ever fully know another human being. The 'outside' is the world we share with our students, though this is not to suppose that they should see the world in the same terms that we have bequeathed to them. Education is crucially bound up with generational change, requiring educators (to borrow from Hannah Arendt) to refrain from denying students 'their chance of undertaking something new, something unforeseen by us' (Arendt, [1954] 1968, p.198). Our task is 'to prepare them in advance for the task of renewing a common world' (p.198). This requires attending to the way they are making meaning out of their experiences, and encouraging them in that effort, sometimes (as Monsieur Patrick did with me) posing questions they may initially find provocative and even confronting, and likewise being responsive to the confronting questions that our students may pose to us (cf. Yandell et al., 2020).

Philip

'Ever the mutable'

I have been extraordinarily fortunate in being able to spend most of my student and working life in literary education. Studying English, American and Australian literature, and then teaching, researching and publishing in those fields, has been a rare privilege. For me, a significant aspect of that experience has to do with the inseparability of learning and teaching. Learning, or learning by reading, is the first stage, but it doesn't cease with the shift into teaching. The classroom has been central to both, although it is not the only site of literary sociability. Teaching involves ongoing learning about language and literature that becomes intertwined with learning about teaching as well. We use the word 'pedagogy' to try to encompass that whole complex of teaching and learning (see Mead & Doecke, 2020). Like the early career teachers who have participated in our project, I was someone who began as a student of language and literature and who turned, like them, into a teacher of those subjects. I think the 'roles' of learner and teacher have remained inseparable throughout my professional life. That was the background – or autobiographical dimension – to the questions I brought to this research project. How are English teachers being made, making themselves, today? How could my own experience of a literary education be useful in understanding their experience?

In the research for this book, we have focused particularly on the experience of the early career English teachers, as a way of understanding the complex moment of transitioning from a student of English to a teacher of English. Our early career teachers have each been students of English in their different ways, but are now also set out on a crucial stage in their learning to be teachers. There were many points where I could easily recognise what they were saying about their own histories. English teachers have experiences in common, whatever their generation:

their own teachers, their students, their own experience of formal English study in different institutional settings, their engagements with reading and writing beyond their formal education, negotiating work at different schools and their power hierarchies. At the same time their making of a literary education – the inter-woven, subjective experience of learning and teaching English – takes myriad forms. It is as singular as the lives of the teachers themselves. My experience of a literary education is that it is, more than anything, processual, and always dialogical, irreversible, full of unknowns, constant shifts in paradigms of understanding, repe-ated encounters with foundational questions, always bound up with our life experience. It, which isn't an 'it', could be said to describe my student and working life, but only in the process, including the doing of learning and teaching English in the classroom, not apart from it in any definitional or abstract way. I can't understand it fully, given its life over such a long time and in so many different institutional and interpersonal settings.

There were not a lot of books in the houses in which I grew up in Queensland, although there was a great reverence for books. My father's family lived mostly in Brisbane, where they had moved from Nindigully, St George and Warwick. They had lived most of their lives in outback south-east Queensland because my grandfather had been a boundary rider on rural properties there and a Cobb & Co. coach driver. Because I was unable to go to school for a time, my grandparents' house in Wilston, Brisbane was also a place of instruction: my grandmother taught me to read and write in the space under the house, where she also washed and ironed. I absorbed from her a sense of the importance of education, if only because she had had so little of it. Later, I would understand the specifically Catholic inflection of this experience. The most visible reading matter in these houses, apart from a breviary, were cheap pulp versions of Zane Grey westerns: *The Lone Star Ranger* and *The Call of the Canyon*, and the like. The movies were as much a source of entertainment and narratives of wonder for my family, particularly *Hopalong Cassidy* films and the weekly stream of Hollywood horse operas. I didn't experience all of this first hand, of course, I was too young, but I absorbed it nevertheless in a form that would turn, years later, into nostalgia. At (then) outer Brisbane state schools I had highly competent English teachers, even if there was little literature studied. We knew about Judith Wright, though.

Then when I was a young teenager my family moved to England, where I found myself at Sutton County Grammar School, the only colonial in the school. In this seriously disorienting, antipodal shift I encountered Shelley and Keats for the first time, but also, memorably, the unquestioning reverence of the other pupils and the English teachers for those icons of English literature. My first class at Sutton Grammar was memorable too; I was given a decrepit old red history book and taken to the classroom, where all the boys were copying a diagram of the Battle of Bosworth field off the board into their exercise books. I recognised that I didn't come from that place. I didn't know where Bosworth field was; it would be a long time before I recognised the assumptions about national and literary history underpinning that school exercise. But I could tell that I came from that language, even if it was a different dialect.

My family then moved to Europe and I was sent back to boarding school in Brisbane, an old-fashioned institution going through a period of Faulkneresque decay. The curriculum was a strange mixture of the vocational and the intellectual: one minute it was technical drawing, the next, one of my English teachers was introducing me to Ingmar Bergman's *The Seventh Seal* with its memorable line about the silence in heaven. There was another strangely antipodal aspect of my literary learning there too. One of the punishments for minor misdemeanours around the boarding house was called 'Tintern Abbey'; prefects could hand it out. I copped this punishment more than once. It consisted of a detention to write out the whole of Wordsworth's poem 'Tintern Abbey', and its full title of course, 'Lines Composed a Few Miles above Tintern Abbey, On Revisiting the Banks of the Wye during a Tour. July 13, 1798' from our poetry anthology, Palgrave's *Golden Treasury of English Verse*. What had the instigators of this punishment been thinking? I can't tell if they thought of it as the worst torture imaginable, writing out a long Romantic poem, or whether it was designed as some kind of moral lesson. Either way, I hardly resented it. For me, the city-remembered Wye wasn't a specific locale, and the address to the poet's sister felt embarrassing, but I certainly found myself going off into reveries over the sound, look and meanings of lots of individual words: *unintelligible, sycamore, dwelling-place, interfused, unborrowed*. And there was the shape of the sentences too, their orchestrated syntax and the billows of affect they produced. Of course, writing the poem out allowed this lingering linguistic absorption, in effect learning about language. Later, when I came across the process writing model, I could see its uses but also its limitations. Wordsworth had no role in that paradigm.

When my parents moved once again, to the US, I was sent to Walt Whitman High School in Bethesda, Maryland. Another shock. Here I entered a brave new world of learning, as well as social and political life. I found myself amid serious tensions and divisions over Vietnam and the politics of busing or the desegregation of the inner DC schools. And English was a core subject, with a lot of American literature content. There were more assumptions here: that you needed to know the history and litera-ture of your own country, a lesson I absorbed, although at an expatriate removal. In the school library, I would work at a table under a print of one of the Matthew Brady photographs of Walt Whitman and a framed poster of his poem 'Eidolons', with its typically Whitmanesque accretion of words around a subject: 'Ever the mutable!/ Ever materials, changing, crumbling, re-cohering'. Whitman High's literary journal, *Eidolon* took its name from this poem. This was a place and a culture, then, where literature and language had an altogether different valency.

But when I think about the stories our interviewees have told of their English teachers at school, a difference occurs to me. It wasn't actually an inspiring indivi-dual who was most influential to me: it was books or texts. In Washington, I would spend as many weekends as I could haunting the P Street bookshops in the old Georgetown terrace houses of downtown DC. These bookshops, sometimes more than one terrace house conjoined, were vast rabbit warrens of books. In one shop there was an attic stuffed with books with a lone attendant who seemed to have little contact with the rest of his own shop. I thought of him as a kind of Bartleby. Another bookshop was so huge it organised its books by publisher, rather than author or subject. I couldn't buy all the books I wanted to, of course, and anyway I wasn't really a book fetishist, it was more the windows onto literary and imaginative worlds that the books represented: Turgenev's light-filled stories of Russian country life; the unforeseeable lives of Stendhal's characters; the poetry sections.

Back in Australia again, for the 1970s. My undergraduate degree at ANU took the form of a double major in English, with an added Honours year. So, it was a pretty intense literary degree. It was structured around year-long historical surveys and language courses (OE and Middle English), with elective special units, like American Literature, and Dante. There was no Australian Literature course during my time as an undergraduate. The mode of English at this time and place was a mixture of New Criticism and Leavisism, with some Oxford textual studies – where I learnt a little about bibliography and the archive. It was also here that I encountered the method of close reading, and how it can be used for good or evil. There is a world of method and theory bound up in close reading, but it rests on knowledge, of any and every kind, about language. And in my experience it always had a sociable dimension, that is, close reading with other students and teachers in the tutorial or seminar. This is not incompatible with the point that Brenton mentions in connection with Fredric Jameson: there is no un-mediated encounter with the text, sure, but there are immediate encounters with its language by people who live differently within language. And that's the beginning of any other kind of reading that might be extended or developed, and of teaching how to read. It was an English course built on the canon but riddled with anxieties and contradictions as well, like the repressed contestation about Australian literature (see Meg Brayshaw [2021] for an account of the ongoing precariousness of Australian literature in the secondary and tertiary curriculum, nearly 50 years on). This degree led on, in a seriously haphazard way, to an MA (American Poetry) and a PhD (Australian Literature), and therefore to learning, first hand, more about the history of the discipline of literary studies in Australia. But the tertiary disciplinary terrain that I ended up teaching in, after experience teaching English in secondary schools in Victoria, and after the tidal wave of theory, had only a few archaeological remnants of the one I had trained in. At this time, as I was learning to become an English teacher across sectors and with myriad professional challenges, I also became involved with the professional association of English teachers and became absorbed in pedagogical theory and the discourse of teaching praxis. My experience of this involvement is a continuing history of discrepancy and commitment.

There was also another university that I was lucky enough to be part of, a dispersed one, outside the various English departments in which I studied and worked, where Australian literature was the core subject. This was the world of contemporary Australian writing, magazines and book production, where I was writing for newspapers and little magazines, and involved in editorial work, in festival and prize culture, in arts policy and international promotion. This is the world of living Australian writers, young and old, whom I was lucky enough to get to know and work with. It was also a world that intersected with anti-Vietnam protest in my ANU days, and other progressive social movements of the time, like the Aboriginal Tent Embassy, and that has continued to have this political and activist aspect. There are a host of tensions between this world and the discipline of literary studies at university. But because of my overriding interest in Australian literature – as something in the process, not just a canon or an archive – I have often tried to foster lines of connection between English studies and the literary world. I taught courses in creative writing, in regional literature, and an Honours course, 'Producing Australian Literature', for example, which tried to give students a knowledge of some of the institutions of Australian literary culture, and included invited writers and guests from publishing, editing and arts administration. Literary education can include a living, sociological content in this way.

A literary education is a constellation of unpredictable, contingent elements, often contradictory and unending, as well as absorbing and self-defining. There's the reality... In my experience literary education has been an imprecise, unknowing journey from fascination to messiness, through ignorance, infatuation and many impasses, with a puzzling and fraught relationship to the epoch I happen to have lived through, am living through. It was always as much social as solitary and scholarly. To connect the literary with education paradoxically attempts to combine this sense of continual uncertainty and unknowing with something that is embarrassingly old-fashioned and heavy with the implicit humanist ideals of growth, progression and self-knowledge.

Of course, we need educational ideals, eidolons Whitman would say. Especially since I seem never to have worked within an institutional setting where English or literary studies was without the most fundamental questions about its value. There was always a politics of knowledge in relation to other disciplines, always the imperative of defence. Just as there was always an unstable internal ratio between Australian literature (including Indigenous) and English, even between English and other versions of a national language. Teaching literature, including Australian literature, within secondary subject English or tertiary literary studies majors, or Australian and cultural studies programs, has always been a matter of working within rapidly evolving theoretical and critical paradigms, where every assumption about the value of literature, the political valencies of subject and discipline English (historically and in the present), and the definition (or relevance) of the national, including language itself, was in question. This reality was always something about which I learnt from my teachers, from colleagues – particularly international ones – and my students. Walking into the English classroom there was always a million possibilities, that was the exciting bit, including the possibility of having to say I don't know what a text might mean. Or, this text comes from a world none of us belongs to. The only response to all this incoherence and uncertainty seemed to be to follow the chimera of learning about language and its literary forms, in whatever historical or cultural setting.

References

Arendt, H. ([1954] 1968). *Between Past and Future*. New York: The Viking Press.

Barnes, D. R., Britton, J. N., & Rosen, H. (1971). *Language, the Learner and the School*. Harmondsworth: Penguin.

Boomer, G. (Ed.). (1982). *Negotiating the Curriculum: A Teacher-Student Partnership*. Sydney: Ashton Scholastic.

Brayshaw, M. (2021). Some thoughts on the (im)possibilities of teaching Australian literature. *Australian Humanities Review*, 68, 45–53.

Department of Education and Science (DES). (1975). *A Language for Life: Report of the Committee of Inquiry appointed by the Secretary of State for Education and Science under the Chairmanship of Sir Allan Bullock F.B.A*. London: Her Majesty's Stationery Office.

Doecke, B. (2004). My English history: Educating the educator. *English in Australia* 141, 9–18. http://hdl.handle.net/10536/DRO/DU:30035802.

Doecke, B. (2020). Missing something: A review essay on Joseph North's Literary Criticism: A Concise Political History. *Changing English*, 27(3), 333–348. https://doi.org/10.1080/1358684X.2020.1732191.

Doecke, B. (2021). Marxism and a literary education. *Changing English*, 28(2), 133–147. https://doi.org/10.1080/1358684X.2020.1848419.

Felski, R. (2008). *Uses of Literature*. Malden, MA and Oxford: Blackwell Publishing.

Gilbert, S., & Gubar, S. (1984). *The Madwoman in the Attic: The Woman Writer and the Nineteenth-Century Literary Imagination*. New Haven, CT: Yale University Press.

Jameson, F. (1981). *The Political Unconscious: Narrative as a Socially Symbolic Act*. New York: Cornell University Press.

McLean Davies, L. (2011). Magwitch madness. In B. Doecke, L. McLean Davies, & P. Mead (Eds.), *Teaching Australian Literature: From Classroom Conversations to National Imaginings*. Kent Town: AATE and Wakefield Press: 129–152.

McLeod, J., & Yates, L. (2006). *Making Modern Lives: Subjectivity, Schooling and Social Change*. New York: SUNY Press.

Mead, P., & Doecke, B. (2020). Pedagogy. In *Oxford Research Encyclopedia of Literature*. Oxford University Press. http://dx.doi.org/10.1093/acrefore/9780190201098.013.1032.

Miller, J. (1995). Trick or treat? The autobiography of the question. *English Quarterly* 27(3), 22–26.

Mishler, E. G. ([1986] 1991). *Research Interviewing: Context and Narrative*. Cambridge, MA and London: Harvard University Press.

Parr, G., & Doecke, B. (2012). Writing and professional learning: A 'dialogic interaction'. In M. Kooy and K. van Veen (Eds.), *Teacher Learning that Matters: International Perspectives*. New York: Routledge: 158–175. https://doi.org/10.4324/9780203805879.

Sawyer, W. (1995). Writing genres, writing for learning and writing teachers. In W. Sawyer (Ed.), *Teaching Writing: Is Genre the Answer?* Springwood: Australian Education Network: 7–24.

Sawyer, W. (2005). Becoming a new critic: Assessing student writing. In B. Doecke & G. Parr (Eds.), *Writing=Learning*. Kent Town: Wakefield Press: 129–145. http://handle.uws.edu.au:8081/1959.7/21990.

Sawyer, W. (2016). The grammar of memory. *Changing English: Studies in Culture and Education*, 23(2), 158–171. https://doi.org/10.1080/1358684X.2016.1162966.

Yandell, J., Doecke, B., & Abdi, Z. (2020). Who me? Hailing individuals as subjects: Standardized literacy testing as an instrument of neoliberal ideology. In S-A. Mirhosseini & P. I. De Costa (Eds.), *The Sociopolitics of English Language Testing*. London: Bloomsbury Academic: 3–22.

Yates, L. (2013). A conversation with the field. In M. Weaver-Hightower & C. Skelton (Ed.), *Leaders in Gender and Education: Intellectual Self-portraits*. Dortrecht: Sense Publishers: 227–239.

Yates, L., Woelert, P., Millar, V., & O'Connor, K. (2016). *Knowledge at the Crossroads? Physics and History in the Changing World of Schools and Universities*. Singapore: Springer.

3

LITERARY KNOWLEDGE DEBATES

Larissa McLean Davies and Wayne Sawyer

Introduction

> What is literary knowledge? Gosh. Yeah, that's huge… So maybe literary knowledge is the knowledge of how you read the world, and expanding your literary knowledge is expanding the ways in which you can read the world… yeah. Literary knowledge is everything.
>
> *(Veronika)*

> I don't really like the word 'knowledge' in terms of… I mean it sort of suggests that there's something to know. I mean… that there's some truth to be learnt that is teachable. I guess I think there is but… 'literary knowledge' sounds to me like knowing the right things about the right books, and I don't think that's what… that's simply not how I've found teaching literature to be, but if I think about literature more as like a way of being or a way of knowing…
>
> *(Katya)*

> Yeah. I don't think it's measurable. I think it's more a way of seeing into things, like making meaning from… yeah, like English (teachers) you know, they look at things a little bit differently (from) others.
>
> *(Rebecca)*

> I think literature is a way of knowing because obviously, it's a way to communicate ideas, whether it be through text or other resources, and it is a way to also share knowledge as well… a very good way to be able to better understand concepts, better understand the world… but I can't really illustrate

DOI: 10.4324/9781003106890-3

a story about how literature might be a way of knowing other than obviously by reading and comprehending you're able to… apply that.

(Scott)

One of the most striking themes from our initial interviews with early career teachers was the different ways in which they approached the concept of literary knowledge in English. For some, like Veronika, literary knowledge is expansive and fundamental, a way of students making meaning in and of the world. This is echoed in the reflections from Katya and Rebecca; however, these early career teachers also trouble the very notion of literary knowledge: Is 'knowledge' the right word? Can it be measured? Does this notion resonate with their purpose as English teachers? While Scott is confident that literary knowledge exists, he is less clear about the specificity of this knowledge, and how this might differ from other ways of understanding the world. This range of views, from just four teachers in the project, resonates with the complex ways in which debates about knowledge have been taken up since the subject became a formal part of schooling in the 19th century (Atherton, 2005a, p.11). Indeed, this equivalence and variety of perspectives on questions of knowledge in English, and, specifically, the knowledge work that is done by literary study, has become an enduring trope in the scholarship about subject English, as it is taught and researched across the world.

To this end, this chapter is guided by a series of critical and inter-related questions that we argue continue to be important to subject English over time, space and place: Does literature 'produce' knowledge? What are school students supposed to 'know' as a result of literary study? We acknowledge that in framing these questions, even the terms 'literature' and 'knowledge' are themselves not stable and that these questions resurface in the history of English and take on new meanings in different social and geographical, as well as historical, contexts. Nevertheless, we argue that this instability, disagreement and tension offers us insights into the ways in which literary knowledge has been understood and, indeed, may be seen as generative and fundamental to constituting the subject. Our focus is to explore these questions through some of the histories and contexts that have brought us to our current moment. As Muller reminds us, 'the forms of the disciplines we have today have their roots in… historical struggles and innovations… and… these shed light on much that seems to us perplexing and intractable today' (Muller, 2009, p.205). In particular, we draw on some of the early history of the establishment of English as a discipline in the northern hemisphere, as well as in Australia.

While the contemporary connections and disconnections between English as an academic (university) discipline and the school subject 'English' will be taken up more fully in Chapter 5, disciplinary and subject histories show us that the interplay between subject and discipline has shaped and informed debates about the role of literature in school English. This conceptual interplay was enabled, in part, by institutional structures and the role of universities vis-à-vis the secondary English curricula through the 19th and into the 20th centuries (Atherton, 2005a; Dale, 2012; Mathieson, 1975). Links between schools and universities were also materially facilitated by people: in England, this includes figures such as Matthew Arnold, who held both academic appointments and a key bureaucratic role overseeing schools, and, in colonial Australia, it includes academics, such as Edward Morris, who started their careers as school principals.

We acknowledge that the readings of the history and present of 'literature' and 'knowledge' that we offer in this chapter are influenced by our Australian cultural context. Questions of knowledge in subject English are often oriented towards, and stem from, the global North; here, we consider the way issues of knowledge have taken root, travelled and been adapted across hemispheres, influencing the teaching of English in colonised contexts such as Australia. By animating 'Southern' perspectives (West-Pavlov, 2018), this chapter offers a particular view on issues of knowledge in English/literature in the 21st century.

Does literature produce knowledge?

Before we approach this question concerning literature and its relationship to knowledge, we reiterate that fundamental issues about the purposes and definitions of English, and, hence, issues of knowledge in this subject, remain contested and problematic (Yates et al., 2019). It is reasonable to say that the dominant discourse and scholarship on subject English suggests that, unlike other school subjects (a point that is taken up further in Chapter 4), this area of the curriculum is not usually seen as focused centrally on 'knowledge', at least not as this term is understood in a propositional sense – an issue introduced in Chapter 1. This position has been taken up and reinforced over decades, with English consequently being characterised as an epistemologically unstable area of the curriculum, despite its enduring and often compulsory status in the secondary years of schooling. In Chapter 1 we quoted the Bullock Report's position that English 'does not hold together as a body of knowledge which can be identified, quantified, then transmitted' (DES, 1975, p.5) along with Peter Medway's argument that English constituted 'nothing less than a different model of education' (Medway, 1980, p.10), comments which have led Doecke to note that '[t]he word "knowledge" is certainly not a word that English educators have ever been able to use comfortably' (Doecke, 2019, p.350).

There are several reasons for this enduring conversation about knowledge in English. One is the relationship of the school subject to academic discipline(s). School subject English, as it is enacted in different national settings, draws together a range of disciplines: literary study, linguistics, cultural studies and creative writing, to name just some. As Garth Boomer once quipped, teaching English requires 'generic promiscuity' (1998, p.20). The knowledge question is particularly highly problematic with respect to literature. The central issues concern the nature of knowledge and understandings of the purposes of literary study that underpin different knowledge claims in school English.

Both the centrality of literary study and debate about what kinds of knowledge (if any) could be accorded to the study of literature was apparent in the campaign to introduce English into established universities in England in the 19th century (Atherton, 2005a). Atherton recounts that a key debate centred on whether the study of vernacular literature (as opposed to Classical literature, which had a firm place in tertiary education) belonged in the amateur (domestic) sphere or professional realm of the university (Atherton, 2005a). If reading fiction belonged solely in the home, or at least outside the institution, arguably it belonged to the realm of personal experience and leisure, rather than 'knowledge' as it was understood in general scientific terms, and therefore there was no basis for its inclusion in professional (tertiary) study. While these concerns were not raised in all settings where English and literature were already taught, such as working men's colleges and mechanics institutes (Dale, 2012; Dixon, 1991), the very presence of the study of 'the vernacular' in these institutions and organisations also cast doubt on the validity, worth and knowledge available through the university study of English literature (Mathieson, 1975).

Thus, the introduction of literary studies in established universities was made possible because those wishing to affirm it as a professional discipline successfully argued that it could be considered alongside disciplines such as science, history and philology (Atherton, 2005a, p.59). When English did eventually enter the institutions of Oxford and Cambridge, the role of the literary remained a problem for the status of the discipline. Although a Chair in English was appointed at Oxford in 1893, the first Professor to hold this role was a scholar of language, rather than literature. A Chair of English at Cambridge was not appointed until 1911.

There is some synergy between arguments and circumstances surrounding the introduction of English literature to universities in the 19th century, which involved scientific notions of knowledge as static and able to be codified, and the debates about 'powerful' disciplinary knowledge made by Young (2013) more than a century later, and which we discussed in Chapter 1 (see also Doecke & Mead, 2018). There is also a link between concerns around literature, and attitudes towards language, both in accounts of the development of English in England, and current institutionalised manifestations of knowledge around English, at least in Australia, where, in the *Australian Curriculum: English* triad of 'Language, Literature and Literacy', Language is privileged over Literature as the 'carrier' of knowledge (McLean Davies & Sawyer, 2018). These contemporary echoes remind us of the ways in which early disciplinary tensions continue to circulate in subject English, and of some of the ways in which the history of English as discipline and subject remains a spectre in current policy and practice. Here we examine some binary positions within that history that reveal, we believe, key underlying beliefs and practices relevant to questions of literature and knowledge.

What kinds of knowledge can literature produce? Some debates

The 'scholarly' and the 'critical': 'knowledge' and 'experience'

Of course, aspects of the teaching of literature do involve propositional knowledge and there are any number of very useful discussions about such knowledge and its uses at the secondary level – for example, discussions of the key terminology of literary study, key literary concepts, or fundamental theoretical issues in the subject (e.g. Marshall, 2014; NSWETA and NSWDE, 2017; Snapper, 2014) – what Kress et al. refer to as key 'curricular entities'(Kress et al., 2005). Moreover, we acknowledge that literature has been strongly argued as presenting us with cognitive propositions (e.g. Medway, 2010; see Sawyer & McLean Davies, 2021). Nevertheless, the role of propositional knowledge about literature, as against the direct experience of, and interpretation of, literary texts has formed one of the key historical binaries of the subject. This has sometimes been played out as 'scholars' versus 'critics', particularly in American historical work (Graff, 1987; North, 2017) with Graff arguing that these terms created a gulf between 'fact and value, investigation and appreciation, scientific specialization and general culture' (Graff, 1987, p.122).

In the 19th-century UK, as we have seen, the study of literary texts in the vernacular was positioned outside 'scholarship' and outside the sphere of specialist academic 'knowledge' itself, focusing 'on the subject's perceived lack of academic validity, and on the belief that it was concerned with judgements rather than knowledge, making it difficult to teach and assess' (Atherton, 2005b, p.221). Hilliard shows that as late as the 1950s in the UK, an examiner could still decline to award a PhD on the grounds of a thesis being 'not a contribution to knowledge, but a piece of literary criticism' (2012, p.10). The positioning of 'science' inside the 'scholarly' in these antitheses is particularly important (Atherton, 2005a, pp.4, 74, passim; North, 2017, pp.22–23) in the privileging of 'factual' knowledge over the 'critical' and in driving a strong emphasis on literary history (e.g. Atherton, 2005b, p.225; North, 2017).

Histories of English in secondary schooling present these debates as being reflected in, or having implications for, the school subject. In the US, of the 1950s, for example, Simmons et al. mark literary study in schools as centred on 'historical approaches versus those of explication de texte' (Simmons et al., 1990, p.96). In the British context major earlier formative factors on the study of English in schools, including the teaching methods of the Classics, the examination system, and the competing claims of literary study and philology (Ball, 1982, 1983, 1985; Homer, 1973; Shayer, 1972; Wright, 1986), effectively mimic much of the contemporary playing out of this history in the universities. This meant early attempts from the late 19th century to WWI to establish the 'integrity' of English by teaching it as if it were the Classics – which meant effectively providing a 'knowledge' for literature in hunting out allusions and in using passages from literature for grammatical analysis – later followed by the 'widespread practice of centring the literature courses on textbooks of literary history' as against a focus on the 'actual reading of texts' for 'real knowledge and appreciation' (Shayer, 1972, p.33). John Adams, for example, is quoted from his *The New Teaching* of 1918 as seeing 'the radical difference between the old teaching and the new' as passing from 'books about books to the books themselves' (in Shayer, 1972, p.60). Due to the influence of examinations, however, important literary knowledge continued to be conceptualised in terms of 'factual information' for some time (Shayer, 1972, p.67). This was a central problem identified by the Newbolt Report:

> We do not emphasise the study of the history of literature, as the danger always is that too much rather than too little attention may be given to it... the essential thing is that the text of the writers should be the first consideration.
>
> *(Newbolt, 1921, pp.118–119)*

All of this has implications for knowledge claims, with one side denying the other's claims to knowledge at all and the other attacking particular manifestations of knowledge as leading away from what was seen as more crucial, the focus on the text. In effect, this binary also resolved into the notion of (textual) 'experience' and 'knowledge' as a key conceptual opposition (Sawyer & McLean Davies, 2021).

'Elite knowledge' and 'knowledge of the masses'

References to the Newbolt Report also open other issues of knowledge in the history of the subject. Newbolt remains one of the most 'significant documents in the history of subject English' in Anglophone contexts (Doecke, 2019, p.340). Though rejecting the study of the history of literature in favour of a central focus on the text, Newbolt nevertheless made particular knowledge claims for English literature in the face of the contemporary dominance of the Classics:

> ...no form of knowledge can take precedence of a knowledge of English; no form of literature can take precedence of English literature: and... the two are so inextricably connected as to form the only basis possible for a national education.
>
> *(Newbolt, 1921, p.14)*

Interestingly, Newbolt's discourse is one of social justice, entitlement and inclusion (McLean Davies & Sawyer, 2020). The Report sees itself as expansive and as having a social justice agenda: literary knowledge was to be available to all students of all backgrounds, whatever their class (Newbolt, 1921, p.60). Nevertheless, though nuanced (libraries in Continuation Schools should have regard to 'the tastes of the adolescent wage-earner' [p.148]), Newbolt ultimately privileges canonical literature over 'the trivial realism... in the ephemeral novels which fill the book-shops today' (1921, p.338) for its aims of developing 'taste' (pp.15, 148, 275, 331, passim) and 'human character' (p.118). Thus, it has been criticised for presenting the culture of the ruling classes as Culture itself (Ball et al., 1990).

This discourse on literature as the gateway to 'culture' positioned schools and English teachers in a particular way. Mathieson's *The Preachers of Culture* famously draws a direct line from Arnold to Leavis via the Newbolt Report (a view reflected in its broad outlines by Baldick [1983]) to position English teachers as 'missionaries' and then 'warriors' of culture, bringing literature as the 'central humanizing experience of the curriculum and critical discrimination as a morally educative activity' (1975, p.138; see pp. 85–139; see also Eagleton, 1983, p.33ff, and

Hodgson, 1974, pp.231–233, 282–314). Centrally for our purposes here, the notion of what 'literature' *is* is not regarded as problematic in this paradigm, which posits a culture and morality that transcends class differences.

Following the rise of Leavis, Ball traces competing orthodoxies from the 1950s to the 1970s represented by Leavis, Thompson and 'Cambridge' on the one hand, and 'London' represented by thinkers such as Britton, Barnes, Rosen and Dixon (Ball et al., 1990, p.58) on the other, as a polarisation of elite and mass concepts of culture (Ball, 1985, 1987), with 'Cambridge', for example, stressing 'high culture' and 'heritage' along with literary-critical methods. Ball et al. (1990) see these orthodoxies specifically as issues of knowledge – as the difference between two opposed knowledge bases: 'elite knowledge' and the 'knowledge of the masses' (p.59). If one accepts this characterisation, then, 'elite' and 'mass' knowledge bases are starkly present at the heyday of the Growth model:

> In the Cambridge vision [are] the English teacher and the great literary heritage with which they are entrusted… In contrast, the London vision celebrates the immediate life, culture and language of the school student. And for many teachers, especially those in the urban centres, that has meant primarily the lives, culture and language of the working class.
>
> *(Ball et al., 1990, p.59)*

The special case of 'Growth'

Ball's historical work then puts the moment of Growth at the centre of the elite knowledge/mass knowledge binary, with the Growth model epitomising one side of that binary. Growth also links into the scholarly/critical binary through the key conceptualisations of 'knowledge' and 'experience'.

John Dixon's *Growth through English* was widely criticised for a number of years following the Dartmouth conference by a literature-centred school who saw his emphasis on pupil experience, and the idea that pupils' own writing was itself suitable literature for classroom consideration, as denigrating the study of literature in the curriculum (Allen, 1980; Hansen, 1979; Inglis, 1975; Whitehead, 1976). Dixon's argument, however, was not a turning away from literature – of the British and Americans at Dartmouth, he says that 'the common ground we found lay in the teaching of imaginative literature' (Dixon, 1975, p.123). Rather, what Dixon wanted to turn away from was the way literature had been deployed as nation-building and as 'civilising' 'a generation that knew largely slums and economic depression' . The two key problems with what he called the 'cultural heritage' approach were that in actual classrooms the 'precious lifeblood of a master spirit (became) a series of inky marginal annotations and essay notes'. The other – more fundamental – is that '[i]n the heritage model the stress was on culture as a *given*'. Dixon's was not a rejection of canonical literature as a category, but rather an emphasising of pupils' interaction with 'the world of the writer' (Dixon, 1975, pp.2–3). Individual response to, and experience of, the text was where literature sat in this view. The contemporary account by Muller refers to the 'British aversion to teaching knowledge about literature', instead 'wanting to concentrate on the understanding and appreciation of particular literary works' (Muller, 1967, p.12) (It was actually a view shared by many of the Americans at the conference as well [see Sawyer, 2019].)

For Dixon, the role of literature is part of the opportunity to use language to explore, order and organise one's experience in Britton's 'spectator' role (Britton, 1970) – where Britton himself also situates literature (Dixon, 1975, pp.4, 8, 9, 28–29). Literature is to add to the store of shared experience in the classroom by 'bringing new voices into the classroom' and 'helping to bring order and meaning to parts of (a student's) experience' (Dixon, 1975, pp.13, 30, 36, 44). Placing pupils' cultures at the centre of the concerns of the classroom was a radical move – but was not unrelated both to Dixon's valuing of literature and to the role of response and 'experience'. The elite knowledge/mass knowledge debate and the knowledge/experience debate are brought together in *Growth through English.*

Not all history, however, simply lines up Growth with 'mass knowledge' and 'experience' in these binary oppositions. Medway (1990), for example, sees 'London' and 'Cambridge' as having common Romantic values in the authority of individual response and the priority of an intelligence of feelings over one of thought (1990, pp.22–23). This was the alliance of a Lawrentian–Leavisite inheritance with a particular construction of 'personal experience' that led, according to Medway, to a construction of English preoccupied with 'feeling', and a certain anti-intellectualism – in effect, in the terms being considered here, a turning away from knowledge (1990, p.25). Moreover, argues Medway, 'Growth' gave English a unique content touched on nowhere else in the curriculum: 'personal experience' with methods and models drawn from literature (1990, p.27). Medway effectively returns us to the specialist/non-specialist terms of the earliest debates around English:

> The strategy was quite different from that which has been well documented for other subjects, the pursuit of academicization… Rather, non-specialism itself became a sort of specialism, one for the handling of which a literary background and trained sensibility were prerequisites.
>
> *(Medway, 1990, p.27)*

The linking of Leavisite traditions with Growth is a not uncommon position in histories of the period (Christie, 1993; Green, 1995, p.397ff; Hamley, 1979, p.347ff; Moon, 2012; Patterson, 1992). Moreover, as we have pointed out elsewhere (McLean Davies & Sawyer, 2020), the examples of literature offered for student reading in *Growth through English* tend to largely reinforce the primacy of the British canon: of the over 30 relevant authors and works referenced in *Growth through English*, almost all are from the UK and only three are published after 1961 – a position reinforced by the monograph from the Dartmouth Study Group on Response to Literature (Squire, 1968; for discussion, see McLean Davies et al., 2019; Sawyer et al., 2016).

The impact of Growth in Australia has been far-reaching (Homer, 1973; Nay-Brock, 1984; Reid, 2003, 2016; Sawyer, 2008; Sawyer & Durrant, 2019). As has been argued elsewhere (McLean Davies et al., 2019), this is apparent in literary curricula of the time. For example, the influence of Growth is evident in the 1975 advice to senior English teachers in the State of Victoria that they focus their attention on the way literature can support an understanding of 'ourselves and the world' (VUSEB, 1975, p.187). Yet, again, this tended to be accompanied by canonical literature as central to students' meaning-making activities. The 28 texts that were selected for this understanding of 'ourselves and the world' are drawn largely from the British or North American canon and published in previous generations (McLean Davies et al., 2019). This has historically arguably framed Growth in a particular imperial way in Australia, and it is this issue of a tension between imperial knowledge and local knowledge to which we now turn.

'Imperial knowledge' and 'local/national knowledge'

Dale's *The Enchantment of English* (2012) shows that the reader's close engagement with the text was the central point of studying literature and any dispute on this point was subsumed by issues of literature as cultural heritage, apparatus and capital in 19th-century Australia. While debates in the UK regarding literary knowledge largely focused on 'how' and 'why' one might engage with literature, in colonised contexts such as Australia, the issue was much more about 'what' was being read, and questions of 'why' took on an even more explicit, imperial cultural purpose. Separated physically from the 'motherland', an understanding of English literature was considered 'the most effective way to strengthen the ties of empire' (Dale, 2012, p.91), and, to take Arnold's 1869 formulation, to guard against 'anarchy' (Arnold, 1971). The notion was that English and its texts would enable any person, no matter their birth or origins, to have knowledge of the 'best that has been thought and said in the world' (Arnold, 1971, p. 6) Writing about the literature to be supported in India, Macaulay argued:

> Whoever knows [English] has ready access to all the vast intellectual wealth which all the wisest nations of the earth have created and hoarded in the course of ninety generations. It may safely be said that the literature now extant in that language is of greater value than all the literature which three hundred years ago was extant in all the languages of the world together.
>
> *(Macaulay, 1835, n.p.)*

The sentiments were carried into all of England's colonial contexts. As one might expect, the force of English in the imperial cultural project in Australia, supported by senior university academics who maintained their professional capital by writing and teaching about English literature, meant that Australian literature was rarely the focus of students' literary experiences. A famous and oft-cited case is Professor J. M. Stewart's avowal, in the 1940s, of the non-existence of Australian literature, in the context of giving a lecture supported by the Commonwealth Literary Fund (see McLean Davies et al., 2021). As Dale writes: 'the dominance of an aesthetic of Englishness structured a sustained disdain for local literature, writers and critical issues' (Dale, 2012, p.19). This continued to be the case later in the 20th century, even when Chairs in Australian Literature were instituted, and had a particular role in advocating for that field. Leonie Kramer, then an Associate Professor of Australian Literature, writing in the national English teachers' journal in 1967, encouraged teachers to identify the value in reading Australian literature, arguing that it had a place in the curriculum even though its quality might be inferior 'to the best of other traditions' (Kramer, 1967, p. 48). Kramer's advocacy for Australian literature, and acknowledgement of perceived tension and disparity – which endures (see Doecke et al., 2011; McLean Davies et al., 2017) – between the quality of locally produced texts and those published in a different hemisphere also communicates an understanding of the kinds of 'knowledge' certain literatures can produce. For Kramer, literature has more than one epistemological purpose: Australian (colonial) literature, as she defines it, can give local students insight into the context and history in which they are living, while British and European literature offers aesthetic insights into 'high-quality' literary writing. At a time when Australian writers, including Australian Indigenous writers, are world-renowned, and questions of quality are not at issue, this argument, intended by Kramer to enable national texts to gain traction in schools, is still used by some teachers and social commentators against their inclusion (McLean Davies et al., 2021).

It is worth noting that Kramer's writing in 1967 argued for the value of Australian literature as a tool for Australian subjectivity and identity development and offered a departure from the English curriculum as it had been enacted in the different Australian States. Green and Cormack note the ways that the early 20th-century primary school curriculum in the State of South Australia approached English and the teaching of literature in a way that would enable students to develop a complementary subject position as Australians within broader allegiance to the Empire (Green & Cormack, 2008). Beavis's examination of the intended curriculum evident in the popular *Victorian Readers*, a series of books set for use in Years 3–8 in the State of Victoria, shows an emphasis on content from England, along with an overall desire to use literature as a means for young colonial subjects to 'travel' beyond Australian shores (Beavis, 1996). Published from 1927–1930, some of these Readers were used in schools until the 1960s.

Debates about the relevance of Australian literature in the curriculum have continued into the 21st century (McLean Davies et al., 2021), and led to the mandating of Australian texts, and particularly texts by Aboriginal and Torres Strait Islander writers, which otherwise remain marginalised in the curriculum (McLean Davies et al., 2017). Reviews of the curriculum by conservative commentators highlight that British cultural heritage texts continue to be prioritised as authentic, valuable literature (DESE, 2014) and analysis of examinations shows that students who write on texts that form the British canon will be more likely to be rewarded by examiners (McLean Davies & Martin, 2017; Teese, 2013). Against this backdrop, we see various interventions designed to unsettle what has become the school canon of English. Groups such as the Copyright Association's 'Reading Australia' (www.readingaustralia.com.au) and AustLit (www.austlit.edu.au), the Australian literature database, for example, offer support for teachers to unsettle dominant colonial narrative. However, such dominant imperial approaches remain difficult to shift (McLean Davies et al., 2020). As part of the *Investigating Literary Knowledge Project*, on which this book is based, we surveyed over 700 teachers across Australia. One survey question asked them to report on the texts that they selected for study. The most commonly referenced texts were (in order of most-cited): *Macbeth* (Shakespeare); *Romeo and Juliet* (Shakespeare); *To Kill a Mockingbird* (Lee); *Animal Farm* (Orwell); *Of Mice and Men* (Steinbeck); *Hamlet* (Shakespeare); *The Outsiders* (Hinton); *Jasper Jones* (Silvey); *1984* (Orwell), and *Othello* (Shakespeare). Of course, this list does not reflect all texts taught or their diversity, but it does indicate enduring canonical allegiances. It is perhaps unsurprising that a report of the most popular texts taught in Britain for Years 7–9 has many of these same titles (Kneen et al., 2021). Of note, the only Australian text to be in the top ten cited in our survey is *Jasper Jones*, by Craig Silvey, a non-Indigenous writer. While this coming-of-age text is named after a young Aboriginal character, the narrator is a young white male. It has been argued that the popularity of this text indicates that teachers want to acknowledge the experiences of Indigenous Australians, but in such a way that does not overtly challenge established narratives and voices (McLean Davies et al., 2021). Issues of whose stories are told, and whose knowledge is privileged, in Australian schools remain significant to debates about literary study in school English in Australia (Bliss & Bacalja, 2021; Truman et al, 2021).

Knowledge: the critical and aesthetic (and the personal)

Just as the Growth approach to English brought with it a range of debates regarding the possibilities of literary knowledge, the advent of critical literacy in schools in the 1990s impacted on the ways that literature was positioned in subject English, and brought about new ways of thinking about the knowledge readers might have about, bring to bear on, and take away from, literature. Central to critical literacy approaches is the understanding that 'all language is socially contextualized… texts are inherently ideological, and… texts are fundamental to the construction of our identity' (Misson & Morgan, 2006, p.ix). Critical literacy was particularly taken up in Commonwealth countries, such as South Africa, Canada and Australia (White & Cooper, 2015), as they sought to 'understand and manage the relationship between language and power' (Janks, 2000, p.175), and enact a social justice agenda. In this way, we see perhaps the first major debate about subject English being generated and perpetuated from outside the imperial centre.

Writing from within the Australian context, Luke argues that these critiques of language, texts and power, from various 'postcolonial, feminist and sociological' standpoints (2000, p.448), culminated in the translation of curriculum critique into the practical creation of critical literacy resources for teachers. Luke argues that sociological, post-structuralist and feminist critiques responded to individualism and the 'emphasis on personal "voice"' of Growth, contending that this was 'at the expense of an understanding about how discourses construct multiple and gendered forms of social identity' (Luke, 2000, p.452). This opposition of 'personal' and 'social' constitutes the most fundamental distinction between the Growth model and critical literacy, as perceived by critical literacy adherents. Specific curricula are suggested with variations on themes such as:

- making explicit the ways in which readers are positioned by texts so that those positionings can be resisted (Mellor & Patterson, 1994)
- making the classroom itself and its curriculum into the 'text' which is explicitly open to discussion and change (Boomer, 1989)
- the 'institutional conditions' of English themselves becoming the curriculum (Patterson, 1990)
- a particular emphasis on 'how particular genres of intellectual and political power work, and how to strategically construct them' (Luke, 2000, p.452).

Growth's emphasis on the 'personal', so goes the argument, leaves students in no position to analyse or critique the institutional parameters of subject English, and thus, ultimately, the basis of the dominant and valued culture, usually as represented by white, middle-class masculine values.

If 'cultural heritage' focused on the text-as-cultural-knowledge and Growth located literary knowledge in the classroom interactions of readers, critical literacy offered a different paradigm located within a much more directly transmissive pedagogy (Boomer, 1989; Patterson, 1992). As a consequence, many resources were developed for teachers, such as the *Chalkface Press* series in Australia, which offered curated collections of short texts with accompanying activities that directed students towards, for example, particular kinds of resistant readings (e.g. Mellor et al., 1987).

Media and political (and often confected) outrage about critical literacy in Australia is well documented (see Gannon & Sawyer, 2015; Lucy & Mickler, 2006, Chapter 1), usually framed as one or more of: the politicisation of the classroom, the scourge of postmodernism, or the loss of the canon (the latter therefore confusing ways of reading with bodies of texts). More importantly, within the academy, key critiques of critical literacy in Australia included a focus on the roles of the aesthetic and of the pleasure to be derived from the text (Misson & Morgan, 2006). Outside of the school subject and in the disciplinary context, Sedgwick has sought to recover literary study from 'paranoid reading' (Sedgwick, 2003) and Felski has also sought to understand the influence of Ricoeur's 'hermeneutics of suspicion' (Felski 2015, p.37) for literary scholarship. Felski critiques contemporary 'criticism' as:

> …a stance incompatible with distraction, relaxation, ease, or indifference. Rather, we are always "on the lookout"—scrutinizing, scanning, searching, surveying, observing, gazing, examining. This looking is not a yielding gaze of pleasure, absorption, or entrancement but a sharp-eyed and diligent hunt.
>
> *(Felski, 2015, pp.37–38)*

It is important to note that arguments such as Felski's are not seeking to return literary studies to a less critical or rigorous engagement with texts, but rather suggest that literary epistemologies and pedagogies need to be understood more expansively – to:

> de-essentialize the practice of suspicious reading by disinvesting it of presumptions of inherent rigour or intrinsic radicalism—thereby freeing up literary studies to embrace a wider range of affective styles and modes of argument.
>
> *(Felski, 2015, p.3)*

Felski's support of affect as a way of knowing and co-creating literature articulates with an affective turn in literary studies (Ahern, 2019; Houen, 2020), which both 'returns' the personal to literary-critical scholarship and offers alternative ways of conceptualising literary knowledge. Recent scholarship has highlighted that Indigenous reading practices offer ways of mediating and drawing together epistemology and ontology in ways that emphasise pedagogies of relationality and community (Philips et al., 2022); however, much more work is needed at curriculum and classroom levels for the potential of these decolonising practices to be realised for all Australian students. For Pitt and Britzman (2003) and Zembylas (2014), literary affect can often lead readers (students and teachers) to experience 'difficult knowledge' including knowledge about privilege, whiteness, race and class, and means that classrooms become spaces for 'pedagogies of discomfort' (Zembylas, 2015) that can open up social justice issues.

The notion of literature producing the conditions to encounter difficult knowledge suggests that literary response is both personal and ideological (and potentially transformative); the nature of the knowledge created through students' engagement with literary texts can still depend on individuals' backgrounds and life experiences. As a result of this, we have seen policymakers, parents and the media in Australia, for example, express anxiety about the kinds of texts students encounter in English, and the potential impact of 'difficult knowledge' (with regard to racism, mental health, social breakdown for example) on students' wellbeing and engagement (Cook, 2017; Medina, 2014; VCAA, 2018). In this context, the idea that literature is, through affect and experience, producing knowledge appears to be a given, and it is the nature and purpose of this form of knowing that is the focus of the debate.

★

In this chapter, we have drawn on the history and present of subject English to explore key debates regarding literary knowledge. While conceptualising knowledge debates as binaries in this way risks some over-simplification, it can nevertheless place into stark focus the central epistemological issues. These include:

- issues of whether literature deals with 'knowledge' at all, and what kinds of knowledge this might encompass
- what the implications of certain kinds of knowledge are for maintaining focus on the literary text, or on the reader and their experience

- whose knowledge is represented by the positioning of particular literature(s) in curricula – including in terms of nation, culture, gender, race and class
- the role that literary knowledge plays in students' understandings of the world and culture, including in settler contexts
- whether knowledge of particular texts needs to adopt, in turn, particular reading positions by focusing on textual rhetorics and discourses that may prompt responses that include surrender, resistance or discomfort.

As we have discussed, debates about literary knowledge have been central to broader debates about the purposes and direction of English since the beginning of the discipline. We consider these debates in relation to the experiences and per-spectives of the early career teachers in our study in later chapters.

References

Ahern, S. (2019). *Affect Theory and Literary Critical Practice: A Feel for the Text*. New York: Springer International Publishing.

Allen, D. (1980). *English Teaching Since 1965: How Much Growth?*London: Heinemann.

Arnold, M. (1971). *Culture and Anarchy*. Cambridge: Cambridge University Press.

Atherton, C. (2005a). *Defining Literary Criticism: Scholarship, Authority and the Possession of Literary Knowledge, 1880–2002*. New York: Palgrave.

Atherton, C. (2005b). The organization of literary knowledge: The study of English in the late nineteenth century. In M. Daunton (Ed.), *The Organization of Knowledge in Victorian Britain*. Oxford: Oxford University Press: 219–234.

Baldick, C. (1983). *The Social Mission of English Criticism, 1848–1932*. Oxford: Clarendon Press.

Ball, S. J. (1982). Competition and conflict in the teaching of English: A socio-historical analysis. *Journal of Curriculum Studies,* 14(1), 1–28.

Ball, S. J. (1983). A subject of privilege: English and the school curriculum 1906–35. In M. Hammersley & A. Hargreaves (Eds.), *Curriculum Practice: Some Sociological Case Studies*. London and New York: The Falmer Press: 61–88.

Ball, S. J. (1985). English for the English since 1906. In I. F. Goodson (Ed.), *Social Histories of the Secondary Curriculum: Subjects for Study*. London and Philadelphia: The Falmer Press: 53–88.

Ball, S. J. (1987). English teaching, the state and forms of literacy. In S. Kroon & J. Sturm (Eds.), *Research on Mother Tongue Education in an International Perspective: Papers of the Second International Symposium of the International Mother Tongue Education Network, Antwerp, December 1986*. Enschede: International Mother Tongue Education Network: 19–36.

Ball, S., Kenny, A., & Gardiner, D. (1990). Literacy, politics and the teaching of English. In I. F. Goodson & P. Medway (Eds.), *Bringing English to Order*. London, New York and Philadelphia: The Falmer Press: 47–86.

Beavis, C. (1996). Changing constructions: Literature, 'text' and English teaching in Victoria. A historical account. In B. Green & C. Beavis (Eds.), *Teaching the English Subjects: Essays on English Curriculum History and Australian Schooling*. Geelong: Deakin University Press: 15–39.

Bliss, L., & Bacalja, A. (2021). What counts? Inclusion and diversity in the senior English curriculum. *The Australian Educational Researcher*, 48(1), 165–182. https://doi.org/10.1007/s13384-020-00384-x.

Boomer, G. (1989). Literacy: The epic challenge beyond progressivism. *English in Australia*, 89, 4–17. https://search.informit.org/doi/10.3316/informit.542851428861996.

Boomer, G. (1998). English teaching: Art and science. *English in Australia*, 122, 15–25. https:// search.informit.org/doi/10.3316/aeipt.90653.

Britton, J. N. (1970). *Language and Learning*. London: Allen Lane.

Christie, F. (1993). The 'received tradition' of English teaching: The decline of rhetoric and the corruption of grammar. In B. Green (Ed.), *The Insistence of the Letter: Literacy Studies and Curriculum Theorizing*. Pittsburgh, PA: University of Pittsburgh Press: 75–106.

Cook, H. (2017). Too many 'depressing messages' in VCE books drives push for trigger warnings. *The Age*, 27 April. Available: www.theage.com.au/national/victoria/too-ma ny-depressing-messages-in-vce-books-drives-push-for-trigger-warnings-20170427-gvtybq. html. Accessed 20 April 2022

Dale, L. (2012). *The Enchantment of English: Professing English Literatures in Australian Universities*. 2nd ed. Sydney: Sydney University Press.

Department of Education and Science (DES). (1975). *A Language for Life: Report of the Committee of Inquiry appointed by the Secretary of State for Education and Science under the Chairmanship of Sir Allan Bullock F.B.A.* London: Her Majesty's Stationery Office.

Department of Education, Skills and Employment (DESE). (2014). *Review of the Australian Curriculum: Supplementary Material*. Canberra: Australian Government Department of Education. Available: www.dese.gov.au/australian-curriculum/resources/review-australia n-curriculum-supplementary-material. Accessed 31 December 2021.

Dixon, J. (1975). *Growth through English: Set in the Perspective of the Seventies*. 3rd ed. London: Oxford University Press.

Dixon, J. (1991). *A Schooling in English: Critical Episodes in the Struggle to Shape Literary and Cultural Studies*. Milton Keynes and Philadelphia: Open University Press.

Doecke, B. (2019). Rewriting the history of subject English through the lens of 'literary sociability'. *Changing English*, 26(4), 339–356. https://doi.org/10.1080/1358684X.2019. 1649116.

Doecke, B., McLean Davies, L., & Mead, P. (2011). National imaginings and classroom conversations: Past and present debates about teaching Australian literature. In B. Doecke, L. McLean Davies, & P. Mead (Eds.), *Teaching Australian Literature: From Classroom Conversations to National Imaginings*. Adelaide: Wakefield Press: 1–15.

Doecke, B., & Mead, P. (2018). English and the knowledge question. *Pedagogy, Culture & Society*, 26(2), 249–264. https://doi.org/10.1080/14681366.2017.1380691.

Eagleton, T. (1983). *Literary Theory: An Introduction*. Oxford: Blackwell.

Felski, R. (2015). *The Limits of Critique*. Chicago and London: University of Chicago Press.

Gannon, S., & Sawyer, W. (2015). Literacy, literature and moral panic in Australia. In M. Yunus & B. Bertram (Eds.), *The International Handbook of Progressive Education*. New York: Peter Lang: 309–324.

Graff, G. (1987). *Professing Literature: An Institutional History*. Chicago: University of Chicago Press.

Green, B. (1995). Post-curriculum possibilities: English teaching, cultural politics, and the postmodern turn. *Journal of Curriculum Studies*, 27(4), 392–409.

Green, B., & Cormack, P. (2008). Curriculum history, 'English' and the New Education; or, installing the Empire of English? *Pedagogy, Culture and Society*, 16(3), 253–267. https:// doi.org/10.1080/14681360802346648.

Hamley, D. (1979). *Changing Principles and Recommended Practice in the Teaching of Fiction in Elementary and Secondary Schools from 1902 to the Present with Special Reference to the Age Group 11–13*. Unpublished PhD thesis: University of Leicester.

Hansen, I. V. (1979). The case for literature study in secondary schools: Some difficulties. *The Teaching of English*, 36(5), 3–16.

Hilliard, C. (2012). *English as a Vocation: The Scrutiny Movement*. Oxford: Oxford University Press.

Hinton, S. E. (2017). *The Outsiders*. Melbourne: Penguin Books Australia

Hodgson, J. T. (1974). *Changes in English Teaching: Institutionalization, Transmission and Ideology*. Unpublished PhD thesis: London University.

Homer, D. B. (1973). *Fifty Years of Purpose and Precept in English Teaching (1921–71): An Overview with Special Reference to the Teaching of Poetry in the Early Secondary Years*. Unpublished MEd thesis: Melbourne University.

Houen, A. (2020). *Affect and Literature*. Cambridge: Cambridge University Press.

Inglis, F. (1975). *Ideology and the Imagination*. Cambridge: Cambridge University Press.

Janks, H. (2000). Domination, access, diversity and design: A synthesis for critical literacy education. *Educational Review*, 52(2), 175–186.

Kneen, J., Chapman, S., Foley, J., Kelly, L., Smith, L., Thomas, H., & Watson, A. (2021). *What literature texts are being taught in Years 7 to 9?* Available: https://ukla.org/wp-content/uploads/Research-Report-What-literature-texts-are-being-taught-in-Years-7-to-9.pdf. Accessed 9 May 2022.

Kramer, L. (1967). The Australian heritage. *English in Australia*, 5, 43–55.

Kress, G., Jewitt, C., Bourne, J., Franks, A., Hardcastle, J., Jones, K., & Reid., E. (2005). *English in Urban Classrooms: A Multimodal Perspective on Teaching and Learning*. London: Routledge Falmer.

Lee, H. (2010). *To Kill a Mockingbird*. Melbourne: Penguin Books Australia .

Lucy, N., & Mickler, S. (2006). *The War on Democracy: Conservative Opinion in the Australian Press*. Perth: University of Western Australia Press.

Luke, A. (2000). Critical literacy in Australia: A matter of context and standpoint. *Journal of Adolescent & Adult Literacy*, 43(5), February, 448–461.

Macaulay, T. B. (1835). *Minute by Hon'ble T. B. Macaulay dated the 2nd February 1835*. Columbia.edu. Available: www.columbia.edu/itc/mealac/pritchett/00generallinks/macaulay/txt_minute_education_1835.html. Accessed 21 December 2021.

Marshall, B. (2014). What does it mean 'to know' in English? In A. Goodwyn, L. Reid, & C. Durrant (Eds.), *International Perspectives on Teaching English in a Globalised World*. London and New York: Routledge: 13–24.

Mathieson, M. (1975). *The Preachers of Culture: A Study of English and its Teachers*. London: Allen & Unwin.

McLean Davies, L., Buzacott, L., & Martin, S. K. (2019). Growing the nation: The influence of Dartmouth on the teaching of literature in subject English in Australia. In A. Goodwyn, C. Durrant, W. Sawyer, L. Scherff, & D. Zancanella (Eds.), *The Future of English Teaching Worldwide: Celebrating 50 Years from the Dartmouth Conference*. London and New York: Routledge: 146–158.

McLean Davies, L., & Martin, S. (2017). Toward worlding settler texts: Tracking the uses of Miles Franklin's *My Brilliant Career* through the curriculum. *Australian Literary Studies*, 32 (2), 1–24. https://doi.org/10.20314/als.8cd522979e.

McLean Davies, L., Martin, S. K., & Buzacott, L. (2017). Worldly reading: Teaching Australian literature in the twenty-first century. *English in Australia*, 52(3), 21–30.

McLean Davies, L., Martin, S. K., & Buzacott, L. (2021). Critical considerations of the challenges of teaching national literatures in Australia in the 21st century. *The Australian Educational Researcher*, 1–17. https://doi.org/10.1007/s13384-021-00448-6.

McLean Davies, L., & Sawyer, W. (2018). (K)now you see it, (k) now you don't: Literary knowledge in the Australian Curriculum: English. *Journal of Curriculum Studies*, 50(6), 836–849. https://doi.org/10.1080/00220272.2018.1499807.

McLean Davies, L., & Sawyer, W. (2020). On being 'well read'. In B. Marshall, J. Manuel, D. L. Pasternak, & J. Rowsell (Eds.), *The Bloomsbury Handbook of Reading Perspectives and Practices*. London: Bloomsbury: 145–166.

McLean Davies, L., Truman, S. E., & Buzacott, L. (2020). Teacher-researchers: A pilot project for unsettling the secondary Australian literary canon. *Gender and Education*, 33(7), 1–16. https://doi.org/10.1080/09540253.2020.1735313.

Medina, J. (2014). Warning: The literary canon could make students squirm. *New York Times*, 17 May. Available: www.nytimes.com/2014/05/18/us/warning-the-literary-canon-could-make-students-squirm.html. Accessed 31 December 2021.

Medway, P. (1980). *Finding a Language: Autonomy and Learning in School*. London: Writers and Readers Publishing Cooperative.

Medway, P. (1990). Into the sixties: English and English society at a time of change. In I. F. Goodson & P. Medway (Eds.), *Bringing English to Order: The History and Politics of a School Subject*. London, New York and Philadelphia: The Falmer Press: 1–46.

Medway, P. (2010). English and Enlightenment. *Changing English: Studies in Culture and Education*, 17(1), 3–12. https://doi.org/10.1080/13586840903556987.

Mellor, B., O'Neill, M., & Patterson, A. (1987). *Reading Stories*. Scarborough: Chalkface Press.

Mellor, B., & Patterson, A. (1994). Producing readings: Freedom versus normativity. *English in Australia, 109*, 42–56. http://eprints.qut.edu.au/53535/.

Misson, R., & Morgan, W. (2006). *Critical Literacy and the Aesthetic: Transforming the English Classroom*. Urbana, IL: NCTE.

Moon, B. (2012). Remembering rhetoric: Recalling a tradition of explicit instruction in writing. *English in Australia*, 47(1), 37–52. https://search.informit.org/doi/10.3316/aeipt.192556.

Muller, H. J. (1967). *The Uses of English: Guidelines for the Teaching of English from the Anglo-American Conference at Dartmouth College*. New York: Holt, Rinehart, Winston.

Muller, J. (2009). Forms of knowledge and curriculum coherence. *Journal of Education and Work*, 22(3), 205–226. https://doi.org/10.1080/13639080902957905.

Nay-Brock, P. (1984). *A History of the Development of the English Syllabuses in NSW Secondary Education, 1953–1976: A Continuum or a 'Series of New Beginnings'?* Unpublished PhD thesis: University of New England.

Newbolt, H. (Chair), The Departmental Committee appointed by the President of the Board of Education to inquire into the position of English in the educational system of England (1921). *The Teaching of English in England*. London: His Majesty's Stationery Office.

New South Wales English Teachers Association (NSWETA) and New South Wales Department of Education (NSWDE). (2017). *English Textual Concepts and Learning Processes*. Sydney: State of New South Wales Department of Education Learning and Teaching Directorate.

North, J. (2017). *Literary Criticism: A Concise Political History*. Cambridge, MA: Harvard University Press.

Orwell, G. (2021). *Animal Farm and 1984*. Melbourne: Fusion Books.

Patterson, A. (1990). Changing the questions: The construction of alternative meanings in the English classroom. *English in Australia*, 94, 59–72.

Patterson, A. (1992). Individualism in English: From personal growth to discursive construction. *English Education*, 24(3), 131–146. www.jstor.org/stable/40172828.

Phillips, S., McLean Davies, L., & Truman, S. (2022). Power of country: Indigenous relationality and reading Indigenous climate fiction in Australia. *Curriculum Inquiry*, 52(1), 171–86. https://doi.org/10.1080/03626784.2022.2041978.

Pitt, A., & Britzman, D. (2003). Speculations on qualities of difficult knowledge in teaching and learning: An experiment in psychoanalytic research. *International Journal of Qualitative Studies in Education*, 16(6), 755–776. https://doi.org/10.1080/09518390310001632135.

Reid, I. (2003). The persistent pedagogy of 'Growth'. In B. Doecke, D. Homer, & H. Nixon (Eds.), *English Teachers at Work: Narratives, Counter Narratives and Arguments*. Kent Town: AATE/Wakefield Press: 97–108.

Reid, I. (2016). Literary experience and literature teaching since the growth model. *English in Australia*, 51(3), 11–18.

Sawyer, W. (2008). English teaching in New South Wales since 1971: Versions of growth? *Changing English: Studies in Culture and Education*, 15(3), 323–337.

Sawyer, W. (2019). Growth through English and the uses of English: Literature, knowledge and experience. In A. Goodwyn, C. Durrant, W. Sawyer, L. Scherff, & D. Zancanella (Eds.), *The Future of English Teaching Worldwide: Celebrating 50 Years from the Dartmouth Conference*. London and New York: Routledge: 27–41.

Sawyer, W., & Durrant, C. (2019). Dartmouth and personal growth in Australia: The New South Wales and Western Australian curricula of the 1970s. In A. Goodwyn, C. Durrant, W. Sawyer, L. Scherff, & D. Zancanella (Eds.), *The Future of English Teaching Worldwide: Celebrating 50 Years from the Dartmouth Conference*. London and New York: Routledge: 65–80.

Sawyer, W., & McLean Davies, L. (2021). What do we want students to know from being taught a poem? *Changing English*, 28(1), 103–117. https://doi.org/10.1080/1358684X.2020.1842174.

Sawyer, W., McLean Davies, L., Gannon, S., & Dowsett, P. (2016). Mid-Atlantic crossings: Some texts that emerged from Dartmouth. *English in Australia*, 51(3), 40–51. https://search.informit.org/doi/10.3316/informit.470257372840048.

Sedgwick, E. (2003). *Touching Feeling: Affect, Pedagogy, Performativity*. Durham, NC: Duke University Press.

Shakespeare, W. (1969). *Hamlet*. Cambridge: Cambridge University Press.

Shakespeare, W. (1977). *Romeo and Juliet*. Harmondsworth: Penguin.

Shakespeare, W. (1992). *Macbeth*. Ware: Wordsworth Editions.

Shakespeare, W. (2008). *Othello: The Moor of Venice*. Oxford: Oxford University Press.

Shayer, D. (1972). *The Teaching of English in Schools 1900–1970*. London and Boston, MA: RKP.

Silvey, C. (2011). *Jasper Jones*. New York: Alfred A. Knopf Books for Young Readers.

Simmons, J. S., Shafer, R. E., & Shadiow, L. K. (1990). The swinging pendulum: Teaching English in the USA, 1945–1987. In J. Britton, R. E. Shafer, & K. Watson (Eds.), *Teaching and Learning English Worldwide*. Clevedon and Philadelphia, PA: Multilingual Matters Ltd.: 89–130.

Snapper, G. (2014). Student, reader, critic, teacher: Issues and identities in post-16 English Literature. In A. Goodwyn, L. Reid, & C. Durrant (Eds.), *International Perspectives on Teaching English in a Globalised World*. London and New York: Routledge: 53–64.

Squire, J. R. (Ed.) (1968). *Response to Literature: Papers Relating to the Anglo-American Seminar on the Teaching of English at Dartmouth College, New Hampshire, 1966*. Champaign, IL: NCTE.

Steinbeck, J. (1984). *Of Mice and Men. 1937*. New York: Bantam.

Teese, R. (2013). *Academic Success and Social Power: Examinations and Inequality*. North Melbourne: Australian Scholarly Publishing.

Truman, S. E., McLean Davies, L., & Buzacott, L. (2021). Disrupting intertextual power networks: Challenging literature in schools. *Discourse: Studies in the Cultural Politics of Education*, 1–14. https://doi.org/10.1080/01596306.2021.1910929.

Victorian Curriculum and Assessment Authority (VCAA) (2018). *VCAA Principles, Guidelines and Procedures for Prescribed VCE Text Lists*. Available: www.vcaa.vic.edu.au/Documents/vce/Principles_Guidelines_Texts.pdf. Accessed 31 December 2021.

Victorian Universities and Schools Examination Board (VUSEB). (1975). *Handbook of Directions and Prescriptions for 1976*. Melbourne: VUSEB.

West-Pavlov, R. (Ed.). (2018). *The Global South and Literature*. Cambridge: Cambridge University Press.

White, R. E., & Cooper, K. (2015). *Democracy and Its Discontents: Critical Literacy across Global Contexts*. Rotterdam: Sense.

Whitehead, F. (1976). The present state of English teaching: (1) Stunting the growth. *The Use of English*, 28(1), 11–17.

Wright, E. (1986). English teaching: Classics in the vernacular. In M. Price (Ed.), *The Development of the Secondary Curriculum*. London: Croom Helm: 49–76.

Yates, L., McLean Davies, L., Buzacott, L., Doecke, B., Mead, P., & Sawyer, W. (2019). School English, literature and the knowledge-base question. *The Curriculum Journal*, 30(1), 51–68. https://doi.org/10.1080/09585176.2018.1543603.

Young, M. (2013). Overcoming the crisis in curriculum theory: A knowledge-based approach. *Journal of Curriculum Studies*, 45(2), 101–118. https://doi.org/10.1080/00220272.2013.764505.

Zembylas, M. (2014). Theorizing 'difficult knowledge' in the aftermath of the 'affective turn': Implications for curriculum and pedagogy in handling traumatic representations. *Curriculum Inquiry*, 44(3), 390–412. https://doi.org/10.1111/curi.12051.

Zembylas, M. (2015). Pedagogy of discomfort and its ethical implications: The tensions of ethical violence in social justice education. *Ethics and Education*, 10(2), 163–174. https://doi.org/10.1080/17449642.2015.1039274.

4

CURRICULUM AND KNOWLEDGE QUESTIONS

Is English peculiar?

Lyn Yates

Much of this book is concerned with the specificity of literary studies in subject English. We began our project intending to explore the thinking, practices and contexts of new English teachers in Australia today, with a particular focus on questions about knowledge. A number of chapters in this book also make a case that English is not just *distinctive* as a subject or form of knowing, but that it is *'exceptional'* (see also Green, 2018; Medway, 2005, 2010). This chapter, however, is written not from inside the subject or discipline or field of English, but from outside it, from the broader field of curriculum scholarship and curriculum policy-making. The aim here is to consider broader rationales and perspectives on curriculum, and particularly on curriculum and knowledge, since the 'knowledge question' for literature was one of the starting points of our own project.

Neither in practice nor the curriculum literature are discussions about curriculum necessarily framed as discussions about knowledge, at least in the sense of some of the specific perspectives on knowledge we will touch on here. This chapter is not intended to be in any sense a comprehensive account of the whole field of curriculum studies, a field whose starting points over time and in different locations have ranged so broadly. Rather, what I am intending in this chapter is a selective discussion of some perspectives of the general curriculum literature that provide context for our own project's starting points and that represent some influential concerns in current times. It is particularly concerned with arguments that are set within or take account of curriculum as part of a schooling and testing *system*. This discussion may capture for readers some elements of what is *not* 'exceptional' about English – of ways in which, as a school subject, it is positioned in and constructed by that very status, which is as an element of the curriculum within a system of compulsory schooling.

Arguably, in so far as school subjects are components of a system of schooling, they participate in three different but overlapping knowledge-related functions of

DOI: 10.4324/9781003106890-4

schooling (Yates, 2017). First, schools are expected to contribute to the capacities of students: the intellectual growth and knowledge, abilities and competencies of young people. Second, the curriculum is expected to contribute to the formation of young people as future members of a particular society (which may be national, colonial, global or other mixes of these). And third, curriculum (via subject choices and streaming and testing) is one of the mechanisms by which young people are sorted into differential opportunities in their future. These three functions of curriculum (which we might summarise as intellect, identity and opportunity) take different forms and relative importance in different places and times, but all have some relevance to the issue of subject English and questions of knowledge.

Let us begin by considering the version of these curriculum concerns that was circulating and much discussed in Australia at the starting point of the current project: the newly developed first national curriculum framework, the *Australian Curriculum* (see ACARA, n.d.; Reid & Price, 2018; Yates, 2018). The *Australian Curriculum* was one of many new national curriculum frameworks and reforms being produced in the early 21st century (Priestley & Biesta, 2013; Yates & Grumet, 2011). These did not take identical forms, but all in some senses were responding to felt concerns to redefine national curricula in the changing 'global' world, and each was also somewhat influenced by the international testing and comparison generated and publicised by the OECD, and by a culture of political and policy thinking that had a new emphasis on measurement and accountability. For example, Biesta and Priestley sum up the new Scottish curriculum in this way:

> When we zoom in on what is happening at the level of curriculum practice and, to a certain extent, curriculum policy, we find trends going in one direction – focusing on children and students and their learning, on teachers and their agency, and on the promotion of wider capacities and capabilities – but when we zoom out to bring the wider socio-political context into view, we see things moving in a different direction – one of narrow aims, central control and measurable outcomes.
>
> *(Biesta & Priestley, 2013, p.230)*

The new *Australian Curriculum* took a less child-centred approach than the Scottish curriculum and spoke more directly to interests in knowledge. But it too reflected some of the tensions to which Biesta and Priestley allude. It was designed around a tripartite structure, named 'learning areas', 'general capabilities', and 'cross-curriculum priorities'. These take up three different elements and drivers of curriculum that were being refreshed in the curriculum reforms of the early 21st century. First, *learning areas* identify and promote forms of knowledge of the kind traditionally represented by school subjects. In the *Australian Curriculum*, these are a recognisable and largely traditional array of subjects, with some updating and collapsing to try to avoid an overloaded curriculum. In relation to each learning area, the document aimed to set out a grid for the years up to Year 10, which would be *systematic* and 'identify both conceptual and substantive topics' as a basis for ensuring that knowledge in each area would 'build or cumulate' over the years of schooling. In this respect the framework was signalling two concerns we will come back to shortly: the value of including contributions from different subject areas/forms of knowledge (as distinct from generic skills or competencies) since they are seen as having some distinctiveness from each other and some specific contribution to make to the development of students; and, secondly, an interest in driving 'effective' (interpreted as cumulative) learning over time, with measurement and accountability orientations being an implicit background to this policy.

A second element of the *Australian Curriculum* framework was what it called *general capabilities*, which it named as 'literacy, numeracy, information and communication technology capability, critical and creative thinking, personal and social capability, ethical understanding and intercultural understanding'. This element tacitly references a strand of thinking about competencies or capabilities that had become prominent in the 21st century. It is seen in the academic literature (Nussbaum & Sen, 2010; Reid, 2012); it is referenced in many reports by politicians and employers, and it is embedded in the work of multinational bodies such as the OECD and the commercially underpinned '21st Century Skills Assessment Project' (Griffin, McGaw & Care, 2012). Thinking of this kind is apparent, for example, in frameworks being developed by the EU, whose own grid of 'transversal competencies' was expected to run alongside or within traditional subjects as a new touchstone across different national curricula (Crick, 2008; Wahlstrom, 2016). Here the driver is thinking about the desired outcome of schooling rather than its content: on what kind of capabilities would be needed to flourish in the 21st century. This was a very popular topic of many education writings as the world entered the 21st century (Yates et al., 2017).

Finally, the Australian framework named a third set of agendas, called *cross-curriculum priorities*. These identified some substantive content or topic foci that should be included across learning areas and were more specifically about identifying what is important content and values for students in this time and place to encounter. For Australia, these priorities were defined as Aboriginal and Torres Strait Islander histories and cultures, Asia and Australia's engagement with Asia, and Sustainability. This part of the framework takes up an element of reform that can be seen more clearly if you look at curriculum documents over time, or across countries: their changing content and emphases as they seek to include something about what it means to be a member of a particular national (and international) entity at a particular time in history. But naming substantive agendas and values in this way is also a strong locus of political contention, as can be seen in the criticism subsequently made of this framework by conservatives in Australia and, from the opposite political direction, in the many criticisms of various UK curricula as trying to present a romanticised past rather than a multicultural present.

Later the *Australian Curriculum* was modified further. The complexity of trying to take up all three perspectives in some detail led to concerns from teachers about over-complexity, and they raised many questions about what the capabilities and cross-curriculum priorities actually entailed within the teaching of a particular 'learning area'. But overall the three named components of the *Australian Curriculum* did, and do, reflect some different missions for curriculum that are potentially part of a knowledge agenda – exposure to different areas and forms of organised knowledge; development of different capabilities; and exposure to content and values and material specifically relevant to students' identity formation. All three of these make appearances in the accounts we hear from English teachers discussed in later chapters.

At the same time, in the Anglo, European and Asian curriculum literature (less so in North America), another debate was flourishing concerning the curriculum and knowledge. This argument was seeking to re-emphasise the central purpose of schools as the first of the three components of the curriculum set out in the Australian framework: knowledge as represented in the school subjects. The argument was that expectations of schools had become unrealistically vast, were too disputed and much too expansive to be actually achieved, and it was time to refocus on what Michael Young called 'powerful knowledge' (Young & Muller, 2010). If that was done, it was argued, the capabilities would take care of themselves and indeed would take a deeper form that was often missing when people focused simply on 21st-century skills and processes such as communication or problem-solving. And, it was argued, the social identifications, the third of the agendas of the *Australian Curriculum*, was not the central role of schools, though these could be taken up at the school level in terms of pedagogical choices.

One reason that the term 'knowledge' may resonate with the public or politicians is precisely the reason that many English teachers in our project felt uncomfortable with it – that it sounds concrete and objective, like facts or propositional knowledge. But the argument in the various accounts by Young and Muller and Moore and others associated with 'bringing knowledge back in' was not simply about students learning 'facts' (see, for example, Young & Muller, 2010, 2013). They argued that 'powerful' knowledge, of the kind that could guide the school curriculum, would demonstrate the following characteristics:

- enable those who acquire it to see *beyond their everyday experience*
- produce *reliable and broadly testable* explanations
- be *conceptual* as well as based on *evidence and experience*
- always be *open to challenge – 'truth-seeking'*
- be *a basis for suggesting realistic alternatives*
- be acquired in *specialist institutions*, staffed by specialists
- be organised into *domains, with boundaries that are not arbitrary, but associated with specialist communities such as subject and professional associations*
- *is often but not* always *discipline-based*.

Clearly, many of these do not fit easily with subject English, and other chapters in this book talk at more length about the problematic assumptions involved in assuming a field has a particular kind of relationship to a discipline, or that 'knowledge' is necessarily 'specialist' or that 'powerful knowledge' is necessarily about reliable and broadly testable explanations. The particular 'social realist' view of knowledge underlying the argument here has been the subject of considerable criticism. Bill Green, in a recent extended discussion of subject English and curriculum inquiry in relation to each other (Green, 2018), makes an argument for a different way of seeing knowledge and curriculum, one in which English, far from being a subject that fails to meet some of the criteria for 'powerful knowledge' outlined above, becomes a model for the curriculum enterprise.

Green argues that in contemporary times the post-structural concern with difference and representation is a better way to think about knowledge than the social realist position of an objective knowledge 'out there'. It is wrong, in this position, to separate curriculum from pedagogy and to see what teachers are doing as primarily translating knowledge from elsewhere. Rather, teachers' work is seen as an active form of knowledge-making for students, given the complexity of meaning-making, and that knowledge involves not just propositional or procedural elements, but the ability of the student (now and in their future life) to act or practice: 'the formation of 'personhood', of a subject-individual, equipped with specific forms of agency and authority' (Green, 2018, p.249).

Green argues that subject English is associated with a practice – 'with doing and making, with reading and writing, talking and listening, viewing and creating as activities' (Green, 2018, p.276). The practice necessarily involves attention both to the students and meaning-making and to their awareness of the public framing and impact of the texts and practices they work with.

Nevertheless, the call to arms for a less relativist and less social message-oriented position on curriculum by Young and colleagues also drew a lot of interest, with special issues in curriculum journals, partnerships with some schools (Young & Lambert, 2014) and some influence on policy-making. It was making a case about the purposes of schools, and about what distinguishes a curriculum that is beneficial for students in the long term. It was meant to be a challenge to school subjects and teachers across the curriculum to think more explicitly about the quality of what they were teaching in ways that were not simply derived from whatever was examined, or from some other contemporary positions on education purposes that Young and Muller argued were problematic.

One such 21st-century common sense is to conceive curriculum wholly or primarily in terms of output skills or competencies or learning. Biesta has called this contemporary fashion 'learnification' (Biesta, 2017), and it is seen, for example in the worldwide popularity of John Hattie's series of books on 'visible learning' (e.g. Hattie, 2012). As Biesta argues, contemporary learning and competencies discourses tend to avoid questions about the aims of education or about the role of teachers (that is, they take these as given). The 'powerful knowledge' interjection tried to disrupt that taken for granted. It argued that 'learner' focused, and 'competencies' focused, frameworks are superficial bases for education. By comparison, a curriculum built on developed fields of knowledge should remain important because these have something distinctive and deeper to contribute to the capacities of students beyond school. In an earlier research project, I carried out, both secondary and tertiary teachers of history and physics strongly echoed this case. They were similarly concerned by an apparent dominance of a more generic skills or competencies approach to school (and indeed university) curriculum (Yates et al., 2017).

When we look at the way English teachers (and stakeholders) talk about their work in later chapters, they seem to be conveying a view of what they are doing which lies outside or is different from either of these two positions. For almost all of the teachers, what they are doing in class and with texts *is* seen by them as going beyond just teaching skills or competencies, and is seen as a subject that will provide a deeper and better foundation to expand students' capacities in their life beyond school as compared with a simple 'skills' focus. But (compared with the history and physics teachers) their claims for the value of their subject do not tend to ground this (explicitly) in terms of their 'discipline' or field and what it has achieved.

A second mantra, which the 'bringing knowledge back in' arguments specifically confronted, is that there can be no basis for a curriculum that transcends politics and political agendas. This had been a core and multi-pronged theme of the sociological curriculum literature since the 1970s and publicly mounted in many critical social movements concerned with feminism, race, Indigenous recognition, disability rights, sexuality, etc. Here the 'knowledge-based curriculum' arguments were suggesting that a curriculum grounded in such concerns is inevitably relativist, and ties students too much to the teachers' (or a curriculum framework's) current way of seeing, without providing firm foundations for young people to move on in their life beyond school. Young was arguing for thinking about curriculum not from a starting point that 'this should be in the curriculum because I like it/am nostalgic about it/it represents my politics' to 'this should be in the curriculum because it has this kind of longer-term knowledge content and role for students that they otherwise may not have access to'. It is arguing for a move from seeing curriculum simply as a means to transfer messages, skills and ideologies of various kinds to students, to one that is interested in what different forms of knowledge make possible for students beyond the messages of the day.

Now it might be argued that the 'knowledge' argument here is putting together two different issues that would be better kept distinct. One is that for students' longer-term interests, they should be introduced to forms of knowledge or ways of knowing that are not simply messages but have some continuing power in their dealing with the world. The second is that it is possible to have a curriculum based on knowledge that transcends social interests. In the case of English, it is evident that one might argue for the former without committing to the latter, and indeed this is the case more broadly. Leaving, for now, the important question of how far 'what is knowledge' is agreed in different disciplines, the case ignores the necessarily selective form which curriculum takes. In any subject area there will still be decisions to be made about *what is of worth* being included in the curriculum, and these cannot be answered only from within a body of knowledge, no matter how reliable. In my earlier project, we found that even in physics, where there is considerable agreement about the fundamentals of the discipline, there are choices of topics that must be made, especially in the senior years, and these are not neutral in relation to their social world they convey, or to their impact on students (Yates & Millar, 2016). This was even more evident in history, where the story of the nation is a traditionally important part of the school curriculum and, in democracies, is always contested. And of course, it is a common debate in relation to subject English and text selections.

As many have noted, the issue of 'what knowledge is of most worth?' is possibly the central curriculum question ('knowledge' here understood in the broadest sense), and this begins with the very selection of subjects or other components that make up the curriculum. For example, Daniel Tröhler draws attention to the different national starting points in 19th-century Europe of what were to be the core components of the curriculum:

> In the curriculum of 19th century France… history, geography, music and even physical education were rarely taught, in contrast to Germany, where national self-assurance had to include the feeling of Germany's heroic historical past, knowledge about the different German States, a feeling of togetherness through community singing (of either religious or national songs) and physical strength as the basis for future soldiers. (Harp, 1998, p.60). France, in contrast, limited itself mainly to the 3Rs, religion and – against the background of France's actual multilingualism – the French language: In the course of the 19th century, the conviction grew to perfect certainty that 'one could not really be French without speaking French'(Harp, 1998, p.33).
>
> *(Tröhler, 2016, p.289)*

Tröhler's historical work on the development of schooling in the 19th century finds that among the national variations regarding what students should learn at school, one commonality was evident: the belief in the foundational significance of the national language and the literature and stories through which it was to be taught – and even more so in countries where the national language and related literature were not already universal. In Australia, Green and Cormack (2011) have shown the work that went into providing reading materials for children in the early 20th century that aimed to develop them as members of an Australian nation, as well as members of the British Empire and inheritors of its traditions. More recently, in the wake of a globalised testing-led and competencies-based curriculum, writers have given attention to the cultural form inherent in that particular approach to knowledge and its deliberate by-passing of cultural specificities. Karseth and Sivesind (2011) draw attention to the way in which these developments are not merely a neutral framework emphasising capability, but actively downplay knowledge that has national cultural specificity, such as the work of Henrik Ibsen for Norwegian students. Similarly, many writers in many countries have written about how the official curriculum silences and under-represents Indigenous knowledge.

Seeing curriculum as a message system that embeds/transmits/reproduces power and inequalities has been a favourite theme of critical social movements and sociologists of the curriculum since the 1970s. And there is a recognition that this is not just about which texts are chosen to represent literature, though that is an obvious part of it. *Whatever* is taught (including ways of knowing) and *whatever* is validated by testing was seen to represent what Michael Apple called 'official knowledge', and to represent a selection from actual social and cultural diversity that represents the interests of the powerful. These arguments are familiar to English teachers through the wide-ranging debates about literacy, about 'standard' and 'non-standard English' and colonial education systems. We will see later (in Chapter 9) that some of these issues continue to be live ones for the teachers in our project.

The perspective that subjects such as literary studies reflect class-based, and race, gender and national/colonial kinds of biases in the content they select and prioritise has gradually been fairly widely accepted, but it is a perspective that functions more readily as a critique, or as a justification for particular inclusions, than as a broader basis for curriculum (Yates, 2018). We will see in later chapters that many teachers continue to be troubled by their inability to resolve their concerns about representation – that is, their awareness of the inevitability of some categories of authors or stories not being included, given the inevitable limits of time and resources in any given curriculum, as well as their awareness of the different kinds of language and life experience some students bring to school compared with others. Young tried to resolve the impasse by making a distinction between 'knowledge of the powerful' and 'powerful knowledge'. He did not deny inequalities of students in relation to curriculum content that was associated with some backgrounds over others but argued that where knowledge was indeed more powerful and deeper, the issue should be about access to this for all (echoing, to some extent, Bernstein's earlier work on 'elaborated' and 'restricted' codes). This argument has been much criticised (e.g. Whitty, 2010; Zipin et al., 2015) and not just for accepting continuing social inequalities in students' success as a likely result of this perspective. For the field of literary studies, it dodges the problem that the changing and contested perspectives on what matters are integral to the discipline itself. And in its perspective on what knowledge is, it is criticised for depending on a view of knowledge as stable and 'out there', and with the role of schools being essentially limited to 'recontextualising' such knowledge for students, rather than seeing schools as having a more dynamic and creative role in relation to students and knowledge (Green, 2018).

An alternative approach to the concern with knowledge as an ideology of the powerful has been to argue for a critical pedagogy, where students are taught to focus on and unpick what is sexist, racist, colonialist etc. in the various subjects they are exposed to. Again, we will see this approach mentioned in some form and variation by many of the teachers in our project, and professors of literary studies interviewed in the project also see this as one mainstream element of their disciplinary work. But many of our interviewees – teachers, professors, other stakeholders – touched on the problem of legitimate critical perspectives or themes in literary studies being turned into something else when they became the answer expected in a high-stakes examination, or when they were taught as a direct instruction to students in how they should read a text.

A further theme of the sociological critique of the curriculum is about 'cultural capital', and this is referenced in some of our interviews in later chapters in reference to a literary canon. Here one argument is that regardless of how powerful or not-powerful or biased certain forms of knowledge or content may be, they may be associated with social power and status. In the Anglo world, the veneration of and facility with Shakespeare is frequently seen as a marker of this. The argument goes in two directions: that an elite or professional upbringing develops the kind of cultural capital that underpins success in school for these students compared with their less-favoured fellow students; and that mastering such elements of the curriculum supports one's opportunities to be an equal of the powerful going forward, especially at university. This is a highly simplified version of arguments particularly associated with the French theorist, Pierre Bourdieu, and there are good questions about whether in the 21st century and countries like Australia, that kind of cultural knowledge has the broad power it was argued to have in the different context of France half a century ago, especially given the significance of mathematics, science, entrepreneurial qualities and the like in current times, and the spread of the culture-free kind of testing and comparisons associated with OECD and PISA. Nevertheless, Richard Teese among others has shown that patterns of subject choice and school results in Australia bear out some of the big directions that Bourdieu showed (Teese, 2000), in particular that class inequalities are stronger in subjects such as literature or physics, for reasons of embedded class-based cultural dispositions and experience. The arguments here are useful to consider because they bear on the questions of knowledge and ways of knowing, and especially on some arguments about knowledge in literary studies.

Bourdieu's body of work was not simply about text selections and hierarchies of content, but much more about the subtler characteristics of what is valorised and rewarded in the education system – and it especially applies to those school subjects whose knowledge characteristics do not seem to be easily made explicit. One of his books was devoted to analysing taste as a historical and socially distributed phenomenon (Bourdieu, 1979). And much of his work on the ways schooling reproduces social inequalities was about subtle cultural/gender/race 'dispositions' that are rewarded in school for some and make school difficult to succeed in for others (Bourdieu & Passeron, 1970). If a student is asked to produce a 'close reading' of a text, the question is what criteria (not necessarily conscious criteria) does a teacher or examiner actually draw on in seeing that work as good or not so good; what are they implicitly holding up as the form and substance of knowing that matters? Bourdieu argued that for students who do not come from already privileged backgrounds, the curriculum often asks them for what they cannot give – the embedded and not necessarily conscious dispositions produced in a home 'habitus' that can produce or inhibit mastery in this area.

A more recent sociological curriculum argument by Karl Maton (2013) pursues some similar arguments, as an argument about the structure of knowledge in different subject areas. Many sociological perspectives on disciplinary knowledge identify knowledge as having a different structural form in the sciences compared with the humanities and social sciences in a way that has a particular significance for the school curriculum. (And incidentally, in so far as this is the case, it challenges curriculum frameworks that try to adopt a common grid of development over the years of schooling as the *Australian Curriculum* did.) The sciences are seen as hierarchical, so teaching topics in a way that ignores the foundational building blocks and the way these underpin higher levels of knowledge would mean that students learn only propositional bits and pieces, or a superficial problem-solving, but not the deeper insider understandings of that field's form of knowing that will allow them to go on developing further understandings themselves. The humanities however are said to have a horizontal logic, where people work on different topics or texts, gradually developing more sophistication, but without a necessary hierarchical order to what they study.

Maton's extension of this argument is that subjects either have what he calls a 'knowledge' structure or a 'knower' structure. Science is an example of the former. For students to advance in science they need to understand the principles and foundational structure, and this is something derived from the discipline; it is 'objectively' part of the structure of the discipline, not dependent on particular teachers or practitioners of the discipline. But for humanities and many arts subjects (Maton uses music as an example), the question of excellence and mastery is not seen as a function of some underlying structure of the field, but of learning to operate in a similar way to those who are accepted as the authorities of the field – he calls this a 'knower' structure. Learning does not have to be advanced by revealing principles or foundations of the form of knowledge, but by giving students examples and feedback to draw them closer to those seen as the leaders of the field. Maton argues that teaching a 'knowledge' subject as a 'knower' subject, or vice versa, will weaken students' success in that subject.

English is often referred to as a hybrid subject, and Macken-Horarik (2011) argued that the new subject English framework in the *Australian Curriculum* confused the principles Maton discussed. She argued that the *Australian Curriculum's* overarching framework was of a 'knowledge' structure (one which wanted to set out explicit principles of how each subject was built from one level to the next). However, Macken-Horarik argued, the critical responses of the professional association of English teachers to the curriculum framework were virtually unanimous that this was not what literature teaching was about, and they appealed to big names in the field to support their case – in other words, she argued, they were asserting a 'knower' structure to the field. Macken-Horarik argued that the *Australian Curriculum: English* lacked 'face validity' because in literature studies (but not in language studies) it tried to impose a structure of knowledge, a form of knowing, that was not accepted by those in the professional field.

While there are different forms of knowledge and knowing in different fields, the case for dividing knowledge into just two main forms, and applying a 'knower' label for the humanities is, I would argue, too dominated by thinking about the kind of scientist view of knowledge seen in Young's dot points above. It does little to elucidate what form of knowledge or knowing is at work in these other fields other than that there is often a reluctance to tie this to neat foundational principles (*why* in a 'knower' structure are some considered authorities, for example). Maton's 'knower' case can come across as if the subject is a black box without identifiable history or shape or context for those seen as 'authorities'. The English professional association responses to the *Australian Curriculum* did indeed cite recognisable authorities as grounds for their response (interestingly these were mainly English educators, not literature professors), but also made substantive identifications of the alternative knowledge structure they understood to be central in English 'that English teachers must acknowledge and draw on students' existing repertoires of language use and textual practices' (see Green, 2018, p.200). Green also notes that the 'knower' question for English elides the issue of whether the ideal 'knower' is seen as an author or a critic.

The arguments about knowledge structures I have outlined here are pertinent to the issue of teaching practices in relation to examinations, discussed further in Chapter 9. If the subject does not expose its principles or foundations to students then judgements of 'taste' to which many students do not have ready access are likely to be dominant. If teachers or frameworks do try to teach directly the 'principles' on which the discipline is built or what counts in terms of assessment (for example, certain forms of critique, or thematic reading or language), they may feel and recognise that they are doing some harm to developing the kind of knowledge which is actually important in that field, namely knowledge which is more nuanced or tacit, and demonstrated rather than reduced to rules. In our stakeholder interviews, a number of the interviewees lamented the tendency towards providing more and more explicit guidance as to what was being looked for in the final high-stakes examination. They argued that this produces a narrowness and a more direct and formulaic type of learning that conflicts with the intentions of the subject, producing a quest for the right answer that first-year university studies in English had to work to undo. But, as one education professor noted, the previous assessment practice, where an overall judgement was made of an essay, and specific criteria were largely tacit, was also not without its problems, of the kind identified by Bourdieu. That stakeholder nevertheless was in favour of a move back in that direction, as a move more in keeping with the knowledge form of this subject, than the detailed specifications of agendas. The problems in attempting to straddle any form of the high-stakes system-wide assessment in these competitive situations may be one reason why teachers, as discussed in Chapter 9, are tempted towards providing scripted answers for the high-stakes final examination in English while also recognising this as wrong, as not what they understand as the form of knowledge in literary studies; and why others lament the impossibility of teaching in a limited time the broad cultural knowledge and 'dispositions' needed to score highly in that examination.

A perspective on different 'structures' of knowledge (a 'knowledge' structure and a 'knower' structure) does not in itself address what of value, if anything, is going on in the latter; what might be the point of this way of knowing that would give students something of value beyond their school days. As the curriculum philosopher Gert Biesta argues:

While the sociology of the curriculum has generated important insights about curricular knowledge, it cannot act as the ultimate arbiter on questions of knowledge. The main unease when everything becomes sociologized and when everything is seen as a social construction is that the idea of knowledge itself begins to disappear.

(Biesta, 2014, p.33)

Biesta's philosophical work on curriculum builds both on Deweyan traditions in the US and the *didaktics/bildung* European traditions. The *didaktics* component of teacher preparation in northern Europe has some resonances with the kinds of sociological interest in the characteristics of knowledge and different forms of knowledge discussed above. However, in this European tradition, the purpose of schooling was never seen simply as a function of knowledge structures and the transferring of these into students, but as a proper and separate question that needs to be addressed in its own right (*bildung*). Stefan Hopmann argues that the curriculum should bring together three concerns: knowledge, students, and purposes of schooling, and must always embed an openness of outcome. As Editor of *The Journal of Curriculum Studies*, Hopmann (2013) argued that the testing-led and economistic framing of contemporary schooling may be 'the end of schooling as we know it', by denying this essentially open-ended and creative element of the teaching and learning mission of schools.

In terms of purposes of schooling, Biesta argues that education has three tasks that teachers must attend to and try to keep in balance: *qualification, socialisation* and what he calls '*subjectification*'. In subjectification, the student is appreciated as an agent not simply an object of teaching and is brought into an encounter with the world which is inherently open-ended in how the student takes it up or refuses it. Conceiving teaching either as purely child-centred or as purely about the transmission of external knowledge is to debase or refuse its main task of bringing these together (Biesta, 2017).

This has been a selective discussion of some curriculum arguments, and I have not discussed many progressive philosophies or pedagogy-centred writings that are not concerned with school subjects. Yet, it might be argued, many cases for the distinctive form of English and literary studies as knowledge have more in common with such perspectives, in their emphasis on language, experience and meaning and on students and their development rather than on subject content. But the sociological and system perspective that has been discussed in this chapter helps to draw attention to mechanisms that are part of the institutional setting of school and that frame the practices and impact of whatever is done within the subject of English.

This chapter is a reminder that 'knowledge' in a narrow capacity-building sense is not the only focus of curriculum concerns. The social formation function tied to the selective nature of what is included in the curriculum is unavoidable, as are issues about inequalities and management of difference and diversity, particularly in relation to systems of examination and selective opportunity for students. These pose issues for English and literature studies. In terms of perspectives on knowledge, the chapter tried to show some different ways of thinking about what is powerful or valuable for students and some ways of enacting this in recent curriculum policy that have their own impact and problems.

References

Biesta, G. (2014). Pragmatising the curriculum: Bringing knowledge back into the curriculum conversation, but via pragmatism. *The Curriculum Journal*, 25(1), 29–49. https://doi.org/10.1080/09585176.2013.874954.

Biesta, G. (2017). *The Rediscovery of Teaching*. New York: Routledge.

Biesta, G., & Priestley, M. (2013). A curriculum for the twenty-first century? In M. Priestley & G. Biesta (Eds.), *Reinventing the Curriculum: New Trends in Curriculum Policy and Practice*. London: Bloomsbury: 229–236.

Bourdieu, P., & Passeron, J. C. (1970). *Reproduction in Education, Society and Culture*. Trans. R. Nice. London: Sage.

Bourdieu, P. (1979). *Distinction: A Social Critique of the Judgement of Taste*. Trans. R. Nice. Cambridge, MA: Harvard University Press.

Crick, R. D. (2008). Key competencies for education in a European context: Narratives of accountability or care. *European Educational Research Journal*, 7(3), 311–318.

Green, B. (2018). *Engaging Curriculum: Bridging the Curriculum Theory and English Education Divide*. New York and London: Routledge.

Green, B., & Cormack, P. (2011). Literacy, nation, schooling: Reading (in) Australia. In D. Tröhler, T. S. Popkewitz, & D. F. Labaree (Eds.), *Schooling and the Making of Citizens in the Long Nineteenth Century*. London: Routledge: 240–261.

Griffin, P., McGaw, B., & Care, E. (Eds.) (2012). *Assessment and Teaching of 21st Century Skills*. Dordrecht: Springer.

Hattie, J. (2012). *Visible Learning for Teachers*. London: Routledge.

Hopmann, S. T. (2013). The end of schooling as we know it? *Journal of Curriculum Studies*, 45(1), 1–3. https://doi.org/10.1080/00220272.2013.767570.

Karseth, B., & Sivesind, G. (2011). Conceptualising curriculum knowledge within and beyond the national context. In L. Yates & M. Grumet (Ed.), *Curriculum in Today's World: Configuring Knowledge, Identities, Work and Politics*. Abingdon: Routledge: 58–77.

Macken-Horarik, M. (2011). Building a knowledge structure for English: Reflections on the challenges of coherence, cumulative learning, portability and face validity. *Australian Journal of Education*, 55(3), 197–213. https://doi.org/10.1177%2F000494411105500303.

Maton, K. (2013). *Knowledge and Knowers: Towards a Realist Sociology of Education*. London: Routledge.

Medway, P. (2005). Literacy and the idea of English. *Changing English*, 12(1), 19–29.

Medway, P. (2010). English and Enlightenment. *Changing English: Studies in Culture and Education*, 17(1), 3–12.

Nussbaum, M., & Sen, A. (2010). *The Quality of Life*. New York: Routledge.

Priestley, M., & Biesta, G. (Eds.) (2013). *Reinventing the Curriculum: New Trends in Curriculum Policy and Practice*. London: Bloomsbury.

Reid, A. (2012). Capabilities and the Australian Curriculum. *Curriculum Perspectives*, 32(1), 50–71.

Reid, A., & Price, D. (Eds.) (2018). *The Australian Curriculum: Promises, Problems and Possibilities*. Deakin West: Australian Curriculum Studies Association, ACSA.

Teese, R. (2000). *Academic Success and Social Power: Examinations and Inequality*. Carlton: Melbourne University Press.

Tröhler, D. (2016). Curriculum history or the educational construction of Europe in the long nineteenth century. *European Educational Research Journal*, 15(3), 279–297. https://doi.org/10.1177%2F1474904116645111.

Wahlstrom, N. (2016). A third wave of European education policy: Transnational and national conceptions of knowledge in Swedish curricula. *European Educational Research Journal*, 15(3), 298–313. https://doi.org/10.1177%2F1474904116643329.

Whitty, G. (2010). Revisiting school knowledge: Some sociological perspectives on new school curricula. *European Journal of Education*, 45(1), 28–45. https://doi.org/10.1111/j.1465-3435.2009.01422.x.

Yates, L. (2017). Curriculum: The challenges and the devil in the details. In T. Bentley & G. Savage (Eds.), *Educating Australia*. Carlton: Melbourne University Press.

Yates, L. (2018). The curriculum conversation in Australia. *Curriculum Perspectives*, 38, 137–144. https://doi.org/10.1007/s41297-018-0057-7.

Yates, L., & Grumet. M. (2011). Curriculum in today's world: Configuring knowledge, identities, work and politics. *Routledge World Yearbook of Education*. London: Routledge: 3–14.

Yates, L., & Millar, V. (2016). 'Powerful knowledge' curriculum theories and the case of physics. *The Curriculum Journal*, 27(3), 298–312. https://doi.org/10.1080/09585176.2016.1174141.

Yates, L., Woelert, P., Millar, V., & O'Connor, K. (2017). *Knowledge at the Crossroads? Physics and History in the Changing World of Schools and Universities*. Singapore: Springer.

Young, M., & Muller, J. (2010). Three educational scenarios for the future: Lessons from the sociology of knowledge. *European Journal of Education*, 45(1), 11–27. https://doi.org/10.1111/j.1465-3435.2009.01413.x.

Young, M., & Muller, J. (2013). On the powers of powerful knowledge. *Review of Education*, 1(3), 229–250. https://doi.org/10.1002/rev3.3017.

Young, M., & Lambert, D. (with C. Roberts & M. Roberts) (2014). *Knowledge and the Future School: Curriculum and Social Justice*. London: Bloomsbury.

Zipin, L., Fataar, A., & Brennan, M. (2015). Can social realism do social justice? Debating the warrants for curriculum knowledge selection. *Education as Change*, 19(2), 9–36. https://doi.org/10.1080/16823206.2015.1085610.

VIGNETTES NO. 1 AND 2 – KATYA AND SCOTT

Katya

Katya recalls a teacher who was especially supportive of her when she was a student. Yet paradoxically this support appears to have occurred on the periphery of the official curriculum and all that she was expected to do to complete Year 12 English and thus gain entry to university. She found English boring, but during the year, when she was required to write an essay on a poem by Wilfred Owen, she looked up his poems on the internet and stumbled across an interpretation by a literary critic that opened up entirely new ways of interpreting the text:

> …I remember… seeing what I now know to be like a critical essay about the poem, and someone had written about how there was a something… like an allusion to ejaculation in one of the like stabbing ones and I was just like… I mean of course it was like you know probably titillating in a sexual way, [laugh] but I remember writing something about it and taking it to my teacher, and we weren't supposed to do that, I think we were supposed to do something else… I used words that we weren't taught… you know this is a symbol of or referencing or whatever, and he was really interested and he loved it, and… and he started giving me things to read… it was very separate to the classroom though, and I don't know if it was something in the curriculum, or there was an assumption that students weren't able to do that kind of work, but I don't think he was like differentiating particularly, I think it was just that was not how what he thought his teaching role of Year 12 English.

Katya's story is more than an account of being inspired by an English teacher to join the English teaching profession herself. Her autobiography could more aptly be characterised as a series of displacements. She was exhilarated by her discovery of commentary surrounding Owen's poetry – she encountered 'this whole other world like oh you can think outside of the thing like it's not just about how many stanzas there are or whatever… it means something bigger'. But she continued to find English boring, and when she commenced university, it was not to enrol in a literary studies course but to do government, something she soon dropped to do women's studies. This involved 'some history, some literature, some culture studies, a lot of literature actually because it was run by people in the literature department'. She then found herself doing a PhD on how creative industries operate within policy frameworks set up by the government, something she eventually abandoned because she 'wasn't enjoying it'. She then worked in the music industry before opening a café in Melbourne, a world away from Queensland, where she had completed her secondary education and obtained her degree.

While working in entertainment and then running her café, she realised that she had 'always wanted to be a teacher actually', which led her to enrol in a teacher education program, and eventually to obtain employment at the inner-city school where we interviewed her. She had also started a family, and when we first met her she was working part-time after an extended period of family leave. She eventually resumed a full-time teaching load, and the stories she told us were often about the challenges of picking up new classes and assuming additional responsibilities within the school.

The continual experience of displacement or decentring that runs through Katya's account of her secondary and tertiary education is also a feature of her stories about the professional learning she experienced through her interactions with students. She does not become the teacher she always knew she was destined to become. Her story is not one about the unfolding of her true self. Her self, rather, is a continual work in progress, involving moments when she radically reassesses her values and beliefs in response to situations she encounters.

Her professional learning is characterised by an openness to experiences that continually challenge her sense of self and her role as an English teacher. She continually weighed up what she said, reflexively monitoring her experiences and tentatively drawing out their meaning, not only for her personally but with respect to English teaching as a cultural praxis. In her first interview, she described herself as being 'full of contradictions' – this was in connection with her felt obligation to prepare students to meet the formal writing demands of Year 12 (the final year of secondary schooling in Victoria) and a desire to respond to the personal impulse behind their writing, which didn't always accord with protocols for essay writing.

Katya reflects continually on the conundrum of teaching literacy in a way that ignores the personal expression and tastes of her students. She tells a story about a girl who 'presents as very sort of cool, very confident talking to adults and teachers, great ideas, funny', who is 'a passionate reader of Manga cartoons':

> ...I just think she's brilliant by the way she talks... I'm really like fascinated in the way she is in the world... she looks like a Manga character. She made friends with all the kids who are into Manga... that's why we're studying an Anime film because she's so passionate about it.

But the point of her story is that this same girl, when she was required to do a test designed to identify students with literacy difficulties, failed miserably:

> ...she scored so low on reading and you know we don't show the students the results or anything, but she just fooled me totally because she presented as brilliant, she can write quite well, but she just can't read... and so that she's obviously learnt how to compensate.

The upshot of this story is that the girl has 'been put in a literacy intervention program because of her test result'. Although Katya does not question the validity of the test, she continues to be intrigued by how this judgement – she 'reads at like a Year 3 level or something' – can be reconciled with the way that Manga has 'really embodied her love of reading', expressing her sense of identity and affiliation with other Manga enthusiasts.

In our last interview with Katya she was still foregrounding the contradictory nature of her practice as an English teacher: 'Have I contradicted myself? Probably in lots of ways'. This was in connection with feeling 'a bit of a cringe at how much what we value is so driven by class' when she concedes that she values 'the middle-class literary or you know literary knowledge as does the curriculum'. Yet her literary sensibility as she characterises it here, namely as one that privileges a certain kind of knowledge or cultural capital, does not appear to prevent her from acknowledging student diversity and the forms of cultural praxis through which adolescents express their identities.

Scott

Scott was encouraged as a reader by his grandparents and family, growing up as he did in a country town south of Perth 'where there's nothing to do'. But it was an English teacher at an outer urban Perth school who had a formative effect on the course of his life. More than one of our interviewees related personal stories of this kind, but Scott's version is strikingly candid. In response to the question 'How did you become an English teacher?', he replied:

> My English teacher… I had her from Year 9 all the way up to Year 12, and she just went above and beyond for me. Coming from a low socioeconomic area as well, she was always willing to put that extra foot forward and help us out, and it wasn't just me, it was all the other students as well. So, I guess the reason why I became a teacher is, so I could help people the way that she's helped me to get to where I am.

Scott didn't enjoy senior English, particularly essay writing, but he remembered his B.Ed studies at university where he took literary studies units alongside curriculum and literacy units. His major in English included a substantial number of literary texts and theory, while the Education strand of his degree included method, curriculum and literacy units. Scott's first school in his first year of teaching was in a 'very low socioeconomic area, a hard-to-staff school because there are lots of challenging kids'. As Scott characterised the school's neighbourhood: 'you can't even drive a Domino's pizza delivery car down the street without getting rocks thrown at you'.

In Years 7 and 8 English, Scott taught *The Freedom Writers Diary* by Erin Gruwell and although he later revealed that he was struggling with behaviour management issues, he was impressed by the level of engagement of his students in the diary entries they wrote, which was just what the students in Gruwell's classes had done. He felt their engagement came from identifying with the characters in Gruwell's text, which reminded him of how he had identified with the young man Chris McCandless in Jon Krakauer's non-fiction narrative *Into the Wild* (and Sean Penn's film), texts that were influential in his own experience of school English.

In his second year, Scott moved to another school which was 'the complete opposite' from his first school, where they'd even been recognised for their good NAPLAN and ATAR results. Here he was teaching Years 7, 9, 10 and 11. By his third year, also at this school, he was teaching a Year 12 class as well. His very first interview shows that he had a clear awareness of being a beginning teacher:

> I'm still like trying to… like learning the whole curriculum in that regard, and so although I have a basic understanding and I hope a decent understanding as well, there will still be gaps in my knowledge that obviously will need to be filled eventually, and I think that will happen by teaching and then reflecting on what I need to do to improve and fill in those gaps.

In his second year of teaching Scott thinks about finding a text that is 'engaging but also accessible and… where I can actually teach to my strengths'. This involves 'thinking a lot more in-depth about my choices moving forward to cater to the needs of more people, whereas last year I was like "Oh well I really like this one, I'm going to pick this text"'. He also expressed a commitment to teaching 'textual concepts as opposed to just teaching texts', developing a metalanguage that he could share with his students because he felt that being more 'explicit' would help them to understand better. He gives the example of teaching Frank Miller's comic book mini-series *The Dark Knight Returns*: 'it's very easy to teach that as the cultural concept idea, as a cultural construct. Then there's the visual text, *Batman*, so the kids love it'. Now he sees his development as involving not only choosing the right text but using the right language to teach it:

> …but I think as I progress in my career and I get a bit more knowledge and a bit more confidence in how to speak about literary texts using the correct language, then I think it will foster a more discursive classroom environment using the right language and not just 'Oh I thought this was really good because it's my favourite genre' or something like that.

Another of Scott's anecdotes about teaching practice reflects his characteristic thinking about his development as an early career teacher. In Scott's words: 'students make meanings themselves, own those meanings. Letting them rate [the text] and talk amongst themselves with just a few guiding questions, they'll be able to make those meanings themselves'. This contrasts with his first year of teaching when he was 'terrible' because he was teaching texts that he 'loved', as though it was enough to communicate his passion for those texts to justify their place on the curriculum:

> …so, I just wanted to tell the kids everything I possibly knew about them. And I had to realise to take a step back, get them started, spoon-feed them and then let them work out a lot for themselves. When they do work it out for themselves, they get that ownership. And that's what comes with that engagement. If they realised their teacher didn't tell them this, they're more likely to continue on and try and find other ways to surprise me. And that came from fostering that enjoyment of the text. I would put a poem on the board one day a week and get the kids to read it without analysing it… the first week I put the poem up on the board I ruined it by saying, 'Do you know what this means?' And then I'd tell them about it. Now I just say 'Read the poem' and then they can talk about it in their own time. Then they work it out themselves. But again, as I learned, they learn.

Scott expressed concern about a focus on literacy that was 'spurred by trying to improve our NAPLAN scores', though he also felt that 'a lot of English teachers… are more than happy to essentially pretend that NAPLAN doesn't exist': 'They want to teach properly as opposed to teaching to a standardised test that means nothing down the track'. He saw an overemphasis on literacy as 'defeating the purpose of teaching good quality literature'. For Scott, teaching literature allows teachers 'to be creative in the way that they teach'. By contrast, 'if they're teaching how to sit a NAPLAN test, it's taking away that creativity, taking away the option to have teacher input in the learning', and 'the kids are too worried about doing the right thing as opposed to actually learning'.

In another reflection on gaps in his knowledge and teaching, Scott gave a detailed account of teaching about Banksy and protest art:

> When we were looking at how voices were constructed through protest I, unfortunately, had to reteach the lesson the next day because I just didn't get it right. And I went and reflected with the person who was running the program and she explained it to me in a different way. And then I could understand it. It was just about certain visual analysis elements that I just completely forgot about from when I was in high school. With a bit more research, looking at Banksy's context and looking at how it's affecting people right now, even though it was

10 years ago that the piece of art was released, I was able to improve the understanding of the students as I improved my own understanding. When we went back over it, it was a great way for me to realise that I don't know everything. Being a second-year graduate teacher, you think 'Oh I know everything'. And obviously, I know nothing! But it was a great way for me to realise that I have gaps in my knowledge, as do the students, and the best way is to work on it together and get help when you need it.

Scott thinks English should be called language arts as opposed to English because 'we're not teaching the English language alone if we teach language arts, we're teaching how language is used for effect in literature, in literacy and everything'.

5

SHIFTING RELATIONSHIPS BETWEEN SUBJECT AND DISCIPLINE

English in Australia

Brenton Doecke and Philip Mead

The relation between subject English as it is taught in schools and the discipline of English as it is conducted in universities is a complex and constantly changing one, with a long history shaped by differing national and international contexts. Our primary focus in this book has been on the variegated experience of the secondary and tertiary spheres of English in Australia that our early career teachers have recently been through. Their progress through these institutions of English education is fundamental to their professional learning and has shaped their thinking about English and the nature of the work they do as English teachers in crucial ways. They are the contemporary embodiments of experience across the sectors of English and literary education.

Their progress has been inflected by the history of the shifting relationships between the secondary and tertiary sectors, even though that history hardly loomed large in their minds in their conversations with us. They were too busy grappling with the immediacy of their day-to-day professional lives. The purpose of this chapter is to relate their experiences to the history of the emergence of English within the school and university sectors in Australia. Subject English at school and the discipline of English at the tertiary level have evolved in the years since Federation into two institutions and discourses with now relatively intermittent and discrepant interactions, even while pre-service teachers transition from one to the other in large numbers (Kuttainen & Hansen, 2020). The stories the early career teachers have told us belie any notion that their studies at the tertiary level provide the foundations for their teaching in any direct or self-evident way. As well, they have come to English teaching through very different life trajectories and their experience of studying English or literary studies at university, in both humanities and education contexts, is likewise distinctive in each instance. Nevertheless, they all share an experience of tertiary literary and pre-service education and of the transition to teaching English in schools that can be read as both the product of shifting relationships between these institutional settings as well as symptomatic of the history of which it is a part.

***

DOI: 10.4324/9781003106890-5

As a way of focusing our sense of the history of the functions and practices of English across the two sectors, we look firstly at two individuals who had a significant, career-long experience of English and literary studies before and after the Australian Federation in 1901. We then consider two individuals in the period after World War II and beyond. The lives of these individuals are variously representative of the historical periods in which they were actively engaged in English education and literary studies, providing windows on the contradictions and complexities that constituted the field at the time and the interface between literary studies and school English. The fact that they are all men means that this analysis can be read as a continuation of Leigh Dale's account of the way the 'English men' put their stamp on English as a colonial and then post-colonial enterprise, but this focus does not mean that we are discounting the role that women teachers might have played in the history of English as a gendered praxis at school and university level (a history that remains to be written).

William Henry Williams and Walter Murdoch each embody the relationship between the discipline of literary studies and subject English that typifies the eras in which they lived. It is a story of male professional experience exclusively because although women were admitted to higher education in the UK and Australia at various points in the second half of the 19th century, they were not awarded degrees until much later (Australia, 1883; Oxford, 1920; Cambridge, 1948). The lens of the lives and work of these individuals allows a historically and locationally specific perspective on the changing relations between tertiary and secondary English that in turn provides a context for understanding the work of educators in subsequent decades.

Education in Australia inherits a number of the structures of its early colonial history. And this history is still reflected in the contemporary perspectives of our teacher interviewees, whose experience of English has been shaped by different State curricula and pedagogical practices. Even today, primary and secondary state schooling is largely governed by 'eight state and territory authorities, each with its own curriculum, syllabus documents, assessment and reporting procedures, and employment practices' (Patterson, 1992, p.311). Except for those whose lives have led them to shift from one State to another, the experience of the early career teachers who participated in our project is strongly embedded in their local communities, as it is probably for the majority of English teachers in Australia. They were understandably preoccupied with how English was done in their particular State jurisdiction, without necessarily being aware that English might assume different forms in other parts of the country. This is a legacy of the history of Australia, which initially comprised separate colonies with distinct histories, which were only brought together with the establishment of the Federation of Australia at the beginning of the 20th century. The various ways in which the 'Australian' or national curriculum engages with this history since the second decade of the 21st century is discussed elsewhere in this study (cf. Ashenden, 2021).[1]

In the different systems of schooling in colonial Australia, English wasn't usually taught as an identifiable subject. Primary schools that were founded in the second half of the 19th century, as part of the movement towards compulsory schooling in the colonies, tended to teach elements of what became 'English', like spelling, reading, elocution, recitation, grammar, sometimes composition. The resources for this teaching at this time included primers and readers like *The Irish School Readers*, 1848–1877, *The Children's Hour* (South Australia, from 1889), and *The School Paper* (Victoria, from 1896). Late in the 19th century, subjects called 'Literature' or 'English' were taught in denominational or church-based secondary schools. Thus, English emerged as a subject within the formation of state secondary education in Australia, colony by colony, State by State and not initially in conjunction with early Australian tertiary educational institutions. This educational history was heavily informed by modes of education and schooling as they were transported by individuals from the United Kingdom and between colonies.

The life in education of William Henry Williams is illustrative of the ways in which this migration of school English to the Australian colonies in the latter half of the 19th century was a developing element in a humanist education dominated initially by the study of Latin and Greek texts and philology. Williams was born in 1852 in Kings Norton, Worcestershire. He attended Newark Grammar School and entered Trinity College, Cambridge, in 1872. After graduating with First Class Honours in the classical tripos in 1879 he became a teacher of Classics, working at the Leys School in Cambridge, a Methodist school established in 1875 (*ADB*); Horner & Williams [1852–1941], 1990). In 1884, Williams was appointed as headmaster of Newington College, in Sydney. Newington was an independent Wesleyan school founded in 1863. The school was shaped by the imperial education plan of the British Methodist Conference, which in 1838 devised 'a general plan of education' for the Church throughout Britain and the colonies (Spaulding, n.d., p.45). Williams started his teaching career at the Leys School as a Classics Master, but at Newington, he instituted a broad curriculum and started a school magazine with a strong 'literary function' that published fiction, essays and poetry, as well as a Debating and Literary Society (Spaulding, n.d., pp.63–64). He also introduced a 'modern form' for students 'not studying languages where the emphasis was on a thorough training in English subjects designed to prepare them for the Civil Service and Junior Public Examinations' (Spaulding, n.d., p.52). Newington's senior curriculum, as in government schools, was shaped by the requirements of the junior and senior Public Examinations in New South Wales, established in 1867 by the Department of Education and the University of Sydney. English was one of the subjects in these examinations.

In 1893, after some differences over employment conditions with the Newington council, Williams resigned from the school. But in the same year, he was one of three lecturers appointed to the new University of Tasmania and in 1896 he became the first Professor of Classics and English at that university, a position he held until his retirement in 1925. As it happens, the Chancellor of the university, Lambert Dobson, was a strong advocate of the study of modern languages and literatures, including English. The undergraduate (BA) program in English Language and Literature Williams developed in Tasmania was organised into historical surveys (Middle English, Elizabethan literature, 18th-century literature) in combination with a focus on philology and the history of the English language. This was also true of similar courses in English at the three other earliest universities, Sydney, Melbourne and Adelaide, where the study of modern languages, including English, was often taught by academics trained mainly in the Classics (see Dale, 2012, pp.63–70). A powerful influence in this development in Australia, including on Williams in Tasmania, was the Glasgow-trained Mungo MacCallum (1854–1942), Professor of Modern Language and Literature at the University of Sydney and a specialist in English literature. Williams maintained the structure of the English courses that he established in 1893 through to his retirement in 1925 (Spaulding, n.d., p.181). Williams's scholarly interests were strongest in pre-Shakespearean early modern drama. The first-year annual examination paper in 'English' at the University of Tasmania for 1892 included questions such as: 'Write an essay on Chaucer's Prologue as typical of manners', 'What do you know about Gower', and 'What is meant by a periodic sentence? Do you prefer short or long sentences?' (Spaulding, n.d., pp.142–43).

It is not until the beginning of the 20th century that English as a distinct discipline is established in Australian universities. The universities were also originally State-based institutions, founded at different stages in different colonies or, later, States (Sydney, 1850; Melbourne, 1853; Adelaide, 1874; Tasmania, 1890). It was only with the establishment of the Australian Universities Commission in 1958–59 that the Federal Government began to take over the administrative and financial responsibility for tertiary education. In relation to the history of tertiary English, Leigh Dale writes in her *The Enchantment of English: Professing English Literatures in Australian Universities*:

> No Australian university commenced operation in the nineteenth century with English as an independent discipline, but academics as diverse as John Davidson, EV Boulger and William Mitchell at Adelaide, Mungo MacCallum at Sydney, HA Strong, EE Morris and TG Tucker at Melbourne, and WH Williams at Tasmania taught in the area at some time in their career. Still, none were appointed only to that role, and (arguably) only MacCallum, Morris and Williams could claim to be specialists in English.
>
> (Dale, 2012, p.65)

The later establishment of tertiary English as an identifiably separate discipline in the first decade or so of the 20th century also coincides in influential ways with the development of secondary English as a subject of study in schools, both shaped by their imperial, colonial and early federation history.

While Williams's career illustrates aspects of the foundation of English within the university sector in the late 19th and early 20th centuries, Walter Murdoch's history as an educator provides another exemplary narrative about the links that emerged between tertiary English and school English. Murdoch was foundation

Professor of English at the University of Western Australia, appointed in 1913. From 1914 until his retirement in 1939 he was also Chief Examiner of senior secondary English or Leaving, as well as chairing the West Australian Public Examinations Board which was responsible for setting exam papers and authorising school sylla-buses, including the syllabus for English, the most popular secondary subject throughout this era. Such close educational and administrative links between those responsible for English education in schools and universities in the early to mid-20th century was also reflected in other States, although there were many differences as well. Williams was responsible for all the examinations in the junior and senior public examinations in Tasmania. In New South Wales, George Mackaness was Senior English Lecturer at the Sydney Teachers' College from 1924 to 1946 and an examiner of that State's Intermediate Certificate. In Queensland, J. J. Stable, lecturer in English at the University of Queensland, and from 1922 till his retirement in 1953, the first Professor of English Language and Literature at the University of Queensland, was centrally involved in the secondary English syllabus and senior English examinations, through the Public Examinations Board. He also edited poetry anthologies for use in secondary English teaching that included Australian poems alongside English anthology classics. In the 1920s, Stable's colleague at the University of Queensland, F.W. Robinson, led 'a group of university and school teachers of English to conduct a local version of the Newbolt Report' under the auspices of Queensland English and Modern Languages Association (Hatherell, 2015, p.4). Also, in the 1920s, Robinson, encouraged by Stable, introduced Australian literature into the University of Queensland's English curriculum, one of the earliest instances of the teaching of Australian literature at the university level.

Walter Murdoch was full of contradictions, some of them explicable in relation to his early experience in Melbourne and his appointment to an inaugural chair at the University of Western Australia. In Melbourne, he belonged to a group of literary intellectuals and cultural nationalists, including Alfred Deakin (later Prime Minister of Australia), Nettie Palmer (Higgins) (later literary critic and essayist) and E. Morris Miller (later Australianist scholar and Professor of Psychology and Philosophy at the University of Tasmania). Deakin was one of his referees for the University of Western Australia founding position. Before his move to Western Australia, Murdoch was a popular assistant lecturer in English at Melbourne University, where he had trained as an undergraduate and had done his MA. But when it came to appointing a professor of English Literature at the University of Melbourne in 1911, the first at that university (and the first in Australia), he was passed over in favour of the Aberdeen and Oxford-trained Robert Strachan Wallace (but like Murdoch, born in Scotland). Leigh Dale suggests that Murdoch's numerous publications – textbooks, anthologies, reviews and articles in the *Argus* – might not have counted for much, given that they were for 'school students or general readers' (Dale, 2012, p.101). Whatever the strength of his identification with the cultural nationalism of the lit-erary coterie to which he belonged in Melbourne, in Western Australia Murdoch felt he needed to implement a narrow Empire version of English studies, at both school and university levels. The 1914 English Leaving Standard exam paper, for example, began with two questions: 'write a short essay on one of the following subjects: a) Ambition, b) What is a gentleman?' and 'what do you know about the following writers: Bede, Cynewulf, John Barbour, John Lydgate, Dunbar'. He did little to initiate the study of Australian literature at his own university, compared with his contemporaries at the University of Queensland. But Murdoch was a theorist of democracy, having published just before he arrived at the newly founded UWA, *The Australian Citizen: An Elementary Account of Civic Rights and Duties* (1912) and was often an advocate for Australian writers in his nationally popular journalism (cf. Dale, 2012). His arrival in Western Australia coincided with the establishment of the first teachers' training College, the first government secondary school and the appointment of Cyril Jackson, an advocate of the 'New Education' (Green & Cormack, 2008) as Inspector General of Schools.[2] Jackson, in turn, appointed the progressive educationist Cecil Andrews as the founding principal of the Claremont Training College (Willis, 1996, p.98). Part of this foundational educational moment, Murdoch went on to preside over public exams and matriculation in Western Australia for 25 years, with a special oversight of English. Yet Murdoch was also outspoken in his criticism of the exam system, particularly in relation to English. In 1929 he wrote in the *West Australian*:

> The fact is that literature is not a subject that lends itself to examinations, and I suppose that my detestation of examinations is due in part to the fact that I am associated with a subject in which, perhaps more than in any other, they are apt to create such a distaste
>
> *(Dowsett, 2016, p.34)*

The era in Australia's history of English education to which Murdoch and his contemporaries belong is about the formation of English as a subject at the secondary level and the role played by inaugural professors of English in the Australian university system. At a time of significant development in education across the nation – the first half of the 20th century – these professors of English are establishing the tertiary paradigm of English studies at the same time as they are involved in shaping English as a secondary subject in very specific ways, including curriculum design, text selection, developing professional networks for teachers, and the design and administration of assessment. And this was happening less than a decade after the establishment of professorships of English at British universities and subject English in British schools and universities (Reid, 1996).

Although there are clearly links between the establishment of English as a subject at both school and university level in England (we have just mentioned the Newbolt report, which provides an important context for the emergence of Leavis's cultural project) and developments in Australia, it is equally clear that the formation of English in Australia had its own momentum, intersecting with an emerging cultural nationalism in complex and contradictory ways. This literary-cultural nationalism often took the form, especially in literary and intellectual communities that were active in the wider public sphere beyond the universities, of a strident assertion of the distinctive quality of Australian literature and culture vis-à-vis that of the 'Mother Country'. Professors in the universities were sometimes targeted as the uncritical exponents of 'imported literature' at the expense of any recognition of an 'Indigenous' literature, to use a binary that P. R. Stephensen posed in his influential tract, *The Foundations of Culture in Australia: An Essay towards National Self Respect* (see Stephensen, [1936] 1986, p.30; see also Doecke, 1993). Stephensen's essay was prompted by an article by G.H. Cowling, Professor of English at Melbourne University, in a series in the *Age* in 1935, 'The future of Australian literature', that asserted that Australian literature was not 'worthy of study because it lacked a Past' (Dale, 1997, pp.108–109). (Leigh Dale remarks that the hostility to university-based critics towards Australian literature in this period was selective – see Dale [1997, p. 108]).

In the Australian States, the responsibility for English wasn't just undertaken by the professors of English and the universities, though. The State education departments in this era were also involved in curriculum design and resource production like the *School Papers, The Children's Hour*, and Victorian and Australian school readers. Murdoch's involvement in subject English in Western Australia may have been conservatively Anglophilic, but as with his senior academic contemporaries in other States, whose influence on secondary English might have differed but was also formative, it was a central part of his job as a Professor of English, a personal commitment for more than 25 years, not just a subsidiary or occasional chore.

***

As Leigh Dale remarks, the years from 1940 to 1950 witnessed a distinct 'changing of the guard', as far as the discipline of English in Australia is concerned, with many of the professors who had been prominent in the decades between the wars (including Walter Murdoch) retiring, to be replaced by a new generation of academics (Dale, 1997, p.92). This generational change signalled a shift in consciousness, as academics responded to the exponential growth of both the university sector and secondary schooling in the post-war years. Parallels might be drawn between the expansion of secondary schooling in Australia, reflecting a commitment to the provision of free, secular education for all, and the growth of comprehensive schooling in the United Kingdom (cf. Medway et al., 2014), which saw some remarkable curriculum development by English educators in response to the challenges of catering for the needs of an increasingly diverse cohort of students.

But there are also continuities between the attitudes and values of the 'English men' (to borrow Dale's characterisation of the professors who dominated the discipline of English prior to World War II) and the views of this new generation of professors. A. D. Hope, whose career serves as another prism through which to view the relationship between the discipline of English and secondary English that emerged in the period of post-war reconstruction, was driven by similarly contradictory impulses to those that figure in Murdoch's career. After an undergraduate degree at Sydney University, Hope won a travelling scholarship to Oxford University, where he seems to have spent an unhappy time. This transnational history of literary education has a personal correlative in Hope's well-known poem

'Australia' (1939), in which the disaffected colonial is finally pleased to 'turn gladly home/ From the lush jungle of modern thought…' and escape 'The learned doubt, the chatter of cultured apes/ Which is called civilization over there'. Returning to Australia in 1931, Hope trained and worked as a secondary school teacher and then, from 1937 to 1944, as a lecturer in Education and English at Sydney Teachers' College. In 1945 he was appointed Senior Lecturer in English at the University of Melbourne, then in 1950 to the Canberra University College. When the College was absorbed into the new Australian National University, Hope was appointed the foundation Professor of Literature.

Yet although he then plays a prominent role in a remarkable moment of cultural renewal in Australia's literary history (a renewal that John Docker has characterised as 'the metaphysical ascendency' in contradistinction to the 'radical nationalist' tradition that had previously been dominant [Docker, 1984]), he never seeks to make Australian literature a singular focus of institutional and disciplinary growth, a reluctance he explains by drawing an analogy between 'the man who graduates B. A. Honours (Aust.Lit)' with a doctor who sets out 'to practise medicine after having dissected (only) the knee and the liver' (cited in Dale, 1997, p.156). His commitment as a poet and critic to supporting the growth of Australian literature and culture in the post-war years was not to be at the expense of training students 'to judge our writers simply as writers and not as specifically Australian writers, and to apply the mature and discriminating standards which are characteristic of the best criticism everywhere' (Hope, 1962, p.7). Hope's frame of reference is not narrowly English – as well as England, he instances France and the United States as countries where an 'educated class of readers' is able 'to support local writers' (p.3) – but it is difficult not to read this as a familiar affirmation, replete with references to Matthew Arnold and William Shakespeare, of the richness of English literature as 'an autonomous literary tradition' (p.12) that rises above the specific social and historical conditions of its emergence to become 'timeless, requiring the application of universal standards of appreciation'(p.13).

Hope's conviction about the salience of standards deriving from the English literary canon arguably lends authority to a significant statement he makes about the conditions necessary for secondary English teachers to be recognised as a profession, which he delivers in a Presidential Address to the Australian Association for the Teaching of English (AATE) in 1967. The formation of the AATE in 1965 is a significant moment in the shifting relationships between the teaching of English in schools and the discipline of English. The text of the address was published in *English in Australia*, which had been established in 1965 as the journal of the association. The AATE thereby flags its right to advocate on behalf of English teachers in Australia by the fact that a distinguished Professor of English is its President. Readers of *English in Australia* learn that Professor A. D. Hope is 'best known as one of Australia's leading poets, and currently holds the chair of English at the Australian National University in Canberra' (Hope, 1967, p.3). Hope's authority as a professor underpins the Association's status as an organisation that has its foundations in a specialist field of knowledge, a claim that is the hallmark of what

Hargreaves and Goodson call 'classical professionalism' (Hargreaves & Goodson, 1996, pp.4–5). This claim by the AATE to represent a profession with a recognised body of knowledge at its core is subsequently extended when Hope, after three years as President, is succeeded by Professor Leonie Kramer, Professor James McAuley and Professor R. D. Eagleson, with Hope remaining the Patron and Public Officer of the Association until his death.

But if Hope and the professors who followed him seem to embody a solid link between secondary English teaching and the tertiary discipline of English, the discourse that unfolds in *English in Australia*, as the journal of the association, is one characterised by contradictions and complexities that often produce a sense of disjunction between the 'knowledge' of the discipline and an emerging professional 'knowledge' about English curriculum and pedagogy. The latter is reflected in contributions by teachers as they reflect on the challenges they are experiencing in their attempts to meet the needs of students within secondary schools that had grown exponentially in the 1950s and 1960s (cf. Doecke, 1997). Tony Delves, for example, writing as the Head of English at Prahran Technical School, provocatively challenges the privileging of Literature (with a capital 'L') that is of interest only to 'a very small and cloistered minority' who are remote from 'modern life', and advocates replacing this with a democratic vision of his students reading, writing, thinking and acting 'literature' (with a small 'l') (Delves, 1966, pp.36–37; Tickell, 1972). The technical school system in Victoria provides a setting in which educators like Delves are prompted to rethink the assumptions they brought to their work as English teachers and to articulate a more inclusive understanding of culture than reified notions of 'the best which has been thought and said', one that has at its centre a recognition of 'our students as vital, spontaneous, social beings' who require more than canonical English literature or the thin gruel of 'literacy'. Students are entitled to have their creativity recognised as writers and readers and thinkers responding to the world around them (a world which Delves typically characterises as 'culture destroying' and 'soul-destroying') (Delves, 1966, p.34). The story of the professional learning that teachers like Delves experience at this time (see also McLaren, 1966) is similar to the story that educators like Rosen, Dixon, Stratta and Barnes tell about their interactions with students in the new comprehensive school settings that were established in the UK in the post-war period (Medway et al., 2014).

Yet it is not as though this contradiction between literature as the province of a cultural elite and a more democratic and inclusive vision of culture as Delves articulates it is reflected in a hard and fast division between the professors and teacher contributors to *English in Australia*. These differences inhabit the contributions that Hope and the other professors themselves make to *English in Australia*. By straddling the divide between secondary English teaching and the field of literary studies, they are crossing two distinct discourse communities, and they are speaking a different language in each. At the very time that they are contributing to *English in Australia*, they are bringing about a major revaluation of Australian literature by rejecting what they deem to be the excessive parochialism of the Australian nationalist tradition and putting more self-consciously 'literary' standards in its place. But although there is evidence of this change in values and standards in the essays they publish in *English in Australia* – Leonie Kramer, for example, confesses to feeling pessimistic about 'the kinds of tests Australian literature should be expected to pass before being admitted to its parents' company' (Kramer, 1968, p.43) – their work as literary critics hardly frames in any significant way their understanding of the challenges facing secondary English teachers in the post-war period.

For all the authority that Hope lends to the AATE as Professor of English at the Australian National University, his Presidential Address registers his concern that 'the teaching of English is not yet a profession in the fullest sense of the word' (Hope, 1967, p.3). The AATE is far from being recognised as the body 'to which the community entrusts its interests' with respect to the teaching of English (p.3). And to address this issue requires more than an appeal to whatever authority might be invested in a degree in English. Hope asks whether 'English is properly speaking a "subject" at all?' (p.6). He then rummages through the habitual practices in which English teachers feel obliged to engage under the pressure of public examinations to clear a space in which other fundamental questions might be asked: 'What don't we teach that we should? What could we do better by not teaching?' (p.6). He contemplates the possibility of jettisoning a narrow focus on inculcating 'the skill of literary judgement' (pp.6–7), though he stops short at articulating the kind of attention he would like English teachers to encourage their students to pay to the texts they read. He nonetheless opens up a space between the machinery of literary scholarship and criticism and the concerns that ought properly to occupy the minds of teachers as they attempt to meet the needs of the increasingly diverse range of students in their classrooms, gesturing towards the diversity of the student population with the exponential growth of secondary schooling in Australia after World War II (p.8). In a similar vein, Leonie Kramer and James McAuley distance themselves from literary criticism to articulate a pedagogy of reading in secondary schools that would lay emphasis (as McAuley expresses it) 'on the interpretation of texts rather than on literary history or evaluative judgements' (McAuley, 1968, p.17; see also Kramer, 1968, p.11).

***

Through its journal and other publications, the AATE plays a significant role in mediating the relationship between subject English and the discipline of literary studies over the next few decades. As an organisation it never gains the recognition that Hope sees as 'the chief mark of a profession' – namely that it 'it is responsible, and is recognised as responsible, for itself as a body to which the community entrusts its interest in one particular field' (Hope, 1967, p.3). It does, however, succeed through its journal and conferences (including an important international conference in Sydney in 1980 [see Eagleson, 1982]) in establishing itself as a significant voice in debates about English curriculum and pedagogy, providing substantial support for research on the teaching of English through disseminating its findings. In this respect, it is significant that the succession of professors of literature who became Presidents of the AATE comes to an end, to be followed by the election of people who are more firmly anchored in teacher education than literary studies (Garth Boomer, Margaret Gill, Claire Woods), and that it also supports significant research arising out of that sector, most notably Jack Thomson's *Understanding Teenagers' Reading* (1987). This was a ground-breaking study, largely because of Thomson's starting point: he had interviewed young people about the novels they had read, treating them as authorities when it came to talking about the pleasures and challenges they experienced when reading, and thus providing a powerful model to English teachers of what you can learn if you listen carefully to what your students have to report about their reading habits and preferences.

This is not to say that literary studies ceases to be a salient point of reference for the discourse community that had formed around the AATE. Thomson's book drew heavily on recent developments in literary studies, most notably Reader Response theory, to provide a framework for interpreting what the young people in his study had told him about their experiences of reading. Through its publications and conferences, the AATE emerges as a forum for an extraordinarily productive dialogue across the sectors of secondary English teaching and literary studies, as is evident by its publication of Ian Reid's *The Making of Literature: Texts, Contexts and Classroom Practices* (AATE, 1984) which, like Thomson's study, had a decisive influence on the way that Australian English teachers understood the role that literary texts might play within their classrooms.

Ian Reid is the fourth Professor of Literary Studies whose career conveniently serves as a small window on an evolving relationships between the tertiary sector and secondary English teaching in Australia. His work brings us close to the moment in which the early career teachers we interviewed are participating. Reid was born in New Zealand, came to Australia to join the staff at the University of Adelaide, completed a PhD on historical fiction in Australia and New Zealand during the Great Depression, before being appointed as Professor of Literary Studies at the newly established Deakin University in 1978. As a Professor of Literature, Reid recognised the importance of the AATE in facilitating a dialogue across the secondary and tertiary sectors directed towards enhancing the literary education of students. This is against the backdrop of a policy environment that was becoming increasingly hostile towards what a literary education might have to offer, as he spells out in a paper published in 1982 in *English in Australia*, entitled 'The crisis in English studies'. Here he invokes the transformation of the social structures that were occurring with the first onslaughts of economic rationalism in both Australia and New Zealand. These he characterises as 'utilitarian bullying' that was rendering traditional rationales for literary studies increasingly inadequate when it came to justifying the legitimacy of English and the humanities within a school and university curriculum (Reid, 1982, p.9).

The role that Reid plays as a Professor of Literary Studies in providing a vital link between secondary English and tertiary literary studies is not simply one of continuing the tradition that had been established by Hope, Kramer and McAuley in the immediate post-war years. It is a response to a different historical moment. And this is not simply a matter of mounting a beleaguered defence of English and literary study against economic rationalism, but of revisiting the purposes of a literary education within a society that is experiencing a 'transformation of the whole social structure' (Reid, 1982, p.9). The rhetoric of the title of the paper he published reflects the tenor of the times when there was a barrage of studies (most notably Catherine Belsey's [1980] *Critical Practice* and Terry Eagleton's [1983] *Literary Theory*) announcing (as Reid puts it) 'a fundamental reappraisal of the very nature of literature and its academic study' (Reid, 1982, p.10). This was the moment of 'theory', with its powerful, transatlantic waves of linguistic, political and philosophical thinking that revolutionised the humanities and social sciences and which from the decades after the 1960s critiqued and largely overthrew the previous paradigm of tertiary literary study shaped by Cambridge Leavisism and to a lesser degree US New Criticism (T. S. Eliot, I. A. Richards and William Empson). Literary theorists, reflecting the broader social movements of the time, argued from feminist, queer, race, ethnic, ecological and other ideological standpoints about the imperatives to develop a new critical lexicon that reflected alternative understandings and histories of the role that literature plays in our lives. (Reid's interventions were informed by a depth of knowledge about the transnational rise of English studies reflected in his later work *Wordsworth and the Formation of English Studies* [London: Ashgate, 2004]).

From the standpoint of the present, Reid's essay might be read as signifying less a moment of 'crisis' than a heightened self-awareness of what we are doing as literary educators. This emphasis on the importance of engaging in a self-conscious 'praxis', involving a reflexive capacity to interrogate the values and assumptions that inhere within our work as English teachers, is articulated more fully in *The Making of Literature*. The subtitle of the book – 'texts, contexts and classroom practices' – announces his intention to shift away from the shibboleths of previous generations of critics and educators, to cease thinking of texts as 'objects' that constitute a canon that somehow exists outside history and to treat them instead as 'media of exchange' within the everyday social settings in which people participate (Reid, 1984, p.56). His position would have been met with incomprehension if not hostility by the previous generation of professors we have just been considering, even though they themselves often doubted the value of literary evaluation for the teaching of reading in secondary schools. But what Reid is doing is drawing on the rich intellectual resources that had become available with the moment of 'theory' to make sense of the social and semiotic transactions that occur in classrooms. A text, he argues, 'is a semantic process by which meanings are transacted through the verbal material, not deposited in it' (Reid, 1982, p.56). The 'crisis of English studies' that he announces in his article in *English in Australia* provides an occasion to rethink the nature and purpose of a literary education in both secondary schools and tertiary institutions in the most extraordinary way. The moment of 'theory' is obviously related to broader movements in society – in schools from the 1970s onwards, for example, there were shifts in thinking about the foundations of education as the result of feminist perspectives and questions about the representation of girls in texts (and women as leaders), including interest in what made for a 'girls'' subject or a 'boys'' subject. All States and governments sponsored inquiries into 'equal opportunity'. These shifts were inflected in the discourses of university English with profound implications for the way secondary English teachers were educated. It was Reid's achievement to make those connections by explicitly locating his reflections on the relationship between texts and contexts – on the complex semiotic transaction that occur around literary texts – within educational settings that were familiar to secondary English teachers (cf. Bellis et al., 2009).

English and literary studies today

The discipline of English or literary studies currently reflects both the global state of the humanities and its disaggregated and differentiated state within the Australian national context. On the one hand, as James Ley asserts, the several recent decades in which 'the study of literature has been the focus of fierce ideological dispute' has taken a toll (Ley, 2020). This intra-disciplinary situation has also intersected with the ideological and instrumentalist attack on the humanities both globally and locally. The Australian Federal Government, for example, like some State Governments in the US, has intervened with financial disincentives to discourage students from studying the humanities. In Australia, this seems to have had little effect so far. The teaching of literary studies at tertiary level has already suffered harm from the institutional effects of reduced course offerings and the casualisation and precarity of teaching staff. This sense of the lack of institutional commitment to the humanities and the 'relentless culture warring [that] has hollowed out the notion that studying literature is an intellectually valid occupation in itself' (Ley, 2020) has led to North American based recovery attempts, like Rita Felski's arguments about the 'limits of critique'. Felski (2015) argues for the positive value of studying aesthetic works against the disillusionments of the hermeneutics of suspicion, critique and identity politics. She argues for forging 'a language of attachment as robust as and refined as our rhetoric of detachment' (p.180). At the least, this 'would require us to treat texts not as objects to be investigated but as co-actors that make things happen, not just as matters of fact but also matters of concern' (p.180).

Within this scenario of struggle and embattlement, literary studies has nevertheless supported or hosted the relatively untroubled growth of creative writing as both a teaching and research field, although it has its issues of disciplinary legitimacy. Growing out of various shifts and developments in higher education since the 1970s, the patronage of Australian writers and the professionalisation of writing teaching, Creative writing is an important and often flourishing element of tertiary literary study. The analogy is with what Mark McGurl (2009) has described in the North American educational context as *The Program Era: Postwar Fiction and the Rise of Creative Writing*, where the growth and effects of creative writing have been much more widespread than in Australian humanities education and more self-reflexively influential in literary studies. There are also links to the development of creative writing within the secondary English syllabus although there creative writing has remained contained within the various regimes of senior English. Sometimes tertiary writing programs co-habit with English or literary studies; sometimes they are separate programs within a 'studies' institutional setting. For students interested in learning about reading and writing, such programs offer a version of literary studies with both professional and intellectual rewards.

Whatever its struggles with perceptions of negativity and the depredation of the humanities, research in literary studies advances according to its own evolutionary logic; it continues to expand in response to new issues and questions that emerge. Australian literary scholars and critics continue to produce leading and influential work in literary theory, in Australian and Indigenous literatures, in environmental, digital, feminist, Modernist, medieval and early modern, Romanticism, poetry and poetics, and world literature sub-fields of literary study. Nor have they lost sight of their own distinctive pedagogical history. The *Australian Humanities Review*'s engagement with Rachel Sagner Buurma and Laura Heffernan's *The Teaching Archive: A New History for Literary Study* (University of Chicago Press, 2021) provides an Australian perspective on '[t]he true history of English literary study', which 'resides in classrooms' (Buurma & Heffernan, 2020, p.2). Buurma and Heffernan assert that 'what we find in the teaching archive overturns nearly every major account of what the history of literary studies has been' (p.6). This is of particular relevance to our thinking about the making of English teachers and their experience of disciplinary English and its uses for teaching subject English. Buurma and Heffernan's re-evaluation of teaching literature

> scrambles existing genealogies for twentieth-century methodological change; the teaching archive dispels our long-cherished accounts of the interminable tennis match between eras in which we championed literature for its aesthetic value and eras in which we modelled ourselves after the sciences by producing knowledge about the world in which texts were written.
>
> *(Buurma & Heffernan, 2020, p.6)*

One of the chief values of their study is that it clears the canopy of disciplinary history that 'blocks the sunshine from ever reaching the seedling of practitioners' own experiences of their teaching and research' (p.7).

Notes

1 See Dean Ashenden's review of *The Quest for Revolution in Australian Schooling Policy* by Glenn C. Savage (Routledge, 2021) for an analysis of how this history was ignored or misunderstood by the education policy of Kevin Rudd and Julia Gillard, as Prime Minister and Minister for Education, respectively (https://insidestory.org.au/school ings-ozymandias-dean-ashenden/).

2 The 'New Education' of the late 19th and early 20th centuries was 'wide in scope and a more or less piecemeal collection of reforms, rather than being a tightly conceptualised project' (see Green & Cormack, 2008).

References

Bellis, N., Parr, G., & Doecke, B. (2009). The making of literature: A continuing conversation. *Changing English*, 16(2): 165–179. https://doi.org/10.1080/13586840902863145.

Belsey, C. (1980). *Critical Practice*. London: Methuen.

Buurma, R. S., & Heffernan, L. (2020). *The Teaching Archive: A New History for Literary Study*. Chicago: University of Chicago Press.

Dale, L. (1997). *The English Men: Professing Literature in Australian Universities*. Toowoomba: Association for the Study of Australian Literature.

Dale, L. (2012). *The Enchantment of English: Professing English Literatures in Australian Universities*. 2nd ed. Sydney: Sydney University Press.

Delves, T. (1966). English as she is not taught. *English in Australia*, 3, 33–40.

Docker, J. (1984). *In a Critical Condition: Reading Australian Literature*. Ringwood, Victoria: Penguin.

Doecke, B. (1993). P. R. Stephensen: Fascism. *Westerly*, 38(2), 17–28.

Doecke, B. (1997). Disjunctions: Australian literature and the secondary English curriculum. In D. Bird, R. Dixon, & S. Lever (Eds.), *CanonOZities: The Making of Literary Reputations in Australia*. Special edition of *Southerly*, 57(3), 67–77.

Dowsett, P. (2016). *The History of Curricular Control: Literary Education in Western Australia, 1912–2012*. PhD thesis, the University of Western Australia.

Eagleson, R. D. (Ed.) (1982). *English in the Eighties*. Adelaide: AATE.

Eagleton, T. (1983). *Literary Theory: An Introduction*. Oxford: Blackwell.

Felski, R. (2015). *The Limits of Critique*. Chicago and London: University of Chicago Press.

Green, B., & Cormack, P. (2008). Curriculum history, 'English' and the New Education; or, installing the Empire of English? *Pedagogy, Culture and Society*, 16(3), 253–267. https://doi.org/10.1080/14681360802346648.

Hatherell, W. (2015). Queensland man of letters: The many worlds of FW Robinson. *Queensland Review*, 22(2), 143–156. https://doi.org/10.1017/qre.2015.29.

Hargreaves, A., & Goodson, I. (1996). Teachers' professional lives: Aspirations and actualities. In I. F. Goodson & A. Hargreaves (Eds.), *Teachers' Professional Lives*. London: Falmer Press: 1–27.

Hope, A. D. (1962). Standards in Australian literature. In G. Johnston (Ed.), *Australian Literary Criticism*. Melbourne: Oxford University Press: 1–15.

Hope, A. D. (1967). Presidential address. *English in Australia*, 5, 3–10.

Horner, J. C., & Williams, W. H. ([1852–1941] 1990). *Australian Dictionary of Biography, 12*. Available: https://adb.anu.edu.au/biography/williams-william-henry-9120.

Kramer, L. (1968). The challenge of English. *English in Australia*, 7, 3–16.

Kuttainen, V., & Hansen, C. (2020). Making connections: Exploring the complexity of the secondary-tertiary nexus in English from the perspective of regional Australia. *English in Australia*, 55(2), 39–51. https://search.informit.org/doi/abs/10.3316/informit.017173931936378.

Ley, J. (2020). Trapped in negation. *Sydney Review of Books*, 13 March. Available: https://sydneyreviewofbooks.com/essay/trapped-in-negation/. Accessed 21 April 2022

McAuley, J. (1968). Evaluation or interpretation? *English in Australia*, 7, 17–26.

McGurl, M. (2009). *The Program Era: Post-War Fiction and the Rise of Creative Writing*. Cambridge, MA: Harvard University Press.

McLaren, J. (1966). From examination to discourse. *English in Australia*, 3, 13–20.

Medway, P., Hardcastle, J., Brewis, G., & Crook, D. (2014). *English Teachers in a Postwar Democracy: Emerging Choice in London Schools, 1945–1965*. New York: Palgrave Macmillan.

Patterson, A. (1992). Individualism in English: From personal growth to discursive construction. *English Education*, 24(3), 131–146. www.jstor.org/stable/40172828.

Reid, I. (1982). The crisis in English Studies. *English in Australia*, 60, 8–18.

Reid, I. (1984). *The Making of Literature: Texts, Contexts and Classroom Practices.* Adelaide: Australian Association for the Teaching of English.

Reid, I. (1996). Romantic ideologies, educational practices, and institutional formations of English. *Journal of Educational Administration and History*, 28(1), 22–41.

Reid, I. (2004). *Wordsworth and the Formation of English Studies.* Aldershot, UK: Ashgate Publishing.

Spaulding, R. (n.d.). *William Henry Williams: Tasmania's First Professor of English.* [unpublished history].

Stephensen, P. R. ([1936] 1986). *The Foundations of Culture in Australia: An Essay towards National Self Respect,* with a new introduction by Craig Munro. Sydney: Allen & Unwin.

Thomson. J. (1987). *Understanding Teenagers' Reading: Reading Processes and the Teaching of Literature.* Norwood, SA: Australian Association for the Teaching of English.

Tickell, W. G. (1972). Literature as a valid field of knowledge. *English in Australia*, 21, 9–24.

Warner, M. (2004). Uncritical reading. In J. Gallup (Ed.), *Polemic: Critical or Uncritical.* New York: Routledge. 13–38.

Willis, K. (1996). The shaping of secondary English in Western Australia: The formative years, 1890s-1915. In B. Green & C. Beavis (Eds), *Teaching the English Subjects,* Geelong: Deakin University Press: 96–117.

6

LITERARY KNOWLEDGE IN THE WIDER FIELD

Reflections from literary studies academics, teacher educators and curriculum authorities

Larissa McLean Davies

> I think anyone who teaches literature is aware that they have a certain body of knowledge. It may be that they find it difficult to articulate, and it may be that the whole profession has been rather sort of slack in articulating it… or have not wanted to… create further barriers. But I think everyone is very aware that… they've acquired knowledge.
>
> *(Owen, literary studies academic)*

Central to this project was the idea that English teachers' perceptions about English and literature are mediated socially by the people, texts and institutions they encounter throughout their education and career. Thus, our methodology included interviews with a diverse group of stakeholders – literary studies and English education academics, and representatives from teacher accreditation and curriculum authorities and English teaching associations – individuals who, through their professional roles, directly and indirectly influence the daily practices of teachers and contribute to perspectives on literary knowledge in the field of English education, and more broadly in public discourses. As Chapter 5 discussed, these relationships between teachers, tertiary institutions, literary studies academics and professional associations have been intertwined, fracturing and evolving in the teaching of English in secondary schools in Australia since the early 20th century (see also Doecke, McCleneghan, & Petris, 2011; Fletcher et al., 2016; Kuttainen & Hansen, 2020).

In this chapter, I explore core questions of the nature and purpose of literary knowledge through the perspectives of these key informants. In doing so, I both build on and distinguish our research from that which has been done previously regarding the professional influences on English teachers' knowledge and identity. Peel et al.'s study, *Questions of English* (2000), which considered English teachers' beliefs and perceptions across three geographic locations – Australia, the United Kingdom and the United States – elicited the perspectives of tertiary academics as

DOI: 10.4324/9781003106890-6

part of an investigation of what should be the core of the English curriculum. My aim here is not to try and reconcile the views of these key stakeholders with the tensions and views of the teachers in our study, but rather to tease out the complexity and nuance of the disciplinary, institutional and textual networks that surround English teachers and intersect with their work with literature in classrooms.

Over the course of the project, 13 key literary studies academics from across Australia were interviewed. These individuals were selected to provide a sense of the diversity and commonalities of their disciplinary field, but we do not claim this to be a comprehensive study at the tertiary level. We particularly sought out literary studies academics who had shown some connection to secondary English teaching through institutional degree structures (for pre-service and in-service teachers), through contribution to the work of curriculum authorities or participation in public debate. Interviews with these academics were focused on their views about: a) the central disciplinary knowledges around literary studies; b) their ideal and actual interface between secondary and tertiary studies of literature; c) their ideal and actual role in preparing secondary teachers of English.

In addition to this, seven leading academics who teach and/or research in the area of secondary English curriculum were also interviewed. These interviews focused on conceptualisations of a 'literary education', and on the most effective ways to prepare English teachers for the literary education of future pupils. Six representatives from State-based curriculum and accreditation authorities and one representative from the national body, which implement (and/or accredit) the disciplinary requirements for secondary English/Literature were also interviewed, to capture other institutional and organisational understandings of literary knowledge. These stakeholders provided key insights into their system's assumptions regarding what constitutes literary knowledge and its contribution to disciplinary knowledge in English. These representatives were also asked how they saw teacher education graduates' literary knowledge shaping their professional practice, and these teachers' responses to, and uses of, the *Australian Curriculum: English* (ACARA, n.d.). Additionally, four key individuals in State English Teachers' Associations (including three Presidents) were interviewed so we might understand their professional associations' assumptions about the status and constitution of literary knowledge and how this is experienced by English teachers. Taken together, these interviews with accreditation, curriculum and professional association leaders offered insights into the nature of a literary education for secondary English teachers.

Placing these interviews in dialogue has enabled us to look across the linked fields of literary studies and English teaching for traces, echoes and tensions regarding the nature of literary knowledge and the professional formation of English teachers. Through discursive analysis we have clustered key themes emerging across these diverse conversations with stakeholders, viz:

a   the layered, distinctive and dynamic nature of literary knowledge, and
b   the forces and practices that create and constrain literary study and knowledge in the 21st century.

In the following section, I will discuss the different ways in which the interviewed stakeholders explored these two themes and will conclude the chapter with considerations of the implication of these insights for English teachers, literary knowledge and teaching in the 21st century.

The dynamic nature of literary knowledge

While our conversations with early career English teachers were initially characterised by an ambiguity towards, or in some cases a rejection of, the term 'literary knowledge' (see Chapters 3 and 7), for the most part, the stakeholders we interviewed were interested in exploring what this concept might mean and in testing the possibilities and limitations of the notion of literary knowledge against their experiences and practices. Like others who have wrestled with the 'knowledge question' in English (Dixon, 1975; Doecke & Mead, 2017; McLean Davies & Sawyer, 2018; Medway, 2010), several of the stakeholders we interviewed sought to distinguish what they perceived as dynamic and 'affective' means of literary knowing (Ahern, 2019; Houen, 2020) from other forms of knowledge. For Oliver, a literary studies academic, literary knowledge provides access to an

> emotional understanding of the world which is actually central to our real existence, ... how we live day-to-day and the kinds of decisions we make and so on, and that you can't necessarily get to that kind of knowledge through the sciences or other ways of understanding... it's not about knowledge as a body of facts, it's about a capacity to understand... a capacity to interpret...

This idea of literary knowledge as a means by which readers/students might develop a transformed understanding of the world, as Fialho notes, 'has been present since human beings realised that they could influence others through discourse'; is a key tenet of humanities education; and is also often specifically associated with the purpose of literary reading (Fialho, 2019, p.3). These sentiments are echoed by teacher educator Natalie, who is also substantively involved in the English teacher professional association in her State:

> So, the idea that we can pin literary knowledge down to something... I can't buy into that. I can understand... literary knowledge [as] a way of thinking, a way of approaching things. I would like my students to leave my Methodology classes knowing how to engage with literature, but I actually would be more happy if they were comfortable with that uncertainty when they approach a text and never think they've got *the* understanding of the text... It's an interactive thing, it's moving... it's dynamic process of meaning-making and understanding and responding... it's about beauty and personal response, it's intellectual and it's about ideas.

For Natalie, literary knowledge is a process, explained through verbs such as 'thinking', 'moving', 'responding' and 'approaching' to achieve a personal response and engagement with art. Literary knowledge as a way of thinking and making meaning is also taken up by Julie, a curriculum bureaucrat, who reflects that English is 'almost about ways of thinking, and we're expanding those ways of thinking with every engagement with texts'. This supports Dale's claim that 'what is actually taught in the literature classroom is not "the text", as we might assume, but the "proper mode of responding to it"' (Dale, 2012, p.24). As we discussed in Chapter 3, what constitutes the 'proper mode' of response has been debated over time, but as these quotes from our participants reinforce, this is a concept that has carriage across the fields of literary reading, teacher education and professional learning.

Like some of the teachers in our study (see Chapter 7), Oliver makes the explicit distinction between literary knowledge and understanding, or knowing (Medway, 2010), and propositional knowledge:

> the idea of knowledge is usually understood as a repository which is kind of clear and discreet and so it's like a collection of facts…, whereas… a word like 'understanding' is… clearer to people because… you don't have to agree with every book you read, but… they may add to your capacity to understand even if it's because you disagree with it… if you learn how to read… you're generating… abilities sort of like exercising… you know you can exercise and use it for this purpose or that purpose.

The distinction drawn out by Oliver can be understood in terms of the difference between knowing 'that' and knowing 'how' (Muller, 2016). For Muller, 'knowing how' concerns both inferential knowledge – an understanding of how the discipline works, the 'epistemic joints that link the knowledge bits together' – and procedural knowledge, where the student 'learns how to find out new things', tests ideas and makes judgements (Muller, 2016, p.103). For the stakeholders cited above, literary knowledge is primarily about 'knowing how' readers engage with literary texts, both intellectually and affectively, to create meanings. Yet, it seems that what Oliver describes goes beyond the paradigm suggested by Muller, which was also identified by Winch (2013) and taken up by Hudson (2018). Literary knowing as described here is also about the intersection of knowing 'how' and knowing 'why'. Knowing 'why' supports an understanding of the role that literature, on a meta-level, can play socially to negotiate meanings.

Some literary studies academics interviewed see these dimensions of 'knowing how' and 'knowing why', alongside more instrumental, propositional knowledge, as part of their conceptualisation of literary knowledge. Owen, who has taught both literature and writing internationally and in Australia, sees the

> tools of technical analysis… alliteration, rhyme, rhythm, those things in poetry, which person it's written in… first person, third person, past tense, … the grammatical features [as] a form of literary knowledge that's very helpful

He reflects that "if you don't have [these tools], you're just going to confuse what other people say... and the wider questions... of audience..."

We have a sense, here, of the layers of literary knowledge conceived by Owen, who sees technical and formal knowledge as necessary to engage with the meanings of others and broader questions of the purpose of engaging with literature. This resonates with ideas by Marshall (2014) and Kress et al. (2005), who discuss the elements of texts that students will find valuable to know in order to make meaning, each suggesting a possible taxonomy for literary knowledge, which places knowing 'that' as an important precondition for further generative and transformative engagement with texts.

Layers of literary knowledge

The notion of 'layers' of literary knowledge, starting with a close reading and understanding of language and moving beyond the text to its uses and purposes, is also taken up by Jordan and Lucas. Jordan initially draws attention to the challenge of 'trying to make and defend knowledge claims when you are dealing with something [the literary]' that 'is by its very nature imaginative and... fictional, constructed'. Jordan teases out the possibilities of literary knowledge as an 'ambiguous concept', suggesting that it encompasses 'knowledge of literature and knowledge of the way in which literature works and the kind of mechanics of it' and also notions of 'literature as a tool or as a lens through which you can gain knowledge of the world'. This multiplicity of meaning and purposes of literary knowledge reflects the perspective on literature offered by Glazener (2015) and articulates both proximities to language and text and movement away from it. For Jordan, the layers reflect the approach to literature his institution is taking with undergraduate students, whom he asks

> to think both about the kind of phenomenology of what they are doing when [they're] reading... a book or a poem... what is this thing that they're trying to think about the world through.

Continuing, he notes that he and his colleagues also 'try to get [students] to think about the world and the ideas... beyond the text that are being activated.' He concludes, '... I think any... good definition of literary knowledge would want to try and draw on those two gravities.' This concept of gravities, as the pull of the 'what' (the form of the literary text – 'the thing that [they're] trying to think about the world through'), and the 'why' (the content of the text, which gives access to the 'world' of 'ideas') identifies the aspects of literary study that teachers must negotiate and balance in their work with students, at any stage of education.

The different levels and focus of literary knowledge are also articulated by Lucas, a scholar who had spent years teaching literature in different Australian States, and also in the United Kingdom. Lucas reflects:

Well, I think there are diverse kinds of knowledge involved in studying literary texts. I mean, I'd see literary texts as generating a kind of knowledge of the world which is quite specific to literary texts. It's different from the propositional knowledge generated by philosophy or by the sciences, but it's a genuine kind of knowledge. It's partly a knowledge of language and the way language works, but it's more than that... it's a knowledge of the way social fantasies work, social myths, the ideological structures that float around in a society. I see literary texts as working upon those raw materials and producing a kind of critical knowledge of them. Then separate from that but allied to it, we teach certain kinds of knowledge in the classroom, we teach in particular the ability to read texts very closely, to read figurative language, to work out what's going on with figurative language, we teach the reading of narrative structures... and we teach more generally a model of interpretation that's widely applicable across other kinds of text than literary text.

While Lucas distinguishes between literary knowledge, which enables a critical engagement with the world, and propositional knowledge in other disciplines, he also communicates propositional aspects of literary knowledge – such as narrative structures – that are aligned with the skill of reading and have a utility beyond the literary work. Indeed, Lucas, Owen and Oliver all frame an aspect of literary knowledge in terms of process and action, as knowing how texts work, as acquiring an ability to read for meaning flexibly outside of the literary field – and employing interpretative practices that are transferrable. This aspect of literary knowledge is also raised by other stakeholders. Julie, working in a State English curriculum role, identifies expert English teachers as those who can see the relevance of literary study beyond the classroom, and beyond literature:

I look at people who can analyse outside of the field, you know that analysis [of] being able to look at a text and find the layers and levels [this] is the transportable skill to life.

Literary knowledge as a social practice

While the literary studies academics we interviewed were interested in exploring, for the most part, the possible temporal, textual and interpretative layers that might constitute literary knowledge, a key theme to emerge from our conversations with teacher educators, curriculum officers and professional association officers, who focused their responses on literary knowledge for school teachers and school students, was the critical dimension of reading and interpretation. Given that post-structuralist theory, which contributed to the evolution of critical literacy in schools (Luke, 2000; Mellor & Patterson, 2004), started in the academy, it is of interest that the critical dimensions of literary knowledge were largely taken up by the other stakeholders, rather than the literary studies academics we interviewed. Reflecting a critical literacy approach (Mellor & Patterson, 1994; Misson &

Morgan, 2006), Julie suggests literary knowledge includes the kinds of questions to ask of a text or a body of works being selected for study:

> Who's been left out of this picture? Who's going to be included? Whose voice is missing from here, and what does this say about the times and what does it say now?

Helena, a teacher educator, also emphasises the importance of critical approaches to literature in terms of her work with pre-service teachers:

> I want them to understand [literature] has been contested, has been problematic in some ways and I think going back to the idea of whose voices are included, whose voices aren't, even like the representation of… women… as authors and characters… what I encourage my [pre-service teachers] to do is to really question why they're teaching something, how they're teaching something, but then… I [also] want them to be equipped to analyse the literature and to show their students how to engage in that process…

And for Stella, representing an English teachers' association, ways of reading literature, and explicit understanding of literary theoretical lenses, are similarly a core part of literary knowledge for teachers. She reflects:

> I think that without actually operating within a literary framework, understanding it and explaining that literary framework to your students, a lot of stuff just becomes activity.

These responses are particularly pertinent when concepts of 'critical reading' or critical literacy have been elided, at the national level, from curriculum documentation in Australia (Lu & Cross, 2014). In contrast to the tertiary literary studies academics we interviewed who were interested in the tensions and possibilities of literary knowledge, for the teacher educators and colleagues in professional associations who were part of our study, tensions existed as a result of the imperative to rethink and reassert concepts of literary knowledge in a secondary context. Consequently, several interviewees placed particular emphasis on literature as a justice-oriented social practice. This focus placed on criticality and politics suggests crucial literary knowledge is beyond an individual's experience of a text and enables epistemological questions of 'why', rather than 'what' or 'how' to be mobilised. Further, it positions teachers as *creators* of literary knowledge, as redefining and forming the field, a point that will be taken up further in the following section, and in Chapter 7.

Curriculum and teaching influences on literary knowledge

Alongside broader conceptions of literary knowledge, our interviews with stakeholders also offered insights regarding the ways in which literary knowledge or 'knowing' is formed, and the forces enabling and constraining this. The different views shared by these stakeholders convey a further sense of the complexity of the role of institutions in both the making of English teachers and teachers' enactments of knowledge in this subject. Across the stakeholders interviewed, there was a strong sense of curriculum decisions and trends, both at the tertiary and secondary level, as shaping and making literary knowledge in a subject area that is unfixed and evolving. Alice, a tertiary literary studies academic, reflects:

> I think about literary knowledge in exactly those [curriculum] terms. Like what needs to be in the curriculum because we don't, … have traditional survey courses, but we have a sequence of core studies and therefore you know, in every curriculum review and discussion, those staff get together… And I've been involved in some of those discussions to look at… not what texts need to be studied, but what needs to be studied for a student to come out with a major in English, which you might say is… with credible literary knowledge at the end of that. What do they need to know? What do they need to have encountered? What do you need to have as the actual learning objectives – not the cocktail ones – at each level… and how do you put those together so it's coherent? So that what they get is not repetition, but building of skills, knowledges – knowledge that… makes sense to them across different areas of study.

Alice's response draws attention to the changing nature of literary studies at the tertiary level (Mead, 2011). She indicates that where there might have once been consistent approaches to 'surveying' bodies of literature in undergraduate courses in Australia, following a British, colonising model (Dale, 2012), the expansion and diffraction of literary studies in recent decades means that the tertiary curriculum is being made anew by those responsible for it.

Further, Alice's reflection indicates the role of curriculum and teaching in informing and shaping the literary field – a point that has been taken up persuasively by Buurma and Heffernan in *The Teaching Archive: A New History for Literary Studies* (2020). While there have been sustained arguments that textual knowledge is formed in dialogic classroom contexts in school settings (for example, Reid, 1984; Yandell, 2013), these arguments have not traditionally been made in the context of tertiary literary education. Consequently, Buurma and Heffernan's contention that 'Classrooms offer us both a truer and a more usable account of what literary study is and does, and of what its value is today' (2020, p.6) seems radical in terms of the history of literary study and fundamentally contests Young and colleagues' notions of powerful literary knowledge (Young, 2013; Young & Muller, 2013) as fixed, agreed and established in the realm of scholarship (see also Jones, 2022). Oliver conveys the significance of teaching to literary knowledge when he explains his own need to return to undergraduate teaching to: ensure the quality of his scholarship; test his own understandings of texts; learn how his ideas are being received; and make new meanings, in the classroom, with students.

...it hurts the research if you don't go back in [to the classroom] and... see what people are making of what it is you're saying [in publications], because if you can't explain something to a first-year student or a second-year student, then it's possible that it's kind of obscure... and...you get... feedback... [on] what they [the students] are thinking and that feeds into how you understand the texts... [The texts are] constantly changing in terms of how people understand them...

Yet, for Frank, in a different institution, the tertiary classroom is not the space for unintended individual and collective meaning-making that it perhaps once was. Frank draws attention to the ways in which high-stakes accountability cultures mediate the nature and openness of the conversation about literature, moderating the claims made by Buurma and Heffernan (2020). Frank notes that

we tend to sort of hold tutorials... and prescribe what the discussion will be about texts... We either nominate specific critical or theoretical things that we want to address... we don't leave enough room for... individual choice... I do think that in some ways we limit certain critical possibilities by telling them how to think and... what to do and not just allowing them to develop their own sense of what the literature is and what it can give them.

The teacher educators we interviewed also lamented the ways in which account-ability cultures have changed the way literary texts are experienced by students in secondary schools, and profoundly influence where secondary teachers are required to place their focus (Teese, 2013). Helena and Fred both communicate that the National Assessment Program for Literacy and Numeracy (NAPLAN) is impacting teachers and students, and Helena specifically raises the issue of the influence of this high-stakes test on secondary teachers' sense of professional knowledge and iden-tity. She reflects:

I think it would be a really positive development if teachers started thinking about their literary knowledge as one of the bases of their expertise because so much of it has been stripped away... it's very important that the profession begins to reclaim some of what is being stripped away through the literacy phenomenon.

In a similar vein, Karoline and Natalie discuss how the final public English exam in their State also stymies personal and creative knowledge-making with literary texts (I take up this point further, in the context of the early career teachers' interviews in Chapter 7). Karoline reflects:

I've seen more and more that literary experience is really being constrained and narrowed by... the external examination requirements. We've always known this, but the more high-stakes they've become, the more formulaic has been the engagement with literature... oh yes, it's gone hand in hand, and teachers understandably are constantly searching for that ideal formula... and to me, that is the antithesis of what literary education should be all about.

A member of the final year examination committee in her State, Natalie remarks on the limiting nature of the high-stakes examination system, saying:

> I continue to be concerned about the impact of high-stakes testing on what's happening in English classrooms... So, I think they're ongoing issues and we grapple with that on the exam committee enormously... I think it flavours so much of what's happening in classrooms.

Thus, across both tertiary and secondary stakeholders interviewed, assessment and curriculum regimes, and the institutions that administer and enact these, were perceived as antithetical to the potential of literary study, and to the kinds of literary knowledge and experiences students might encounter in classroom contexts.

Teacher professional preparation influences literary knowledge

In institutions where there was a structural alliance between the general arts curriculum (where potential teachers study literature) and education faculties (where preservice teachers study English education), we sometimes saw the influence of both teacher Standards and school curriculum preferences on the ways that tertiary students developed literary knowledge. Jordan shares that the undergraduate literary studies curriculum at his institution was intentionally designed to serve the needs of beginning teachers. He explains:

> ...the majority of our students... are on the pathways to secondary teaching or on the pathways to primary or even some kind of early childhood [teaching], so we redesigned the curriculum a couple of years ago so that the four core units that they take from first through to third year try to tick off a lot of the major boxes... conceptually that we would want them to have... particularly with the high school teachers... So, there is... an awareness of scaffolding... across the four years, certainly in terms of the complexity and the difficulty of material and our expectations of their engagement..

Here we have a sense of Jordan working alongside teacher educators to shape the disciplinary curriculum, but also of the secondary English curriculum, and notions of knowledge and understanding communicated in these policy texts, pragmatically shaping the undergraduate literary studies offering. This offers a different perspective on the linear notion, proposed by Young and colleagues (Young, 2013; Young & Muller, 2013), of the discipline informing the content and rendering of the school subject. Jordan's language, of 'scaffolding' and a developmental continuum, further shows the influence of dominant educational – rather than literary – discourses. His insights here offer a further perspective on literary knowledge as it is understood broadly, and specifically within a tertiary disciplinary context. While his earlier response conveyed the challenge of the word 'knowledge' in the context of literature and explored 'two gravities' that might be used to consider the expansive breadth of literary knowledge, his account of the pragmatic ordering of the curriculum, here, suggests a hierarchical approach to literary knowledge – a vertical, rather than a horizontal (Hudson, 2018) or a heterarchical (Dimock, 2007), ordering of the disciplinary field that impacts on the way knowledge is conceived and framed.

Like Jordan, Elizabeth is conscious of the role of the undergraduate literary studies courses she is responsible for at her institution in the preparation of future English teachers. At the time of the interview, Elizabeth was the convenor of the 'English' major, which draws on literature and television and film studies and is distinct from a major in 'Literature'. This is a bespoke offering that has longevity in the curriculum as it was 'created primarily for secondary teachers of English'. Elizabeth, like Jordan, has worked closely with teacher educators in her institution to determine the content of her course. In the early days of her appointment to this administrative role, Elizabeth set up an advisory board, which included colleagues from the State-based teacher professional association. In more recent times, yearly meetings with her key contact in the School of Education in her institution have enabled Elizabeth to modify the literary studies major, so that it reflects the kinds of practices and foci of the secondary curriculum:

> …she'll [the teacher educator] say, 'Well, secondary teachers do a bit of creative writing now. So, this course, this first-year course should have a bit of creative writing tucked in there'. And we've done that, you know, in a first-year Lit course. So, students will do, say, a creative response to a novel and that sort of ticks that box.

This reflection indicates the ways that creative writing had been reduced in subject English (antithetical to the shift at tertiary level, which will be discussed further below). Both Jordan and Elizabeth, operating in very different institutional contexts and in different States, refer to framing disciplinary content and knowledge for potential teachers as 'ticking a box', echoing the structure and compartmentalisation of Teacher Standards (AITSL, 2011). While they don't refer explicitly to the Standards-based reform underpinning this approach, it is nonetheless reflected in their discourse and the notion that for teachers, knowledge and content needs to be 'checked off'.

Elizabeth made a further modification to the major based on other information her education colleague gave her:

> My colleague said, 'Well the teachers are probably going to have to teach Shakespeare'. So, we have… sort of recommended… [that] BA/BEd students do the Shakespeare course. So that's on the major. And she said that they

probably have to do some sort of Australian Lit. or Australian culture. So…
[we] recommend one of those courses… we make sure we have an Australian
Lit course.

On the one hand, this approach can be viewed pragmatically as the ordering of a
discipline that, as Alice said, does not offer an immediate or consistent organising
principle. On the other hand, though, this approach may result in downplaying the
expansive potential of literary knowledge and increased attention to the epistemological 'what', rather than the more ontological questions of 'how' or 'why'.

It is worth noting, by way of an aside, that Elizabeth's reference to the place of
Australian literature in her major is one of the few references to national literary
texts, broadly defined, that we encountered in our conversations with stakeholders.
While Jordan talks about the teaching of Indigenous Australian literatures and
canonical Australian texts as part of a general first-year course that is taken by those
wanting to become teachers, for the most part, literary knowledge, in our conversations, was not grounded in place, or time beyond generic references to the
value of teachers and students understanding literary history. Clearly the long
shadow of imperial literature in Australia (Dale, 2012) remains. The imperative for
teachers to have a critical engagement with the literary field, raised independently
by Helena, Julie and Stella, discussed previously, is the closest the dialogue moves
to grounding literary study and knowledge temporally and geographically.

Competing disciplinary knowledges and the fate of literature

While subject English is mandated across the years of schooling, and thus remains
the largest curriculum area, this is not the case in the tertiary sector, and literary
studies academics discussed the challenge of 'making' or doing literature in the
marketised university, where, as Noah says, 'there are pressures on the humanities
and pressures on English because English departments are kind of dissolving'. He
continues:

> I think it's demonstrable globally that you know the financial concerns of the
> corporate university are big factors in what will happen to English… some
> people have written very positively about that… about how English has a great
> future but it will change, and… more vocational and communication and digital
> literacy and literate citizens and all that sort of stuff will be part of what English
> does. Literature will shrink to a more niche space. And I think that seems pretty
> likely… and at the same time, creative writing is just booming.

Like Noah, Elizabeth and Jordan also register the perceived threat of creative
writing to literary studies. Elizabeth notes that creative writing has 'really altered
the power balance in the School', and Jordan notes that creative writing is the
'thing that everybody [students] wants to do' and as a consequence, 'literary studies
is… declining in terms of its position'. In his survey of English programs across the

(mostly Anglophone) world, James English (2012) discusses the ascendancy of writing and sees this as part of a global move towards re-orienting and re-defining the discipline of English (English, 2012). English argues that creative writing, is potentially positive for the study of literature in the academy (if the literary remains central to inquiries into language and creativity – a point also raised by Everett, 2005); however, it could ultimately result in the decline of literary study should the nature of the writing focus shift the disciplinary orientation further towards a more vocational, and less literary, basis for the study (English, 2012, pp.167, 171–172). It is the disaggregation of reading and writing that Jordan laments, he sees some students of creative writing as captured by the romance of production, and not able to

> see the actual things that you learn from reading and taking apart texts as being… significant… we try to… talk to the students about [the idea that] being a good reader… makes you a good writer; the two things… can't be taken apart.

Jordan argues for a form of literary knowing or knowledge of how literary language works as central to production as well as reception, however, he notes that this is not a generally agreed position and that in Australia, the Australian University Heads of English, and the Australasian Association for Writing Programs are quite separate organisations that are not often in dialogue.

If there is value in shared conversations about discussions about the future of the discipline and subject and generative knowledge in this context, as has been argued strongly for more than a decade (see Doecke, McLean Davies, & Mead, 2011; Kuttainen & Hansen, 2020), then it is important to have all who are influencing this future as part of the conversation. This becomes particularly important when we consider that undergraduate experiences of writing, as well as other discipline areas such as drama, can be used by intending pre-service English teachers to satisfy the entry requirements of graduate-entry teacher education programs (see for example NESA, 2018).

In his interview, Charles, an English curriculum bureaucrat, argues that the different approaches to English taken by tertiary institutions, and the imperatives they face, mean that teachers come to pre-service preparation with diverse conceptualisations of what constitutes literature and English:

> People are coming in with different levels of literary knowledge by dint of… the program that they've been under in that particular time of what curriculum was. So the notion of depth of curriculum knowledge, of literary understandings or literary knowledge is a very relative thing for individual students.

By contrast, the range of discipline areas able to be utilised by pre-service teachers, raised as a concern by Charles, was assessed by James English, in his analysis of the discipline worldwide, as a positive interdisciplinary aspect of the approach to tertiary English undertaken in Australia. However, English also noted that in the Australian tertiary context, this interdisciplinary disposition is 'characterised by a strong bias towards vocationalism' (2012, p.153). This point is reflected in the enthusiasm for creative writing across Australian institutions, discussed above, and has been stridently reinforced in the context of the Humanities more generally in recent years, with the Australian Federal Government increasing the cost of arts degrees, to incentivise students to undertake more 'job-ready' courses (Khadem, 2020). Frank's experience reflects this zeitgeist, and he talks about the impact of vocational pragmatism on his teaching of literature within the discipline of English in Australia, noting that in the United Kingdom, literature remains popular, even with the government charging more for humanities degrees:

> …in the last five or ten years, we've had to agree to let go of certain things that we can't teach anymore, because… English itself… and not just at schools, not just because of literacy and all the other things at school, because at university there are so many other subjects that they're finding more appropriate, more vocational, you know communication, media, cultural studies…

In a similar vein, Charlotte, located in a different State again to Elizabeth and Frank, says that 'a big conversation in the first year is how do we retain students into second year?' She notes that while there is a 'natural flow' from secondary school into university English, this interest is not maintained and that university staff in English have to strategise about offerings that will continue to draw students into literary subjects.

Implications for literary knowledge and the making of English teachers

Charting of the key concerns and issues to surface through the project's stakeholder interviews offers a perspective on how literary knowledge is variously shaped, experienced and understood in contemporary Australian contexts. We see that across these conversations, an expansive, transformational (Fialho, 2019) under-standing of the potential of literature was communicated. Yet, at the same time, the interviews also highlighted that neoliberal imperatives, including account-ability cultures and high-stakes assessment, impact on all sectors, and limit and constrain the development of literary meaning-making. This means that while history of English teaching (as discussed in Chapter 5) shows that the literary priorities of academics in universities previously influenced practices in schools, largely through the senior examinations systems in operation in different Aus-tralian States, in the contemporary moment, what is valued in terms of literary knowledge in schools can impact quite substantially on the curriculum in some universities, particularly if there is a strategic alignment between undergraduate education and arts degrees. Thus, although professors of literature, as Chapter 5 showed, were accustomed to having authority over the secondary curriculum, communicating what Young and Muller have expressed as 'powerful knowledge' (2013), we see that the power balance, at least in some places, has shifted, and teacher educators and practices in schools are currently influencing university curricula and the literary experiences made available to tertiary students. This is not to say a change in direction of curriculum influence is intrinsically valuable, or even benign: the secondary curriculum and assessment expectations that are influencing tertiary offerings often reflect external pressures and expectations that are outside the remit of individual schools or teachers.

In light of this, the interviews discussed in this chapter reinforce the value of a shared, cross-sectoral conversation about the teaching of literature and the forces that are shaping future teachers' perceptions of literature and its purposes. In the last decade, arguments have been made for this collaboration based on its value to students, as they traverse the stages of their formal education, or to share new understandings of reading practices or texts (see, for example, AUHE, 2014). These reasons for greater networking and shared understanding of practice remain valid. However, it seems imperative for teachers of literature, and other tertiary disciplines taken up by future English teachers, to mobilise across sectors if we are to understand and contest the ways in which regimes of value and capital (Guillory, 1993), perpetuated by standards-based reforms and neoliberal cultures, are being manifested in tertiary and secondary institutions, and the impact this has on the development of generative, transformative literary knowledge, particularly in settler contexts.

References

Ahern, S. (2019). *Affect Theory and Literary Critical Practice: A Feel for the Text*. New York: Springer International Publishing.

Australian Curriculum Assessment and Reporting Authority (ACARA). (n.d.). English – Foundation to year 12 (Version 8.4). Available: www.australiancurriculum.edu.au/f-10-curriculum/english/. Accessed 21 April 2022.

Australian Institute for Teaching and School Leadership (AITSL). (2011; revised 2018). *Australian Professional Standards for Teachers*. Available: www.aitsl.edu.au/teach/standards. Accessed 21 April 2022.

Australian University Heads of English (AUHE) Secondary-Tertiary Nexus Working Group. (2014). *Secondary-Tertiary Nexus AUHE Discussion Paper No.2*. Available: https://auhe555190908.files.wordpress.com/2022/02/auhediscussionpaper2nov.-2014-version_secondary-tertiary-nexus.pdf. Accessed 21 April 2022.

Buurma, R. S., & Heffernan, L. (2020). *The Teaching Archive: A New History for Literary Study*. Chicago: University of Chicago Press.

Dale, L. (2012). *The Enchantment of English: Professing English Literatures in Australian Universities*. 2nd ed. Sydney: Sydney University Press.

Dimock, W. C. (2007). Introduction: Planet and America, set and subset. In W. C. Dimock & L. Buell (Eds.), *Shades of the Planet: American Literature as World Literature*. Princeton, NJ: Princeton University Press: 1–16.

Dixon, J. (1975). *Growth through English: Set in the Perspective of the Seventies*. 3rd ed. London: Oxford University Press.

Doecke, B., McCleneghan, D., & Petris, L. (2011). Teaching small 'l' literature: Lessons from English in Australia. In B. Doecke, L. McLean Davies, & P. Mead (Eds.), *Teaching Australian Literature: From Classroom Conversations to National Imaginings*. Kent Town: Wakefield Press: 266–292.

Doecke, B., McLean Davies, L., & Mead, P. (2011). National imaginings and classroom conversations: Past and present debates about teaching Australian literature. In B. Doecke, L. McLean Davies, & P. Mead (Eds.), *Teaching Australian Literature: From Classroom Conversations to National Imaginings*. Kent Town: Wakefield Press: 1–15.

Doecke, B., & Mead, P. (2017). English and the knowledge question. *Pedagogy, Culture & Society*, 26(2), 249–264. https://doi.org/10.1080/14681366.2017.1380691.

English, J. (2012). *The Global Future of English Studies*. Malden MA and Oxford UK: John Wiley & Sons.

Everett, N. (2005). Creative writing and English. *The Cambridge Quarterly*, 34(3), 231–242. https://doi.org/10.1093/camqtly/bfi026.

Fialho, O. (2019). What is literature for? The role of transformative reading. *Cogent Arts & Humanities*, 6(1), 1–16. https://doi.org/10.1080/23311983.2019.1692532.

Fletcher, L., Clarke, R., Crane, R., Gaby, R., Milthorpe, N., & Stark, H. (2016). The teaching of English in Tasmania: Building links between senior secondary and tertiary teachers. *English in Australia*, 51(1), 25–33.

Glazener, N. (2015). *Literature in the Making: A History of U.S. Literary Culture in the Long Nineteenth Century*. London: Oxford University Press.

Guillory, J. (1993). *Cultural Capital: The Problem of Literary Canon Formation*. Chicago: University of Chicago Press.

Houen, A. (2020). *Affect and Literature*. Cambridge: Cambridge University Press.

Hudson, B. (2018). Powerful knowledge and epistemic quality in school mathematics. *London Review of Education*, 16(3), 384–397.

Jones, K. (2022). The teaching archive: A new history for literary study. *Changing English*. https://doi.org/10.1080/1358684X.2021.2013161.

Khadem, N. (2020). Government uni changes mean some students will pay more than their degree costs. *ABC News*, 19 June. Available: www.abc.net.au/news/2020-06-20/study-arts-and-humanities-government-fees-tertiary-education/12374124. Accessed 30 January 2022.

Kress, G., Jewitt, C., Bourne, J., Franks, A., Hardcastle, J., Jones, K., & Reid., E. (2005). *English in Urban Classrooms: A Multimodal Perspective on Teaching and Learning*. London: Routledge Falmer.

Kuttainen, V., & Hansen, C. (2020). Making connections: Exploring the complexity of the secondary-tertiary nexus in English from the perspective of regional Australia. *English in Australia*, 55(2), 39–51. https://search.informit.org/doi/abs/10.3316/informit.017173931936378.

Lu, W., & Cross, R. (2014). Making sense of mixed messages: Literacy within the Australian Curriculum. *Literacy Learning: The Middle Years*, 22(2), 41–50. https://doi.org/10.3316/informit.317851040328241.

Luke, A. (2000). Critical literacy in Australia: A matter of context and standpoint. *Journal of Adolescent & Adult Literacy*, 43(5), 448–461.

Marshall, B. (2014). What does it mean 'to know' in English? In A. Goodwyn, L. Reid, & C. Durrant (Eds.), *International Perspectives on Teaching English in a Globalised World*. London and New York: Routledge: 13–24.

McLean Davies, L., & Sawyer, W. (2018). (K)now you see it, (k)now you don't: Literary Knowledge in the Australian Curriculum: English. *Journal of Curriculum Studies*, 50(6), 836–849.

Mead, P. (2011). What we have to work with: Teaching Australian Literature in the contemporary context. In B. Doecke, L. McLean Davies, & P. Mead (Eds.), *Teaching*

Australian Literature: From Classroom Conversations to National Imaginings. Adelaide: AATE/ Wakefield Press: 52–69.

Medway, P. (2010). English and Enlightenment. *Changing English: Studies in Culture and Education,* 17(1), 3–12. https://doi.org/10.1080/13586840903556987.

Mellor, B., & Patterson, A. (1994). Producing readings: Freedom versus normativity. *English in Australia,* 109, 42–56.

Mellor, B., & Patterson, A. (2004). Poststructuralism in English classrooms: Critical literacy and after. *International Journal of Qualitative Studies in Education,* 17(1), 85–102. https://doi.org/10.1080/0951839032000150248.

Misson, R., & Morgan, W. (2006). *Critical Literacy and the Aesthetic: Transforming the English Classroom.* Urbana, IL: NCTE.

Muller, J. (2016). Knowledge and the curriculum in the sociology of knowledge. In D. Wyse, L. Hayward, & J. Pandya, (Eds.), *The SAGE Handbook of Curriculum, Pedagogy and Assessment.* London: SAGE Publications: 92–106.

New South Wales Education Standards Authority (NESA). (2018). *Subject Content Knowledge (Abridged).* Available: https://educationstandards.nsw.edu.au/wps/wcm/connect/a e7db0fc-4a6d-4904-b635-f70147e0dc3c/subject-content-knowledge-requirements-re cent.pdf?MOD=AJPERES&CVID=. Accessed 30 January 2022.

Peel, R., Patterson, A., & Gerlach, J. (2000). *Questions of English: Ethics, Aesthetics, Rhetoric, and the Formation of the Subject in England, Australia, and the United States.* London and New York: Routledge Falmer.

Reid, I. (1984). *The Making of Literature: Texts, Contexts and Classroom Practices.* Adelaide: Australian Association for the Teaching of English.

Teese, R. (2013). *Academic Success and Social Power: Examinations and Inequality.* North Melbourne: Australian Scholarly Publishing.

Winch, C. (2013). Curriculum design and epistemic ascent. *Journal of Philosophy of Education,* 47(1), 128–146.

Yandell, J. (2013). *The Social Construction of Meaning: Reading Literature in Urban English Classrooms.* London: Routledge.

Young, M. (2013). Overcoming the crisis in curriculum theory: A knowledge-based approach. *Journal of Curriculum Studies,* 45(2), 101–118. https://doi.org/10.1080/00220272.2013.764505.

Young, M., & Muller, J. (2013). On the powers of powerful knowledge. *Review of Education,* 1(3), 229–250. https://doi.org/10.1002/rev3.3017.

VIGNETTES NO. 3 AND 4 – JANET AND CLARE

Janet

Janet told a story at the end of her final interview about 15 boys who were in a program called the Victorian Certificate of Applied Learning (VCAL). This is an applied learning program specifically designed for students who are judged to be more suited to a vocational pathway than doing the Victorian Certificate of Education (or VCE) for entry to university. VCAL is all about 'hands-on learning', to use the language with which schools typically promote the program.

Janet recounted that the 15 VCAL students had been encouraged to join the much larger cohort of students who were doing VCE to enjoy a performance of Shakespeare's *Romeo and Juliet*. But the boys mucked up badly, with the result that they were kicked out of the auditorium and even suspended from school. Janet felt 'really bad... I wanted them to enjoy it [laugh] but I couldn't force them to... I think I felt like saying...., you're being VCAL students, stop it! [laugh] I didn't want them to be yeah, I didn't want them to... yeah so dreams have been crushed and that's okay [laugh]...'

From our very first interview, Janet evinced a commitment to working with students who lack the cultural capital of those students who successfully complete the VCE and go on to university. She insisted that it was not that these students weren't bright. They simply did not have the language that would persuade examiners to give them high marks. They had good ideas, but they were wrapped up in poor spelling and mangled syntax or simply not expressed in a form that sounded right.

Each year, students across the State sit for the VCE exams and those who achieve the top marks are feted in the newspapers. Most of those students come from elite private schools and their scores are an important marketing tool for influencing parents' choice of a school for their children. Janet was teaching in a regional denominational college that catered for kids from the town and the surrounding districts, many of whom lived on farms and caught a bus each day to get to school. So, she was hardly working in a school whose demographic matched that of elite private schools in Melbourne. The town was a couple of hours away from Melbourne, which meant that the kids had little or no experience of city life. The social life of the town centred on football, and on Saturday nights the older students often found themselves with little to do. During the time that we were interviewing Janet, the region had gone through a severe drought, which had resulted in considerable strain being placed on families.

Janet, however, was no newcomer to this culture. After completing a double major in English at a university in Melbourne, she eventually found herself working in London as an editor for a major publisher specialising in medical textbooks. Her students were fascinated when she told them about the work she had done before becoming a teacher, including writing blurbs. Her story gave them a sense of a point in doing English. But the fact is that Janet herself came from this town, and although she had not attended this particular school, her decision to take up a position was a return to the rural culture and scenes of her childhood and adolescence.

Janet spoke fondly about her university education and the opportunity it gave her to read widely. She completed her degree in the 1990s, and the stories she told about her university education reflect the culture of that time. She sat for hours in the basement of the university library, chasing up critical commentary on books she was reading. Her degree behind her, she backpacked around Europe, spending most of her time in Germany, re-reading German novels that she had read at university in locales where the atmosphere seemed to match that of the book she was reading (in Eisenach she re-read Kafka's *The Castle*). It is difficult to imagine a more literary pursuit or one that contrasts so markedly to everyday life in the region where she was now living and working, which comprised talk about crops and cattle and milk production.

Yet here she is. She is even living on a dairy farm and in our first interview with her, when she was working part time and was yet to secure a full-time position at the school, she was milking cows:

> Yeah, so I think the boys, particularly because I milk cows… that's the other thing about me [laugh] so I still milk cows… Yeah, so I grew up on a beef farm, and when we moved back to Australia we built a house that was in the centre of a dairy farm… they knew who I was, and they said, 'Would you like to do some work with cows?' And I had two young kids at home, and it was great work that I could do while they were asleep in the morning, so I'd get up at four, milk, and then be home by eight… and I won't milk every morning these days because I'm here every day, but on the weekends I'll milk, yeah.

She remarked that 'there's no messing around with Miss Simpson because swear words don't really impress her, she's not shocked by anything'. The students 'knew that I was still milking cows on weekends and that it wasn't completely divorced from their world yeah… hopefully it shows that you can still be interested in reading books and literature'.

The growth that Janet experienced over the three years we interviewed her was reflected in an ever more refined appreciation of the conflicts facing her students as they try to negotiate a pathway between the demands of the curriculum and the values and expectations of their community. Janet understands her role as one of enabling her students to see themselves differently, to recognise that they too are capable of success at school.

She is capable of standing up to the school leadership when she feels that the directions they are pursuing conflict with the provision of a worthwhile English curriculum. She has been consistently critical of the standardised testing that all schools in Australia are obliged to implement (or what is known as the National Assessment Program Literacy and Numeracy [NAPLAN]). Because of the nature of the school community, the results that students achieve fall below expected standards, prompting the principal to insist that English teachers devote one period a week to drilling and skilling students. Janet's response to this was to email her objections to the English Coordinator. Even though she was immediately rebuffed – her Coordinator told her not to dish up her 'airy-fairy bullshit' about literature and the imagination, and to focus instead on improving those scores – it was obvious that she remained committed to facilitating classroom activities that reflected a richer understanding of the relationship between language and meaning than that embedded in standardised testing.

Clare

Clare is an early career teacher who is actually in her second career. She had decided to enrol in a Master of Teaching after some years working in the travel industry, where it was her responsibility to deliver professional development. This was something she enjoyed. Recognising that she wanted to do more than teach people 'how to make money and run a business', she consulted her university transcript and discovered, much to her relief, that she had taken enough units in her undergraduate degree to enable her to teach English, with History as her second method.

Clare realised that her motivation for becoming a teacher was different from that shared by most of her (often younger) peers. She could not recall an inspirational or charismatic English teacher who set her on the pathway to becoming a teacher. And, she was a bit troubled by fellow pre-service teachers who were apparently consumed by a desire to play such an inspirational role in their students' lives. While Clare wanted to 'empower' her students to 'become articulate… and amazing people', she was not motivated primarily to 'form a relationship with them or to be memorable to them'. This standpoint is reflected in the mantra Clare developed in her first year: 'be the teacher that your students need, not the teacher that you think you should be'.

Clare had not enjoyed English at school. Attending a private girls' secondary school in country Victoria, her experience of English had been 'very much just a… chore… something that had to be done'. She still, however, developed a great love of reading, as she was surrounded by 'an abundance of books in the house', adults who were committed readers and friends who were involved in the publishing industry. It is her love of reading and the possibilities of texts that she wants to share with her students:

> …you know you can't have all those experiences yourself as one human being, so that's why you read isn't it, so you can get all these other experiences and live vicariously through all these characters and have all this amazing insight and empathy into other people around you?

This dual purpose, to share her love of literature and to be the teacher her students need her to be, creates tensions, questions and challenges for Clare that played out differently across the three years that we interviewed her.

In her first year of teaching, Clare is allocated a Year 10 English class for those with identified 'literacy needs'. She is uncomfortable with the deficit language and the emphasis on commercial literacy tests and programs, but she is also confronted by the literacy needs of the students themselves:

> I've got students who are reading at a Grade 2 level, and I'm not sure I'm equipped with the skills I need to teach the rudiments of reading. I'm not sure I'm the teacher that those students need, but I'm the teacher that they have, so we just have to muddle through together.

Teaching this class also highlights the challenge of expanding students' experiences and understanding through texts. The set text for the class is *Growing up Asian in Australia*, an anthology of short stories edited by Alice Pung. She recounts that the Asian Australian students in the class are delighted to see themselves in a text for the first time. As the study of the text commenced, and Clare outlined the School Assessed Task (SAC), she recounts that one student said:

> Miss, that's bullshit. The EAL students have got such an advantage, I can't believe they get their own text. They're going to do so well on this SAC because they know all about this and it's got nothing to do with me.

This incident raises questions for Clare about students' perceptions of reading, the ethical role of English, and white privilege and text selection practices in the school.

When we meet Clare again in her second year of teaching, she has been made Director of English and is managing a department of 26 teachers. Encouraged to apply for the position by the departing director because of her 'managerial... corporate background', Clare was appointed because of these strengths:

> I said 'Obviously there's not that much I know about the teaching of English just yet because I've been doing it for 12 months, but I do know a lot about these things... if that's what you're looking for, then have a go', and they decided that that would be a good idea.

Clare acknowledges that she is 'in a really different headspace to where we were last year', and this is evident through her language, which reflects her responsibilities: five essays across Years 7–11 are not enough to prepare for Year 12; there are 13 classes of Year 7s and 8 teachers – how can consistency of student experience be assured? Numbers and data become the means by which she can argue for curriculum changes. Early in her second year of teaching, Clare presents a 'business case' that shows the literacy program has not made any measurable differences to student attainment, and the program is axed.

In her third year of teaching, Clare retains her role of Head of English and also becomes Head of Literacy (which is considered a separate department in the school). As she develops in these leadership positions, her commitments to both 'being the teacher her students need to be' and engaging her students in reading and expanding their experiences through texts are variously strengthened, nuanced and negotiated. As Head of English, Clare is obliged to teach Year 12 and her first class consists mostly of high-achieving maths and science students. Clare finds it challenging to involve the class in discussion – hyper-aware of class ranking and ATAR scores, the students are reluctant to share ideas in case it causes them to lose a competitive advantage. Clare persists by bringing butchers' paper into the classroom and setting tasks on character and theme that require students to talk to one another. She is encouraged by the dialogue that emerges, and the new understanding being built by what she perceives is an unorthodox approach to senior English pedagogy. When comparing her class with those of other colleagues, who favour the silent writing of practice essays, Clare worries that she may be disadvantaging her students when it comes to the VCE exam.

As an English leader, Clare becomes more conscious of the tension between selecting texts to expand students' lived experiences and develop empathy, and choosing texts that will enable them to draw on their existing knowledge and understanding in an exam. She recognises the risk of setting texts such as *I for Isobel*, which was chosen by the previous Head. She is conscious that 'so much is at stake', and feels that, as a cohort, the students at her school do not have the necessary background or contextual knowledge to write well on this text, and will be competing with private girls' schools, who are well versed in the book's themes of Catholic guilt and recognise its sophisticated intertextual references. For Clare, the challenge at VCE is 'trying to find things that are not too similar but not dissimilar', so that students are engaged, but not locked out of rich readings.

7

TEACHERS' CONCEPTIONS OF LITERARY KNOWLEDGE

Larissa McLean Davies

It was our privilege to visit vastly different institutional contexts in which students' and teachers' experiences of literature were being shaped. Some schools were newly built and we were greeted in the reception area by uniformed mannequins, attempting to bring consistency to diversity through blazer and bomber jacket; in other more established schools English teachers had their own staffroom and apparent autonomy over the curriculum; and in different contexts again, teachers had access to cutting-edge technologies and felt the weight and expectation of an educational environment in which students were selected for academic success. As we met with our early career teachers over the course of the longitudinal study, it became clear that their perceptions of what literary knowledge might be and mean for students were influenced by several factors, including the diverse institutional context in which they were teaching; the texts available and selected; curriculum intentions and high-stakes assessment regimes; their understanding of the purpose of English; their roles within the school community; and also their own experience of literary reading and meaning-making. Each teacher had a different story (as the *vignettes* through this book highlight) and as their own classroom experience grew, their approach to the question 'What constitutes literary knowledge?' and their perception of the relevance of this term changed.

In this chapter, I will draw on the scholarly debates about literary knowledge foregrounded in Chapter 3 and think with the literary theoretical framework 'deep time' proposed by Wai Chee Dimock (Dimock, 2006) to analyse how teachers articulate both the possibilities and challenges of students' encounters with literature in school English, and their own roles in these engagements. The chapter will conclude with a consideration of what this analysis might mean for questions of powerful or empowering curriculum knowledge (Young, 2008, 2014) with regard to the teaching of literature in schools, and specifically in settler societies such as Australia.

DOI: 10.4324/9781003106890-7

English teachers' concerns about literary knowledge

A core interest of our research was in how early career English teachers made sense of and engaged with the notion of literary knowledge. We wanted to know if, and how, this concept resonated with their praxis, and their professional identity as English teachers, and whether this changed or developed over time. Having said this, we did not come to this inquiry with a fixed sense of what literary knowledge might be. We deliberately did not seek to define 'literature' and avoided suggesting limits and possibilities for the word 'knowledge' when conjoined with an inquiry about texts. Consequently, the early career teachers in our study responded in a range of ways to our questions about knowledge and literature. Indeed, it is fair to say that most of the 40 early career teachers[1] we interviewed, at least initially, expressed uncertainty and caution, or at times rejection of the concept, and its relevance to their students or their perception of their role as an English teacher.

In the first year of interviews, some of our teachers felt challenged by the ways students were responding to the non-propositional nature of textual study. Clare reflects: '…I think that's the thing that students get really frustrated with [in] English… [they ask] "Am I right or am I wrong? Am I correct or incorrect?"' Her qualified answer, 'Well you're correct to a degree' only leads to further student anxiety: 'Well, what can I do to make myself more correct?' Clare registers the challenge in clarifying the nature of knowledge in English, how this might be experienced, and for what purpose:

> It's so intangible… I think it's very difficult to actually articulate… I feel like it happens sometimes almost by a process of osmosis, you know like the more you read the better your writing becomes, the more familiar… I don't know, that's what I mean, it's very hard to measure…

Clare's anecdote suggests that her capacity to explain the role of texts in supporting meaning-making is made, somewhat paradoxically, more complex by her own literary education and formation. She shares with us that her family home was filled with books, and that family members worked in publishing. She acknowledges the gap between her students' experiences and her own when she finds herself needing to express explicitly the value of engagement with texts. This is not something she is prepared for, and she finds it difficult to identify the specific role of literature in and beyond English, which in her own family and school experience was uncontested.

For other teachers, however, questions about literary knowledge prompted them to turn to the specificity of texts and to feel that they might not be 'well-read' enough (McLean Davies & Sawyer, 2020). Although like Clare, Debra has grown up in a home filled with books, and recounts her father reading Orwell's *Animal Farm* to her after dinner when she was in primary school, she registers concern about her knowledge and experience as an English teacher, as she focused on history in her undergraduate degree. Yet, it is not simply their academic background that determines some teacher's sense of textual preparedness. Rebecca majored in literary studies, but despite this, she tells us that she felt she hadn't read widely and was anxious that this might be discovered.

> I was so terrified the Headteacher was going to [say] 'Have you read this?' And I was going to say, 'Oh no'… and… even though I'd read heaps at uni… still… feeling… unprepared in that way.

These concerns reflect various assumptions and issues regarding English teachers, knowledge and texts that are worth explicating. As we have written elsewhere (McLean Davies & Sawyer, 2020), significant reports and texts in the history of teaching English over a period of 50 years – the Newbolt Report (Newbolt, 1921); Newsome Report (CACEE, 1963); John Dixon's *Growth through English* (Dixon, 1975); the Bullock Report (DES, 1975) and the Cox Report (DESWO, 1989) – all emphasised the importance of an English teacher being 'well-read', and with each report, the possible texts a teacher might engage with was expanded, incrementally increasing the 'knowledge' required. We can infer from our teachers' comments that this long history of expectations to read 'well and widely' continues to have its legacy and is exacerbated by the ways in which texts often act as a substitute for knowledge in English (see Yates et al., 2019; Chapter 9). Indeed, in our previous research, which considered the ways mid-career English teachers in Australia and England were conceptualising literary knowledge, it was common to see that teachers, weighed down by the performative culture associated with neoliberalism, felt worried about the so-called 'limitations' of their textual knowledge (McLean Davies & Sawyer, 2020). They reported feeling compelled to engage in subterfuge, even when they were well-established in a school, so that students, parents and colleagues would not become aware of what they perceived as absences – particularly around canonical literature – in their reading history (McLean Davies & Sawyer, 2020).

Further, in addition to the nervousness many teachers feel when they commence practice, the policy context in Australia could arguably be understood to have contributed to our teachers' sense of the 'limitations' of their literary subject knowledge. In 2011, the Australian Institute of Teaching and School Leadership (AITSL) introduced the Australian Professional Standards for Teachers (APSTs). Standard 2.1 – 'Know the content and how to teach it' – requires graduating teachers to 'Demonstrate knowledge and understanding of the concepts, substance and structure of the content and teaching strategies of the teaching area' (AITSL, [2011] 2018) and assumes a stability of 'content' that is not possible in English (as we discussed in Chapters 1 and 3). The second level of the APSTs – 'Proficient' – which teachers are awarded at the end of their first year of practice following the submission of a portfolio, further reinforces that content knowledge was achieved on graduation, and thus the focus going forward is on pedagogy. The Standards don't allow for the building of knowledge in practice, or the dialogic and sociable nature of English. In 2014, the Teacher Educational Ministerial Advisory Group (TEMAG) report (2014), commissioned by the Australian Federal Government of the time, made 38 recommendations to improve the quality of pre-service teacher education programs and teachers, and introduced the rhetoric of 'ready to teach'. Taken alongside the Professional Standards, the notion of 'ready to teach' further reinforces that teachers will commence practice with a stable and comprehensive knowledge of content (as well as of pedagogical and classroom management aspects).

However, while questions concerning literary knowledge prompted some teachers to reflect on the number and nature of the texts they had read, not all the early career teachers in our study felt pressure to be well-read in a traditional sense. Indeed, some actively contested the enduring role of the canon in schools, arguing that subject English needed to be understood in the contemporary moment. Amaris took the view that her journalism degree had enabled her to see what English *should* be focusing on in the 21st century. Arguing that the intention of English is to support the development of students' communication skills, Amaris railed against the term 'literary knowledge' not because of its intractability, but because she felt that it conveyed an inappropriate allegiance to cultural imperialism. This results in her dismissing not just the notion of literary knowledge, but also the place of literature in subject English. Drawing on the specificities of her undergraduate study in journalism, Amaris explains that she sees literature as divorced from the core business of subject English, which she believes is to teach students to critically engage with the world. Her text choices reflect this understanding:

> …they're not from this… canon list… I'm not teaching literature, … they're not old school… *Macbeth* and … *The Crucible*… I'm not teaching those texts… I don't teach literature, I teach English…

In her first-year interview, Nicole also questions the relevance of literary knowledge as a concept in subject English. Although she is more tolerant of traditional texts than Amaris, she sees these as perpetuating imperial understandings of race and class (see McLean Davies et. al., 2022). Indeed, both Amaris and Nicole reject the role of 'preacher of culture' (Mathieson, 1975), the teacher who dutifully plays a moral, civilising and culturally homogenising role through the teaching of aesthetic texts. Conceiving their professional roles as contesting, rather than confirming a cultural heritage approach – 'the induction of readers and writers into the great works of the literary canon' (Macken-Horarik, 2014, p.10) – they initially dispense with the term 'literary knowledge', seeing it as evoking what Guillory (1993) has argued is the key role of schools and teachers in creating and maintaining cultural capital.

Literary knowledge and deep time

While our teachers registered concerns about the term and scope of literary knowledge in English, they also shared generative and productive possibilities for what an understanding and experience of literature might mean for students, drawing from their lived experience in and out of the classroom. Like Amaris and Nicole (above), Katya takes issue with a notion of literary knowledge that is grounded in the canon. Rather than rejecting the literary, though, as Amaris does, she imagines literary knowing as fundamentally ontological and affective – 'like a way of being'. When Rebecca focuses on the way her students might experience literature and the knowledge they might encounter and take away, she sees this in expansive terms. However, she did not apply this paradigm to herself, at least initially, but rather, as we saw above, in the context of high-stakes curriculum and assessment expectations, defaulted to a quantifiable notion of literary-cultural capital (Guillory, 1993).

The idea of literature as a way of knowing that brings together epistemology and ontology, suggested by Katya, Rebecca and others, resonates with Medway (2010), Fialho (2019) and with Walsh, who observed that 'the kind of knowledge and the mode of knowing afforded by successful literary art seems to have an intimacy and an immediacy not characteristic of knowledge as knowledge about this or that' (Walsh, 1969, p.138). These concepts are also synergistic with Wai Chee Dimock's notion of the deep time of literature (Dimock, 2006). Dimock argues that literature can be understood as

> 'a set of longitudinal frames, at once projective and recessional with input going both ways and binding continents and millennia into many loops of relations, a densely interactive fabric'.
>
> *(2006, p.3)*

This framework challenges discreet and stable concepts of epistemology and extends the parameters of literary knowledge beyond individual texts, geographies and histories. This notion of the 'deep time' of texts offers us a framework for exploring how the early career teachers interviewed articulate the value and purposes of literary study, when the notion of 'knowledge' sat uneasily for many. Indeed, Dimock's provocation that 'literature is the home of nonstandard space and time' (2006, p.4) helps us to think with some teachers' more expansive conceptions of the literary and their focus on students as the starting point for literary knowing.

Our conversations with teachers thus revealed that the value, purpose and knowledge created through textual engagement goes beyond the space and time of the individual text. For many teachers, the power of literary study existed precisely in using the text as a starting point, or as a vehicle to enable them to access different worlds. Amanda shares with us the way she uses literature to open up '… a way of understanding, interpreting our world and seeing how people work and how society works'. Using the example of Shakespeare, Amanda explains how literary study enables students to move between the present and the past, making meaning across times and spaces: 'being able to look at Shakespeare and the way the things within that are still relevant today… we can use that as a lens to understand power struggles or family conflict'.

While Amanda is interested in connecting the texts of the past to students' own experiences, supporting them to interpret the present, Rebecca sees the expansive potential of literature as taking students beyond their current contexts:

…it's that idea that texts can transport you to different times, to different places in the world, and I think just being able to see the world from a different person's perspective that's the most valuable no matter where they are.

Similarly, Eva reflects:

…there's definitely lots of teaching moments for life in literature of course, and there's understanding the world, there's becoming more tolerant in understanding the world… But I think also being able to understand oneself, identity, like understanding and being able to create a personal narrative… you learn that, I think, by reading other narratives.

Although Dimock's notion of 'deep time' gestures towards the sociable and expanding possibilities of literature, this concept takes on an additional dimension in the classroom, where students' own embodied texts and lives mediate the ways they and others are reading, enabling both an expansion of knowledge of the world and how they might move within it. Rebecca reflects on the way in which one student spoke in the final assembly about the idea that, through studying the concept of literary representation in English, she came to adopt this as a way of making meaning of her daily interactions and major life events. For Rebecca, this was 'literary knowledge in practice'. She reflects

… that idea of representation in text translated into the rest of the world for her [the student] and she realised [that] all these things we do in society are also constructed in a way. So, I thought that is of value, … there's something you can learn from literature that can help you in your life… it can be a very turbulent part in your life, leaving school, especially if you're very comfortable here, and the idea that she was going to lose touch with all these friends was what was… really worrying her. So, saying… 'This isn't the end, you know everything about this graduation ceremony is saying we're going to end… but we're not, this is just a representation'… and I think of all the things you learn from literature, that idea of representation is probably the one [that] is valuable in real life… [and] I liked that… she'd attached it to real life.

This idea of personal transformation through literature resonates with Fialho's research on the 'purpose' of literature (Fialho, 2019). Synthesising various scholarly accounts of the meaning readers make with texts, Fialho argues that 'reading can be woven into the texture of readers' lives. The experience [of reading] seems to have transformative powers as it deepens our understanding of the position of the self in the world' (Fialho, 2019, p.2). Clare conveys these sentiments when she explains that literature 'allows you to access parts of yourself that you might not access in other ways' as well as allowing you access to 'parts of the world you might not be able to access in other ways'. The implication here, and in Fialho's research, is that each student will have a distinct experience of texts through this engagement. As Dimock writes:

> Literary relations are idiosyncratic relations… They bring distant words close to home, give them a meaningfulness that seems local and immediate even though they could not have been so initially, objectively. The distance between readers and the words they read is anything but a number. In this domain, at least, time is made up not of fixed lengths but of lengths variably generated by each reader.
>
> *(2006, p.133)*

Clare sees the role of school in this exchange as facilitating a 'common experience', not of insights into the world and the self, but the role of literature in connecting the individual with the deep time of texts. If knowledge can be considered common in English, it is in terms of this broader notion of literary knowing – that is, knowing what literature can do and make, rather than the knowledge that is made by individuals through the classroom experience. This use of texts as a gateway to other texts and meaning is in itself not a new concept or discovery of practice. English teachers will certainly be familiar with the spontaneous interplay between the text as an artefact, the texts that circle around it in time and space, and the texts the students embody and bring with them into the classroom. What is significant here, though, is that this rich literary experience is not often considered in terms of literary knowledge, or as knowledge at all, and nor is this way of knowing validated in curriculum documents or assessment practices.

For Dimock, this development of one's sense of themselves in relation to others is a key affordance of deep time literary reading. She proposes that reading is a multi-layered, multi-temporal and multi-textual activity that

> alert[s] us to our long sojourn on this planet, a sojourn marked by layers of relations, weaving our history into our dwelling place, and making us what we are, a species with a sedimented imprint. Honouring that imprint, and honouring also the imprints of other creatures evolving as we do, we take our place as one species among others, inhabiting a shared ecology, a shared continuum.
>
> *(2006, p.6)*

It is this sense of a 'shared continuum', and the possibilities of community through and with literature, that is evoked by Sophie when she reflects on the role of literary education for students:

> Part of what we're doing [in English] is opening windows, opening doors into worlds that some kids have never heard of, some kids kind of dabbled in, but certainly connecting their experiences to a wider lived human experience that helps them to… see a bigger picture of the world… open their eyes, lift their eyes a little bit… that they're not alone, and that… there's value in seeing things from a different perspective and through different modes.

Thus, for the early career English teachers in our study, productive formulations of literary knowledge, or knowing through literature, are conceived as expansive, enabling a simultaneous knowledge of the self and the world. This is made possible because of the 'deep time' and unbounded properties of literature, where powerful knowledge lies in variety and instability, rather than in propositional claims.

Literary deep time in the classroom.

As a literary theory concerned with the nature and production of literature, and the effect of literary texts on readers, however, Dimock's conceptualisation of deep time does not extend to pedagogical or institutional contexts. Rather, like the theory of literary sociability that we also animate in this book, it is primarily concerned with the nature of the relationship between texts and readers, assuming a productive engagement, even when the reader must work hard, navigating time and space, to make meaning. Of course, English teachers cannot assume students will naturally, or consistently, have a productive or transformative engagement with texts.

Several of our teachers commented that to experience their story as part of a shared continuum, as Dimock imagines, they felt students needed to be challenged or made uncomfortable to develop key critical capacities. Debra reflects:

> I think they… get an understanding about themselves, and if they can recognise themselves in a character or not recognise themselves in a character, they get an understanding of where their perceptions about the world, where their attitudes, values and beliefs come from and how they are applied, and then also [about] prejudices they might be applying to other people around them.

Michael also takes this up when he expresses a desire for his students to

> reflect on who they are, knowing who they are, knowing what their place is in the world, how to challenge things… to understand there are multiple interpretations of the world… I want them to question, and I think texts especially allow them to question themselves and the world around them.

These ideas are echoed by Lily, who wants her white students to be challenged to view themselves and their world differently and understand what Indigenous narratives and the narratives of people of colour might mean for their own sense of identity. Lily raises concern that selecting texts that are perceived as 'relevant' to engage her group of students meant that

> they learn about themselves and no one else, which you know is good and we do need that, but I just think it's too narrow. And… teaching Indigenous texts… some of the kids struggle with because that's outside of them, and at the moment that's the only way that they're looking outside of themselves.

Like Lily, Angela wants students to encounter new ways of knowing that tests their assumptions and their experiences and she sees the strategic selection of texts as part of this. Angela tells us that her decision to teach the film text *Gayby Baby*, told from the perspective of students with same-sex parents, was motivated by the imperative to

> Get them [the students] thinking for themselves. I want to challenge them, and I want to provoke them because to me English isn't just building empathy, it's about critical thinking...

In this context, having access to the deep time of literature, experiencing a sense of being embedded and nested in a heterarchical structure (Dimock, 2007), can't simply be considered as a natural process, or as an aspect of literature that students will experience through reading. Rather, the breadth and possibilities of literary knowing are determined by a critically sociable encounter with literature in the classroom, and by the teacher's part in this. Angela shares that she wants to 'challenge herself and be part of that journey with the kids', recognising that transformative encounters with literature include herself as the teacher.

For Katya, Chloe and Leo, critical theory provides an important framework for supporting students to see larger meanings in a text, and moving into a closer 'proximity', to use Dimock's term, with the literary work. This is not a simple, instrumental rendering of critical literacy which results in students being removed from the aesthetic and affective dimensions of texts (see Chapter 3), but rather these teachers use literary theory to enable students to see the relevance of the literary work to them as readers, and to their lives more generally. In their third-year interviews, Katya recounts bringing psychoanalytic theory into the classroom to help students engage with and make meaning with Hitchcock's film *Rear Window*; Chloe talks about the feminist interpretations her students engage with when studying Chevalier's *Girl with a Pearl Earring*, and Leo discusses his use of Judith Butler's notion of gender performativity in conjunction with Watson's *Montana 1948*. He shares that through this introduction to feminist frameworks, several of his students were

> Questioning... the views and values that they had been brought up with, thinking... 'Well it's not necessarily the way I'd go anymore, no. [I] don't have to have this view if it's negatively impacting somebody else. I don't have to be this person'.

Our teachers' investment in students experiencing themselves as part of a broader continuum and community articulates with notions of 'difficult knowledge' (Pitt & Britzman, 2003; Zembylas, 2014) – knowledge gained through encounters in classrooms that are unsettling and even confronting, and also resonates with literary theoretical ideas of global south reading practices which provide 'access to discourses, places, and speakers in such a way as to generate new subject positions, fields of agency, and possibilities of action' (West-Pavlov, 2018, p.2).

The examples shared by the teachers suggest that to experience the transformative and reflective potential of literature, they need to provide opportunities for students to experience 'pedagogies of discomfort' (Zembylas, 2014). This draws attention to how students' experiences of literature are mediated by teachers and the texts they select in the context of the classroom. Unlike Dimock's paradigm of 'deep time', which imagines the textual relationship entirely between readers and texts, our study shows the significant mediating role English teachers play in school-based literary encounters. This highlights the limitations of conceptualisations of powerful knowledge as fundamentally disciplinary, and outside ontology, for both the student and the teacher (Young, 2014), and positions the teacher not as the carrier of knowledge, whose responsibility is 'knowing the content and how to teach it', but rather one who is contributing to the nature of the content and knowledge to be encountered.

The nature of English, and the key role that text selection plays in shaping students' experiences of literature (McLean Davies et al., 2021), means that teachers' own reading experiences, preferences and priorities matter. To take up Alfred Tatum's notion of a 'bookprint' – 'a reading and writing autobiography which shows that who you are is in part developed through the stories and information you've experienced' (McLean Davies,et al., 2019, n.p.) – English teachers have been formed by the stories and texts they have been exposed to, and these unique experiences, in combination with their school, university and teaching contexts, impact the way their students experience the subject (McLean Davies & Buzacott, 2021). This means the literary knowledge that students develop across the years of schooling is the amalgam of the classrooms they have been part of, the texts they have studied, the literary experiences of the teachers who have taught them, and their own experiences of literary deep time. Laura raises this perspective when we first ask her about her understanding of literary knowledge. She reflects:

> I guess literary knowledge is quite subjective… because… New Scheme teachers, Old Scheme teachers, they have different knowledge of what literature is… and even where we're educated at universities or… wherever we've been educated and our experiences… it's all made up of where we come from or where we have been, it's always going to be different… I guess that's a good thing for the kids, I think it's a good thing, but it can be quite confusing for them because there's no sort of 'this is what English is', and even though we have a Syllabus that says this is what English is and this is you need to know in order to be considered a student of English and they need to meet these Outcomes, it doesn't necessarily mean that these kids are always going to meet these Outcomes in the way that the government or whoever writes the Syllabus wants… or even to teachers teaching content to the content markers or to the Outcome or whatever they're doing, it's not going to be the same anywhere, it's never, ever the same. Teaching at this school is different to teaching at other schools.

We know that the knowledge students build in all subjects is dependent on the way the teacher presents material and their understanding of any given topic; however, what we see emphasised in Laura's reflection is the connection between ontology and epistemology. Teachers are 'read' as they simultaneously read the literary work with their students (McLean Davies, 2008a). For Laura, this material variety in how teachers approach questions of literature and define 'the literary' is ultimately 'a good thing for the kids'. Amidst standardisation and accountability cultures, it is worth teasing out what it might mean to see such variety as 'good'. Just as students are more likely to experience the transformative and affective potential of literature through multiple engagements with texts that enable them to make connections and have a sense of their part in what Dimock refers to as 'the continuum', it stands to reason that a range of teacherly perspectives and engagements will also broaden the potential for connection and meaning-making.

In her final interview, Nicole takes up similar issues to Laura regarding the value of the diversity of literary knowledge carried into classrooms by teachers. She reflects:

> I think I was a bit too prescriptive with what I considered literary knowledge, then, because I've realised that among English teachers, we all have different types of literary knowledge... I think it depends on our personal reading preferences and interests and the types of culture we consume... we bring those interests and those strengths to the texts that we suggest and the way that we teach.

This rich and intersecting paradigm of literary meaning-making is not emphasised in discourses that centre on the text as a substitute for knowledge in English (Yates et al., 2019), or even on students' dialogic engagements with the text. It also offers a different and more nuanced perspective on teacher knowledge of literature to that offered in the 20th-century reports on English teaching mentioned earlier, which emphasised the need for teachers to have a breadth of reading experiences so that they could effectively engage students and teach the content required. We are reminded in the interviews with our teachers of the ways in which their ontological experiences of text, how they have encountered literary knowing, as well as the texts they have read, will impact the literary experiences of students and the knowledge they build (Truman et al., 2021). This is aligned with, but not the same as, an argument about pedagogy: that what matters for students' experiences of texts it what is done with them in the classroom (Yandell, 2017).

Of course, it would be naïve to suggest that while the diversity of teachers' literary knowing is of value, this link between teacher and student epistemology and ontology, through and with the study of text is naturally or reliably benign. Craig speaks at some length about the need to act covertly to use texts that he believes will meet the needs and interests of his students, but that he believes would not be prioritised by his Head of English or those he perceives as more conservative colleagues. Similarly, when she becomes Head of English, Clare talks about having to remove *The Hate Race* by Maxine Beneba Clarke (2016), which details Clarke's experiences of racism in Australia, because staff felt too uncomfortable teaching it, although for many students,

Clare says, this was the first time that they had related to a text in secondary English. We see here that what teachers encounter as 'difficult' knowledge can impact the literary knowing students can access, and more broadly the maintenance of colonial frameworks and ideologies in English.

It is in response to the issue of teacher influence in English that, in his final interview, Leo shares with us his intention to give his students responsibility for selecting texts for the following year of study. He says:

> When I'm thinking about how we work and how we prioritise particular types of literary knowledge, I think that's a dangerous way of making decisions by ourselves, and I've kind of come to the conclusion that it's not just us… and it would be useful to ask students. So, for me, one of the questions was about the selection of texts and also thinking about the voice of students.
>
> [We should be]… more focusing on how we affect them… their emotions. 'How do we change them?' is fraught… they don't necessarily have to change. [It is more about] them thinking, 'Who am I?' … for me the purpose of English is inherently… well it's political, and the politics side of it is the individual growing and how do I as the teacher allow that particular individual to grow? … It would be giving it to them. So, giving them the selection. What do they want to read? What types of literary knowledge do they want to focus on?

Leo registers a level of discomfort with the idea of imposing difficult knowledge on his students, feeling he has too much power when determining their textual experiences. His solution, to offer students the opportunity to meet and discuss the kind of texts that will be set for study, to determine the nature of their own 'growth', seems democratic, but it can't guarantee that students have a transformative and generative literary experience. The texts that become part of the students' 'continuum', to return to Dimock's term, are also those which are present through the bodies and experiences of teachers and other students, and how these are brought together in the classroom.

By paying attention to the complex relations between texts and individuals, we have the opportunity to consider the intersecting experiences of literary knowing that are coalescing, being mediated and being brought into tension through the sociable spaces of the classroom. Thinking with Dimock's concept of 'deep time' in the context of secondary school English, therefore, adds a different dimension to considerations of the ways students build knowledge in English, and how we understand that development and input of teachers over time. In the next section, I will turn further attention to some of the challenges teachers identify regarding students' access to literary knowing.

Institutional, assessment and curriculum challenges to deep time literary knowledge in school English

The interviews with our early career English teachers, taken together over the three years, showed a strong sense that teachers valued the transformative potential of literary knowing for their students. However, they also surfaced the limitation or impediments to students experiencing and teachers facilitating inquiry into the deep time of literature within current institutional structures, assessment regimes and curriculum contexts.

The impact of the high-stakes examination system on students' experiences of texts and framing of valuable literary knowledge was apparent from the first year of our interviews, in the ways in which teachers discussed students' attitudes to essay writing. Several teachers shared the challenge they were facing in convincing students that English, and its core literary studies, was supporting them to develop relevant knowledge and skills that would be useful to them beyond the classroom. For example, Freya reflects:

> I've got some… students… who are just… they don't see the point in English… [they say] 'But we're never going to use an essay in real life'.

Similarly, Nicole recounts one student asking her:

> How's this going to help me? You know I want to be a carpenter, why do I need to know how to write an essay?

Bound by a system in which what is valued in English is ultimately determined by a final exam (Teese, 2013), these teachers, in their first year, find themselves defending English and literary reading through the utility of the pragmatics of literacy. Brittney does this when she tells a student, 'Even though you go into a trade, you still need to be able to read and write and you need to be able to understand and express yourself', and Tim takes this approach when he tells an aspiring scientist

> …you will be given a scientific dissertation and you'll have to read it and you'll have to understand the words, and you'll have to break down what it means, but you'll also have to understand its consequences upon science and your job.

This is not to say, of course, that reading literary texts in English, or the English curriculum more generally, does not lead to practical, skill-based outcomes (for further discussion on assessment, see Chapters 10 and 11, and for discussion of the essay, see Chapter 11). It is rather the case that more expansive concepts of ontologically transformative literary knowing, which follow the development of the skills of reading and writing (two of the three 'Rs' that are always the jurisdiction of English) are obfuscated in this high-stakes environment, where students' knowledge of texts is dominantly framed by a five-paragraph essay structure (McKnight, 2021; Phillips et al., 2022 et al).

In the context of examination expectations, an issue to surface in our interviews was the challenge of teaching the background of the text and its intersections with other texts, so that all students could respond in ways that would be recognised and rewarded by assessors. While Dimock's imagined reader comes to the text with the resources to engage with it, the teachers in our study drew attention to the ways in which students' unfamiliarity with the historical context of both traditional and contemporary texts limited how they could express literary knowledge. For Clare, this issue is brought into sharp focus when she is required to teach Amy Witting's *I for Isobel* to her Year 12 students. She explains:

> [the novel] relies on literary allusion to convey so much because the character Isobel is this avid reader; she has this amazing fantasy world which is constantly informed by the books that she's reading, and as she sort of transitions through her rite of passage, all of the texts that she's reading tell you so much about her... but of course, 90% of our students hadn't read any of those... It just really highlighted to me that my kids were going to be writing on that text in an exam and being compared to students from other schools who have that breadth of depth and have read some of these texts which were being referred to.

Clare's anecdote draws attention to the intertextual understanding expected by English examination systems (McLean Davies, 2008b; Teese, 2013). To support her students to be successful in this system, Clare creates a 'key' for reading the novel which explicitly tells students that when the character Isobel is 'reading Sherlock Holmes it tells us this, and when they are studying *Twelfth Night* it tells us that'. Amanda is similarly explicit when teaching Dickens' *A Christmas Carol* to Year 11 students. She shares that she found herself teaching the historical context of the Industrial Revolution, and then looking specifically at how this is symbolically and metaphorically manifest in the novel. Amanda reflects the tensions she experiences in the high-stakes environment, between generative pedagogy and pragmatic outcomes:

> I kind of almost went against what I like to do in telling them that this is the point of the book before we started, but I think for Year 11 it helped them to notice those things as they read through and to understand the purpose of some of the symbols and imagery that Dickens used because they knew... the overall point.

Amanda's reflection communicates that in this system, there is specific knowledge, 'an overall point', which is to critique the sociocultural period in which it was written. Students must communicate this point, through an understanding of literary language, under exam conditions. While much scholarship has raised concerns about the continued selection of canonical texts (see for example Bliss & Bacalja, 2021; McLean Davies et al., 2021), Clare's and Amanda's anecdotes remind us that examination systems not only privilege certain texts but also shape responses in such a way, in some State contexts, that it leaves little time for students to encounter the 'deep time' of literature, particularly in the high-stakes senior years of school.

Leo raises this point when he laments the ways in which the high-stakes system requires students to reproduce certain sanctioned readings rather than expressing their own experience of texts. He reflects:

> the students' ability to understand what you're looking for is what is prioritised as opposed to who they are or what their opinions and their arguments are, and that for me if that's what we're looking for, focusing on textual knowledge… that's more looking for an answer, more than it is looking for who they are.

Leo contrasts this approach of teaching for a particular reading, which ignores the students' affective responses to texts, with a more open, less prescriptive 'way into' tests, by reflecting that students' responses, when allowed to engage with the text on their own term, were more generative:

> I remember teaching Plath last year and not addressing the context and the history of Plath's work before we did the text got a very different response to when we looked back on it after they had the historical context, and I thought the interpretations we were having at the beginning were much more fruitful and diverse than when we'd actually given them the context of who constructed the text and all those types of issues.

This is not to argue for dispensing with historical context, or that teachers should not support students to understand the deep time of literature through intertextual work. Rather, the reflections of our teachers pertain to issues of emphasis and weight, and to the role of examinations in shaping what is rewarded as literary knowledge. In a high-stakes system, where English is mandated and important in students' scores in final assessments and, at least in the first instance, determine their pathways beyond school, we can see how the 'knowledge' assessed in examinations becomes symbolically and materially powerful.

Fialho raises the issue of disjunction between what readers see as the purpose of literature and the assessment and curriculum dimensions associated with studying it in the context of her research into transformative reading. Fialho writes:

> The problem is that when it comes to an education in literature, such a [transformative] purpose is not always expressed or have [sic] a place. Literature students may acquire the skills necessary to analyse narrative techniques, and to distinguish modernist from postmodernist novels, but they are not asked to read for personal relevance. Traditional literary studies have centred around questions such as "What is this text about?". In fact, why one would study literature in the first place is an issue that is notoriously ignored in curricula. Questions such as "What is this text about for you?", "What does it mean for your life?", "What can I learn from this story", and "How could this novel change the way I live?" are seldom considered.
>
> *(Fialho, 2019, p.3)*

As we see through our teacher interviews, current curricula and high-stakes testing take time away from considering what 'growth' in English – still considered to be fundamental to this curriculum area (see Doecke & Yandell, 2018; Goodwyn, 2016) – might look like in 21st-century decolonising contexts, and limit how the transformative possibilities, the 'deep time' of literature, might be articulated and experienced. Personally powerful literary knowledge (as opposed to examined literary knowledge) is not necessarily measured or assessed but is found in the spaces in and outside the classroom, in conversations and accounts of meaning-making, such as in Rebecca's student's address to fellow Year 12s about literary representation, which show new understandings of language and meaning that can be taken beyond English and school.

Reflecting on the nature of powerful literary knowledge in English

Fundamental to arguments about a knowledge curriculum made by Young and colleagues is the claim that tertiary disciplines should structure and underpin knowledge in schools (Moore & Muller, 1999; Moore, 2013; Muller & Young, 2019; Young & Muller, 2010). Green (2017) and others have disputed this relationship in terms of English and, as we argued in Chapters 1 and 3, knowledge *per se* is contested and debated in subject English, Yet, as I have discussed in this chapter, our early career teachers' account of their practice indicates that while the term 'knowledge' may cause a sense of consternation, teachers do have a sense of what powerful literary knowing can be. Thinking with Dimock's concept of 'deep time' has offered a way of framing literary knowledge as both ontological and epistemological and enables us to explore the kinds of relationships between texts, teachers and students that contribute to literary knowledge and empowered or powerful knowing. In classrooms, however, 'deep time' literary experiences are not guaranteed. They require the coalescence of texts (both material texts set for study, and texts symbolically and imaginatively carried by humans and animated in the classroom) to be working in a productive relationship and to not eclipse, or silence, 'difficult' textual knowledge experiences (for students or teachers).

Taken together, the perspectives offered by our teachers show both the possibilities of literary knowing for students and the challenges they face, professionally and personally, in enacting these in high-stakes contexts and in colonised contexts. These insights, as we will take up later, have implications for teacher preparation and teacher professional learning.

Note

1 This study interviewed 24 early career English teachers over three years of the project. A further 16 teachers were interviewed once in the first year of the project. This group was known as 'Cohort 2' and was included to supplement the longitudinal study and to allow for attrition in the longitudinal group.

References

Australian Institute for Teaching and School Leadership (AITSL). (2011; revised 2018). *Australian Professional Standards for Teachers*. Carlton South: Education Services Australia. Available: www.aitsl.edu.au/docs/default-source/national-policy-framework/australian-p rofessional-standards-for-teachers.pdf. Accessed 27 May 2021.

Bliss, L., & Bacalja, A. (2021). What counts? Inclusion and diversity in the senior English curriculum. *The Australian Educational Researcher*, 48(1), 165–182. https://doi.org/10.1007/s13384-020-00384-x.

Central Advisory Council for Education (England) (CACEE). (1963). *The Newsome Report: Half our Future*. London: Her Majesty's Stationery Office.

Clarke, M. B. (2016). *The Hate Race*. Sydney: Hachette Australia.

Department of Education and Science (DES). (1975). *A Language for Life: Report of the Committee of Inquiry appointed by the Secretary of State for Education and Science under the Chairmanship of Sir Allan Bullock F.B.A.* London: Her Majesty's Stationery Office.

Dickens, C. (2003). *A Christmas Carol: And Other Stories*. London: Penguin.

Dimock, W. C. (2006). *Through Other Continents*. Princeton, NJ: Princeton University Press.

Dimock, W. C. (2007). Introduction: Planet and America, set and subset. In W. C. Dimock & L. Buell (Eds.), *Shades of the Planet: American Literature as World Literature*. Princeton, NJ: Princeton University Press: 1–16.

Dixon, J. ([1967] 1975). *Growth through English: Set in the Perspective of the Seventies*. 3rd ed. London: Oxford University Press.

Doecke, B., & Yandell. J. (2018). Language and experience: Re-reading *Growth through English*. In A. Goodwyn, C. Durrant, W. Sawyer, L. Scherff, & D. Zancanella (Eds.), *The Future of English Teaching Worldwide: Celebrating 50 Years from the Dartmouth Conference*. London: Routledge: 159–172. https://doi.org/10.4324/9781351024464-13.

Goodwyn, A. (2016). Still growing after all these years? The resilience of the 'personal growth model of English' in England and also internationally. *English Teaching: Practice & Critique*, 15(1), 7–21. https://doi.org/10.1108/ETPC-12-2015-0111.

Green, B. (2010). Knowledge, the future, and education(al) research: A new-millennial challenge. *The Australian Educational Researcher*, 37(4), 43–62.

Green, B. (2017). *Engaging Curriculum: Bridging the Curriculum Theory and English Education Divide*. London: Routledge.

Guillory, J. (1993). *Cultural Capital: The Problem of Literary Canon Formation*. Chicago: University of Chicago Press.

Macken-Horarik, M. (2014). Making productive use of four models of school English: A case study revisited. *English in Australia*, 49(3), 7–19.

Mathieson, M. (1975). *The Preachers of Culture: A Study of English and its Teachers*. London: Allen & Unwin.

McKnight, L. (2021). Since feeling is first: The art of teaching to write paragraphs. *English in Education*, 55(1), 37–52. https://doi.org/10.1080/04250494.2020.1768069.

McLean Davies, L. (2008a). Teaching Australian writing: Polemics and priorities. *Idiom*, 44 (2), 23–28.

McLean Davies, L. (2008b). Telling stories: Australian literature in a national English curriculum. *English in Australia*, 43(3), 45–51. https://search.informit.org/doi/10.3316/ielapa.599789065824489.

McLean Davies, L., & Buzacott, L. (2021). Rethinking literature, knowledge and justice: Selecting 'difficult' stories for study in school English. *Pedagogy, Culture & Society*, 1–15. https://doi.org/10.1080/14681366.2021.1977981.

McLean Davies, L., Gannaway, J., Buzacott, L., & Truman, S. (2019). 5 Australian books that can help young people understand their place in the world. *The Conversation*. Available: https://theconversation.com/5-australian-books-that-can-help-young-people-understand-their-place-in-the-world-127712. Accessed 29 May 2020.

McLean Davies, L., & Sawyer, W. (2020). On being 'well read'. In B. Marshall, J. Manuel, D. L. Pasternak, & J. Rowsell (Eds.), *The Bloomsbury Handbook of Reading Perspectives and Practices*. London: Bloomsbury: 145–166.

McLean Davies, L., Truman, S. E., & Buzacott, L. (2021). Teacher-researchers: A pilot project for unsettling the secondary Australian literary canon. *Gender and Education*, 33(7), 814–829. https://doi.org/10.1080/09540253.2020.1735313.

McLean Davies, L., Yates, L., & Sawyer, W. (2022). Investigating literature as knowledge in school English. In B. Hudson, N. Gericke, C. Olin-Scheller, & M. Stolare (Eds.), *International Perspectives on Knowledge and Quality: Implications for Innovation in Teacher Education Policy and Practice*. London: Bloomsbury: 109–127.

Medway, P. (2010). English and Enlightenment. *Changing English: Studies in Culture and Education*, 17(1), 3–12. https://doi.org/10.1080/13586840903556987.

Moore, R. (2013). Social realism and the problem of knowledge in the sociology of education. *British Journal of Sociology of Education*, 34(3), 333–353.

Moore, R., & Muller, J. (1999). The discourse of 'voice' and the problem of knowledge and identity in the sociology of education. *British Journal of Sociology of Education*, 20(2), 189–206. https://doi.org/10.1080/01425699995407.

Muller, J., & Young, M. (2019). Knowledge, power and powerful knowledge re-visited. *The Curriculum Journal*, 30(2), 196–214. https://doi.org/10.1080/09585176.2019.1570292.

Newbolt, H. (Chair), The Departmental Committee appointed by the President of the Board of Education to inquire into the position of English in the educational system of England (1921). *The Teaching of English in England*. London: His Majesty's Stationery Office.

Phillips, S., McLean Davies, L., & Truman, S. (2022). Power of country: Indigenous relationality and reading Indigenous climate fiction in Australia. *Curriculum Inquiry*, 52(1), 171–186. https://doi.org/10.1080/03626784.2022.2041978.

Pitt, A., & Britzman, D. (2003). Speculations on qualities of difficult knowledge in teaching and learning: An experiment in psychoanalytic research. *International Journal of Qualitative Studies in Education*, 16(6), 755–776. https://doi.org/10.1080/09518390310001632135.

Shakespeare, W., (2008). *Twelfth Night: or, What You Will*. New Haven, CT: Yale University Press.

Teacher Education Ministerial Advisory Group (TEMAG). (2014). *Action Now: Classroom Ready Teachers*. Canberra: Australian Government.

Teese, R. (2013). Academic Success and Social Power: Examinations and Inequality. 2nd ed. North Melbourne: Australian Scholarly Publishing.

Truman, S. E., McLean Davies, L., & Buzacott, L. (2021). Disrupting intertextual power networks: Challenging literature in schools. *Discourse: Studies in the Cultural Politics of Education*, 1–14. https://doi.org/10.1080/01596306.2021.1910929.

Walsh, D. (1969). *Literature and Knowledge*. Middletown, CT: Wesleyan University.

West-Pavlov, R. (Ed.). (2018). *The Global South and Literature*. Cambridge: Cambridge University Press.

Yandell, J. (2017). Knowledge, English and the formation of teachers, *Pedagogy, Culture & Society, 25*(4), 583–599. https://doi.org/10.1080/14681366.2017.1312494.

Yates, L., McLean Davies, L., Buzacott, L., Doecke, B., Mead, P., & Sawyer, W. (2019). School English, literature and the knowledge-base question. *The Curriculum Journal*, 30(1), 51–68. https://doi.org/10.1080/09585176.2018.1543603.

Young, M. (2008). From constructivism to realism in the sociology of the curriculum. *Review of Research in Education*, 32, 1–32.

Young, M. (2014b). Powerful knowledge as a curriculum principle. In M. Young, D. Lambert, C. Roberts, & M. Roberts (Eds.), *Knowledge and the Future School: Curriculum and Social Justice*. London: Bloomsbury Academic: 65–88.

Young, M., & Muller, J. (2010). Three educational scenarios for the future: Lessons from the sociology of knowledge. *European Journal of Education*, 45(1), 11–27. https://doi.org/10.1111/j.1465-3435.2009.01413.x.

Zembylas, M. (2014). Theorizing "difficult knowledge" in the aftermath of the "affective turn": Implications for curriculum and pedagogy in handling traumatic representations. *Curriculum Inquiry*, 44(3), 390–412. https://doi.org/10.1111/curi.12051.

8

LITERARY SOCIABILITY

Making meaning in English classrooms

Brenton Doecke and Philip Mead

Literary works are sometimes characterised as 'unmasking' everyday phenomena, enabling us to see our world in new ways (Eagleton, 2012, pp.91, 103; cf. Bennett, 1979, p.50). This view of 'literariness', as Terry Eagleton remarks, derives from the Russian Formalist understanding of 'making strange': reading a poem supposedly involves 'estranging our perceptions', 'retrieving them from the workaday staleness in which they are commonly sunk' and turning them into 'arresting objects of investigation in their own right' (Eagleton, 2012, p.91). Literary language, in this sense, can renew our perceptions of the familiar and the everyday. Like Les Murray's poem, 'Shower': 'only in Europe is it enjoyed by telephone'. Or Craig Raine's postcard from a Martian about life on earth: 'Rain is when the earth is television'.

Yet the notion of 'making strange' not only serves to describe what poets sometimes do with language. The influential sociologist, C. Wright Mills, characterises the work of the sociological imagination in analogous terms, as a matter of rendering what we take for granted in new ways (Mills, [1959] 2000, pp.7–8). Mills hardly has in mind the unveiling perception of the world that we associate with a poetic image. He is instead invoking a capacity to recognise social structures and relationships in ways that were not previously visible to us. Yet it is still significant that he uses the word 'imagination' to name the re-envisioning of everyday life that he sees as the sociologist's work. In a similar vein, Dorothy Smith, whose concept of 'institutional ethnography' played an important role in our thinking when we were initially attempting to envisage our inquiry into the teaching of literature in secondary schools, describes her mode of investigation as one 'that works from the actualities of people's everyday lives and experience' (Smith, 2005, p.10), allowing us to discover 'just how our everyday worlds are being put together within social relations beyond the scope of our experience' (Smith, 2005, p.32). And although she gestures towards understandings of the social structure that are 'beyond' the experience of everyday life, she still sees these concepts as playing a

DOI: 10.4324/9781003106890-8

role in enabling us to view the world differently. It is as though, once achieved, we can bring those concepts back into our everyday lives in order to open up dimensions of which we had not previously been aware.

The term 'literary sociability' can be understood in ways similar to these defamiliarisations of everyday life and experience, opening up the possibility of re-envisioning the interactions that take place in English classrooms around the reading of literary texts. The word 'sociability' names a disposition to 'seek and enjoy the company of others', to be 'willing to converse in a pleasant manner' (see *The Shorter Oxford English Dictionary*). In this sense, the word has a positive resonance, in much the same way that Raymond Williams characterises the word 'community': as 'a warmly persuasive word to describe an alternative set of relationships' (Williams, [1976] 1983, p.76). To couple the word 'sociability' with 'literary' might therefore be taken to name an ideal form of communication that people enjoy when they gather together, for example, in book clubs or on occasions that centre on sharing and enjoying literary texts. In the context of an inquiry into literature teaching in secondary schools, it might thus be understood to refer to ideal moments when the exchanges that pupils and their teachers experience in reading and talking about the texts chosen for study are particularly pleasurable. The term might be interpreted as signifying those moments when a text or texts have proven to be especially generative in stimulating classroom discussion and everyone finds themselves rubbing along together in a congenial manner.

Our teacher-interviewee 'Olivia' gives an account of her attempts to encourage her Year 7 students to do wide reading that might serve as an example of 'literary sociability' in this sense. The routine is one with which all English teachers would be familiar: she and her students read for ten minutes at the start of every lesson. This is not something that Olivia has chosen to do, but a school-wide policy promoted by the headteacher. Olivia, however, has become mindful that there are kids in her class who have the attitude: 'I don't read… I haven't read for ages, why should I read?' And vis-à-vis this resistance, she tries a new tack:

> And I've found I just got some butcher's paper and I just chucked it up and I wrote book recommendations and those kids who are really big readers started writing some books that they wanted to recommend for their peers, and then once they sort of got up, all of the kids started getting up, and I was sitting back like this is excellent, my board's getting filled up. And some of them wrote little blurbs on like you know what the book was about, and I found that after doing that… like all of my class was reading, and I haven't had that much success in my last two years. The first year it was just sort of like there's the books in the box. You know we got told we had to read them, we had to read them, how do I engage you with the text? So, like it was just sort of this is what my headteacher's making you do, but I didn't see how I could get the kids connected with the books, even though I was really trying to push reading, whereas this year getting the kids to recommend stuff I've only had one

kid who you know I've really struggled to find a book for, and I think that's just because… I don't know, he's not really big on reading and I tried… I'm still trying.

Such moments of sociability have become significant because of the way they've multiplied over the duration of the project, prompting us to consider them not simply as a result of teaching strategies that these early career teachers apply in classroom settings that are otherwise run along traditional lines. They also open up alternative ways of understanding the relationships that constitute those settings and how literary texts are involved in them. Whether it has taken the form of enabling students to talk with one another when they can draw on their own experiences to make meaning from texts, or (as in Olivia's anecdote) seizing opportunities for them to share their reading – they all seem to reflect a similar logic, prompting us to ask: what does this say about these teachers' understanding of the role that the literary imagination and literary language play in our lives? Why should there be such a strong emphasis on promoting reading as a scene of social interaction and the sharing of experiences of reading literary texts? And why, vis-à-vis the machinery of standardised testing, are such opportunities for the students to share and learn from their experiences of literary knowing not particularly valued? Why does the compulsory ticking of a box in a standardised literacy test count for a more valid representation of a student's ability to make meaning from language than the insights that students share when responding to texts in class?

The everyday world of the early career teachers who have participated in our project has been shaped decisively by standardised literacy testing. Although they promote reading as a sociable activity (presumably as a result of their socialisation into reading at home and school), they are also supremely mindful of their responsibility to ensure that their students perform successfully on standardised tests. And in this respect, they are hardly unusual (see e.g. Allard & Doecke, 2014; Auld et al., 2014).They experience a tension between 'literacy' and the understanding of the 'literary' that they have developed through their education and upbringing that has sometimes prompted them to tell fairly disturbing stories about their struggles with the machinery of standardised literacy testing and the assumptions about language and meaning which underpin such tests. This is not to say that any of them see themselves as fearless champions in the fight to prevent English being reduced to the construct of literacy embedded in standardised literacy tests – though some have indeed shown themselves to be pretty feisty when reacting to such testing. We need only think of Janet's exchange with her English Coordinator when the school leadership team decided that a period of English a week should be set aside for drilling and skilling that would improve the school's test results (see vignette).

***

Janet's resistance opens up dimensions of her professional practice as an English teacher that might enable us to develop our understanding of 'literary sociability' as it gets played out in classroom settings. Yes, a tension between 'literacy' and the 'literary' (broadly defined) has characterised the stories that many of the early career teachers have told us about their professional practice. Yet it is obvious that these same teachers are still driven by a relatively sophisticated understanding of language and literature, and specifically of the potential of literary language to enhance their students' understanding of language through their exchanges with one another, whatever pressures might exist to improve their standardised test results.

Janet related to us a strategy she used to facilitate discussion in her Year 9 class, which she called 'the Texta of Death'. She developed this strategy in a bid to facilitate class discussion of Niccolò Ammaniti's *I'm Not Scared*. This is how she explains her strategy:

> …it's set in Italy, and there's a lot of complicated town names. One of the classes was doing a spelling test on the town names included in the book, and I've decided not to do the spelling test… we do a thing that I call 'Texta of Death' where the students write a response to one of my questions, and if they feel like it they can take a whiteboard marker and write their response on the board. If someone's struggling with it, they're free to copy that student's work, and then we sit down and talk as a class… about what makes that a good response and what was that person thinking. The student has a chance to talk about it.

As with Olivia's attempt to promote wide reading, Janet's strategy is instantly recognisable to any English teacher who has sought to prompt discussion around texts within classroom settings, but within the context of our project, such strategies have become especially significant for the way they reflect alternative forms of meaning-making, in contrast with the practices that tend to characterise a competitive academic curriculum, where the dominant form of communication is typically one that privileges a preferred reading of a literary text that students are expected to reproduce by writing an essay under examination conditions. By the same token, this recognition of the value of classroom talk and other forms of social interaction strikes us as being more than an attempt by these early career teachers to achieve pre-conceived outcomes that stipulate (say) 'discussion' or 'performance' as legitimate ways of responding to stories or poems, along with other forms of engaging with literary texts. Rather than seeking to justify such activities by referring to official curriculum documents, which typically comprise lists of skills that the curriculum is meant to cover, these early career teachers are drawing on all that they have learnt about the complexities of meaning-making as accomplished readers and university graduates. This includes a recognition of the unpredictable complexities of literary language and the possibility of entertaining discrepant readings as students attempt to make meaning from a text through conversations with one another.

Yet we do not want to set up false binaries. Practising English teachers would be entitled to say that they are hardly in a position to choose between 'literacy' and the 'literary'. The fact is they are obliged to teach both. Many of our interviewees made precisely this point when they told stories about the pressures they experienced to improve their students' literacy scores. They proved very adept at adjusting the narrow requirements of literacy teaching to their broader under-standing of English in their teaching. This kind of pragmatism is reflected in the name that Janet has given to her activity: if you are one of her students and the 'Texta of Death' falls into your hands, you feel more or less obliged to put your comment on the whiteboard, just as you have no choice when it comes to attending school each day. The name conveys a playfulness that reflects the con-tradictory nature of the situation she shares with her students, showing her com-mitment to facilitating sociable meaning-making in a school setting that is often not very sociable at all. This is not to refer specifically to her school, but schooling as an institution within our society. 'Oh, school, Miss, everything's rules in schools', as one student remarked to 'Debra', another early career teacher we interviewed when she told us a story about her attempts to initiate a discussion about the rules that govern life on the island in *Lord of the Flies*.

***

'Literary sociability' names more than those moments when the exchanges that occur within classrooms seem especially convivial. As well as referring to the plea-sures that students might derive from the conversations they have around literary works, it sensitises us to the ways a text's meaning is negotiated within formal educational settings and how that meaning-making is mediated by the social dynamics of the classroom. This is without initially pushing us to judge the quality of the relationships that constitute those settings or the teaching and learning that might be happening there. A classroom organised traditionally, with the teacher out the front asking questions about a set text and pupils putting up their hands to answer, is just as much a scene of 'literary sociability' as a classroom organised to facilitate small group discussion around a poem or a short story that the pupils themselves may have chosen to read.

Douglas Barnes's observations of the talk that occurs within classrooms perhaps provide a useful reference point here. In *From Communication to Curriculum*, Barnes famously evokes an image of classrooms that are characterised by complex exchanges among pupils, as places where the curriculum 'enacted' by them far exceeds what a teacher may have planned for pupils to learn (Barnes, [1975] 1992, p.14). This difference is not necessarily a sign of a teacher's failure to realise what he or she had intended but highlights the potential of classroom negotiations to open up dimensions of language and meaning that might not have been anticipated by a teacher's planning. Yet what is often forgotten when people celebrate Barnes's vision of the classroom as a language community is that his starting point is not some ideal moment when everything in a classroom is humming and buzzing. He starts by saying that 'schools are places where people talk to one another', making his readers aware of the everyday protocols and conventions that typically obtain when it comes to determining who can speak and what might be said (Barnes, [1975] 1992, pp.11–12). He begins with observations about the hierarchical rela-tionships and talk that characterise most classrooms. He renders the exchanges that comprise everyday classroom life 'strange' in much the same way that an accomplished sociologist or ethnographer might do. And on this basis, he begins to tease out other dimensions of communication that might more productively be the focus of classroom life. Barnes begins with the everyday, showing how multi-faceted it is, and then returns to it with an enriched sense of its possibilities.

So with the concept of 'literary sociability'. The term implies the primacy of social relationships for understanding the dynamic of institutional settings like English classrooms and the linguistic exchanges that take place within them. This is to say that the communication between people within those settings should be understood as arising out of the relationships that constitute those settings. This is most obviously the case with respect to the roles that people play as they interact with one another – the 'self' that 'I' perform as I relate to others within the social space of the school. Such recognition is also bound up with how those relationships shape the reading of texts and how they stretch beyond the immediacy of a school setting, prompting us to conceptualise the school as a context within larger social and cultural contexts. We might think of the community in which a school is located, which in turn might lead us to think about where that community is situated within a larger social structure. It makes a difference whether you are teaching in a small state school in regional Victoria or an elite private school in Sydney.

None of these observations is startlingly new – the sociology of education has produced countless studies on the role that schools play in shaping the lives of young people through their institutional practices and the ways those practices intersect (or fail to intersect) with the values and beliefs of particular school com-munities. We begin to see the familiar in new ways – to make the familiar 'strange' – when we try to cultivate a sensitivity towards how the relational nature of schooling mediates the exchanges that occur within English classrooms, how the meaning-making that occurs around literary texts within classrooms settings is shaped by the social relationships that comprise them. And this is not in the first instance to see those relationships as either constraining or enabling or totalising in any way when it comes to exploring the complexities of any literary text. Social relationships are a precondition for any meaning-making to occur, just as language is unthinkable outside society or community.

Literary sociability as it is enacted within classroom settings may or may not involve enjoyment in the company of others (to hark back to the dictionary definition of 'sociability'). Indeed, sociability can paradoxically take unsociable forms (cf. Schiller, 2016, p.xxiiii, p.170). At its heart, however, is a recognition of the contingent, unsystematic, impure, 'untutored' or 'uncritical', sometimes collaborative, and often unpredictable meanings that occur when students in classroom settings share their responses to the texts chosen for study. Their responses to the language of the text might often seem discrepant or aberrant. Whether or not they are prompted to develop such responses into more formal 'interpretations' of the text will partly depend on the approach taken by their teacher and the requirements specified by a particular curricular framework. Should the class's responses primarily be directed towards the language of the text or should they reflect (for example) awareness of its genre or its narrative structure or other formal aspects? Is the point of studying a text to identify themes within it that might then provide the focus of an essay? How much should the students know about the historical context at the time of the text's production? How much of a role should the English teacher play in meaning-making? For our purposes, literary sociability names the way that any work around texts within classrooms has a relational and dialogic character. And this can include people arguing or even behaving anti-socially to one another – such actions still presuppose a world that is constituted by social relationships. And obviously, the literary sociability of the classroom connects with that other way of experiencing literary texts through solitary reading of an intensely personal kind. That experience, which remains valuable and formative, is carried into the classroom as a site where multiple private experiences of reading are mediated and potentially transformed by the social relations of the classroom. Yet we might also argue that the intensely personal engagement associated with solitary reading only becomes possible when readers are socialised into such habits.

A heightened awareness of the social relationships that comprise school settings can give rise to a reconceptualisation of the meaning-making that occurs around literary texts within the English classroom and a better understanding of the work that English teachers might do as they mediate students' responses to a text that has been chosen for study (cf. Doecke, 2019). Such a recognition, however, can only emerge from the experience of ordinary classroom life. We are not positing some ideal condition for interpreting literary texts but drawing attention to precisely the opposite: the realities of linguistic and textual engagements. This re-envisioning of the meaning-making that occurs around texts chosen for study draws on what the early career teachers involved in our inquiry have had to say about their day-to-day teaching practice. We also use the concept to try to understand what they have told us about their education and upbringing and the professional learning they have experienced on joining the profession and making the transition from being students of literature to teachers of literature when the experiences they have related to us – you could call them the 'literary events' that abide within their memories – almost invariably reflect a sociable character (cf. Rosenblatt, 1978, pp.135, 153; cf. Eagleton, 2012).

The concept of literary sociability begins with the everyday and allows us to return to it, enriched by our efforts to understand the larger contexts that mediate what happens in English classrooms and how literary knowing takes place.

***

A key impulse behind the work of many of the early career teachers we interviewed is a desire to facilitate sociable conditions that enable their students to engage with literary works in their classrooms in ways that aren't pre-determined by conventional forms of responding to the texts chosen for study. Debra told a story about teaching *Henry IV* when she discovered what she could learn by walking around the class and listening to the kids' conversations as they talked about key themes within the play:

> …a kid comes back from suspension you're not really allowed to talk about it, and I had the kids talking about it, and I just sort of went through and was

listening to his group, and I think he might have been doing... he might have been in one of the groups doing masculinity, and he just started talking to the people around him about his suspension, and he goes my dad's just got a very different view of masculinity to me. He thinks it's following the rules and doing the right things and being a leader, but I don't think he remembers that you know you do stupid things when you're young, and that's why I do stupid things, and that's... you know that's what's happening here as well, and you know you need your crazy people to help you out and sort of push you on the right path. And he didn't realise that I was standing behind him at the time, but I was very, very impressed by the way that he sort of made that connection.

This student's relationships with his father and the peers with whom he is sharing his experience of being suspended provide a context for his insights into the relationship between King Henry and Hal as it is represented in the play. Debra initially appears to experience some hesitancy about the direction that this small group discussion is taking, but she does not intervene, with the result that she gains valuable insight into how students read texts based on the experiences they bring to class.

This is to push the word 'sociability' to mean far more than providing a convivial learning environment. The conversations we had with our early career teachers suggest that sociability is integral to engaging with literary works, that the very process of making meaning from literary texts is inherently a linguistic and sociable act. Indeed, it could be argued that the full potential of the literary imagination can only begin to be realised when the teaching of literature is reconceptualised around talk and the other forms of sociolinguistic interaction that typically occur when people engage with literary texts, such as at writers' festivals or other examples of what we might specifically call a 'literary sociability'.

With the term, 'literary sociability', we are drawing on a body of literary theory that prompts us to refocus on the nature of reading as both an event in time and space and a dimension of the autobiographies of readers. The stories told by Janet, Debra and Olivia accentuate how meaning emerges through students sharing their insights. Such activities might thus be characterised as a shared construction of meaning (Barnes, [1975], 1992; Mercer, 1995), without supposing that everyone finally agrees or that people do not feel entitled to hold dissonant views (indeed, Janet's 'Texta of Death' seems designed to encourage a diversity of responses to a literary text). Teachers typically find themselves fielding a range of responses in their efforts to encourage students to participate in constructing meaning around a literary text, a meaning that often remains contested and unresolvable. Indeed, students can sometimes feel impelled to defend discrepant or aberrant readings of the text without necessarily grounding their opinions in a close reading of the words on the page (Doecke & Yandell, 2020).

Crucial to our understanding of the concept of 'literary sociability' is the opening chapter by Peter Kirkpatrick and Robert Dixon to a collection of essays that looks at how the reading and writing of literary works are typically embedded in particular communities. Kirkpatrick and Dixon use the term 'literary sociability' to 'shift attention from individual writers and great books' – both often fetishised in literary knowing – 'to examine the various forms of community that facilitate and sustain writing and reading, and also the kinds of communal identities that are formed by the practices of writing and reading' (Kirkpatrick & Dixon, 2012, p.v). They then go on to instance 'networks of writers and readers that cluster around literary journals and little magazines… reading groups and book clubs, writers' festivals, and the various forms of sociability generated by institutions such as libraries, schools, universities and writers' associations' (Kirkpatrick & Dixon, 2012, pp.v–vi).

This reorientation of literary studies has the potential to inspire a fundamental redesign of the traditional secondary school English syllabus. It is not difficult to imagine a change in the content of the syllabus that might enable students to study (say) the modes of literary engagement as they are manifested in book clubs and other diverse social settings where people come together to talk about writing and reading, instead of focusing exclusively on set texts and a predictable range of authors. As Kirkpatrick and Dixon observe (quoting Russell & Tuite, [2002]): 'sociability is not just the context for the writer's work but "a kind of text in its own right"' (Kirkpatrick & Dixon, 2012, p.vi). Such a change would mean revisiting certain categories that currently determine the selection of texts for study and opening them up for scrutiny, including the category of the 'literary' itself when it is used to name a certain body of writing that has a privileged status vis-à-vis travel writing or sports journalism or popular fiction or comic books and so on. Yet the concept signifies far more than a change in the content of the syllabus, or even an opening up of the syllabus to include writing with which students might more readily connect than the texts that typically figure in school syllabuses. Nothing very significant is achieved by requiring students to explore the clusters of the activities that surround the production and consumption of literary texts if such a shift sidesteps the question of the social semiotic at the heart of such activities and the role that language and other semiotic activities that figure within these examples of cultural praxis play in the formation of identity and our relationships with others.

By the same token, it is literary sociability that allows us to recognise the kinds of meaning-making that can happen with the most predictable or traditional of English texts set for study, once the various norms of reading and reception are ignored or evaded and different kinds of meaning-making are acknowledged. As Michael Warner observes, the students who come to his first-year university literature classes read in all sorts of ways:

> They identify with characters. They fall in love with authors. They mime what they take to be authorized sentiment. They stock themselves with material for showing off, or for performing class membership. They shop around among taste-publics, venturing into social worlds of fanhood and geekdom. They warm with pride over the national heritage. They thrill at the exotic and take reassurance in the familiar. They condemn as boring what they

don't already recognize… They grope for the clichés that they are sure the text comes down to. Their attention wanders; they skim; they skip around. They mark pages with pink and yellow highlighters. They get caught up in suspense. They laugh; they cry. They get aroused (and stay quiet about it in class). They lose themselves in books…

(Warner, 2004, p.13)

Warner's job is to teach his students so-called 'critical reading' in contradistinction to 'these modes of their actual reading' that would largely be classified as 'uncritical reading' (Warner, 2004, p.13). Warner usefully relativises the fetish of 'critical reading' and the political project that underpins it. The paradox is that none of the practices associated with so-called 'critical reading' can be observed in 'any empirically describable practice of reading', but that the thrust of literary studies at a tertiary level seems to be towards replacing 'the raw and untrained practices of the merely literate with a cultivated and habitual disposition to read by another set of practices' (Warner, 2004, p.15). There does not even seem to be evidence of a productive engagement with reading as it is actually practised in multiple ways beyond the academy. The practice of 'critical' reading appears to be premised, rather, on forgetfulness of the pleasures of 'uncritical' reading. 'Identification, self-forgetfulness, reverie, sentimentality, enthusiasm, literalism, aversion, distraction' – all these dimensions of reading as it typically experienced by readers in their everyday lives are dismissed as 'unsystematic and disorganized' (Warner, 2004, p.15).

Warner is not alone in raising such questions concerning the dominant emphasis in the field of literary studies on a 'critical' engagement with texts (see Felski, 2015). Within the context of German education, Thomas Zabka also raises concerns about the apparent inability of both literary scholarship and secondary education to show 'interest in reading as ordinary people experience it'. In both universities and schools, the emotional pleasures of reading have 'been displaced by an emphasis on supposedly more scientific or analytical approaches to literature' (Zabka, 2016, p.230). Within Anglophone educational systems like Australia, this has been most evident in rhetoric relating to so-called 'critical literacy' that similarly constructs everyday reading practices as somehow unreflective and therefore dangerous because they expose young people to the risks of ideological manipulation. It is the job of teachers to enable their students to exercise a critical distance from the pleasures of the text. This requires teaching their students to develop analytical skills that accentuate the ideological work a text is doing while exercising a sceptical attitude towards the allure of the 'aesthetic' or the 'literary'. Students need to build a capacity to resist the emotional engagement that we name when we use words like 'empathy' or 'identification' with the characters in a novel or play.

***

The intellectual challenge in recognising the realities of literary sociability in the school English class consists in the questions it generates about English education and schooling, including how classrooms are organised and the nature of the structures that mediate what happens in schools. The concept prompts us to try to reconsider the nature of a literary education and the acquiring of literary knowledge as they are shaped by the institutional setting of the school. In this respect the range of activities that Kirkpatrick and Dixon list as instances of 'literary sociability', though richly diverse and inclusive, only takes us so far when it comes to thinking about the exchanges that occur within English classrooms. The very diversity of the situations that Kirkpatrick and Dixon list demands a sensitive analysis of how literary sociability is realised in each of these settings. With regard to schooling, such an analysis begins with a recognition that the hierarchical structures that mediate what happens in schools cannot be ignored, that the English educational practices that schools promote, involving ritualised activities such as competitive examinations and writing formal essays in response to questions about set texts, cannot easily be equated with situations where people with an interest in reading and writing literary texts come together voluntarily. As Debra's student remarks: 'everything's rules in schools'.

But with this observation, we want to forestall any recycling of old images of schools as institutions exclusively geared towards regulation and control, where the mechanisms directed towards producing a citizenry with the requisite skills and dispositions (such as those typically specified by neoliberal education blueprints) supposedly determine everything that happens. There is no doubt that schools have historically performed this role and continue to do so – they 'interpellate' individuals (to borrow from Althusser's influential essay on the ideological function of schooling within capitalist society) – requiring them to take up the roles and identities specified for them by the system as a whole (Althusser, [1971] 2008, p.44; cf. Yandell et al., 2020). Yet at the same time, it is also vital to acknowledge that schools are settings constituted by the social relationships between people who gather together within them. This is what the stories told to us by the early career teachers who have participated in our project have continually reminded us. While those relationships are mediated by organisational structures that can produce tensions, they nonetheless provide the context for social interactions and meaning-making that cannot fully be contained by policies and practices that attempt to prescribe what will occur. At the level of everyday classroom life, this means that the aims that a teacher might specify 'in advance of instruction' (to invoke Barnes again) will always give rise to meaning-making that exceeds what she or he may have planned. And while Barnes's recognition of the difference between the intended curriculum and the enacted one might be applied to classrooms across the subjects that comprise the school curriculum, it is played out in a peculiarly intense way within English classes, where the focus is typically on texts and everyone's interpretation of them, where the meaning-making in which everyone is engaged itself becomes a subject of reflection and the focus is peculiarly on *language*. The dynamic of classroom life intersects with the activities surrounding literary texts in ways that are specific to subject English and the English classroom as a site of literary knowing and interpretation.

The anecdote that Debra told about the contribution one of her students made to a small group discussion centred on *Henry IV* serves to illustrate how classrooms can provide a scene for this kind of intensity of engagement in language and meaning. Debra could certainly justify this activity in terms of mandated outcomes for English, but it is not as though she has orchestrated this activity to achieve those outcomes. The conversation she describes occurs without any intervention on her part beyond the decision to organise her class into groups and to assign each group a thematic aspect of the play – like 'masculinity' – to discuss. What comes out of those discussions is unpredictable. She is in the position of wandering around the room, monitoring the conversations that are taking place, though again without any inclination on her part to direct the students towards achieving understandings of the play that she has specified to herself beforehand. As she tells her story, it is as though she has been eavesdropping, picking up the drift of a conversation in which she has not been involved. She is receptive to what her students have to say, showing a capacity to be surprised by the quality of their insights.

The meaning-making that is occurring here, as Debra's student draws connections between Hal's conflict with his father and his struggle with his father's expectations and the school's rules, might be seen as a result of the way she has organised her classroom. But it also emerges crucially out of the dynamic of the conversation between this student and his peers, as he draws on his recent experience of suspension to respond to the nature of masculinity as it is dramatised by the play. Debra does not recount his peers' reaction to his story, but it seems reasonable to assume that they have shown an understanding attitude towards his revelations about his relationship with his father. They have granted him his 'storytelling rights' (Rosen, n.d., p.18), recognising that the experience he is recounting provides a perspective not only on the relationships represented by the play but on their own lives. That this experience involves a transgression of the accepted boundaries typically imposed by schooling underlines the way that this exchange is both shaped by the institutional setting in which it takes place and transcends that setting as a moment of insight into the play's representation of the relationship between a father and his son. But perhaps 'transcends' is not the right word. For it is clear that this very act of transgression is formative, that this student's sense of 'self' is being shaped by the experience of schooling itself and his reaction to the rules imposed on him. It is, in short, a product of this school setting. The conversation that Debra overhears is one in which this student and his interlocutors are reflexively engaging with the version of 'self' that school and their parents require them to perform, most notably the 'very different view of masculinity' that this student's father holds. This involves 'following the rules and doing the right things and being a leader', all adult precepts, to an extent backed up by the school, that involve a forgetfulness about how the world looks to you when you are young, and all precepts that should be open to scrutiny as these young people struggle to find out whom they might become.

Literary sociability prompts us to reconceptualise classrooms as interpretive sites, where the meaning of literary texts is understood as a product of the relationships in which a text is read and appropriated. That, at least, seems to us to be the key conceptual challenge posed when we begin to think about the exchanges that occur around texts within classrooms as sociable meaning-making.

References

Althusser, L. ([1971] 2008). *On Ideology*. London: New Left Books.

Allard, A., & Doecke, B. (2014). Professional knowledge and standards-based reforms: Learning from the experiences of early career teachers. *English Teaching: Practice and Critique*, 13(1), 39–54. Available: http://education.waikato.ac.nz/research/files/etpc/files/2014v13n1art3.pdf.

Auld, G., Doecke, B., & MacGilp, R. (2014). Engaging with tensions: Tensions are the norm. In B. Doecke, G. Auld, & M. Wells, (Eds.), *Becoming a Teacher of Language and Literacy*. Port Melbourne: Cambridge University Press: 19–36.

Barnes, D. ([1975] 1992). *From Communication to Curriculum*. 2nd ed. Portsmouth, NH: Boynton/Cook.

Bennett, T. (1979). *Formalism and Marxism*. London: Methuen.

Doecke, B. (2019). Rewriting the history of subject English through the lens of "literary sociability". *Changing English*, 26(4), 339–356. https://doi.org/10.1080/1358684X.2019.1649116.

Doecke, B., & Yandell, J. (2020). The English literature classroom as a site of ideological contestation. In A. Al-Issa & S-A. Mirhosseini (Eds.), *Worldwide English Language Education Today: Ideologies, Policies and Practices*. London and New York: Routledge: 35–52.

Eagleton, T. (2012). *The Event of Literature*. New Haven and London: Yale University Press.

Felski, R. (2015). *The Limits of Critique*. Chicago and London: University of Chicago Press.

Kirkpatrick, P., & Dixon, R. (Eds.) (2012). *Republic of Letters: Literary Communities in Australia*. Sydney: Sydney University Press.

Mercer, N. (1995). *The Guided Construction of Knowledge: Talk amongst Teachers and Learners*. Adelaide: Multilingual Matters.

Mills, C. W. ([1959] 2000). *The Sociological Imagination*. New York: Oxford University Press.

Rosen, H. (n.d.). *Stories and Meaning*. Sheffield: NATE.

Rosenblatt, L. (1978). *The Reader, the Text, the Poem: The Transactional Theory of the Literary Work*. Carbondale, IL: Southern Illinois University Press.

Russell, G., & Tuite, C. (Eds.) (2002). *Romantic Sociability: Social Networks and Literary Culture in Britain, 1770–1840*. Cambridge: Cambridge University Press.

Schiller, F. (2016). *On the Aesthetic Education of Man*. Trans. Keith Tribe with an Introduction and Notes by Alexander Schmidt. : London: Penguin Books.

Smith, D. E. (2005). *Institutional Ethnography: A Sociology for People*. Lanham, MD: AltaMira Press.

Warner, M. (2004). Uncritical reading. In J. Gallup (Ed.), *Polemic: Critical or Uncritical*. New York: Routledge : 13–38.

Williams, R. ([1976] 1983). *Keywords*. New York: Oxford University Press.

Yandell, J., Doecke, B., & Abdi, Z. (2020). Who me? Hailing individuals as subjects: Standardized literacy testing as an instrument of neoliberal ideology. In S-A. Mirhosseini & P. I. De Costa (Eds.), *The Sociopolitics of English Language Testing*. London: Bloomsbury Academic: 3–22.

Zabka, T. (2016). Literary studies: A preparation for tertiary education (and life beyond). *Changing English*, 23(3), 227–240. https://doi.org/10.1080/1358684x.2016.1203618.

VIGNETTES NO. 5 AND 6 – CRAIG AND AMARIS

Craig

Craig was more interested in teaching history or critical skills than being an English teacher, but in his first appointment at a school in a disadvantaged area in Western Sydney, he found himself teaching only English, and at all levels from Years 7 to 12. He found the low literacy of students, the high turnover of teachers and headteachers, and the lack of time and collegiality available for working up new curricula quite confronting. The next year he was at the same school but teaching a more restricted range of different subjects. By his third year, he had taken a year's leave without pay to build up a private online tutoring business he was developing, while earning some money from teaching subjects other than English at another school. In the three interviews we had with him he often turned to the same themes, and even the same examples, to illustrate the points he was making, though he also mentioned an increasingly diverse number of texts, films, television shows and podcasts as he reflected at length on the interview questions and his own teaching experiences.

Craig had two agendas as far as his teaching was concerned. On the one hand, he was very concerned about explicitly teaching 'fundamentals' and 'scaffolds' – his online business had developed in part from his interest in providing support of this kind to his students. He put up posters about essay structure, with thumbnail definitions of genres and other elements that students might need to know for examinations. But he was critical of teachers who tried to steer students to the right answer. He wanted students to think for themselves, but with support – support of the kind he provided by his decoding of the tacit assumptions embedded in what schools mean by 'explain' or 'argue' or 'context' or 'thesis'.

Craig's second big repeated theme was about what English (and schooling generally) was for. He wanted it to be 'relevant' and to develop critical and moral kinds of thinking. He believed critical skills could and should be taught and he did not see these things as exclusive to English. He repeatedly mentioned psychology, philosophy, anthropology and his experience of doing history as important. In our third interview with him, he was involved in project-based learning, an integrated studies subject, and was promoting that way of learning in his tutoring business:

> The model I'm doing with Year 7 to 10 is completely different, it's project-based learning. The kids come up with their own driving question or come up with their own problem they want to solve, and I just have some set activities that are largely often very formative, and so it gives them the opportunity to explore their interests at the same time as learning the skills they need.

Craig repeatedly criticised English teachers for valuing literature over other aspects of the subject, saying that they had a 'paternalistic' view that made students do Shakespeare rather than looking at contemporary media of various kinds. He thought that it was no wonder that student motivation was low. In his view, English teachers were rooted in a *Dead Poets Society* kind of world that had a 'missionary', 'paternal', 'colonial' orientation. He valued moral questions – he valued his Catholic schooling – but not in the form of paternalism. He objected to the 'really pervasive bias that English has in believing that it has some particular unique almost biblical knowledge that everyone has to have access to, and I personally think that's quite… it's quite a middle class, middle-upper class, often white, male…'

Craig often reflected on his influences. He was 'not from a reading family'. His belief in scaffolding and trying to decode the basics of arguments and the like were related to both his mother who taught in special education with autistic students and his experience of travelling and teaching in Thailand and Sweden. He also coached sport and often drew analogies between coaching and teaching English:

> In the push for progressive teaching, terms like 'fundamentals' and 'basics' are derogatory. They're seen as negatives and I think it's done a real detriment… I played sport for years, and same with people that I know that did music, a lot of what you do is rote because some of the things that are fundamentals you need that automaticity, that ability to do it without having to think… to me it should be balanced.

For English 'you need to give them the metalanguage so it's automatic'.

At university, Craig was particularly influenced by his exposure to gender studies, which opened his eyes to new critical thinking and the value of having tools and knowledge to make new critique possible, by providing 'lenses to look at… power and big moral and philosophical issues'.

Two other things emerged from our interviews with Craig. He seemed to be on a ceaseless intellectual quest – always seeking out new readings and viewings and listening to podcasts – operating almost as an autodidact in the way he wanted to explore ideas. And at the same time, he was a contrarian. He often told his English teacher colleagues that they should not regard themselves as special and that they valued literature too much, and that there were other more relevant purposes for schooling. And he extended this to blogging to his professional association, where, he noted, he only received about 20 'likes' in response to his posts in an association that has thousands of members.

Overall, Craig was frustrated by all the really big problems he saw in the world and in the way schooling was organised, and the huge gap between those things and what was actually achieved by schools. He was only in his mid-20s and by the time of our third interview with him was thinking that he might not continue being a teacher:

> I've sadly become probably quite obviously increasingly demoralised, cynical and depressed [laugh]. I can't help but see a curriculum that doesn't address the needs of students much at all… teachers associate literature with critical thinking and intelligence, yet in reality is a very narrow, largely highly Western, middle to upper-class view that looks down upon people who relate to more accessible texts.

Amaris

Amaris remembers her first experience of having her understandings challenged and transformed through English. It is a story she returns to in each of her interviews. She was in senior high school, in a regional coastal town, four hours from the capital city, when she was introduced to *No Sugar*. This award-winning play, written by Aboriginal writer Jack Davis in the 1980s, tells the story of an Aboriginal family's experience of racism and marginalisation in the 1920s and 30s. When Amaris, who is of white settler heritage, encountered this play, her eyes were opened to their history and the present. She both knew, and was related through her extended family to, Aboriginal people in her community – 'they were my friends – but this just wasn't something that I even really considered'. Studying *No Sugar* changed her 'perception on Indigenous Australians... it was a sort of turning point for me'.

After completing high school, Amaris was unsure about what to study, but she eventually decided to enrol in a degree in Journalism 'because it was about the world around me, and... I was good at writing, but not creative writing'. However, while she enjoyed the course, her internship made her aware of aspects of journalism that she found alienating: a competitive and unsupportive work culture and a marked propensity to expose and exploit the narratives of the marginalised and hurting. She had discovered feminism, but her intention to write for a women's publication proved unviable. So, after her degree, Amaris enrolled in a DipEd, feeling that she could make a social contribution by promoting critical thinking in the classroom.

When we meet Amaris in her first year of teaching, she is on a short-term contract at a well-resourced private secondary school. She is teaching in the school's general English program, taken by students pursuing vocational pathways rather than those who wish to compete for a place in a university course. Amaris is determined to ensure each of her students understands that they have a story to tell and she sees the strength of her teaching in the way she connects with individuals. She also prides herself on her ability to instil in her students a capacity to analyse the texts of popular culture that make up their world. For Amaris, English is about the development of the whole person, which means cultivating a capacity to be kind to and respect one another. Within this framework, she feels that it is possible to challenge aspects of their discourse when necessary:

> The other day... they were doing... group work on their own, and one kid said dabbing was gay. I said hold up, that's not the language that we use to describe an activity. We don't use the word 'gay' to negatively depict or describe something... there are potentially people in this classroom who identify as gay and you're using their sexuality to describe something that's negative.

Amaris nonetheless feels somewhat of an outsider to the discipline and subject of English. This is most apparent when we talk about teaching literature. She emphatically rejects the word 'literature', which she relates to canonical texts. When other teachers talk about texts such as *The Crucible* and *Macbeth*, this confirms her sense of herself as someone who 'does not teach literature'.

This does not mean that she rejects the value of knowing about texts and textuality or that she denies that books can play a transformative role in people's lives, such as when she read *No Sugar*. In her view, a knowledge of how to analyse and deconstruct a text enhances students' sense of what it means to be 'human... and interact with the world around you'. This is facilitated through discussing and sharing readings.

At the time of her second interview, Amaris has changed to another well-resourced, 'independent' public school, which is part of a growing body of government schools in the State run by school boards and given greater financial independence and responsibility. This school is academically ambitious. Amaris notes, however, that this does not reflect the aspirations of all students. On another short-term contract, Amaris's teaching allocation includes students in both the academic and vocational pathways. One class largely consists of students who have disengaged from school, including many who have been in the juvenile justice system. Amaris is conscious that these students sit outside the overtly conservative culture of the school and seeks to engage them in English and convince them of its relevance to life beyond school.

While her focus previously had been on broadening experience, with these students she prioritises connection and a sense of belonging. She wonders if she has been given this class because no other teacher wanted to take them, but she appears to relish the opportunity. She recounts a highly successful lesson where she had the most disengaged Year 10 students writing their own stories. Students generate narratives by explaining the moment of acquiring a scar on their body and then provide the back-story. Amaris starts the process by recalling her encounter as a three-year-old with a broomstick, which has left a scar on her head. It is the sharing of personal stories that Amaris recalls as 'the most memorable' for her as a teacher– she feels her students were 'doing… English … without even realising it'.

At the same time, in this new school, she has been required to teach a university-style elective literature course on modernity. Amaris's background means that she has had to do significant preparation for this unit, teaching herself key literary concepts and texts. 'I had to find knowledge', she remarks, 'having never really engaged in the history of literature'. It is perhaps as a result of this experience, and her varied classes and cohorts, that in her second year Amaris's notion of literature has expanded: 'there is contemporary literature and like traditional literature, maybe. Um, so I'm still, I'm happy now to call them both literature… but I'm not necessarily engaging with that tradition'.

So, Amaris reaches her third year of teaching. She secures a permanent position at her first school, and she speaks more like a member of the school community, seeing herself as contributing to decision making and the ethos of the school. Specifically, she sees herself contributing to the culture of the English department, recognising that each teacher brings different expertise to their job. She finds the more experienced teachers are both willing to support her and to learn from her knowledge of popular and media texts. She recommended a film to her experienced colleagues and a group of them discussed the merits of this text from their different perspectives. While this text is not one they have decided to teach, she nonetheless values the conversation between them and the insights that emerged that she can take into her teaching.

Although Amaris still refers to herself as 'a weird journalism undergrad', she feels affirmed by the respect she has gained from her colleagues. While, in previous years, Amaris had lamented her lack of literary studies experience, she is now happy to admit to her students that there are aspects of literary theory or language she is uncertain about and needs to check. She stresses that English teachers possess a variety of expertise, that she knows some things, but not others.

Although she had no intention of being an English teacher, Amaris talks in her final interview about the ways in which, since starting teaching and participating in this project, she has developed a professional identity with which she feels comfortable. As part of her English teacher identity, Amaris reflects that she has gained clarity on what is important literary knowledge for English teachers. She argues that teachers must have both knowledge of texts and knowledge of their students.

9

KNOWLEDGE PROXIES

Text selection and assessment

Lyn Yates

Coming to this project not as an English specialist but as a curriculum sociologist, I was interested in how literature teachers talked about their work and their field compared with what teachers in other subject areas say about those subjects and fields (Yates & Miller, 2016; Yates, 2018; Yates et al., 2017; Yates et al., 2019) and compared with general themes that have been a focus of the curriculum literature (discussed above in Chapters 2 and 4).

One familiar finding is the pervasiveness of these teachers' concerns about assessment regimes (that is, the programs of assessment originating outside their school or classroom). The assessment regimes are an inescapable point of reference that influences what teachers do. They know that the assessment priorities and scores of the final certificate literally count as literary knowledge for the students, and the 'literacy' emphasis of the earlier national testing regimes also impacts heavily on what space they have for literature study in their school contexts. But the teachers also are clear that something important about the knowledge or knowing in this subject will be lost or made meaningless if the whole focus of the classroom becomes the maximising of test scores. This tension was already evident in the large survey of over 600 teachers we did at the beginning of this project. Preparing students for assessment was a priority for the respondents but was ranked below and in tension with other priorities related to students' gaining insight and understanding of their life experiences and developing their enjoyment of literature (McLean Davies & Buzacott, 2021).

Another issue familiar from the broader curriculum literature is the problem of social diversity and social inequalities as a challenge for school education. Literary studies have long been identified as a subject where these challenges are most overt and least escapable, a subject which in some ways most directly engages with and depends on the cultural knowledge and dispositions students differentially bring to school (Bourdieu & Passeron, 1990; Teese, 2000). For the teachers in our project,

DOI: 10.4324/9781003106890-9

reflections about social inequalities and diversity pervade their thinking and their commentaries on their practice. Diversity and inequalities are central themes when they talk about knowledge in relation to this subject and the issue of the selection of the texts that students will be required to engage with.

Trying to identify what these teachers understand as 'knowledge' or 'literary knowing' as they describe their work can be difficult, at least for an outsider. The way teachers talked about these concerns in the longitudinal and qualitative part of the project conveyed a sense that both 'knowledge' and 'skills' seemed too neat and too narrow as labels of what the teachers were aiming for in their work with students and literary texts. At different points in the interview, teachers would seemingly bring up quite different takes on this, or even apparently contradict themselves – and they would recognise and comment on this later when they read their previous transcripts, without disowning the different and conflicting comments they had made. This points to something in their overall approach to their work, their sense of literary knowing and the distinctive purposes of literary studies to which we will return.

A lot of what teachers convey is implicit or to be read in the overall stories they tell us; in what they say and do over the three years we followed them. This chapter focuses on two concrete touchstones from which teachers speak about knowledge in this area – text selection, and assessment.

Text selection as knowledge substitute

Many of the teachers in our project rejected or wanted to avoid answering a direct question about what they understood by literary knowledge, but they cannot avoid the very concrete issue of text selection. Debates about which texts should be set are very familiar in the public domain, frequently pitting exposure to the classics against reflecting student lives today or addressing contemporary issues. In school English departments the topic of which texts will be used is often the source of more discussion and disagreement among teachers than anything else. When a new State or national curriculum framework is released, the issue of which texts are specified on (or omitted from) the list commonly draws the most fierce attention. Interestingly, the *Australian Curriculum* (designed for up to Year 10) chose to not name specific texts; and for Year 12 subjects State traditions vary both as to whether texts are specified, and which ones are chosen. But the choice not to have texts specified for the final examination itself has an impact on what kinds of questions or emphases can be used (thematic rather than 'close reading' for example). And even where teachers have some choice of texts, the 'knowledge' implications of the selection they make are a subject of their discussion in interviews with us, and in their networks of colleagues.

One way these debates are sometimes interpreted is that the text choices mark different allegiances in the culture wars: tradition versus modernity; standards versus relativism; high culture versus popular culture; appreciations versus deconstructions. These are live issues in the press and among curriculum authorities, and there are certainly some different opinions on these matters among English teachers. As Sawyer and McLean Davies (2021) have argued, these familiar debates about texts often serve as a substitute for a discussion of knowledge in literary studies. This substitution, unfortunately, implies that the value of what is done in literary studies is wholly a function of the text, or at least forecloses attention to what teachers and students do in conjunction with the text. The substitution diverts attention from the teaching of English or the students' experience of English to the background culture from which the subject has to draw. But although teachers may have strong views on text selections, they also understand this is only one part of the way they approach 'literary knowledge':

> At this school I would say that what determines the way literature is taught is… I think it is partly the interest of the teacher, I think it is partly what the syllabus dictates, and I think it is partly the expectation of what the students will enjoy.
>
> *(Brittney)*

In Australia, different States have had different traditions in relation to the degree of teacher autonomy in text selection, and this is also influenced by the resources and culture of different schools. However, our initial national survey showed that State differences did not appear to greatly influence how teachers rated their broad priorities in their literature teaching. And it also showed quite a lot of convergence on which texts teachers themselves had studied at school (*Macbeth, Othello, Hamlet,* and *Romeo and Juliet* repeatedly topped the mentions, while other 'classics' such as *To Kill a Mockingbird, Lord of the Flies, Animal Farm* and *Of Mice and Men* were also regularly referenced. Texts by Australian authors received fewer mentions (McLean Davies et al., 2021).

Although the debate over texts often seems to pit those with a 'canon' agenda against those with a 'contemporary relevance' agenda, the longer comments teachers in our longitudinal study made on texts and text selection were less binary and more nuanced than this. For example, Brittney talked about three-fold drivers of what is done in literature – the syllabus, the teacher, the students – and has several agendas about these that she keeps in play. She is interested in the qualities and possibilities of different kinds of texts and wants to expand students' repertoires of engagement with different texts and their vocabularies by which texts are analysed or argued about. But she is also interested in students' own contexts and meaning-making and the need to extend her own repertoire and judgements about different kinds of texts.

Brittney is teaching at a school with a strong vocational and trade orientation, where 'the conversation that I have *a lot* is: even though you go into a trade, you still need to be able to read and write' (first interview, 2017), offering students what might seem to be a skills-based or instrumental justification for this study. At the same time, over the three years, she spends a lot of time trying to see what students are interested in, including reading up about sci-fi literature which she previously had not been drawn to. Similarly, she does not personally like the young adult *Twilight* novels,

…but if that's the only book a child has read between the ages of 11 and 15, then that has a lot of value for them. I've certainly learnt to value all types of literature in terms of not necessarily the literary value, but what they're actually allowing the child to be exposed to.

She tries to find material that is 'relatable'; and she believes in aiming for some diversity in terms of the kinds of authors and themes that are introduced.

But Brittney is not solely driven by what she sees as the students' agendas and experiences. After she talked about the value of diversity of materials, genres and authors, Brittney adds that she also worries that bringing in some kinds of texts (visual, for example) may be at the expense of 'more traditional forms of literature'. She wants to include texts that are meaningful to students, that they see themselves in – but also sees the purposes of literature as a form of expanding their repertoire about 'the human condition'. She wants students to have some literary vocabulary they can use when justifying why they like or don't like texts. And she is critical of using a simplified *No Fear Shakespeare* resource rather than finding ways to have kids appreciate the language and the rhythm in the original. She tells us about her success in getting her class to enjoy the Shakespearean insults (after first using a graphic novel to allow them to get on top of the overall story). Brittney wants to see and understand what the students find value in, but she also wants them to see that liking or not liking a text is not the end of the story, and she insists that they make arguments and justify their responses both in class discussion and in writing:

…conveying the idea that just because we're presenting the text to you, doesn't mean that you have to agree that it's a good text. And I think that what a lot of kids don't realise is that the value that's placed on a text is not necessarily universal, and even in the literary community there's disagreement as to what makes a good text.

In the national survey, we found over 60% of respondents had included Australian literature, Shakespeare, poetry and 20th-century literature among their under-graduate studies, though in Australia these are generally elective-based degree structures. Many teachers themselves valued literary works associated with a canon or high culture and/or recognised a cultural value (cultural capital) of exposure to Shakespeare. Yet the same teachers would also talk about the value of students working with modern or Australian or diverse stories whose protagonists were more familiar to them. Some teachers in our project began with a clear sense of what kinds of texts should be taught but revised this as they encountered and thought further about the specific students they were teaching, or when they moved to a different school and encountered students from different backgrounds. In her second-year interview, Brittney says she believes knowledge of the canon is important but knows other English teachers disagree and comments that what she had learned from her experience teaching in this school was

I think it's taught me that there is a very subjective element to value, and I think there's perhaps a bit of arrogance involved in people standing up saying this is a quality text.

Nicole comments in her second year of teaching

Perhaps I've changed my mind about what I think. Like, a canon of literary knowledge – I think I've broadened my view of that. I think I was a bit too prescriptive with what I considered literary knowledge then, because I've realised that among English teachers we all have different types of literary knowledge... and I think it depends on our personal reading preferences and interests and the types of culture we consume. I know that within my circle of friends here who are colleagues, we are all interested in completely different things and we bring those interests and those strengths to the texts that we suggest and the way that we teach. And I don't know if I really believe that there's a hierarchy of knowledge like that. I think that in some ways the tea-chers who have more pop culture knowledge that I don't really have, they can bring that into their classrooms more successfully than I can. So, I think that's probably one thing that I would say I have changed my thinking about.

These teachers were not repudiating their own earlier pleasure in or valuing certain texts but expanding that. They were rethinking the dynamic of literary knowing in a specific institutional context with a specific group of students.

English is traditionally a subject where issues of national identity are expected to be part of its purpose, and this is particularly fraught in Australia, a country with a colonised past, a difficult history of lack of recognition and attention to Indigenous people, and where at least half the population were either not born in Australia or have parents not born in Australia. For the 'discipline' of literary studies, and for the curriculum of schools more broadly, the last half-century has seen fierce debate about representation. In this project too, many teachers were concerned about diversity in Australia today and the inadequacies of a list drawn from another time and place. Sometimes their initial response to a question about text selection began by giving a long list of types of authors, experiences or identities they would ideally like to include – gender, ethnicity, sexuality, Indigenous, refugee experiences and so on. This was often followed by a recognition that this type of categorical approach to 'inclusiveness' raises impossible problems of representation given the actual limited school day (akin to their concerns about gaps in their reading they apologised when we asked about literary 'knowledge'). But teachers did want some evident variety and diversity of texts/genres even as they were aware of the impossibility of including everything.

Clare said:

I want them to read everything. I want them to read everything... I want them to have... you know you can't have all those experiences yourself as one human being. So that's why you read isn't it, so you can get all these other experiences and live vicariously through all these characters and have all this amazing insight and empathy into other people around you. I feel like I'd like to do more texts than we do here.

She is interested in finding contemporary texts and some diversity but acknowledges 'you're right, there is never the right text for the right student at the right time – that's really a simplistic way of looking at it' (2017). And she supplies an anecdote of how her choice of a text with central Asian characters (the school has many students of Asian background) did prove quite off-putting to some other students:

> So, one of my white Australian students said to me, and I was quite appalled, but it is what it is, in front of the whole class she said to me when we [read] *Growing up Asian*, she was like 'Miss, that's bullshit. The EAL students have got such an advantage, I can't believe they get their own text. They're going to do so well on this SAC because they know all about this and it's got nothing to do with me…' Like just went on this huge diatribe, and I was like WOW!!! And for her, she felt really affronted that she couldn't connect with that book because [she saw it as] that was their story.

Clare comments that she (the teacher) had assumed that reading and empathy were very heavily linked, but here it did not work that way, even though she tried to get the student to see that this is what the other students had been feeling about other texts that the student herself identified with. In another school, Katya gave similar examples of boys who were unhappy with a choice of texts with a feminist theme; and that she had been concerned about texts with death, suicide and trauma themes when she knew that some students in that class had recently lost a parent.

Some teachers too were critical of a 'tick box' kind of approach to representation. Leo commented:

> …for example, in our school, we have a growing group of Pacific Island students. Therefore [some say] in order to engage them we must find a text by a Pacific author because then they will enjoy it, and it's us thinking about them [rather] than what they want, and they like… Just because you have a particular religion, culture or geographical background doesn't really tie you into a particular context because there are contexts within those contexts themselves.

Leo's response to the problem of making possibly arbitrary assumptions about what would be of interest to students was to set up a new process where students themselves, as well as staff, had a say in which texts were used. Rupert, however, was dismissive of the whole idea of 'trying to give them texts that reflect their lives' (year 3, 2019) and thought the emphasis should be on introducing students to quality texts and the sort of 'textual joy' that will help them to understand their experiences. However even Rupert acknowledged that just forging ahead with 'quality' texts is a 'struggle':

My experience is that the moment students have to start working hard they will turn off... You have to persuade them as a teacher that the struggle is worthwhile to get there.

Most of the teachers in our study saw it as important that students could recognise themselves more readily in at least some of the texts, usually alongside making some judgement about better and worse qualities of particular texts for those purposes. Even here their responses illustrate that the judgements they were making were somewhat context-specific. For example, many teachers remembered enjoying *To Kill a Mockingbird* in their school days, but they did not all think it had a similar resonance now:

No one's going to say *To Kill a Mockingbird* is not an amazing literary work but is it the best for our students?

(*Heather*)

I mean, *To Kill a Mockingbird* again? ... It's not to say that they don't bring value when they are great texts, it's just there's more out there.

(*Veronika*)

It's good to have Australian texts too ... *To Kill a Mockingbird* is still a really good text, but can it be connected to something we've got here?

(*Jen*)

Some of the teachers work with this text but pair it with another more contemporary text or compare different student ages where they think it works or does not work. Chloe remembered 'hating' it and being bored when she first read the book as a student herself, but later re-read it as an adult and now.

I just think it's so relevant, like it's always one that I make reference to in my classes, even if the kids haven't read it, I just think that it encompasses so many... just English techniques and conventions in it, it's just a really great book [but] Harper Lee is also racist at the same time, so I always love [being able to say that as well] [laugh] like Shakespeare.

And some have parents who come into a parent-teacher meeting and say, 'I studied that when I was at school, it's brilliant' (James); while others such as Amanda report a different reaction from a parent:

'I told them when they came home, I hated *To Kill a Mockingbird* in school, so why should you like it? [laughs]' [to which Amanda adds] And I'm like, thanks a lot [laughs] ... just undermine everything I'm trying to do here! But I think that general culture of reading's not something that's really highly valued by our families.

Clare is also aware of how texts may be chosen because they are the right length, or the resource is available, or they address a particular issue, and she is critical of the tokenism that can generate. She does not want to ignore representation, nor does she want to treat it as ticking the box or something that just resided in the text rather than also in what teachers and students did with the text. So, she was trying to address student resistances of the kind quoted earlier by having her students look at gaps and silences in the texts.

Many teachers not working in elite or selective school contexts were strongly aware of the inequalities of different starting points for different kinds of students. 'Inequalities' here are not the same as 'diversity', which was also an issue for them. Teachers' concerns about diversity are seen in some ongoing rethinking by them of the nature of 'literature' and 'literary quality'. In the comments above, they were not rejecting the qualities of some classic texts but rather recognising the breadth and changing scope of literature, and the selection from this corpus that was being made available to the students they taught. And it was related to thinking about one implicit aim of the national curriculum (as discussed in Chapter 4), its identity-making role, as well as literature's role in exploring the human condition.

But 'inequality' as a concern is more specifically related to disadvantage and impediments: teachers' awareness of what kinds of background experiences make it difficult to enter the subject expansively.

> Getting a student that struggles to read a novel, or saying they have to read a novel, is like asking someone that has never done gym to go do a hundred kilo bench-press.
>
> *(Craig)*

In the national survey, teachers from private schools were much less likely to rate sociocultural diversity or class size as a challenge; and those teaching in government schools and in regional schools were more likely to see behaviour management as a challenge. Those from comfortably bourgeois backgrounds and teaching in similar settings had little trouble having students engage with literature from another time and place. But two teachers who had themselves grown up in such environments and were now working in government schools (Clare in Victoria and Craig in NSW) each independently commented that they could now see that the so-called universal themes of the classics are more readily accessible if students have been brought up Catholic (and in Catholic schools) as they had, and been more explicitly immersed in certain types of big moral questions.

Many discover from their experience in actual schools and with actual students that abstract discussions that put the value in the texts rather than in the triumvirate of texts, teachers and students are inadequate. It is not just that some settings or groups of students are handicapped compared with others. Rather, teachers see the purpose of their subject as undermined if they are facing so much of an entry hurdle by the texts selected that they cannot even engage the students. The issue is not simply about which texts but the kinds of interactions and teaching that are able to occur with specific texts in specific contexts.

Clare, for example, confronted the difficulty of immigrant students who are just learning English and who have trouble with literal meanings of English words yet are being asked to move to the figurative. She turned to pop music as a way of teaching metaphor. Leo made his own videos to 'translate' different literary perspectives and put them on YouTube for his students. What these teachers are doing is not giving up on the project of literary studies but finding ways into it.

Finally, in the junior secondary years, there are quite practical constraints on text selection: which resources are already owned by the school and whether the school can afford to buy new ones. A consequence of this is that texts that are chosen at one point for their contemporary relevance can still be on the curriculum 20 or 30 years later for a quite different generation and cohort of students. And younger teachers are aware of the generational changes – both the extent to which their own literary exposure is different from the students they teach and their awareness that older teachers can resist changing the texts because of the workload implications when they already have their plans for existing lessons well-established.

Interestingly, Charles, one of the curriculum authorities people, interviewed for this project, put a more positive spin on the resource problem: he valued the way in which that starting point of limited and given resources forces English teachers to be creative:

> As a new teacher, your starting point is the books that are in the bookroom…
> So, I think as you develop as a teacher, the constraint even in a tiny little universe to have to use certain texts, and I go back to my own experience of not caring for a number of short stories and then going aside, where can I find extra stuff, what can I do?

Overall, there is an inevitable topic and text selection issue for school curriculum which is different from tertiary studies, even for the sciences (Yates & Millar, 2016) but especially in the humanities. School is compulsory, and what students are exposed to, or mandated to be exposed to, is a different kind of issue than in undergraduate study. And the issue of text selection is especially fraught for literature teachers, working with the constraints of time and resources and examinations, and who are aware that they cannot include everything they would like to, but who do also take seriously concerns about which texts they and their students can connect with and develop meaningfully from.

Assessment, gaming and over-direction

One of the most prominent discussions in the recent curriculum literature has been about the rise of certain kinds of testing and test-related accountability in schools, and the negative effect of this test-driven curriculum on teaching practices and the culture of schools (Lingard et al., 2016; Yates et al., 2017).

In Australia, the main program of such testing is NAPLAN, the National Assessment Program – Literacy and Numeracy. This is a national testing program administered in Years 3, 5, 7 and 9. It was originally intended to monitor national standards rather than individual or school performance but has subsequently been used as a published measure of school performance, and frequently has generated drives within schools to improve their performance on those measures. The testing has also been controversial, with some parents and teachers maintaining it is unfair and/or inappropriate in its focus; and some schools apparently taking steps to manipulate results by asking some students to stay home! In the literature, there have been many accusations that these tests reduce the quality of student experience because, especially in disadvantaged schools, too much time is devoted to teaching to the test, rather than broader curriculum purposes.

The second form of external assessment that is highly visible in Australia is the final (Year 12) school examination, the Higher School Certificate (HSC) or equivalent.[1] In Australia, the scores in different subjects are used to produce a single ranked score (ATAR[2]) that is used for university entrance. As entry to university and prestigious courses has become increasingly competitive, individual and school results on the HSC are published in the press. The content and assessment form of the HSC examination often permeates what is done in earlier years. Many teachers we interviewed, whether they taught a Year 12 course or not, were aware of and commented in detail on the focus and assessment of that final-year subject and what was needed to get a good score.

What is evident from both the survey and the interviews is the ubiquity of NAPLAN and HSC as points of reference for teachers when discussing knowledge and their purposes and practices. Often, they were very critical of these assessment forms. The majority of teachers argued that the 'literacy' assessed in NAPLAN was a kind of 'back-to-basics' focus that did not capture what they were trying to do in engaging their students with literature, and rather sought a kind of technical grammatical knowledge that in their view was not necessarily needed to be a good reader or writer (and that in some cases they did not themselves have).

There has been a widespread critique of NAPLAN by teachers in terms of the narrowness and social unfairness of what is tested. However, many parents support the testing, and so far the program has been maintained across governments of different political persuasions for more than a decade. The issue of external testing is much debated, and there is also an argument that *not* making these relativities visible has contributed to some poorer education for disadvantaged students (discussed further in Yates, 2013). A few teachers in the project were critical of the way other teachers were dismissive of NAPLAN. Craig for example saw such criticism as too much of a 'progressive group think'. And Katya, who was working at a school that was selective and with good overall results, criticised the teachers who had prided themselves on being above the tests. She thought the tests did reveal some gaps in what these students knew, even though the school's overall results were strong. Rupert too feels the criticisms of NAPLAN by English teachers are overdone:

I've actually got no problem with NAPLAN. I'm one of those people who, I wouldn't say I support it, but what it does is it measures what you should have been teaching anyway. So, the question is, if you're not teaching skills up to that point when are you going to do it? Because going through the NAPLAN I was just amazed by how straightforward it was. It didn't want anyone to be doing anything we shouldn't already be doing. The question is, are we doing it? Are we teaching skills?

However, teachers in disadvantaged schools often felt discouraged by this testing program. Whereas students from backgrounds with cultural capital did not have to spend time focusing on the test to get high results, these teachers felt their students would be discouraged by seeing in black and white where they were on the scale compared with their more advantaged fellow students.

In a few cases, the early career teachers in our study were given some school-level role of responsibility for improving NAPLAN results, and this tended to produce a more nuanced reaction to the testing. Clare was made Head of English and her two 'KPIs' were the school scores on NAPLAN and VCE English. Katya had been involved in some NAPLAN professional development and worked as an assessor for NAPLAN while she was on maternity leave. She argued that teachers were incorrect in their claims that the test only rewarded technical knowledge. She agreed that these tests were somewhat narrow, and regretted that they have such prominence, but she nevertheless saw them as having some value, or at least that they could be used to have some value.

Overall, while several teachers expressed criticisms or reservations about NAPLAN, by the third year of our study it was also evident that some schools had brought it more centrally into the curriculum of the school, either by mandating lessons on 'literacy' as such or by adding new strategies specifically directed to improving NAPLAN scores. Katya found that her previously highly teacher-autonomous school environment had become more data-driven. Amaris in her second interview reported that her school had two people 'specifically dedicated to literacy and NAPLAN'. These strategies reduced the time available for teachers to do more open-ended work on literature. (Incidentally in her third interview Amaris had changed to a different school where she said she hadn't heard anyone even talking about NAPLAN!)

Where NAPLAN impacted what was prioritised in school English in junior and middle school, the final HSC examination influenced what students learn to count as literary knowledge in the final years. In Year 12, teachers recognise the real impact of grades on students' opportunities beyond school, and consequently, they had learned to look closely at and share tips about what counted for examiners as good work. This extended beyond any explicit list of criteria set out in the schedule. For example, the specified curriculum might allow students (or their teachers) to choose from a number of alternative texts as their focus, but teachers' experience was that some texts (e.g. classics) were more likely to draw high scores than others. And they were conscious that the use of specific vocabulary and ways of stating a point would be evidence of higher knowledge.

We are so influenced by the VCE and the examiners' reports… And so, the things are very much designed to focus on what is going to get a tick in the exam. You've always got to push a kid from a seven to an eight or an eight to a nine or a nine to a ten, and that often leads to… a focus on parts of texts that are of questionable relevance… students are rewarded if they write about the construction of a text in their essay… and [there is] a quite formulaic way of doing that, and students, especially the boys at this school appreciate the formula…

(James)

James argues that this approach leads to an overly micro-focus that can ignore the overall text and 'misses the forest for the trees'. Or again, Craig comments:

…you know the way the system kind of judges success is HSC, and that's kind of how all of those things relate and filter down… they're often forced to write essays that only teachers will read, with no ability to disagree with statements or concepts provided, often limiting their interpretation or just reconfirming common and fairly logical interpretations of texts discussed by English teachers and English majors or critics at university.

Some drew comparisons between what they saw as the specific agenda of Year 12 assessment, and what they saw as the broader purpose of teaching literature in the junior and middle years on the one hand, and university study on the other.

I think my goal is to balance engagement and enjoyment and building a love of literature in our students, but I want that to be very evenly balanced with the skills and requirements that they need for VCE because as much as I would love it to just be building toward a love of literature, if we're making them love literature but they don't know how to write an essay in the way that the VCE examiners will expect them to, then I also think we're doing them a disservice.

(Amanda)

Teachers enjoyed the opportunity to teach HSC, but they were critical of two aspects of this high-stakes phase. One was that here above all, the social inequalities and demographic diversities that students brought to school were inescapable and sometimes disheartening. What was being examined in HSC in a sense brings in the world: the broader cultural understandings and language nuances that, as one teacher put it, can't simply be taught in one year. Here above all, they were caught by wanting students to do and appreciate the world that literature had to offer but disheartened by the impossibility of a level playing field. These are issues that have been written about at great length by sociologists since the 1970s. Indeed, the reality of teachers' perceptions of this stubborn set of inequalities is reflected not just in the continuing pattern of score distributions to students of different demographics, but also in the demographic distribution of schools that teach higher-level literature courses compared with those who do not. (This is discussed further in Chapters 10 and 11.) Increasingly in my State, the Year 12 literature subject is being abandoned in most schools, and only being offered to students from a limited number of private, selective and girls' single-sex schools.

Teachers were also aware of and sometimes critical of the kinds of test gaming and strategies being used to achieve good scores. Some refer to other teachers producing 'scripted answers' for their students to learn and reproduce. The State authority where this seemed particularly rife recently changed the form of the examination to try to avoid rote-learned answers, but it is a constant issue at the HSC level where teachers face pressure from their schools, students and parents to produce good results. All of the teachers accepted that some specific examination orientation was necessary when teaching at this level, but a number distinguished between strategies that gave students tools (for example, vocabulary, the structure of essays, and concepts that could be relevant) and strategies were effectively trying to tightly guide students to a 'right' answer – an answer that would score highly regardless of what the student themselves might think about the text in question.

Debra was critical of a colleague who aimed to maximise students' skill with essay writing by spending the year doing essay after essay and without the class discussion where students explore and develop their understandings and perceptions in dialogue with others. For her, this solo approach might maximise some technical facility, but it reduced the richness of engaging with texts that she saw as the heart of this form of knowledge.

In so far as the final school examination is a high-stakes competitive test for entry to university it sets up pressures and distortions that are widely recognised but impossible to avoid and difficult to navigate. Curriculum authorities and professors of literature (also discussed in Chapter 6) were unanimous in their concern about the use of 'over-direction' or 'backward-mapping' and 'scripted answers' as a way of maximising scores. Some criticised the use of prescribed themes where students' engagement with texts is narrowed to looking only for what is relevant to the theme. They all conveyed a sense that they wanted more openness to how students engage with the texts, alongside some technical vocabulary and genre understandings that are reasonable to expect for this level of schooling. But an external high-stakes competitive examination of this kind propels an examination-related focus, especially at the upper end, as Oliver, one of the professors of literature we interviewed acknowledged. He began by lamenting the fact that in Year 12 his son (at a 'good' private school) does not read whole books but rather is directed to extracts and other materials that will underpin 'good' answers on the examination. But Oliver ends up supporting that approach – seeing it as necessary if you want 'standards' or to maximise students' scores:

> I think this is partly because of the model of the examination is how you can answer the exam, and… so there's kind of a range of questions and a range of responses. Of course, the teachers, the pressure there is… and they've got really good teachers at his school you know… it's their duty if you like to

kind of teach them how to answer the exam questions… It's a difficult thing because I kind of don't mind at all the model of exams, and… but then when you are looking to assess and standardise in various ways that's… there's a different kind of understanding of how you approach that text.

(Oliver)

Oliver, incidentally, was critical of the university rankings and citation pressures that he sees as distorting literary studies in university education, but sees the distortion as unavoidable when it comes to the competitive final school certificate!

One teacher, Debra, came from a system in another State that had not had an external examination at the time she was at school. She sees the examination as being too dominated by the big idea and funnelling students towards this, and talks of her belief that teaching to the text and maximising scores is in tension with instilling a love of literature in students. Interestingly, she talks of her 'Extension' class (that is, the most advanced students) as having a fear of getting it wrong. As with the professor quoted above, there is a sense that it is those students who are most likely to go on to tertiary studies in literature who will mostly be driven to focus on the gaming or essay template aspects of study at the HSC level (perhaps that is part of their advanced status – that they are quick to pick up on the sub-text of an activity!). A number of the professors interviewed talk of having to spend the first undergraduate year reorienting students away from the idea that they need to focus on the right answer.

Teachers cannot ignore external testing because it has ramifications for the school and the students. But at the same time, the teachers all saw the purposes of literary study, and their hopes for why students would do that and what they would take into their life beyond school from it, as not able to be encompassed by the testing but something that must be developed in tension with it. And this is one of the things that feeds some apparent contradictions in how they talk about what they value in different parts of the interview.

In this chapter, I have considered two of the concrete, institutional issues that confront teachers, text selection and assessment regimes. The institutional setting of schooling, which includes these examination and testing programs, is not something that teachers can simply ignore: they provide the conditions, enabling and constraining, in which teachers and students engage with literature.

Notes

1 This currently is organised and named differently in different States: Higher School Certificate (HSC) in NSW, Victorian Certificate of Education (VCE) in Victoria, Western Australian Certificate of Education (WACE) in WA. Here we will simply use the abbreviation 'HSC' as a generic term.
2 Australian Tertiary Admission Rank.

References

Bourdieu, P., & Passerine, J. C. (1990). *Reproduction in Education, Society and Culture*. Trans. R. Nice. London: Sage.

Lingard, B., Thompson, G., & Sellar, S. (ed.) (2016). *National Testing in Schools: An Australian Assessment*. London: Routledge.

McLean Davies, L., & Buzacott, L. (2021). Rethinking literature, knowledge and justice: selecting "difficult" stories for study in school English. *Pedagogy, Culture & Society*, 1–15. https://doi.org/10.1080/14681366.2021.1977981

McLean Davies, L., Martin, S. K., & Buzacott, L. (2021). Critical considerations of the challenges of teaching national literatures in Australia in the 21st century. *The Australian Educational Researcher*, 1–17. https://doi.org/10.1007/s13384-021-00448-6.

Sawyer, W., & McLean Davies, L. (2021). What do we want students to know from being taught a poem? *Changing English*, 28(1), 103–117. https://doi.org/10.1080/1358684X.2020.1842174.

Teese, R. (2000). *Academic Success and Social Power: Examinations and Inequality*. Carlton: Melbourne University Press.

Yates, L. (2013). Revisiting cCurriculum, the nNumbers gGame and the iInequality pProblem., *Journal of Curriculum Studies*, 45(1), 39–51.

Yates, L. (2018). History as knowledge: Humanities challenges for a knowledge-based curriculum. In B. Barrett, U. Hoadley, & J. Morgan (Eds.), *Knowledge, Curriculum and Equity: Social Realist Perspectives*. London: Routledge: 45–60.

Yates, L., McLean Davies, L., Buzacott, L., Doecke, B., Mead, P., & Sawyer, W. (2019). School English, literature and the knowledge-base question. *The Curriculum Journal*, 30(1), 51–68. https://doi.org/10.1080/09585176.2018.1543603.

Yates, L., & Millar, V. (2016). 'Powerful knowledge' curriculum theories and the case of physics. *The Curriculum Journal*, 27(3), 298–312. https://doi.org/10.1080/09585176.2016.1174141.

Yates, L., Woelert, P., Millar, V., & O'Connor, K. (2017). *Knowledge at the Crossroads? Physics and History in the Changing World of Schools and Universities*. Springer: Singapore.

10

LITERATURE AND LITERACY: THE EVER-VARYING CONSTANTS

Wayne Sawyer

Introduction

In many ways, 'literature' and 'literacy' have historically been two pillars of the subject called 'English'. It is arguably because of these two concepts that English has gained its purchase as the central subject in the school curriculum in the English-speaking world. Yet already – only two sentences in – qualification is needed. In referring to 'literacy' in this way, I am referring to a range of specific *practices* to which, if only in retrospect, we have come to give the name 'literacy'. For, despite its current ubiquity, 'literacy' as a term has a relatively short history in English education. It was not used as a term in the seminal 1921 *Newbolt Report* on 'the teaching of English in England' for example. 'Literacy' was still a relatively new term in 1921, coming in the late 19th century as a back-formation from the term 'illiteracy', which had actually been in currency for over 200 years. It was the other term – 'literature' – that, according to Raymond Williams, until the late 19th century, was associated with what today we call 'literacy' (the normal adjective associated with 'literature' was 'literate') (Williams, 2009, pp.46–47).

Nevertheless, commentators looking at the period from the late 19th century to the 1970s do label certain practices and knowledges as 'literacy'. When Dixon famously called one prominent historical model of English 'skills', he defined this model specifically in terms of 'literacy' (Dixon, 1975, pp.1–2) and listed what traditionally characterised this 'model' as involving spelling, vocabulary, punctuation and comprehension, for example (Dixon, 1975, p.2). Ball et al., too, argue that the 'school-builders' of the 19th century founded their education on 'literacy' and that '[i]n time reading, writing, literacy, would become the subject English' (Ball et al., 1990, p.49). Even Newbolt referred to 'illiteracy' and the context for this was explicitly that of abilities in written 'composition' (Newbolt, 1921, p.88). Thus,

DOI: 10.4324/9781003106890-10

English has been historically underpinned by practices of reading and writing and accompanying knowledges and skills that have come to be understood as 'literacy'.

That other 'pillar' is what Dixon nominated alongside 'skills' as the second of the previously influential models of the subject – 'literature' in the form of the 'cultural heritage' – a label echoed in Mathieson's well-known reference to English teachers as 'preachers of culture' (Mathieson, 1975). Similarly, for Ball et al., standing alongside 'literacy' from the late 19th century were 'the values and morality of "literature"' (Ball et al., 1990, p.49). In fact, Ball et al's identification of educational 'moral technologies' in late 19th-century England cites literature and literacy as playing key complementary roles in teaching the working classes 'to behave'. Literacy was a form of 'social insurance against criminality' (Graff in Ball et al., 1990, p.50), and came to be linked to the values and morality of literature as reinforcing national solidarity (Ball et al., 1990, pp.48–50).

'Literature' and 'literacy', however, have not always reflected the alliance suggested by Ball et al. Green sees 'literature' and 'literacy', their relationship with each other and with 'language' as constituting a 'conceptual field' for the subject (Green, 2018, p.272), but within this conceptual field, Green sees '"literature" operat[ing] as a reflex counter-balance to "literacy"' (Green, 2002, p.26). This begins to open up the tensions between the two. If Dixon, in the context of reporting on the Dartmouth conference, saw the 'skills' and 'cultural heritage' models as more or less historically complementary (Dixon, 1975, p.2), American Herbert Muller, in his report on the conference, argued that for teachers, literature is at 'the very heart of their subject' though 'the ordinary citizen regards it as only a kind of elegant pastime, not really essential to an education... [compared to] the practical importance of writing and speaking well' (Muller, 1967, pp. 4–5; see also Kitzhaber, 1966, pp.2–3). In reference to earlier versions of England's National Literacy Strategy, English teachers interviewed by Andrew Goodwyn saw a huge divide between a focus on 'literacy' and their belief in the value of a literary education:

> The NLS (and literacy as defined by the NLS) is actually very dull stuff, which does little to nurture children's imaginations. It neglects the aesthetic experience of English.
>
> It is lamentable that the term 'English' and 'Literature' are progressively (like a spreading fungus) being usurped by the term 'Literacy'.
>
> *(Goodwyn, 2003, p.125)*

As represented in the title of the essay from which these statements came, these teachers saw themselves as teaching 'English', not 'literacy'. Goodwyn makes clear that in these teachers' eyes at that time, the threat posed to 'English' was the lack of acknowledgement of the 'value of literature', and 'the potential loss of opportunities for students to be "creative" and "imaginative"' (Goodwyn, 2003, pp.130–131). This was not an over-simplistic dichotomy on the part of Goodwyn's teachers. As he says, they distinguished between literacy as 'social good' and 'educational entitlement' and what they regarded as the reductive practices of 'capital "L" Literacy' as enshrined in public policy and in practices such as the Literacy Hour. Similarly, in relation to their privileging of literature, the profession was not arguing for a very narrow notion of cultural heritage, and, in fact, had already opposed this manifestation of literature in the second National Curriculum of 1995 – their distinction between 'literature and 'L'iterature echoing that of the distinction between 'literacy and 'L'iteracy (Goodwyn, 2003, pp.130–131). Their responses here, then, were not those of die-hards who saw the canon as the only justification for English but were a specific reaction to the definitions of literacy issuing out of public policy and the practices that followed from such policy.

The relationship between these two dimensions of the field, then, is partly constitutive of the field, reflecting some of the range of concerns at the centre of the work of English educators. But, as we've seen with Goodwyn's teachers, neither dimension is a culturally or politically neutral concept, with an always stable set of characteristics. This relationship between 'literature' and 'literacy' among the teachers discussed in our current project is the topic of this chapter, but first a brief diversion into current understandings of the term 'literacy'.

What is literacy?

For some time, understandings of literacy within the profession itself have embraced dimensions of practice that go well beyond the exercises imposed by areas of public policy, in particular by standardised testing regimes that treat literacy as decontextualised, usually low-level, skills. A brief selection of the richer conceptualisations of literacy from the last 30 years or so could include – very broadly defined:

- *a sociocultural view of literacy as social practice contesting a psychological-individualist model* (Gee, 1990; Street, 1997): the way form, function and the meanings in literacy events differ across cultures, communities, social groups and 'literacy domains'
- *the concept of 'multiliteracies' contesting a monocultural, generic print-based model and highlighting both the growing significance of cultural and linguistic diversity and the influence of new communications technologies* (Cope & Kalantzis, 2000; New London Group, 1996): the understanding of language and literacy codes, multimodal reading and writing practices drawing on a range of semiotic resources, multimedia authoring skills and critical analysis
- *the critical literacy paradigm* (Peim, 1993; McCormick, 1994; Morgan, 1997): broadly, contesting the ideological neutrality of reading practices and examining how texts themselves position readers to help create identities and belief systems
- *the notion of curriculum literacies*, in which English has not just a generalised role in the development of literacy but has its own repertoire of literacy practices, which distinctively define 'English' – such as in the realm of the imagination,

of metaphor and narrative (Green, 2002) – and that these practices parallel specific 'disciplinary literacies' (Moje, 2015) in other subject areas.

Some of these approaches to literacy sit behind calls for a model of English itself that is based on *rhetoric* (Andrews, 2014; Green, 2018, p.174ff), such calls seeing the subject as focusing on the arts of communication, and accounting for context, mode, media and technologies, audience etc. Furthermore, aspects of these different areas of literacy are occasionally brought together in particular *models of curriculum* – such as the 'four resources' model of reading (text decoder; text participant; text user; text analyst: Freebody & Luke, 1990) or the '3-D' model of literacy (operational; cultural; critical: Green & Beavis, 2014).

Public policy around literacy in Australia

The reference above to Goodwyn's interviewees from the early 2000s highlights the contextual issues raised for one group of teachers as a result of public policy. For the teachers we are concerned with within this book, among the important public policy contexts are Australia's own national curriculum and its own machinery of standardised testing.

Australia's first, and, at the start of our project, still relatively new, national curriculum – the *Australian Curriculum: English* (AC: E) – is not Australia's first centralised curriculum, since individual Australian States had a variety of forms of curriculum implementation prior to the AC: E, with a variety of approaches to prescription. It is simply the first centralised curriculum to be mandated nationwide – though, in fact, the States continue to implement the national curriculum in their own different ways, from adopting it wholesale to adding its individual elements to their own local syllabuses/ frameworks. The *Australian Curriculum* in general is an attempt to reinstate disciplinary knowledge as the foundation of the school curriculum, in contrast to what Yates and Collins (2010) characterised as an 'absence of knowledge' in curriculum development over the prior two decades in Australia. The specific curriculum in English was conceptualised in its initial papers as a question of knowledge, of developing 'an active working knowledge of a common language and literature' (NCB, 2008, p.6). English had a 'core knowledge base' defined as 'knowledge about the English language, knowledge about literature, and knowledge about how to use English actively and effectively across a broad range of settings' (NCB, 2008, p.7). *Language, Literature* and *Literacy* eventually became the overall organising 'Strands' of the AC: E. In terms of knowledge, McLean Davies and Sawyer (2018) have argued that the individual elements of the phrase 'knowledge, understanding and skills' (ubiquitous in the AC: E) connect very specifically to the individual Strands *Language, Literature* and *Literacy* in that order, so that 'knowledge' attaches very specifically to *Language*. Certainly, 'understanding' is a form of knowledge (Gibson, 2009) and quite specific areas to 'know'/'know about' are referred to in the *Literature* Strand of the AC: E. Nevertheless, knowledge about language is conceived of as the fundamental disciplinary knowledge in the total subject *English* in the AC: E and this knowledge is continually seen to underpin *Literacy*.

The other key area of public policy relevant to literacy in Australia is standardised testing via the *National Assessment Plan: Literacy and Numeracy* (NAPLAN) for all students in Years 3, 5, 7 and 9 in *Reading, Writing* and *Language Conventions* (spelling, punctuation, grammar). Writing is assessed through a very particular approach that focuses on text structure and devices purportedly appropriate to the nominated 'genre', vocabulary, cohesion, paragraphing, sentence structure, punctuation and spelling, all of which presuppose correct answers. NAPLAN results are on public record in the *My School* website of the Australian Curriculum, Assessment and Reporting Authority (ACARA – see ACARA, 2020), allowing the media to publish league tables of schools. Further, though ACARA advertises that 'the content assessed in (NAPLAN) tests is aligned to the Australian Curriculum: English' (ACARA, 2016), NAPLAN testing was introduced in Australia before the AC: E. NAPLAN therefore effectively pre-empted the AC: E, constructing a particular version of literacy before the curriculum itself was put in place, thus seriously compromising any statement that the AC: E itself had to make about the nature of literacy and the forms of assessment best suited for judging the capacity of students to handle language (Doecke et al., 2018). Both NAPLAN and the AC: E are currently overseen by ACARA. Readers in other jurisdictions would be familiar with the ways in which the mandating of standardised testing effectively, in turn, mandates a particular version of literacy, whatever particular curricula in English/language arts may lay down. This marked the context into which our early career teachers were stepping.

Teachers' accounts of the role of literacy in schools and how they see this in relation to literature

We invited our early career teachers directly in their Year 3 interview to reflect on the following extract from one teacher's interview from earlier in the project (it was one of a number of extracts that we gave to the teachers to prompt reflection):

> …they're always talking about how important literacy is across the curriculum, and that you need literacy skills in all subjects, and I agree with that, but this is literature and that's something different. I suppose maybe literature is at the heart of English, but literacy is just the basics of spelling and grammar and the boring stuff that the English Department wants you to improve your NAPLAN scores on, whereas literature is the core… it allows you to be critical and it allows you to have your own thoughts and it allows you to be creative, it allows you to practise the words for spelling, it allows you to read… literature provides the context to teach everything else… if you have a good book you can cover every single dot point on the curriculum with it…

The following discussion largely grows out of teachers' responses to this prompt (a small amount of the discussion issues from other questions). The teachers in the project saw literature as central to their project of teaching English. For Morgan, 'imagination is our sixth sense and literature allows us to imagine'. Veronika talks of 'learning about the world through a book'. Laura says, 'literature is the meaning' and she is not referring to the meaning of individual texts, but to the very meaning of the subject itself. Nevertheless, despite this strong favouring of the literary, teachers' responses to this extract enacted something well beyond a simple binary opposition between literature and literacy. One set of responses echoed the prompt itself in seeing literature as a context for developing literacy, even at the level of the development of skills such as spelling and punctuation:

> ...it's definitely more interesting to study literacy in the context of a text rather than sort of on its own... they can be inspired by great writers and think 'Well I want to write like that, how do I do that?'
>
> *(Rebecca)*

> I tend to think of literacy as looking at maybe the mechanics of language... and I would teach those skills within the context of a novel that you're studying... I don't necessarily think they need to be pulled in different directions.
>
> *(Brittney)*

> I would never teach the skills in isolation... grammar... I tend to teach... within the texts that we're doing.
>
> *(Katya)*

Laura's picking up of this theme in the following extract is particularly interesting in the way that she sees standardised testing working against its own aims:

> ...one of the things that was really frustrating last year about literacy [was] taking it out of the context that might actually help kids be more literate... we were... doing a lot of literacy... programs but pulled apart from say... reading a book or reading texts... a lot of the kids just don't see those skills as being important because they're taking it out of the context where it actually is important. They're not taking it seriously.
>
> *(Laura)*

Laura, as we have seen, clearly believes in the centrality of literature to English, but even she does not view literacy as a kind of necessary, but second-rate, aspect of her work. On the contrary, she argues that students 'have to actually get the basics... first before they can then engage with anything in English'. Here, though, she is making the crucial point that standardised testing is failing on its own terms because the practices that can be forced on a number of schools such as hers mean that literacy development becomes about skills and knowledges removed from the contextualisation that is fundamental to a meaningful understanding of texts. The result is her students not taking literacy seriously and broader aspects of English, such as to 'read and think a bit more critically', are neglected. Laura thus gestures towards the reality that literacy itself is also being increasingly narrowly defined by policy, especially by standardised testing and the kinds of practices often forced on teachers by their schools' (understandable) focus on their results in such testing. This was a very strong theme among a number of teachers and did give rise to concern over how such aspects of literacy were both driving curricula in their schools, and how this was often at the expense of other – broader – areas of their subject, especially literature:

> …the English department wants you to improve your NAPLAN scores… and it's always that disparity of… conceptual-based programming but then…these very measurable scores as well, and… one can be a foundation for the other, but do we have time? … We need to achieve both goals and… a love of reading and a love of language… And while we're in a marks-focused world I… think we [are]… possibly ebbing too far one way… you know, rote learning, teach-the-test.
>
> *(Debra)*

Timothy broadened this point in his State's context to the 'lack of alignment… between the expectations of NAPLAN and how the syllabus is constructed for high school' – and argued that meeting the demands of both is actually 'not… achievable'. Teachers are then torn between following 'their syllabus' and 'social expectations' around achievement in standardised testing. Rebecca also highlighted the tensions with which teachers worked when trying to balance government policy priorities around 'grammar… punctuation and literacy' with the demands of her local State syllabus which, she thought, focused centrally on 'understanding texts'. Ideally, again, literacy would be 'completely integrated and… all of your literacy lessons would be embedded in… the study of a novel or… poetry'. In all her classes, she saw a fundamental need simply to give students the opportunity to engage in more extended writing, seeing this very lack as a large contributor to students' problems with writing, partly reflecting Donald Graves' famous complaint that the 'problem with writing is not poor spelling, punctuation, grammar and handwriting. The problem with writing is no writing' (Graves, 1978, p.636).

Janet, too, spoke of 'hav[ing] a problem' not with the curriculum, but with the way standardised testing influences how the curriculum is 'enacted in the school', requiring teachers in her institution, for example, to work with particular text-books reflecting the form of that standardised testing. In addition, she argued that however the profession might recognise and aim at developing a broad range of literacy practices, the very form of standardised testing turns attention away from a more contemporary view of the texts with which students need to engage and in which they need to develop skills, in turn shifting the profession away from deeper considerations about the purposes of literacy which might then drive dif-ferent approaches to the curriculum. She objected to 'teachers who are taking points off students' work because of spelling mistakes, when actually… if you look beyond the spelling errors it's a masterpiece there'. This in turn relates to a larger complicating issue of students who may enthusiastically engage in areas such as classroom discussion surrounding a text chosen for study, but who struggle when it comes to areas of written work – from simple spelling errors to expressing ideas in written form:

> …we've got some students here who can read a book and formulate opinions and ideas… but they can't actually write them down… So, they sit in with an aide and talk through… and I've kept recordings of lots of them and they're quite astounding the thoughts they have… And then NAPLAN doesn't allow for that. They would say that student is actually illiterate.
>
> *(Janet)*

Katya's experience was similar:

> I actually think even students that struggle with the mechanics can be great readers in a lot of ways and be very literate in lots of ways… I've come across a lot of students over my career that might not be very skilled writers but they're great readers of texts and they show that in other ways… they might not yet have the skills to write an essay… even… students we would identify as 'low literacy' can be creative, critical.

Katya, it is worth noting, very much recognises the importance of a focus on functional literacy in the classroom. The 'mechanics' and the 'creative, critical' are not areas she sees as mutually exclusive in any way, just as they rarely are with the other teachers. Janet's and Katya's views here simply highlight that the judgements made by standardised testing rarely tell a whole story about students or even about the curriculum. They show that the playing out of the relationship between literature and literacy in classrooms is rarely simple. In her first interview, Katya spoke about a particular student – one mentioned elsewhere in this book – for whom popular culture had a strong place in the development of literacy (see Beavis, 2015):

> …a young woman I teach… presents as very sort of cool, very confident talking to adults and teachers, great ideas, funny, and then… she scored so low on reading… but she just fooled me totally because she presented as brilliant. She can write quite well, but she just can't read… very well… but she is a passionate reader of Manga cartoons… and to me, there's something really powerful in that. She has real shame about her reading ability. She's been put in a literacy intervention program… She made friends with all the kids who are into Manga… it's really embodied her love of reading, yet we would call her a failed reader… [H]ow can we… harness that energy and passion she has for reading in a classroom?

Providing a particularly interesting perspective on this overall issue was Clare. Despite being an early career teacher, during the project, she became Head of English at her school, which might be seen as necessarily positioning her in particular ways towards standardised testing. Though she believed that what English teaches, and values, is 'not necessarily... easily defined and measured in... standardised tests... a frustration... most English teachers will experience', she also argued that 'if we're doing the things we should be doing, then we should be seeing traction and growth... with those numbers'. She sees standardised testing as a simple contextual reality – part of the complex makeup of the world English teachers negotiate daily ('we work within the constraints that we work within, don't we?'). Though necessarily focused on improving her 'numbers' ('that one number is very important to the people who employ me'), her strategy is not simply to target the tested skills in any kind of 'cramming' way, but rather, with respect to reading, to implement independent reading in classes alongside 'some explicit... reading strategies', while wanting to expose students to a 'wide variety of texts'. She also wants this work in reading to feed into students' experience of writing – again, not just relentlessly practising those aspects of writing that appear in standardised tests.

It would be simplistic to view Clare as simply acting out her executive role in the school. As we have seen, the reality is that our teachers had a widespread concern with their students' literacy whatever their position. Freya, for example, felt that 'without the spelling and grammar being clear and concise in what you're trying to say, then the meaning of what you're saying doesn't have any weight'. Rebecca embodied a range of these complexities. Of her Year 9/10 class, she said this:

> ...with Year 9/10 it's always lower level, but getting to talk to them about... issues of gender and how... people should behave in... relationships because we're watching... and reading *Taming of the Shrew*... it is... a lot of talk because my classes... often are... much better at talking about issues or texts or anything other than writing responses, but I still think it's important... my focus maybe last year was more on... analysis of text and now I'm thinking 'Okay I've got to... focus a bit more on writing as well... how to articulate... your thoughts on the texts in writing', and particularly... the lower-level ability, [this] is something they struggle with...

Again, here we see a teacher's concern that students in literature classes who struggle with the written expression of ideas are not excluded from what is seen as the essential work of literature around the discussion of 'issues or texts' and around the thinking through of meaning(s). For Rebecca, literature carries the key intellectual work of the subject. While addressing her students' literacy problems ('people take your views more seriously when you can express them using correct grammar'), she is concerned that they are not excluded from that intellectual work. She argued that 'in order to be able to express these complex thoughts that come from analysing literature, you need to be able to express yourself in a... more sophisticated way'. Importantly, then, for her, literacy was not just about improving NAPLAN scores, but helping 'kids [to] express themselves the way they want to... [it's] important, ... we study literature... but if you can't express it on paper you know we're doing them a disservice'. Literacy is 'a vehicle', and, of herself, she felt that as she was becoming more experienced, 'literacy (was) becoming more of a priority':

> ...the problem is in school it's always about the output, so we've got to write about it... So, trying to give them a vehicle to actually express those ideas that they get from a text is becoming more important. So not just sort of having that knowledge but being able to translate that knowledge... it's becoming, 'Okay how do I get them to write well?'

Yet Rebecca continues to express the complexities, the contradictions, the balancing act that our teachers generally represented as she argued at the same time that literature remained 'the heart of English' and that 'understanding texts and the things you can take away from them [is] so important from a personal level that... we can't just do away with that and just teach... grammar.... that's not going to help them either'. She continued to see in literature opportunities for 'texts [to] transport you to different times, to different places in the world, and I think just being able to see the world from a different person's perspective, that's the most valuable... and... that is unique to English'. Rebecca by her third interview felt that focusing on literature while focusing on literacy remained a professional tension. She expressed the history of her teaching in these terms:

> ...when I first started I was... 'Okay... got to be able to break these things down really well... for the kids and it can all make sense'... and... so I guess... analysis was my main focus... So, then it [became] 'Okay, writing' and I was freaking out because the kids here do struggle to write. But now... I want them to be able to write so that they can express all that lovely analysis we've done in class... because they'll say it to me aloud but then I ask them to write it down a lot of the time and they're..., 'Well what do you mean – and how?'... so, I see them as more related now than I may have previously.

There was some support for standardised testing on the part of some teachers. Rupert had 'no problem with NAPLAN... it measures what you should have been teaching anyway... if you're not teaching skills up to that point when are you going to do it?'. He felt that '[s]ome of the things they're asking for I don't think we do'. Note that the extract from earlier interviews which was the prompt for this discussion named literacy as 'the basics of spelling and grammar and the boring stuff'. Katya saw this as 'quite a narrow view of what literacy is'. As a former marker of NAPLAN, she felt that 'it does reward students who have critical literacy and have more complex ideas than just the "boring stuff" of spelling and grammar' and that 'it does really reward students who are wonderful writers, and it's more of a complex sort of literacy that it values'. Katya rejected the binary opposition of literature and literacy that this particular discussion prompt set up and Craig argued even further that '[t]he "boring stuff" is actually the stuff that allows you to function in society...

People need literacy more than they need literature in my view, and the view of literacy as just grammar is, I would say, a very traditional narrow view of literacy that isn't at all helpful in this day and age'.

Timothy's position at a selective high school rendered even more complex the tensions discussed in this chapter, and he demonstrated how many of the issues raised here play out in teachers' practice. On the one hand, many of his students are obviously 'proficient in terms of their literacy skills', even 'top performers in the year', but of course, the literacy being discussed here is literacy in the English language, and at home some of Timothy's students 'hardly ever speak… in English', or, in some cases, 'couldn't speak English' at all until relatively recently. Here is yet another level of complexity: literacy defined in Anglophone terms, and EALD students constructed as deficient by the testing regime, and the potentially rich complexities of language interfaces rendered inadmissible. Further, Timothy did not feel that concern for literacy should only be a focus in the junior years, but that literacy issues could persist into Year 12, even at his selective high school. It was a place, he felt, where literacy issues for EALD students struggling in writing academic English might easily be initially overlooked because students could appear so capable in a discussion. Alternatively, others may simply 'get really lost' initially among the academic content of senior English. This is a problem that can be compounded by 'the expectation around marks and the content that's covered' in his school. In specifically addressing a question about students who might lack confidence in working with literary texts, Timothy provided a good example of how the issue of literacy is never a simple one. Here he is not speaking exclusively about his current teaching context in a selective high school, but it is worth keeping that context in mind as he discusses the complexity of an issue that we can too easily associate only with weaker students:

> I think it's not just whether we're concerned about being able to write in an eloquent or thoughtful fashion, it's about understanding the material that's contained within the novel, and you know if you find it hard to read, you're struggling with that component. And so, I think the kids that have an ease in breaking down a text and then talking about it and writing about it, they generally have the better literacy levels… This kid that's not performing well in English, who isn't speaking in class discussion, who doesn't seem to be able to get to very deep insights when breaking down a text, their literacy has always been an issue. So, I think that's the first one that you've got to address. And then sometimes you find the kids who are articulate don't write all that well. So that's another level of literacy – but that's not the kids who… really, really struggle to read, that's the kids who can read, who can articulate their thoughts but then writing a sentence that is cohesive and communicates a message or some meaning, they find real problems there. And that's surprising for a teacher. I think you go a little while without marking their work and you're thinking 'Oh this kid's going to be a good performer, and they get it', and then you read their work and you think 'Holy cow there is so much work

to be done here'. So, I think literacy definitely has to be considered the first impactful element in this... the NAPLAN and high school syllabus are at odds... but still we need to take care of it and make sure that through 7, 8 and 9 they're getting the additional support they need, which is hard with funding and hard with differentiation and... just the amount of time a teacher has...

...[In studying literature] you construct what that world would be like in your head. So that's kind of like a higher-order mode of synthesis that the kids who are really strong in this subject can do... it's like an imaginative and analytical capacity fused together. But I feel like literacy determines that. I think literacy in a way in your earlier years determines how imaginative you can be with language.

The complexities Timothy raises here are many: the relationship between under-standing and expressing that understanding; the students whose weaker facility with writing can be hidden behind good oral communication; the question of support and funding for students struggling with literacy; the sheer logistical difficulty for a teacher of addressing all their individual students' needs; the imaginative and ana-lytical capacities needed to engage with literature, and the relationship between these capacities and (early) literacy. Timothy's extract indicates the ways in which these teachers highlighted some complexities around the place of literacy in schools and how that literacy rarely has a simple relationship in practice with how students might engage with the texts themselves.

Overall, too, these teachers argued the need for a broader sense of literacy than is contained in the quote that prompted their reflections – a sense that includes the conceptualisations of literacy that have gained currency in the last 30 years or so. These views of literacy saw some teachers link literacy and literature in ways that went beyond seeing literature as a context for developing functional literacy, but as the central site in which these broader literacies are developed – in literature, for example, as the central site in which more sophisticated notions of reading can be developed:

I know they talk about 21st-century literacy and digital literacy and all those things, but if we're thinking about literature and the place of... literature in a curriculum, I would say the literacy there is political, economic, philosophical as well... spelling, punctuation and grammar is part of literacy, but looking at the examiners' reports you're seeing 'high's' and 'very high's' with sometimes basic spelling and grammar errors, so I think literacy is much more than just functional things... literacy is about the way in which people can think and interpret and express themselves... literature has a role in allowing critical lit-eracy... it's the discussion that comes out of looking at texts, looking at lit-erature, that allows for those types of literacies to come out.

(Leo)

Here Leo is referring to the VCE, not the standardised literacy testing of NAPLAN. He begins to highlight some of those areas which our teachers saw as giving literature its importance in the curriculum. These are, in his eyes, socially and culturally oriented ('political, economic, philosophical'), related to aspects of cognition ('the way in which people can think and interpret and express themselves') and even to the formation of citizens ('critical literacy'). Importantly, they are themselves forms of literacy in Leo's view and define the subject in important ways.

Conclusion: Where is English currently sitting with this... 'intersection'? 'binary'? 'relationship'?

I have argued that recognition within the profession (as represented by our early career teachers) of the importance of the literacy needs of students goes beyond any simple adherence to a literature/literacy dichotomy. These teachers were telling us that recognising the importance of one does not mean jettisoning the other. It is not as if, for example, Muller's 'practical importance' of 'writing and speaking well' is regarded as a social justice imperative with literature simply Muller's 'elegant pastime'. Neither does teachers' regard for literature as Muller's 'the very heart of their subject' prioritise cultural imperatives over a fundamental literacy that is simply 'instrumental'. The tensions and complexities they carry into their thinking are necessarily even further complicated by the approach to literacy seeming to be enforced by standardised testing and by some schools' (again understandable) obsession with results (notwithstanding the views of teachers like Katya that NAPLAN in Australia reflects a larger version of literacy than it is often credited with). Such testing and its effects on schools via ranking is perhaps the most curriculum-intrusive aspect of the Global Education Reform Movement ('GERM': Sahlberg, 2011) bringing, as it so often does, pressure to narrow teaching and learning (Hursh, 2008), and thus distorting the work of the classroom. The (Australian) former Director for Education at the OECD has often argued about Australia's apparent decline in PISA, for example, in the following terms:

> Australia's rank dropped because the Australian mean performance declined… This decline, which was statistically significant, occurred primarily because of a decline in performances at the highest level… it [is] at least clear that [the decline] is due to schools focusing more on basic achievement levels and not so much on the development of sophisticated reading of complex text.
>
> (McGaw, 2009; see Fitzgerald, 2013, p.13)

This distortion can take a particular toll on classrooms in disadvantaged communities, who then focus on (to adapt Paul Willis [1977]) 'working-class education for working-class kids'. In studying the teaching of literacy in Australia, for example, Luke et al. (2011) found that teachers in low SES schools in Queensland spent more time on direct alphabetic instruction and drill of grapheme/phoneme generalisations than their middle or high SES counterparts. Far from students in poorer communities lacking attention to 'basic skills', they in fact receive more work on decoding at the expense of other critical aspects of reading and literacy (Luke, 2010; Luke et al., 2011). Teese has shown that in the State of Victoria, the number of students choosing the VCE more specialist subject Literature (a separate subject from English at that end-of-schooling level) declines with socioeconomic status (Teese, 2011, p.17). Similarly, in the State of New South Wales, there is, in effect if not in intent, a curriculum hierarchy in the HSC such that 'there is a collection of subjects that are predominantly studied by students of higher average SES, and that also have greater value to students' ATAR… Similarly, there is a collection of subjects studied by students of lower average SES that have less value to students' ATAR' (Roberts et al., 2019, p.10).

These are all Australian examples, but this is a phenomenon of (at least) the English-speaking world:

> …poor districts… offer stripped-down drill-and-practice approaches to reading… rather than teaching for higher-order applications… critical thinking and problem-solving; collaboration… effective oral and written communication; accessing and analysing information; curiosity and imagination. The kind of curriculum that supports these qualities has typically been rationed to the most advantaged students in the United States.
>
> *(Darling-Hammond, 2010, pp.52–54)*

It is not a long stretch to translate this last quote into specifically English terms, including those specifically English terms used by our early career teachers – and it looks remarkably like (lower-order) 'literacy' and 'literature' being rationed to different groups. It is precisely the kind of scenario that our teachers largely seek to avoid playing out in their own contexts. In their early careers, their own thinking about curriculum has moved beyond such a policy legacy.

References

Andrews, R. (2014). *A Theory of Contemporary Rhetoric*. New York and London: Routledge.

Australian Curriculum Assessment and Reporting Authority (ACARA). (2016). Language conventions. Available: www.nap.edu.au/naplan/language-conventions. Accessed 12 June 2020.

Australian Curriculum Assessment and Reporting Authority (ACARA). (2020). My school. Available: www.myschool.edu.au. Accessed 15 June 2020.

Ball, S., Kenny, A., & Gardiner, D. (1990). Literacy, politics and the teaching of English. In I. F. Goodson & P. Medway (Eds.), *Bringing English to Order*. London, New York and Philadelphia: The Falmer Press: 47–86.

Beavis, C. (2015). Young people, online gaming culture and education. In J. Wynn & H. Cahill (Eds.), *Handbook of Children and Youth Studies*. Singapore: Springer: 815–827.

Cope, B., & Kalantzis, M. (Eds.) (2000). *Multiliteracies: Literacy Learning and the Design of Social Futures*. South Yarra: Macmillan.

Darling-Hammond, L. (2010). *The Flat World and Education*. New York: Teachers College Press.

Dixon, J. (1975). *Growth through English: Set in the Perspective of the Seventies*. London: Oxford University Press.

Doecke, B., McLean Davies, L., & Sawyer, W. (2018). Blowing and blundering in space: English in the Australian Curriculum. In A. Reid & D. Price (Eds.), *The Australian Curriculum: Promises, Problems and Possibilities*. Deakin West: Australian Curriculum Studies Association: 33–42.

Fitzgerald, D. (2013). *Taking the Lead: A Future for Public Education*. Surry Hills: NSW Teachers Federation. Available: www.nswtf.org.au/files/13187_ttl_revised.pdf. Accessed 9 July 2020.

Freebody, P., & Luke, A. (1990). Literacies programs: Debates and demands in cultural context. *Prospect*, 5, 7–16.

Gee, J. P. (1990). *Social Linguistics and Literacies: Ideology in Discourses*. London: The Falmer Press.

Gibson, J. (2009). Literature and knowledge. In R. Eldridge (Ed.), *The Oxford Handbook of Philosophy and Literature*. Oxford: Oxford University Press: 467–485.

Goodwyn, A. (2003). We teach English not literacy: 'Growth' pedagogy under siege in England. In B. Doecke, D. Homer, & H. Nixon (Eds.), *English Teachers at Work: Narratives, Counter Narratives and Arguments*. Kent Town: AATE & Wakefield Press: 123–134.

Graves, D. (1978). We won't let them write. *Language Arts*, 55(5), 635–640.

Green, B. (2002). A literacy project of our own? *English in Australia*, 134, 25–32.

Green, B. (2018). *Engaging Curriculum: Bridging the Curriculum Theory and English Education Divide*. New York and London: Routledge.

Green, B., & Beavis, C. (Eds.) (2014). *Literacy in 3-D: An Integrated Perspective in Theory and Practice*. Camberwell: ACER Press.

Hursh, D. (2008). *High-Stakes Testing and the Decline of Teaching and Learning*. Lanham, MD: Rowman & Littlefield.

Kitzhaber, A. R. (1966). What is English? In A. R. Kitzhaber et al., *Working Party Paper No. 1; Response, Report to the Seminar, and Supporting Papers One through Six*, ERIC document number ED082201. Available: http://files.eric.ed.gov/fulltext/ED082201.pdf. Accessed 1 June 2020.

Luke, A. (2010). Will the Australian curriculum up the intellectual ante in primary classrooms? *Curriculum Perspectives*, 30(3), 59–64.

Luke, A., Dooley, K., & Woods, A. (2011). Comprehension and content: Planning literacy in low socioeconomic and culturally diverse schools, *Australian Educational Researcher*, 38 (2), 149–166.

Mathieson, M. (1975). *The Preachers of Culture: A Study of English and its Teachers*. London: Allen & Unwin.

McCormick, K. (1994). *The Culture of Reading and the Teaching of English*. Manchester and New York: Manchester University Press.

McGaw, B. (2009). The place of reading in the Australian national curriculum. Address to *Effective Reading for All: National and International Perspectives*, Learning Difficulties Australia seminar, September. Available: https://archive.ldaustralia.org/client/documents/Sir_Jim_Rose_visit/mcgaw___lda.pdf. Accessed 12 May 2022.

McLean Davies, L., & Sawyer, W. (2018). (K)now you see it, (k)now you don't: Literary knowledge in the Australian Curriculum: English, *Journal of Curriculum Studies*, 50(6), 836–849.

Moje, E. B. (2015). Doing and teaching disciplinary literacy with adolescent learners: A social and cultural enterprise. *Harvard Educational Review*, 85(2), 254–278.

Morgan, W. (1997). *Critical Literacy in the Classroom: The Art of the Possible*. London and New York: Routledge.

Muller, H. J. (1967). *The Uses of English: Guidelines for the Teaching of English from the Anglo-American Conference at Dartmouth College*. New York: Holt, Rinehart, Winston.

National Curriculum Board (NCB). (2008). *National English Curriculum: Initial Advice*. Available: https://docs.acara.edu.au/resources/English_Initial_Advice_Paper.pdf. Accessed 12 June 2020.

New London Group. (1996). A pedagogy of multiliteracies: Designing social futures. *Harvard Educational Review*, 66(1), 60–92.

Newbolt, H. (Chair), The Departmental Committee appointed by the President of the Board of Education to inquire into the position of English in the educational system of England (1921). *The Teaching of English in England*. London: His Majesty's Stationery Office.

Peim, N. (1993). *Critical Theory and the English Teacher: Transforming the Subject*. London and New York: Routledge.

Roberts, P., Dean, J., & Lommatsch, G. (2019). *Still Winning? Social Inequity in the NSW Senior Secondary Curriculum Hierarchy*. Canberra: Rural Education and Communities research group, University of Canberra.

Sahlberg, P. (2011). *Finnish Lessons What Can the World Learn from Educational Change in Finland?* New York: Teachers College Press.

Street, B. (1997). The implications of the "New Literacy Studies" for literacy education. *English in Education*, 31(3), 45–59.

Teese, R. (2011). The new curriculum for English in Australia and student achievement under the old curriculum: Understanding inequality and addressing it. In B. Doecke, G. Parr, & W. Sawyer (Eds.), *Creating an Australian Curriculum for English: National Agendas, Local Contexts*. Putney: Phoenix Education: 5–20.

Williams, R. (2009). *Marxism and Literature*. Oxford and New York: Oxford University Press.

Willis, P. E. (1977). *Learning to Labour: How Working-Class Kids Get Working Class Jobs*. Farnborough: Saxon House.

Yates, L., & Collins, C. (2010). The absence of knowledge in Australian curriculum reforms, *European Journal of Education*, 45(1), 89–102.

VIGNETTES NO. 7 AND 8 – REBECCA AND LEO

Rebecca

Rebecca's history is reminiscent of many histories that have become part of a collective narrative about the formation of dedicated English teachers. She grew up in a house where books were valued, she was read to as a child and, in turn, loved reading herself. When she reached high school, she enjoyed exploring 'texts and what they mean'. She had the same English teacher for four years who nourished her love of reading both in the classroom and beyond, providing her with books in addition to those set for study. Looking back, she felt that the end-of-schooling public examinations resulted in a narrowing of focus in comparison with the 'freedom' she experienced in her early years, but this didn't deter her from enrolling in a double degree in Arts and Education with majors in English and History after she completed her secondary education.

What Rebecca had loved about English before those exam years was discussion. From about age 16 she'd thought about becoming a teacher and when she started university her aim was initially to teach in primary schools. But she decided she missed the kinds of discussion she'd enjoyed at high school and so she switched to high school teaching. The role of talk in learning was a continual theme in her interviews with us and by the time of her second interview, she felt that in her senior classes she had more or less succeeded in establishing a classroom culture characterised by spoken interaction. She still felt, however, that she could do more to encourage junior students to interact with one another rather than depending on her to initiate discussion: 'they'll happily talk back and forth with myself, but to talk about it together… they don't do a lot of that until they get into Year 12'. Her dilemma was that 'sometimes there's so much for me to say', which limited the opportunities for students to talk with one another. She also sensed that younger students only felt that they were doing 'work' when it was directed by the teacher.

When she was a school student, Rebecca had been a higher achiever in a number of subjects including maths and science, but she opted for English teaching because she thought English was a place where 'you learnt something about the world, about humanity which was different to what you would learn in another subject… it was sort of like a school in life'. She was being 'reconfirmed' in this belief every year now that she was a teacher. It was in these terms that she affirmed the role that literature can play in her students' lives:

> Knowing about literature is like knowing about the world… when you're reading something it's like another viewpoint… and I guess growing a greater perspective, which I think's valuable. And then there's that moment… you find … a novel or something and it just really resonates with you because it's … very similar to your own viewpoint, and you find just recognising yourself in that text, and… you know you're not alone in the world and all of that silly stuff… but it's also interesting to see very different ideas about the world and society and … the whole idea you're transported to other places and times.

For Rebecca, this emphasis on the importance of being able to relate to a text at an experiential level was combined with a commitment to enhancing students' awareness of the complexity of representation and textuality, dimensions that she saw as central to subject English.

Rebecca was teaching in a comprehensive co-educational and multicultural public high school in an area of Sydney's south-western suburbs that was being converted from a public housing estate to an area of more mixed housing, though it would still be regarded as 'disadvantaged'. Students often come into the first year at her high school with relatively poor reading ability and an accompanying reluctance to read. For a large number of them, English is an additional language, which means that they 'really struggle' with the literacy demands placed on them. The crucial challenge, as Rebecca saw it, was to provide students with texts that 'are going to appeal to them in their life'. She felt that a 'fundamental move' on her part as a teacher was to think firstly about her students' relationship to a text. This meant providing them with texts that were 'meaty' and not simply giving them a 'basics' curriculum. She mentioned 'angsty kids' who are 'drawn to the existential problems' or students who are otherwise regarded as poor with literacy taking on 'issues of gender' through watching *The Taming of the Shrew*. She also mentioned students who in this 'multicultural school... really empathis[ed]' with the racial issues in *To Kill a Mockingbird*'. Her students admitted to crying over *The Paper Menagerie* and *Blue Winds Dancing* 'because... a lot of kids from sort of mixed racial backgrounds... feel like they don't really belong [and] they found... a story that captured that feeling or explored those emotions'.

Rebecca continually questioned her own teaching, specifically how her focus on discussion might productively be combined with her obligation to teach literacy:

> My classes... often are much better at talking about issues or texts or anything than writing responses, but I still think it's important... my focus maybe last year was more on like analysis of text and now I'm thinking 'Okay I've got to ... focus a bit more on writing as well... how to articulate... your thoughts on the texts in writing', and particularly... the lower-level ability [this] is something they struggle with.

But she remained committed to ensuring that the students in her literature classes who struggle with written expression should not be excluded from discussion of 'issues or texts'. She recognised the problems those students were experiencing and saw her role as addressing them –('people take your views more seriously when you can express them using correct grammar') – but this should not be at the cost of excluding them from the kind of curriculum offered to other students regarded as more capable.

By the time of our final interview with her, she saw herself as strategically handing over the conversation more completely to students, getting them 'to a point where they can have these thoughts and express them with others and... tweak them and explore them'. She still saw herself as being 'out front too much, ... you need to be out front quite a bit, but I think it sticks in their head better if they hear it from a friend than if they hear it from me, or certainly if they have a really cool idea and somebody else thinks it's cool'.

Leo

In his second-year interview, Leo says that when he read his previous year's transcript he felt he must have been having a cynical day. 'It's easy to blame other people, but I feel like I'm taking more ownership now. To do something with the kids I've got.' Like many new teachers in his state, he is on a one-year contract, but the school clearly values him. In his second year, he is asked to take over the important final-year English subjects, and in his third year he is given a formal position of responsibility for 'student voice' and 'student leadership'.

Leo grew up in a migrant working-class family and neighbourhood where many, including his parents, had limited English and literacy. He says his initial drive to be a teacher came from seeing people he knew being exploited by contracts they did not understand, though he also mentions valuing a book he read at home, with characters in a similar immigrant situation to his own. He went to the local university that is dominated by 'first in family' students and recalls his undergraduate English studies as having little focus on language or technical elements but instead using novels as a jumping-off point for students to discuss big, Marxist-oriented ideas.

Leo was, characteristically, being overly self-critical in calling his first interview cynical. Throughout the three years, he does maintain a critical view of the institution of schooling and social inequalities inside and outside schooling. But he also maintains and builds a strong sense of what can be done in English teaching, and of trying out (and largely succeeding in) new strategies of working towards goals that he values – practical skills agendas; opening up critical and big ideas; using English as a base for students to investigate 'who I am', and genuinely trying to find ways to promote and enact the issues for which he was given the position of responsibility – developing student voice and leadership.

His critical view of schooling is to recognise that it is a kind of prison, compulsory, and that a lot of students don't get much out of it. He mixes with people like that – his old school friends – and recognises that they have successful lives, that the promise of schooling with its emphasis on getting an 'A' and becoming a doctor, as though this is all that matters, is hollow. He sees the Year 12 external examination as rewarding a formulaic approach and objects to his working-class school (pre)replicating it every year from Year 10 – not least because this is clearly ineffective with the students, who are bored and forget what they have done. Instead, he wants to find ways of making the experience of school more satisfying for the students – and also believes that this will produce better outcomes: 'If students take ownership they actually do really well, and their marks improve.'

Leo says that many of his students are the most literate person in their family, but they come to their senior years not having read a whole book at any time. He works tactfully to persuade other colleagues to include some voice by the students in decisions about which books they study: 'The best writers are ones you feel a connection with'. He has found by experience the importance of not designing activities that last more than 20 minutes. He builds student engagement by setting up small groups to have opinions about the selected texts and to defend these ('in an academic way') against others he knows will differ. He sees having an opinion (as compared with regurgitation) as an important foundation for having an argument. He sees such argument as something that is particularly rewarded in the Year 12 examination and he also sees it as an important foundation for having an active rather than passive life, and as important to a democracy. But Leo is conscious too that he must create a safe space for this kind of discussion to work.

Leo is active in designing strategies both to improve students' writing skills and to find ways of engaging them in the big ideas and the pleasures of reading. On the former, he includes five-minute 'skill builders' in his lessons, and has developed his own videos on YouTube that 'translate' into a more accessible form the perspectives of various critical approaches to literature. But he is most pleased with an experience he developed for students in his second year, and successfully repeated the following year. He took these outer suburban students into a contemporary art gallery in the city to look at some powerful post-colonial art so that they could start talking about post-colonial ideas via their reactions to this, rather than first being told about post-colonial concepts in a textbook in relation to literature. And his students did indeed get engaged and extended the discussion as he had hoped to their literature texts.

Through the interviews, Leo maintains a strong self-critique about his own power and assumptions. He grapples with the problem of having a 'deficit' view of his students and about a too pervasive institutional sense that school success is all that matters. Even though he believes in the value of literature studies, he raises the issue of deciding what is good for students as a problem: 'It's like your wife goes to the trouble of making you a nice meal and forgets you are allergic to one of the ingredients in it'.

But Leo does want students to see that life is open to be made by them and is excited about literature as something that allows this exploration, something that 'problematises the discourse that we have in education and in everyday life'. He is pleased that his strategies in the classroom seem to be building a greater enjoyment and community among the students: 'They all seem to hang out together now as opposed to, they didn't before. Everyone seems to be going out with each other'. And he likes 'getting to know who these kids are through their reading and writing and watching them grow as intellectuals'.

11

KNOWING AND MAKING

Classroom curriculum and pedagogy

Wayne Sawyer

Introduction

In this chapter, I consider specific tensions around curriculum and pedagogy that are highlighted by our early career teachers as they talk about engaging with the teaching of English. In particular, how do they describe the kinds of engagement with students and texts and interpretations and meaning-making that they set up? I hope to show that the kinds of work and intentions that are described by the teachers embed complex views of meaning-making and purposes for literary studies that raise questions about both the relationship between literary studies and language in subject English, and the gaps between formal curriculum documents and the dynamics through which teachers understand their work. The chapter elaborates on some of the arguments raised in Chapter 1 on 'knowing' and 'making' in the contemporary era. In preparing this chapter, I began by seeking out key areas related to 'pedagogy' and 'engagement' in the interview responses of these teachers. This analysis highlighted a number of discordances, tensions and ambiguities in the interview data and I begin here by firstly asking, 'What do they name as key tensions?'

Tensions arising from teacher interviews

One of the key tensions that arose from the interviews with our early career teachers was that between 'literature' and 'literacy', which has been dealt with in the previous chapter in terms of the specific practices of our early career teachers, but which I briefly take up here as part of more general issues around curriculum and pedagogy. As we saw in the previous chapter, some teachers placed literature (or 'the literary') firmly at the centre of English curriculum and pedagogy. This is not to say that they constructed 'literature' and 'literacy' in binary opposition, in which literacy was deemed less important. Most teachers discussed the place of literacy,

DOI: 10.4324/9781003106890-11

and some specifically saw the teaching of literature as supporting the acquisition of literacy. One strong theme was the problematical nature of standardised testing and the possibility that such testing actually undermined students' literacy development rather than supporting it. Teachers also saw such testing as driving increasingly narrow notions of 'literacy', leading in turn to a narrowing of what constitutes 'English' itself. This narrowing occurs against the backdrop of a recognition by educators in the early decades of the 21st century that literacy is a far more complex notion than is captured in such testing. This complexity includes recognition of the multiliterate (multimodal and multimedia) practices in which teenagers engage in their everyday lives. One consequence of this is that students often have skills that are not recognised by the nature of such testing.

Among the skills of 'English' not recognised are many which teachers feel comprise the key intellectual work of the English classroom, such as those involved in the exploration of literature. While most teachers would not countenance the neglect of basic literacy for the exploration of ideas in literature, their fear was more often that the reverse of this might occur. As Katya argued, 'I don't think that all that we owe them is the nuts and bolts of language so that they can write CVs... that stuff is really important... being able to write, being able to read... it goes without saying. But I think that they all deserve... to bask in ideas and each other's ideas and have the language to do that'. Katya's use of the word 'language' here is interesting: for her, 'language' is something which students 'deserve' in order, ultimately, to engage with each other and with ideas. The phrase 'nuts and bolts' allows her to see this part of the 'brief' of English as still related to 'language' (note that she doesn't call it 'literacy'), while also recognising that what is offered by a microscopic focus on tools alone (as is often the case in standardised testing) can forego a concern with what is to be built with them. Katya echoes Andrew Wilkinson's famous distinction between students as 'communicating beings' rather than 'spelling-punctuation-grammar producing machines' (Wilkinson, 1987, p.3). Katya's statement also serves to remind us that the tripartite division between Language, Literature and Literacy of the *Australian Curriculum: English* (AC:E– ACARA, n.d.) does not really serve to represent the professional practice of English teachers. Where do these categories begin and end when it comes to curriculum and pedagogy as they're implemented in classrooms?

Laura, too, told us of her students arguing that 'we're actually not just here to learn how to write sentences; we're actually here to learn how this is in our lives and why this is relevant', while Veronika argued for the importance of her students being 'connected to the texts and to the subject and to each other or to life'. She went on to talk about the need for English to address such areas as 'You're a person. What do you already know? What do you already think? What do you feel? What do you do? What do you wonder about? And we never have those conversations, we don't make *time* for those conversations. I *made* time for those conversations in my literature lessons because I felt I needed to'. Sophie thought that even when students believed that they 'can't write, and so, therefore... can't be good at this subject', that English was also 'where you get to watch and learn and build empathy and hear people's stories [and] that bit should be engaging'. This connecting of the text to students and of students to a larger world via literature is obviously important to English teachers. Morgan spoke to us about a student whose attitude to English – indeed, to her education generally – was turned around by her engagement with Patrick Ness's *A Monster Calls* and Chloe felt it a matter of some regret that some students were unable to find in texts 'someone that [they] relate to or understand or… [that enables them to] feel like [they're] understood for a while'.

Related to the literacy/literature issue is that of assessment in the larger subject 'English'. Success in 'English' depends as much on areas of 'literacy', such as writing essays competently, as it does on 'literary knowledge'. For Rebecca, this tension impinged on the depth to which literature could actually be explored through discussion. She felt that 'you could really dig in deep with some of these texts we do, but it's a matter of different priorities and time and assessment and… just getting them to have all the pieces they need to form a really good argument'. Consequently, 'you don't explore as much as you could… in the end it comes down to their results… and… the final assessment… the priority's more to do with that than increasing the literary knowledge because that's not really measurable, is it?'. Clare thought that 'one of the great challenges in the subject of English is that there's a lot of nebulous stuff that's not necessarily so easily defined and measured in those standardised tests… a frustration I think most English teachers will experience' (see Mead et al., 2020). Clare's 'nebulous stuff' can probably be interpreted as referring to aspects of student understanding, which at any one moment for any one student can be partial, tentative and very often shifting in the interactions of the classroom – a reality that for the teacher needs to be multiplied by the number of students in the class. Oddly enough, such indefiniteness is often assessed through its expression in a specialised form of literacy – the 'lit.crit.' (referring to literary criticism) essay – which can often reward a defined range of readings of literary texts, as well as rewarding particular forms of expression. Students' partiality and tentativeness and the shifting nature of meaning and interpretation in classroom exchanges we would want to see as a necessary sensitivity towards literary language, but these can be deprivileged by assessment pressures to identify measurable knowledge.

Moreover, as Rebecca suggested, this is not just an issue of the kind of skills that need to be developed for assessment success, but the way in which forms of assessment can impinge on the curriculum. Timothy wondered whether his own experience as a student at school would have developed his current 'literary knowledge and… love of literature' if English had been as assessment-driven as the (national/State/school) culture in which he now taught. Laura argued that 'we're so bound in high school by NAPLAN, or by the HSC, or by assessment tasks, that we can't actually have fun with the literature… and I think that's a disservice'. She thought 'how much fun it would be just to read a book just for the sake of reading a book in class, not having to do a test on it… and just go, "Okay…Let's talk about what happened in this book"… like a book club'. Chloe told us, 'I often go, "Okay girls, it doesn't matter what the assessment is. We're not talking about that right now, we're just going to look at the text"… but at the same time I'm very aware that I'm teaching to that assessment and, if I'm not, I don't feel like I've prepared them enough'. For Debra, time devoted to preparation for standardised testing in a 'marks-focused world' with its emphasis on 'measurable scores' threatened the development of 'a love of reading and a love of language'. Scott was adamant that standardised testing had 'a negative effect on the culture of reading and the culture of literature'.

Laura's reference to 'book clubs' has some resonance here because it is activities like this that Kirkpatrick and Dixon (2012) list as exemplifying the 'literary sociability', which we discuss in this book (see Chapter 8). But in picking up the concept of 'literary sociability' we were also mindful of the way the institutional nature of schooling mediates the activities surrounding books in distinctive ways. Laura goes on to say, 'I don't think you'd be able to do that… in… a classroom…, which sucks because… reading for pleasure is [an] Outcome'. Here, Laura hits not just on a note of regret, but also a kind of irony. The Outcomes she refers to are the content Outcomes of the New South Wales (NSW) *English K-10 Syllabus for the Australian Curriculum* (NESA, 2019). On the one hand, one wants to celebrate a syllabus that sees pleasure as an Outcome for composing, and responding to, texts (this is a long tradition for NSW Syllabuses, in fact). Laura reminds us that sometimes what teachers may see as valuable beyond the practices of their own school can be available and legitimised even by centrally mandated curricula, which could then be used to negotiate those local conditions in a variety of ways. With greater experience and/or when teaching in different schools, the possibilities offered by this syllabus might seem more achievable to Laura. On the other hand, the notion of making 'pleasure' a mandated Outcome in school contexts, which almost by definition are not replete with the kinds of freedoms inherent in book clubs, contains a kind of irony that sits behind what Laura says here. It is precisely such institutional imperatives – sometimes manifested as a clash between central and local imperatives – that create the tensions these teachers negotiate in their everyday practice. As Morgan – teaching in the same State as Laura, with the same mandated curriculum – said, 'the love of literature creates a connection on a social level, and… what we see in book clubs and literary festivals happens in schools as well', but 'it's more forced'. Why it is more forced in Morgan's eyes has to do with assessment – 'judgements made about their approach to books' – but also with the day-to-day institutional realities of how much 'student agency' and 'choice in what they read' is usually available to students compared to such agency and choice outside school.

And it is to this general issue of text selection – and its place in discussions of literary knowledge – that I now turn. When our teachers spoke about literary knowledge, they often spoke about what their students were learning/being exposed to through engaging with particular literary texts. The issue of text selection can be one place in which debates about literary knowledge and the teaching of literature gain on-the-ground purchase. Yet many factors impinge on the pedagogical ideal of matching texts with students. The first, in public ('state') schools especially, is the simple cost of texts. As Clare says, 'in an ideal world, text selection would be based on what is the appropriate text for the students… I feel like in this school… maybe more so in the past, text selection is all around, "What resources do we have?"'. Students' levels of literacy development can be, as we have seen, another obvious issue with regard to text selection. Leo felt his students had 'no stamina' for reading literature. Nicole argued that 'in some schools, literary knowledge and exposure to the world of literature would be very important and very practical. Here… it's very much, "How do we get these kids through?"'. An additional issue is the fact that text selection in an examination regime is often set by a central authority rather than by the teacher (which can often also restrict a text's availability to earlier years: the fact that the text is set in the senior years often means that it cannot be used earlier in the curriculum).

One wider issue more directly related to the knowledge question which teachers discussed with us was the perennial one of whether texts should 'reflect' or 'broaden' students' worlds – i.e. whether they should be texts in which students can recognise themselves and aspects of their experience, or texts which represent worlds beyond that experience, or perhaps texts that represent either or neither of these but are challenging with respect to the form they take or the style in which they are written. This is often glossed around issues such as 'engagement' or opening up a student's 'imagination'. Clare saw 'trying to find that balance between broadening their worlds and offering them texts where they can see themselves' as a 'real tension' in her school. This is often put forward as a particular tension in low-socioeconomic-status (SES) schools when teachers feel their students may not have access to the cultural capital of canonical texts, which can reflect specific worlds and values. It can't be forgotten, however, that these students are already negotiating complex semiotic practices and understandings in their everyday lives. The teachers in our study did not provide a simple answer to this issue; it is another of the ongoing tensions which they inhabit and within which they develop their practice. Scott spoke of 'a lot of the kids [having] absolutely no idea about [a particular] context'. For Clare, 'exposing them to texts that we feel they need to have exposure to and exposing them to texts that they have the capital to access' is the thing she 'grapple[s] with the most when it comes to text selection'.

Seeing one's world reflected in a text is felt by teachers to be an important way to enable students to gain access to a text and is thus an important factor in the provision of a literary education for all – and is an issue taken up below in the discussion of engagement. But some teachers, such as Clare, also see access to the canon for less privileged students as equally a question of social justice and entitlement, however remote particular worlds and cultures might be. Text selection is a question of curriculum, as we saw from Chapter 10. The work of Teese (2011) and Roberts et al. (2019) show a curriculum hierarchy in at least two Australian States that, in effect, reflects a correlation between SES and more 'specialist' or higher 'status' or greater 'value' (in the sense of contributing to university entrance scores) courses in end-of-schooling curricula. In English in these States in Australia, this correlation also reflects the selection of such courses *within* the broader (usually compulsory) subject English.

This, in turn, often reflects the degree to which such courses contain texts that are both canonical and which are embedded in an extensive literary-critical debate:

> Teachers in disadvantaged schools are caught in a dilemma. On the one hand, they choose texts for their accessibility – the language is familiar… Little historical knowledge is required… But on the other hand accessible texts have no rich tradition of interpretative literature behind them. This makes every student of these texts a pioneer critic.
>
> *(Teese, 2011, p.16)*

There are a number of issues raised by this notion of curriculum hierarchy. One is the culturally loaded nature of what is valued. Teese is partly arguing that certain forms of literary sensibility are privileged within the English curriculum – in his State of Victoria, this is reflected in the status of 'Literature' as a separate subject from 'English' in the publicly examined senior curriculum, the Victorian Certificate of Education (VCE). This involves a select range of texts. But it also involves a certain kind of attention or mode of appreciation – a privileged kind of response that is rewarded by examiners in the form of the 'lit.crit.' essay as discussed previously.

For some of our teachers, like Scott, 'quality' was a second-order issue: encouraging reading meant taking an attitude of 'as long as they're reading, I'm happy'. Similarly, Brittney argued strongly for the value of texts she referred to as 'transitional':

> …if that's the only type of thing they read, then at least that's a starting point to then introduce them to other types of texts… I wouldn't call it 'literature' as such, but it's still important.

In contrast, Timothy, in a selective-entry school, 'banned' graphic novels during wide reading periods as not providing a 'sustained enough' reading experience. (Some other teachers feared that students were becoming too used to the 'short, sharp and available' and that there was a move away from setting longer texts, or even full texts.) Ultimately, both Timothy and Brittney clearly value 'quality' (that's why Brittney provides a 'starting point'), yet their very different approaches again demonstrate complicating tensions around the place of particular texts in schools. Even issues of 'What's worth studying?' do not exist in a social and cultural vacuum.

Another tension for teachers was the perennial issue of the 'status' of individual interpretation, especially in an exam setting. When Rebecca recalled from her own schooling a time when her class went on an excursion to hear one of the 'set' poets for her HSC speak in person and he contradicted particular interpretations they had taken in class, or which were taken by academic speakers at the same event, her key memory was that 'as teenagers, we just wanted the right answer… it was all about… getting good marks in our exams'. And for many of her own students now, the question still is just wanting 'to be told the answer and want[ing] it to be the right answer' because 'they don't trust themselves enough to find their right answer'. When Jen raised this issue of students having different views about a text from what seemed to emerge from class discussion, she contextualised it as 'fear of failure [being] massive' and told of one student who demanded that, as her teacher, she 'tell [her] what the answer is'. Morgan argued that the approach to interpretation encouraged in English is 'a great freedom, but for a student that needs "one plus one equals two", that's scary'.

This issue also relates to how the emotional and intellectual intersect in reading. It is widely acknowledged in both the fields of education and literary studies that meaning-making in reading includes drawing on a 'tacit knowledge of the world' (Eagleton, 1983, p.76; see also Goodman et al., 2016, p.39, passim). This notion has implications for the issue of traditionally 'authorised' meanings for any particular text, but it also opens a broader issue of the way students engage with texts at an emotional level. Our early career teachers generally acknowledged the importance for their students of personal connections to texts as a primary level of engagement, quite apart from the role that 'knowledge of the world' played in making meaning. They saw the roles played by the values and experiences their students brought to their reading as multi-faceted.

Engagement

Thus, 'experience' has at least two meanings peculiar to English when we think about literature in the classroom. The first has to do with interpretation and the role that prior experience (including experience of the literary) plays in making meaning; and the second is to do with 'connection', raising in its turn the issue of how students engage with texts. As briefly mentioned above, the nature of the texts available in a school was seen by our teachers as having a key role in engaging students. Rebecca, in moving from a senior school as an intern (and briefly as a casual teacher), entered a context where Years 7–10 students were now to make up the bulk of her teaching load. She identified her current school as having in Year 7 'a lot of reluctant readers, and then a lot of EALD students as well'. To address 'trying to get them engaged more', English teachers there turned to 'multicultural texts'. With the resources to do this and based on the notion that students ought to see themselves reflected in the literature they encounter, this is clearly an important way of enabling students to engage in their reading.

In a similar socioeconomic context, Laura also found engagement an issue and depended on getting 'buy-in' from students around 'context': a focus on the context in which a text is set (a point echoed by Timothy) or, like Rebecca, focusing on parallel themes/events in the students' own world(s). Though engagement often included the need to read the text to/with some students for initial comprehension, Laura's key practice remained focused on 'context'. She felt in her first interview that 'they're actually making connections… now into their own worlds, which is what I think English teaching has to do because we have to engage these kids'. Sophie would begin a study of *Macbeth* by connecting it to stories of loyalty and power that students already knew. Olivia said that when she could 'relate it to their lives or put them in the shoes of certain characters, there's a huge discussion'. Engagement, she argued, was strongly related to students' understanding that 'there's elements in it that relate to everyday life'. 'Kids', argued Laura, 'connect with the story and with the characters or with what they go through or their issues and their problems'. As

Rebecca said, 'you hook them with the empathy'. Timothy also talked about 'real-world application' and 'the importance of… finding something for themselves in [literature]', but elaborated on this issue less around empathy specifically and more around opportunities provided by literature to broaden students' perspectives on the world more generally:

> I care about literature because it reflects the world really and the people you meet, and if you're in a different circumstance but you've tried to put yourself in that context or understand those people, then you can acclimate… your version of reality… and change that and change your perceptions, and try to engage in an authentic manner in that context.

Jen, who saw herself in a context of teaching highly reluctant, and often weak, readers, had her students choosing and working between silent reading, listening to audiobooks and reading to each other in small groups. She also emphasised the need to have an interesting range of books available for students. Olivia would often talk to her students about the point of studying literature being in the particular skills it was developing: identifying issues, creating meaning and taking different perspectives. Another linking engagement with 'relevance' was Amanda, who focused her students on what she called 'real-life application now and in the future' from the study of literature. Olivia added the notion that genuine teacher engagement with a text was a necessary step to fostering student engagement. Brittney, too, felt that 'showing that you're really passionate about literature and English' was important to student 'buy in', while Debra argued that text choices should be partly based on 'what *we* can be passionate about as teachers'.

Olivia believed that the kind of freedom of text choice available in the junior years (7–10) compared to the HSC (in NSW) was another key factor in engagement. Her classes would have four books 'going… at the same time' to 'appeal… to the kids… meet their abilities and their needs, and… that they are going to be interested in… and [that] get them to *love* a text'. Janet felt it was valid to occasionally say 'let's have a talk about the books that we love rather than let's talk about (X) which we all *have* to read'. By her third interview, Janet felt that she'd turned around reluctance to read in her class by basing text choice on recommendations made by students from the school library. Timothy, too, felt that students having a 'text that *they* choose' was an important factor in engagement. While 'literacy' is often treated in public discourse as fundamental to simply operating in the world, English teachers also see reading as something they wish to develop in students to take into their post-school lives for its sheer enjoyment. Given this, there is something of a paradox in the teacher/the system choosing texts on students' behalf at all as the default position. Clare, though someone who felt that 'there is some value in everybody… read[ing] certain things because they have artistic merit', also argued that her 'students choosing texts… is a much more authentic way of doing things than me telling them what I think they should study'.

Debra believed that in her current school in the junior years the approach to assessment was a strong factor in engagement since it drove interesting pedagogical practices:

> …in the junior years… it's not just essay after essay… Shakespeare's the one that we really try to make different, so in Year 9 they all do *Romeo and Juliet*, and… they're given a scene and they have to create a film to appropriate that scene, and it's brilliant… they put it… into their own context, and they just absolutely… love it.

Engaging pedagogical practices such as these – reflecting a broader range of means through which students can reflect engagement – often depended on the notion of sociability as meaning-making that we have been highlighting in this book. In working together to create a war between two well-known fast food outlets (one of the *Romeo and Juliet* scenarios from Debra's class), students are also exploring their responses to *Romeo and Juliet*: a connection made explicit when they 'rationalise' the decisions they make in designing these re-creation scenarios based on their reading of the text. Freya nominated as her most successful lesson one in which Year 8 engaged in literature circles involving discussion and note-taking, after which students produced written pieces based on the texts under consideration – such as writing about the freedom of flight from the point of view of the bird in Maya Angelou's poem 'Caged bird'.

Tensions, engagement and knowledge

Through the processes in which English engages students – and, indeed, through the nature of reading itself, however much content is prescribed, individual meaning-making remains at the centre of English. The 'making' of literary meanings through classroom processes remains an important part of what the study of literature is about, often derived from socially oriented practices such as discussion. Nevertheless, policy overlays a framework on local practice that can be more or less constraining, particularly through mandated forms of assessment. As we have noted, Laura's comment about 'pleasure' being the desired Syllabus Outcome for reading and textual creation is potentially enabling. However, policy frameworks are not necessarily consistent. Laura pointed out the inconsistency between a syllabus with such Outcomes and the constraints, in particular, of standardised testing for literacy. Timothy explained (see Chapter 10) that for his context in NSW, meeting the requirements of the subject *English* and the expectations of national standardised testing around *literacy* may drive quite different practices, cultures and knowledges that may be sometimes complementary, but equally may be quite divergent.

We have seen also that pedagogical choices in English can be intimately tied up with certain conceptions of knowledge, whether such links are fully intended by teachers or not. In 1980, Medway claimed that the 'unique[ness]' of English consisted in its enacting 'nothing less than a different model of education: knowledge to be made, not given; knowledge comprising more than can be discursively stated… educational processes to be embarked on with outcomes unpredictable; students' perceptions, experiences, imaginings and unsystematically acquired knowledge admitted as legitimate curriculum content' (p.10). This 'remains a powerful and succinct statement' (Green, 2018, p.279) in many ways about the potential of the subject, albeit one that has been complicated at a policy level by those neoliberal imperatives enacted through the Global Education Reform Movement, such as standardisation, a focus on 'basics', and high-stakes accountability (Sahlberg, 2011) Since a literature curriculum foregrounds questions of interpretation and 'making' meanings, then literary encounters epitomise the idea of knowledge being 'made' through classroom processes in the ways described by Medway. Thus, pedagogy becomes crucial and, as Green argues, becomes inseparable from the curriculum itself (Green, 2018, pp.246–248).

Possibly apart from classroom discussion, there are no particular pedagogies in literature classrooms that one would want to label as *always* 'characteristic'. Nevertheless, practices have emerged in the literature classroom, since the 1970s, for example, that one might see as 'mainstream', around the issue of expressing a response to literature, such as various forms of textual intervention. Pope (1995), in the context of tertiary studies in literature, has written about reading texts as a form of re-writing and acts of interpretation as acts of intervention. His approach to textual intervention has included activities such as students changing the point of view of a poem or of creating an interior monologue for characters in a novel or considering alternative endings to a play. Knights and Thurgar-Dawson's (2006) 'active reading' is in a similar vein. In secondary school, such textual interventions in literature have had a history as 'imaginative re-creation'. Imaginative re-creation has held an important place at least since the term was coined by Stratta, Dixon and Wilkinson in 1973 to refer to students having 'a creative role in relation to the work of fiction' to 'imaginatively re-create for [themselves] the experience of the novelist' (Stratta et al., 1973, p.70). This family of activities envisaged a kind of response to literary texts in which students created texts 'alongside' the authors of the original. Others addressing secondary English specifically have extended such ideas under different labels, such as Reid's (1984) 'Workshop' model for teaching literature or Adams' (1995) notion of 'dependent authorship'.

Though focused on the notion of responding to literature through creating literature (see Adams' [2013] subtitle) these practices are firstly acts of reading: modes of interpretation. Pope's argument, for example, is that the re-writing and reading entailed in such textual interventions are 'the best way to understand how a text works'. The practice is to 'play around with it, to intervene in it in some way… and then try to account for the exact effect of what you have done' (Pope, 1995, p.1). Stratta et al., too, argue that this work requires 'the reconsideration of the original text… interpretation by re-creation and re-creation by interpretation. The pupils must *ask themselves* [original italics] questions of interpretation before they can bring their new creation into being' (1973, p.87). Thus, this work is crucially a matter of working with the form and language of the original text. 'Interference' with the text in Reid's Workshop gives readers 'a licence to read in a way that is alert to the processes of writing, to the structural or stylistic options chosen or rejected or ignored' (1984, p.25). In fact, the idea of 'creating' is intimately tied to reading in the study of literature. 'English composition' at Harvard began its history rooted in the study of literature, not so much as a way of 'modelling' writing, but as a way of coming 'to a fuller and deeper understanding of literature itself by approaching it from the inside' (Haake, 2006, p.158).

Such activities are also built on the assumption that responding to texts in ways other than the 'lit.crit.' essay offer opportunities to deepen engagement with the original texts. The normalised default position in discussing literary responses from our early career teachers seemed to be the academic 'lit.crit.' essay – what Debra referred to as 'essays and essays and essays'. Their own teaching of writing was most often talked about by our teachers in terms that distinguished 'essays' (in response to literature) from 'creative writing' (usually personal, imaginative, fictional) or from areas of literacy (such as in 'writing sentences' or 'writing paragraphs'). It may be that in discussing the expression of literary knowledge, our teachers were also defaulting to thinking about their senior students, but this was not always the case: Tash discussed essays in relation to texts more usually used in the 'junior' school, such as Louis Sachar's *Holes* or S. E. Hinton's *The Outsiders*. This is touched on in Chapter 10, but it is worth noting here the extent to which ways of responding to literature through writing appear to have been narrowed by the requirements of examinations (or 'assessment tasks') to this 'lit. crit.' academic essay, which can often involve a closing down of meaning rather than a recognition of the polysemic character of a text. Even where the essay may not act to close down possibilities of meaning, this narrowing of the range of expressing response, especially in writing, can also reflect an ongoing assumption 'that a "mature" response to literature somehow involves moving beyond personal response to more analytical forms of engagement' (Zabka, 2016, p.227). I would go slightly further than Zabka. For me, the keyword here is 'forms'. It is not that types of response, such as 'imaginative re-creation', are necessarily less 'analytical' than formal literary criticism, but simply that they are expressed in ways other than those traditionally rewarded in high-stakes assessment. The most extreme expression of the dominance of forms of assessment in our project was from one teacher whose school had separated reading and writing into separate areas of the curriculum and where the set text was 'just the vehicle for learning to write a text response essay'. All of this is further exacerbated today by the tendency sometimes across whole jurisdictions to have students write in very formulaic ways. These are often centred on the artefact of the paragraph, such as in the demand for topic sentences or structures such as PEEL (Point Evidence Explanation Link) or TEAL (Topic Sentence Evidence Analysis Link) – both common examples in Australia. While one might see some value in these in introducing students to essay writing, they soon – like 'genres' in writing pedagogy – become reified into formulas, with the particular problem here of entirely taking the focus off the structuring and flow of a total argument across a whole piece of writing (see McKnight, 2020).

The subject here is English and particular things need to be at the centre of classroom concerns:

- the semiotic practices of students
- the relationship between language and meaning, including a notion of textuality: *how* texts represent experience

In relation to the latter, certainly, there is a plethora of discussion among our teachers of 'analysis' in linguistic terms, of 'technique[s]', and generally of 'how language is functioning' (Leo) in texts. However, making connections to students' worlds is obviously a key concern for English teachers. Such connections highlight these teachers' sense that literature still speaks to something important in their students' lives, even if those teachers do not see themselves as Mathieson's (1975) 'preachers of culture'. There is no doubt that for some teachers in our study, discussion about the larger social/philosophical/historical/psychological issues arising in literature is an important pedagogical practice. The teachers in this project approached literature as an 'impulse to make sense of [human experience]' (Misson & Morgan, 2005, p.25), largely highlighting what Harold Rosen once called students' 'need to find in literature an illumination (not a reflection) of their lives' (Rosen, 1981, p.8). As Yandell argues, 'What subject English provides, particularly in its textual or literary dimension, is the opportunity to look afresh at concepts that are encountered as much in everyday existence as in the classroom... not just recognition but re-cognition – a thinking again' (Yandell, 2017, p.597). This notion of re-cognition, of looking again, is an important one in discussing the particular knowledge claims of literature as helping to understand a world with which we are already familiar (of 'everyday existence'), but which presents that world in conceptually new ways:

> As readers, we deploy re-cognition to take us out of the forest of hermeneutic uncertainty, back home to a fresh understanding of the already known... Literary knowledge, in sum, is distinctive; it's dialectical; and it depends as much on what is already known by the reader as on what's new in the text.
>
> *(Simpson, 2013, pp.41–42)*

Practices such as activating prior knowledge return us to the question of how the intellectual and emotional can intersect in the study of literature – of knowledge and experience as embodied, lived, situated. This is not a question of sentimentality, but has some affinities with Polanyi's (1958) notion of 'personal knowledge', positioning some knowledge as related to 'experience' rather than simply positing 'experience' as in opposition to 'powerful knowledge' (Young & Muller, 2013). As we saw earlier, an important aspect of practice for these teachers issues out of the belief that understanding a text depends partly, and at first, on caring about it. Thus, we are brought back to the centrality of students as 'beings' communicating with their texts, rather than being positioned, such as through standardised testing, as Wilkinson's 'spelling-punctuation-grammar producing machines'.

References

Adams, P. (1995). *At the Far Reach of Their Capacities: Case Studies in Dependent Authorship*. Norwood: AATE.

Adams, P. (2013). *At the Far Reach of their Capacities: Responding to Literature through Writing Literature*. Putney: Phoenix Education.

Australian Curriculum Assessment and Reporting Authority (ACARA). (n.d.). Australian Curriculum: English. Available: www.australiancurriculum.edu.au/f-10-curriculum/english/. Accessed 29 August 2021.

Eagleton, T. (1983). *Literary Theory: An Introduction*. Oxford: Blackwell.

Goodman, K., Fries, P. H., & Strauss, S. L. (2016). *Reading – The Grand Illusion: How and Why People Make Sense of Print*. New York and London: Routledge.

Green, B. (2018). *Engaging Curriculum: Bridging the Curriculum Theory and English Education Divide*. New York and London: Routledge.

Haake, K. (2006). Creative writing. In B. McComiskey (Ed.), *English Studies: An Introduction to the Discipline(s)*. Urbana, IL: NCTE: 153–198.

Kirkpatrick, P., & Dixon, R. (Eds.) (2012). *Republic of Letters: Literary Communities in Australia*. Sydney: Sydney University Press.

Knights, B., & Thurgar-Dawson, C. (2006). *Active Reading: Transformative Writing in Literary Studies*. London: Continuum.

Mathieson, M. (1975). *The Preachers of Culture: A Study of English and its Teachers*. London: Allen & Unwin.

McKnight, L. (2021). Since feeling is first: The art of teaching to write paragraphs. *English in Education*, 55(1), 37–52.

Mead, P., Doecke, B., & McLean Davies, L. (2020). Contingencies of meaning-making: English teaching and literary sociability. *Australian Literary Studies*, 35(2).Accessed 12 May 2022. https://doi.org/10.20314/als.00225a9681.

Medway, P. (1980). *Finding a Language: Autonomy and Learning within School*. London: Writers and Readers Publishing Cooperative and Chameleon.

Misson, R., & Morgan, W. (2005). Beyond the pleasure principle? Confessions of a critical literacy teacher. *English in Australia*, 144, Summer, 17–25.

NSW Education Standards Authority (NESA). (2019). *NSW Syllabus for the Australian Curriculum: English K-10 Syllabus*. Sydney: NSW Education Standards Authority. Available: https://educationstandards.nsw.edu.au/wps/portal/nesa/k-10/learning-areas/english-year-10/english-k-10. Accessed 20 August 2020.

Polanyi, M. (1958). *Personal Knowledge: Towards a Post-Critical Philosophy*. Chicago: University of Chicago Press.

Pope, R (1995). *Textual Interventions: Critical and Creative Strategies for Literary Studies*. London and New York: Routledge.

Reid, I. (1984). *The Making of Literature*. Norwood: AATE.

Roberts, P., Dean, J., & Lommatsch, G. (2019). *Still Winning? Social Inequity in the NSW Senior Secondary Curriculum Hierarchy*. Canberra: Rural Education and Communities research group, University of Canberra. Available: https://researchprofiles.canberra.edu.au/en/publications/still-winning-social-inequity-in-the-nsw-senior-secondary-curricu. Accessed 21 August 2020.

Rosen, H. (1981). *Neither Bleak House Nor Liberty Hall: English in the Curriculum*. London: University of London Institute of Education.

Sahlberg, P. (2011). *Finnish Lessons: What Can the World Learn from Educational Change in Finland?* New York: Teachers College Press.

Simpson, J. (2013). Cognition is recognition: Literary knowledge and textual "Face". *New Literary History*, 44(1), 25–44.

Stratta, L., Dixon, J., & Wilkinson, A. (1973). *Patterns of Language*. London: Heinemann Education.

Teese, R. (2011). The new curriculum for English in Australia and student achievement under the old curriculum: Understanding inequality and addressing it. In B. Doecke, G. Parr, & W. Sawyer (Eds.), *Creating an Australian Curriculum for English: National Agendas, Local Contexts*. Putney: Phoenix Education: 5–20.

Wilkinson, A. (1987). The quality of language: Some considerations for Kingman. *English in Education*, 21(2), 3–11.

Yandell, J. (2017). Knowledge, English and the formation of teachers, *Pedagogy, Culture & Society*, 25(4), 583–599. https://doi.org/10.1080/14681366.2017.1312494.

Young, M., & Muller, J. (2013). On the powers of powerful knowledge. *Review of Education*, 1(3), 229–250.

Zabka, T. (2016). Literary studies: A preparation for tertiary education (and life beyond). *Changing English*, 23(3), 227–240. https://doi.org/10.1080/1358684x.2016.1203618.

12

CROSSING INSTITUTIONAL BOUNDARIES

Negotiating a professional identity as an English teacher

Brenton Doecke and Philip Mead

There is a fable about the life pathway of English teachers that circulates in various versions among educators and the wider community: a young child grows up in a household of books, responding with wide-eyed enthusiasm when her mother or father reads her stories at bedtime. As a student she is inspired by her English teacher's passion for literature to become an English teacher herself, moving from secondary school to study English at university, perhaps completing an Honours degree in English, and after that a teaching qualification. Such individuals return to school imbued with a passion for literature that they are committed to sharing with their students. A teaching qualification admittedly is a bit of a nuisance, a tiresome government regulation with which they are obliged to comply in order to secure a job. The chief quality English teachers require is a capacity to instil a joy in all things literary into their pupils. In this scenario the teacher is a kind of aide; the real teacher is literature itself through the powers that it exercises directly over young imaginations. As the Newbolt Report put it in 1921, teachers of literature should try to stand by their pupils 'sympathetically, directing or moderating' their reading of literature without standing between them and the author they are reading (Newbolt Report, [1921] 1938, p.24).

Though some elements of this mythic narrative can be traced in the accounts that our early career teachers give of themselves, by and large, they tend to provide counternarratives to this story. The bulk of our interviewees has certainly evinced what we might call a literary sensibility that is at the heart of what they are doing as English teachers. They have told us stories about how as children they enjoyed reading at home, about an influential English teacher, or their attraction to literary works of various kinds. Yet their heightened sensitivity to the play between language and meaning, even the tentative privileging by some of literary and language study over the teaching of literacy, can hardly be equated with the missionary zeal to open

DOI: 10.4324/9781003106890-12

up the richness of literature and the literary imagination that has historically been ascribed to teachers of English as 'preachers of culture' (Mathieson, 1975).

This is not to say that the English teaching profession as a whole has remained captive to this story about impassioned individuals whose mission is to bring their pupils in touch with the riches of the literary imagination. There is another less inspiring version of this story that Terry Eagleton relates in his influential book, *Literary Theory* (Eagleton, 1983, pp.22–36). This version of English teaching sees it as promoting an apolitical ideal, a community of literature lovers and a literary culture in which everyone can share at the expense of any recognition of social divisions. In this view, the humanist story of English teachers as 'preachers of culture' is fundamentally self-deluding, compromising any capacity on their part to recognise the nature of the work they actually perform in society. Eagleton's account of the 'rise of English' was influential at the time that it was first published, one of a number of critical studies that highlighted the ideological role that English has played since its inception (see e.g., Anderson, 1969, Baldick, 1983; Ball et al., 1990; Batsleer et al., 1985).

But this critique of the 'preachers of culture' story is also heedless of important realities of English teachers' experience. Because it is not as though every English teacher has become disillusioned by this narrative of disillusionment. Many English teachers have remained committed to the value of their subject and the welfare of their students, even while they have grappled with perceptions of their role as functionaries in the reproduction of existing society. Those teachers are deeply aware of how their own education and upbringing have shaped their values and beliefs and they continually question whether their literary knowledge is genuinely inclusive or whether the literary imagination is even worthy of attention given the massive social dislocation and inequality that characterise contemporary society. They live and work within the politics of contemporary English education. There are plenty of examples of English educators who have reflexively interrogated their own literary education in an effort to recognise and engage with the understanding of language and worlds of experience their students bring into their classrooms. Their goal has been to realise the potential of a literary education as part of a social-democratic project (cf. Barnes, 2000; Medway et al., 2014).

So where do the early career teachers we have interviewed fit into this complex and variegated history of subject English? To do justice to the subtlety of their dispositions as they have been shaped by the literary, historical and theoretical knowledge they bring with them from university, it is obviously necessary to find new ways to represent the varieties of their professional identities. Yet it is also obvious that the reflexivity they have shown by sharing their stories with us locates them within a history of subject English in which English teachers have continually interrogated their praxis (cf. Doecke, 2019). That history reveals how English teachers and their pupils perform many identities in school settings other than those that may have been determined for them. The stories that teachers tell about themselves – even when they might be recycling aspects of the myth about preachers of culture – can be read as having a Utopian dimension. By telling such stories, teachers affirm the possibility of imagining life differently from the way that it is organised at present. At the least, those stories reflect a belief in the possibility of their own agency, rather than a resigned or unknowing acceptance of the role ascribed to them. And that belief in the possibility of agency, including a capacity to imagine alternative identities and practices, is something they often see as inherent within the way they have learnt to read and respond to language as part of their literary educations. As Fleur Diamond remarks about her memory of studying S. E. Hinton's *Outsiders*: 'Over the years, this moment has come to crystallise what became a key part of my pedagogy once I became an English teacher – that interpreting a text can also be an occasion for critically interpreting one's life and world' (Diamond, 2020, p.237).

***

It is useful to understand the praxis of early career English teachers as emerging out of the cultures of the schools in which they are working. Their praxis has a richly situated character – this, at least, is the abiding impression that we take away from the corpus of stories they have told us about their struggles to negotiate a professional identity within the institutional settings where they find themselves working. They each bring a certain set of beliefs and values to their teaching, but their continuing professional learning emerges out of a dialectic between 'inner' and 'outer', between their sense of an emerging professional 'self' and the relationships they are required to negotiate within their school communities. One of the important emphases of our study has been its focus on the first stages of this dialectic. These early career English teachers' professional 'selves' are not to be understood solely as inner, privatised sub-jectivities, but emerge more fully in the 'in-between' space of their relationships with those around them (Hourd, [1949] 1968). Nor do they think of the values and beliefs embodied in those 'selves' as constant or consistent. Those 'selves' remain works in progress that they sometimes experience as deeply contradictory.

In this context, it is also worth noting that the bureaucratic apparatus of profes-sional standards (e.g. the Australian Institute of Teaching and School Leadership [AITSL]) hardly seems to connect with these teachers' sense of themselves as English teachers. Early career teachers are typically only aware of these standards to confirm their teacher registration. The standards did not provide a point of refer-ence in our conversations with them, and the accounts they gave of their experi-ences could only loosely be mapped onto the sequential stages of professional learning those standards define. Those standards construct professional development as essentially a matter of individual progression through stages without any regard to how that development might be decisively shaped by the specific school settings in which a teacher is working. Nor, given the fact that they have been constructed as generic standards that apply to all teachers across the subject areas, do they pro-vide any kind of framework for understanding the way English teachers specifically might experience their professional learning through their interactions with stu-dents (cf. Doecke, 2016). The immediacy of the demands made on beginning teachers from day to day doesn't seem to allow them to situate their work within the discourse of professional standards.

'Amanda' attended a non-denominational Christian school in the south-eastern suburbs of Melbourne. She now finds herself teaching in another non-denominational Christian school on the fringes of the Melbourne metropolitan area. The school is located in a rural setting, on land that only a few years ago was used for farming. With Federal Government funding, such schools have sprung up around Australia, the result of bipartisan education policy directed at providing parents with the capacity to choose the right school for their children. The standardised test results that are published online each year have been a key mechanism of this change, since they supposedly enable parents to exercise that choice, rather than simply sending their children to the local state school, as occurred in the past. The effect of this policy has been the steady residualisation of the state school sector and the undermining of the post-war ideal of provision of a free, secular education for all (Teese & Polesel, 2003).

What kind of professional praxis is Amanda able to enact within this setting and what does it owe to her experience as a student of English? To some extent she is driven by her memories of teachers who inspired her at her own secondary school – she was recognised as being 'talented' at English and one teacher actually gave her individual attention designed to extend her abilities. She might thus be said to be living the old story of a student whose love of literature has inspired her to share that love with the students she is now teaching. But this story needs to be combined with another story that shows her gradually adjusting to a culture that she does not experience as fully receptive to her ideas. Much to her astonishment, she is made the English Coordinator in her second year of teaching. The school is a fairly small one that is slowly building up its numbers as more parents enrol their children. She is not coordinating a large number of staff, but she still experiences a struggle with older teachers who have their favourite books along with a file of resources they have accumulated over the years. But the chief obstacle she encounters in her role as coordinator is a certain *ad hocery* – nobody has thought very carefully about which texts should be taught at which year levels and how the English curriculum might be organised sequentially to provide students with a varied and meaningful experience over the years of their schooling. In the course of our interviews with her, she takes the opportunity to articulate a rationale for text selection, including reasons as to which books should follow which, arguing the importance of offering the students texts that have been written in their life-times when she instances a range of contemporary Australian titles, while also affirming the value of teaching texts that are more remote from their lives such as Charles Dickens' *A Christmas Carol* and Elizabeth Gaskell's *North and South*.

The most memorable stories that Amanda told, however, concern the exchanges she has had with both parents and students relating to texts chosen for study and the activities she has devised to encourage her students to engage with them. Not many of the parents at her school have university degrees. She describes the school community as comprising tradespeople or farmers from the surrounding district. So, although she can identify students who enjoy reading the books set for study, she also tells many stories about students who resist engaging with these texts. When she invites her students to find quotations within *To Kill a Mockingbird* that might support certain statements about themes within the text, nudging them beyond merely generalising about themes in the book to a close reading of the words on the page, one boy asks how such an exercise could possibly be of use to him when he wants to become a plumber. Her answer is that when he is a plumber he will need to have a good knowledge of the building code and be able to locate stipulations within it should any customer query what he is doing. With another class, she organises a Great Gatsby party, preparing mocktails and canapés and asking the students to come along dressed up as one of the characters, equipped with quotations that will enable them to stay in character. At the end of the lesson, one of her students concedes that it has been a lot of fun but wants to know how the activity could possibly serve any purpose as far as their learning is concerned. At a parent-teacher night, when she is trying to impress on parents the importance of encouraging their children to read at home, one mother remarks that they can't possibly expect their kids to read any books when the family is just about to go on holiday. At another parent-teacher night, Amanda admits that the students have struggled with *To Kill a Mockingbird*, only to have one parent nod her head knowingly: 'I told them when they came home, I hated *To Kill a Mockingbird* in school so why should you like it?'

These are all stories that experienced English teachers would recognise, and they prompt any number of questions about the strategies a teacher might use to encourage reluctant readers to participate in classroom activities around texts chosen for study. But for this analysis, we want to suspend such judgements and the assumptions they might imply about effective English teaching and look at Amanda's account of her teaching alongside the accounts that other early career teachers in our project give of their professional praxis. The point of the project has never been to identify the best examples of English teaching. Nor do we have any desire to single out those early career teachers who might have told especially reflective accounts of their teaching – just about every teacher who has participated in our project has provided an impressive example of reflective practice. Nearly all of them, including Amanda, took the opportunity with each interview to articulate their insights into the complexities of their professional practice to understand their work better. But to read Amanda's account of the culture of her school community alongside, for example, Katya's reflections on the culture at her school (see the vignette) is to be confronted by a more fundamental question: how can these cultures be compared at all?

For, on the one hand, we encounter a world of Year 11 students shyly drinking mocktails and eating canapés, where the meaning-making that occurs around literary texts is inevitably mediated by a fairly deep-seated resistance to literary-historical knowledge, not to mention the non-denominational Christian values espoused by the school community. Just about everyone looks the same at Amanda's school. When the students experience difficulty with a book that takes refugees and Australia's history as a multicultural society as its themes, she strives to enable them to make connections with the text by mentioning the market at Springvale, a suburb in the south-east of Melbourne with a large Vietnamese community. Surely their parents must have taken them there at least once? This is in marked contrast to the diversity at Katya's school, where she is busy organising a book club as an extra-curricular activity for transgender students. We might also think of Katya's story about the girl who identifies as a Manga character and the relationships she has formed with other teenagers who share her passion for Manga. The culture of Katya's school is completely different from the culture at Amanda's school where the meaning-making in which the students engage is mediated by other values and beliefs.

We have continually highlighted how the meanings of texts are shaped within the social relationships in which they are read and appropriated (see Chapter 5 and 8). Texts, as Ian Reid has argued, 'are not – except in a trivial sense – objects, and so cannot contain anything definitively'. A 'text' names 'a semantic process by which meanings are transacted through the verbal material, not deposited in it' (Reid, 1984, p.56). 'A literary text', Ulf Abraham remarks, 'is not by any means simply there, before we begin to talk about it, but only comes into existence as literature in the course of our exchanges with one another' (Abraham, 2016, p.213). The semantic transactions around a literary text within a classroom are mediated not only by the contingencies of the classroom context in which they occur – the teacher's literary knowledge and her aims in a particular lesson, the knowledge (or lack of knowledge) and experience students bring to the classroom, the time of day when a lesson takes place, the personalities of the students who make up the class – but also by larger contexts embracing both the school community and society beyond. The stories the early career teachers have told us about their teaching challenge any assumption that teachers and their students across diverse communities ever experience the 'same' text or indeed the 'same' English curriculum.

***

The language of educational policy reform hardly promotes any recognition of the diversity of schooling and the culturally specific character of the exchanges that are a feature of everyday life in classrooms. Although such policy rhetoric might make noises about valuing diversity, the emphasis falls overwhelmingly on what is good for everyone. The focus is typically on giving every student 'a real chance of becoming a successful learner, a confident and creative individual and an active and informed citizen', to borrow the language of the 'Melbourne Declaration of Educational Goals for Young Australians', a document that established the framework for bipartisan educational policy in Australia for over a decade (MCEETYA, 2008). This involved a commitment to implementing large-scale testing (what became known as NAPLAN) to ensure that students achieved universally accepted educational standards. The 'Melbourne Declaration' acknowledges the need to 'appreciate Australia's social, cultural, linguistic and religious diversity', but the chief focus is on the importance of students achieving educational outcomes at a complete removal from the culturally specific conditions that shape their lives. The cultures of specific communities are either reduced to something that receives token acknowledgement or they are constructed as sources of 'disadvantage' that may undermine the efforts of students to achieve universally recognised educational outcomes.

This is not exclusively a contemporary phenomenon. As Alison Griffith and Dorothy Smith observe, the development of the school system in the United States was 'in large part driven by the perceived need to homogenise the language and culture of heterogeneous immigration'. Schools were organised to produce 'a generalized level of skills and cultural background oriented to the emerging relations of ruling' (Griffith & Smith, 2005, p.19). A similar argument can be made about the growth of the Australian school system (Green & Cormack, 2011). Griffith and Smith accentuate the middle-class character of school reform, seeing schools as instruments for 'reproducing the new middle class' (Griffith & Smith, 2005, p.25), at the expense of any recognition of minorities. The emergence of schooling was 'an active process', constructing culturally specific 'relations between family, work, and school' as though they applied to the whole population, while effectively transforming the public school system into 'an engine of inequality' (Griffith & Smith, 2005, p.28) because of its systemic incapacity to recognise and cater for the needs of students from diverse communities.

This scenario might seem to emphasise the ideological function that schools play in determining the roles that individuals will be assigned, but the emphasis in the work by Dorothy Smith and her collaborators falls consistently on the standpoint of people as they actively participate in these social structures, suggesting that they can consciously intervene in their situation to bring about change. She characterises the method of inquiry she calls 'institutional ethnography' as starting from 'where we are in our everyday lives' and then on this basis going on to explore social relations and organisational structures that 'are not fully visible to us' (Smith, 2005, p.1). She distinguishes between her approach and sociology that treats people as 'objects' whose behaviours can be explained only by knowledgeable experts outside their everyday world. By contrast, her approach recognises the potential of people within their social or institutional settings to become more knowingly engaged in the conditions that shape their lives. The stories the early career teachers in our project have told provide a similar vantage point from which they have become conscious of the structures that organise their work from day to day, including the machinery of standardised testing and other aspects of school organisation. Their stories might be characterised as an 'embodied knowing' (Smith, 2005, p.7) that gives rise to the possibility of a critique of the reified structures of neoliberal educational reform and the generalising sweep of its policy pronouncements, though it would be wrong to ascribe to them in any blanket fashion the kind of socially critical awareness that Smith sees as emerging through this type of inquiry.

The language Smith uses when she distinguishes between the type of 'embodied knowing' emerging out of everyday life as distinct from the knowledge produced through established fields of inquiry such as sociology or ethnography can still serve to represent the professional learning these early career teachers experience as they grapple with the institutional settings of the schools in which they are working. Smith characterises her approach as an example of a 'feminist sociology', drawing on Sandra Harding's work to argue the capacity of women to re-envision the study of society from a 'women's standpoint' that produces knowledge of society from 'a position in it' (Smith, 2005, p.8). Their learning, however, never constitutes a 'given and finalized form of knowledge' but should be understood as 'a ground in experience from which discoveries are to be made', involving a continuing dialectic between the rich particularities of their everyday experiences and their efforts to achieve an understanding of larger contexts that mediate their lives (Smith, 2005, p.8). We have already observed that several of the early career teachers who participated in our project describe their standpoint as contradictory, as a work in progress, rather than anything resolved or certain.

That the standpoint of these early career teachers potentially provides a point of entry into 'discovering the social' (Smith, 2005, p.10) is accentuated by the fact that they have literally stepped into an institutional setting that they must somehow begin to 'know' if they are to negotiate the social relationships that comprise that setting and handle the responsibilities they are expected to assume. The paradox is that their recognition of the complex social processes they experience as they and their students negotiate their relationships with one another sometimes brings them into conflict with reified structures (most notably the rituals of standardised testing and State-wide examinations in the final years of schooling) that are geared towards containing and regulating everything that happens in this social space. They are torn between a burgeoning recognition of their lives as a continuing process in which they participate with others, requiring an ever-increasing capacity on their part to be responsive to everyday contingencies, and institutional structures that are designed to iron out those contingencies in advance, almost before they step foot in the classroom (Doecke, 2016). They experience a tension between the claims of standards-based reforms to comprehend everything that happens in schools and all that they are learning through their interactions with students.

Situated as they are within institutional settings that are regulated by standards-based reforms, the early career teachers we interviewed struggle to articulate a perspective on those reforms. For one thing, standardised literacy testing is something for which they feel underprepared. This is not least because the 'knowledge' underpinning literacy testing is owned by anonymous measurement experts who are located outside school settings. The test results are then delivered to schools as a set of numbers that then prompts all sorts of strategising on the part of school administrators with regard to targeting year levels and focusing on areas for improvement, requiring another body of expertise that hardly exists within the repertoires of ordinary classroom teachers, let alone early career teachers who have just stepped into those settings. The supposedly 'scientific' discourse underpinning standardised testing hardly recognises what these early career teachers 'know' as graduates of literary studies programs, even bringing into question the salience of their disciplinary knowledge for their work as English teachers. This sense that their knowledge as graduates does not have the same legitimacy as the knowledge that underpins standardised testing is further compounded by the way standardised testing constructs 'literacy'. Many of the early career teachers confessed to not knowing how to teach 'literacy', as though what they are doing when they devise strategies that enable their students to learn from reading literary texts does not count when it comes to teaching them how to read. On the other hand, the teachers also found ways to ameliorate the functionalist aspect of the demands of literacy teaching with other kinds of teaching strategies. Amanda's story about her response to the boy who could not see any point in reading *To Kill a Mockingbird* when he wanted to be a plumber is one such instance.

As well, the universalising pretensions of standards-based reforms never completely achieve their ambition to classify and control everything that happens in schools. Schools are sites where policy intersects with everyday life without ever being able to contain the experiences of people who participate in those settings. We have refrained a couple of times from ascribing a socially critical consciousness to these early career teachers as Smith envisages it. Yet this is not to say that they are not continually seeking to understand their work, that they are not engaged in intense reflection that yields insights into their situation. It would be wrong to suggest that they provide examples of critical engagement as Smith understands it, even though parallels can be drawn between their inquiries into their own praxis and Smith's attempt to envision a form of inquiry that is anchored in the particularities of specific settings. It nonetheless remains the case that through the stories they tell the early career teachers challenge the status of knowledge that is (as Smith puts it) 'stripped of local and biographical particularities' (cf. Miller, 1995).

***

The early career teachers who participated in our project provided us with research interviews that are complex 'speech events' in which narrative plays a crucial role in a joint construction of meaning between interviewee and interviewer (Mishler, 1986, p.4). The purposes that an interviewee brings to an interview are just as important as the interviewer's intentions (Mishler, 1986, p.52). They are interlocutors in a conversation that involves the usual protocols: an effort to establish a shared basis for understanding; turn-taking; the telling of stories, some more or less fully developed, others that remain mere fragments when the conversation moves off in another direction. The meaning-making arising through our conversations with these early career teachers might be characterised as happening in the space between us, a product of the professional discourse that we have enjoyed with them and the multiple contexts that mediate that discourse.

To acknowledge the intellectual and imaginative work that the early career teachers invested in their stories is to foreground their roles as actors in their own lives who are continually seeking to make meaning from their experiences. The stories they tell involve a play between their provisional judgements as to the significance of what they have experienced and contingencies that always escape the generalisations they make. Their reflexivity adds another level of complexity to their stories, as they continually seek to qualify any generalisations they have made, even at the very moment of making them.

By telling their stories, the early career teachers are performing their identities (cf. Allard & Doecke, 2017). It is just as significant to attend to 'how' they are making meaning as to 'what' they might be meaning. The form of their stories – the narrative strategies they employ, even the grammatical choices they make (e.g. grammatical person) – is just as important as the content of their stories. This is to acknowledge how their stories embody their standpoints. Through their storytelling, they are critically engaging with their situations and generating insights into their praxis as English teachers.

Rebecca tells a story about her experience as a Year 12 student when all the work the class had been doing on Peter Skrzynecki's poetry seems to unravel when their teacher takes them to a study day to hear Skrzynecki himself talk about his work. Their confusion doesn't arise simply because Skrzynecki gives a different account of his poetry than the one the class had been developing, but because of what an academic, at the same forum, says about his poetry. This is how Rebecca recounts the event:

> We were studying his poetry for Year 12. He got up, he spoke about all his poems and we're thinking oh this is great, write down everything he says, but a lot of things he was saying was not what we'd interpreted in the class, you know he was saying, no, I really wasn't upset you know as a young man, you know I wasn't depressed, that poem isn't about you know wanting to cut myself or anything and all these things we thought. And then straight after him, like an academic got up and spoke about what she'd thought about his poetry, and you could see him in the front row getting all really annoyed, and we were kind of going well what's all this about? It was pretty interesting, but I think as teenagers we just wanted the right answer.

Before Rebecca tells this story about the way she was unsettled by the instability and contested nature of the meaning of Skrzynecki's poetry, she tells another story in which she relates how her father had encouraged her to read when she was little – 'even though he's like a council worker, very sort of Australian, loves his literature, he's always reading the classics'. Her pleasure in reading was then enhanced when she had the good fortune to have a secondary teacher who shared her passion for reading, opening up the world of science fiction, as well as introducing her to challenging texts like *To Kill a Mockingbird* (ubiquitous in Australian schools) and *The Kite Runner*. But this evocation of her unfolding awareness of the pleasures of reading is disrupted by her story about that forum in Year 12, which she presents less in the form of another episode on her way to becoming an English teacher than as a moment that she is still struggling to understand.

Janet recalls the time when she was completing her final year at St Agnes' College, an elite all-girls private school in rural Victoria, and her English teacher declared that girls at St Agnes would not be having a debutante ball: 'St Agnes girls do not need men to lead them into society'. Janet confesses to being taken aback, that she secretly wanted to 'do' her deb ball, but then she thought:

> What am I doing? And it was the first sort of thought about oh texts can not only give you adventure and that sort of thing, but they can also enhance you as a human being, you can become more learned, you can use them… you could read a novel about someone's struggle and you can become… I can't

remember her name... holding up the books and talking to the girls about these amazing feminist novels and... Oh we read *Jane Eyre*, but it wasn't anything about *Jane Eyre*, it was really about feminism and that kind of analysis of text that wasn't really about what's going on in the plot and what is a metaphor and what is you know write an essay, it was all about what does this mean, what does this mean? And that really stuck with me, it stuck with me.

As with Rebecca, Janet's growth as a reader also involves a supportive parent who encourages her to read as a child. Her parents divorced, and books became a means of escape for her from this unhappy situation as well as (in her words) the 'dreary' little country town where she grew up. Yet although in the account she gives of herself there are traces of a familiar story of a child who has always loved books becoming an English teacher, even including an encounter with an inspirational teacher, the moment she recounts here disrupts a linear narrative of that sort. Her autobiography is in any case complicated by the fact that she does not become an English teacher after completing an Honours degree in English but eventually finds herself in London, where for over a decade she works for a publishing company specialising in science textbooks (see vignette). By constructing this moment in her secondary education Janet is doing much more than answering the question: why did I become an English teacher? A literary education, to borrow loosely from the Bullock Report (p.5), always points beyond itself, and in Janet's case her auto-biography is not simply a matter of the books she read, but 'it was really all about feminism'. Even her account of her parent's divorce, when her mother provided her with an inspiring 'model' of a woman who was able to reinvent herself after the breakup of her marriage, is set against the backdrop of the masculinist culture of a small country town, where 'it was all about getting married and having children and that sort of thing'. Through the stories Janet tells about her education and upbringing, she argues for the continuing salience of a feminist standpoint not only for her work as an English teacher but for her engagement with the community beyond her school, the very community in which she grew up, to which she has now returned after her years away.

Such moments multiply throughout the corpus of stories the early career teachers have told us, prompting us to reconceptualise their praxis as English teachers as involving a repeated confrontation with autobiography (cf. Doecke & McClenaghan, 2011, p.41). The fascination of these stories for us has been the way they transcend the people and circumstances they evoke to resonate so strongly as dimensions of the professional selves they are performing in the present. The term that we have found ourselves frequently using as we have pondered how strongly such stories shape the 'selves' of these early career teachers is that of a literary 'event', which we borrow from Louise Rosenblatt (1978, p.135; cf. Eagleton, 2012) to accentuate the way in which their own experience has been entangled with a sense of the way literary texts act in the world. Indeed, the force of the literary 'events' that Rebecca and Janet relate is underlined by the way that those events continue to raise questions in their minds as to what was really happening. We have already commented that Rebecca still seems to be struggling to explain exactly why her initial experience of the discrepant meanings surrounding a literary text has stayed with her. In Janet's case, the insistent way in which she poses the questions that she was first prompted to ask as a teenager – 'it was all about what does this *mean*, what does this *mean*?' – and then her remark that it 'really stuck with me, it stuck with me' lends her story the same kind of open-endedness. She is not (to draw on Dorothy Smith's characterisation of Sandra Harding's feminism) pretending to articulate a 'given and finalized form of knowledge' but 'a ground in experience from which discoveries are to be made' (Smith, 2005, p.8).

We have been attempting to draw similarities between the critical impulse that Dorothy Smith sees as potentially leading to a re-envisioning of everyday life and the work that these early career teachers invest in their storytelling without collapsing these forms of critical engagement (or 'embodied knowing') together. Smith's understanding of institutional ethnography provided a generative framework for our project not simply because she highlights how institutional structures mediate the practices of people operating within school settings but because of the way she affirms the possibility of critical engagement within those settings. So with the early career teachers who have participated in our project. Although the everyday cultures at their schools provide an inescapable starting point for an understanding of their praxis, their identities as early career teachers are not simply a function of those cultures. The stories they tell show them resisting such determinism. Their schools are sites where their lives intersect with the cultures of the schools in which they are working without completely merging with them.

***

There are many variations of the 'preachers of culture' story and many aspects of it that might profitably be revisited by re-reading key texts within the history of the English curriculum and pedagogy that advocate the value of a literary education. Rather than an exclusive emphasis on the capacity of individual teachers to instil in their pupils a sense of the civilising effects of 'great' literature, those texts can be read as affirming the importance of social relationships as an ineluctable condition for pupils to engage in the literary works chosen for study (Doecke, 2019). But (to hark back to Kirkpatrick and Dixon's definition of 'literary sociability' discussed in Chapter 8), there is no doubt that to shift from a focus on books and writers to foreground the social relationships in which literary works are read and appropriated means rethinking fundamental aspects of a literary education. Such an education is about more than a cultivation of a 'self' conceived as an individual sensibility that is peculiarly open to the language of a poem or the world of a novel, a 'human subject who is sensitive, receptive, imaginative and so on… *about nothing in particular*', to draw on Eagleton's parody of a certain type of literary education (Eagleton, 1985–86, p.98; emphasis in original). As Katya shows us (see vignette), to become an English teacher does not entail an unfolding of her true self, as though she has become the teacher she always knew she was destined to become. In her case, her becoming comprises a series of displacements as she reinvents herself through her active engagement in a variety of social settings, involving a continuing dialectic between her 'self' and the relationships around her.

Her various 'selves' might each be interpreted as a product of the situation in which she happens to be working without supposing that she is not active in the invention of them.

The autobiographies of these early career teachers comprise literary events that resist any attempt to see them as stages on the way to somewhere else, as though they can be mapped onto a developmental continuum that culminates in a fully accomplished English teacher. As we have seen in the case of Rebecca and Janet, the stories they tell evoke moments in their lives that exist in their own right. They have a dialogical character, not only deriving from the professional discourse in which we participated with them but because of their sense of obligation to the pupils in their care. Their worlds are constituted by a relationship between 'I' and 'you' (cf. Hourd, 1968). The teacher, as the Newbolt Report declared in 1921, 'must exist before the pupil' (Newbolt, 1921, p.25) – the argument the authors of the Report were mounting related to the necessity for proper 'training' that would equip teachers to perform the role of a sympathetic companion to their students in the manner in which the Report desired. But, as our early career teachers have reminded us, to say that the teacher must exist 'before' the pupil not only evokes a temporal sequence but a sense of physical space and proximity. In other words, it signifies the relationship between a teacher and his or her pupils and all the responsibilities that inhere within it.

The question that has motivated our research concerns the experiences of early career teachers as they move from being graduates to teachers of English. Sitting behind this question is a belief that your autobiography is more than simply the unfolding of a 'self' that lies deep within you, as though it is a personal trajectory that you have been able to pursue regardless of the people with whom you interact and situations in which you find yourself. There is a sense in which you are instead the product of those people and situations, including institutional settings like the school and university you attended, and the school at which you are now teaching. Your relationships with others within those settings are mediated by hierarchical structures and obligations that are not of your own choosing but pre-exist you as a set of 'objective' conditions with which you must subjectively come to terms.

The stories that English teachers often tell when they are asked about their motivations for becoming a teacher typically involve recalling how a passion for reading was instilled in them by their education and upbringing. But while such formative experiences obviously continue to exist in the stories about being English teachers that these teachers tell, they constitute a sense of 'self' that is also a function of the relationships and settings in which they are now located. This is not to say that one (institutionalised) version of self completely displaces the others. The remembered events that proliferated in our interviews with early career teachers remain a crucial reference point for them now as they attempt to negotiate developing professional selves and pathways within the institutional settings and school communities in which they find themselves working.

References

Abraham, U. (2016). On their own but not alone: The difficulty in competence-oriented approaches to teaching reading and writing of thinking of 'performance' in communal terms. *Changing English*, 23(3), 209–226. https://doi.org/10.1080/1358684X.2016.1203619.

Allard, A., & Doecke, B. (2017). Telling tales: The value of storytelling for early career teachers. *Pedagogy, Culture & Society*, 25(2), 279–291. https://doi.org/10.1080/14681366.2016.1253602.

Anderson, P. (1969). Components of the national culture. In A. Cockburn & R. Blackburn (Eds.), *Student Power: Problems, Diagnosis, Action*. Harmondsworth: Penguin: 214–284.

Australian Institute for Teaching and School Leadership (AITSL). (n.d.). Available: www.aitsl.edu.au/. Accessed 29 May 2020.

Baldick, C. (1983). *The Social Mission of English Criticism 1848-1932*. Oxford: Oxford University Press.

Ball, S., Kenny, A., & Gardiner, D. (1990). Literacy, politics and the teaching of English. In I. F. Goodson & P. Medway (Eds.), *Bringing English to Order*. London, New York and Philadelphia, PA: The Falmer Press: 47–86.

Barnes, D. (2000). *Becoming an English Teacher*. Sheffield: National Association for the Teaching of English (NATE).

Batsleer, J., Davies, T., O'Rourke, R., & Weedon, C. (1985). *Rewriting English: Cultural Politics of Gender and Class*. London and New York: Methuen.

Departmental Committee, Board of Education. ([1921] 1938). *The Teaching of English in England*. London: His Majesty's Stationery Office. [Cited in text as Newbolt Report]

Department of Education and Science (DES). (1975). *A Language for Life: Report of the Committee of Inquiry appointed by the Secretary of State for Education and Science under the Chairmanship of Sir Alan Bullock F.B.A.* (The Bullock Report). London: Her Majesty's Stationery Office. [Cited in text as Bullock Report]

Doecke, B. (2016). What I 'know': Literary studies and the teaching of English. *Changing English*, 23(3), 292–308. https://doi.org/10.1080/1358684X.2016.1203612.

Doecke, B. (2019). Rewriting the history of subject English through the lens of "literary sociability". *Changing English*, 26(4), 339–356. https://doi.org/10.1080/1358684X.2019.1649116.

Doecke, B., & McClenaghan, D. (2011). *Confronting Practice: Classroom Investigations into Language and Learning*. Putney, NSW: Phoenix Education.

Diamond, F. (2020). Cultural memory in English teaching: A critical autobiographical inquiry. *English Teaching: Practice & Critique*, 19(2), 231–244. https://doi.org/10.1108/ETPC-05-2019-0061.

Eagleton, T. (1985–86). The subject of literature. *Cultural Critique*, Number 2, Winter: 95–104.

Eagleton, T. (1983). *Literary Theory: An Introduction*. Oxford: Blackwell.

Eagleton, T. (2012). *The Event of Literature*. New Haven and London: Yale University Press.

Green, B., & Cormack, P. (2011). Literacy, nation, schooling: Reading (in) Australia. In D. Tröhler, T. S. Popkewitz, & D. F. Labaree (Eds.), *Schooling and the Making of Citizens in the Long Nineteenth Century*. London: Routledge: 240–261.

Griffith, A. I., & Smith, D. E. (2005). *Mothering for Schooling*. New York and London: Routledge Falmer.

Hourd, M. L. ([1949] 1968). *The Education of the Poetic Spirit: A Study of Children's Expression in the English Lesson*. London: Heinemann.

Lee, H. (2010). *To Kill a Mockingbird*. New York: Harper Perennial Modern Classics.

Mathieson, M. (1975). *The Preachers of Culture: A Study of English and its Teachers*. London: Allen & Unwin.

Medway, P., Hardcastle, J., Brewis, G., & Crook, D. (2014). *English Teachers in a Postwar Democracy: Emerging Choice in London Schools 1945–1965*. New York: Palgrave Macmillan.

Miller, J. (1995). Trick or treat? The autobiography of the question. *English Quarterly: Teachers: Stories and Reflexions*, 27(3), 22–26.

Ministerial Council on Education, Employment, Training and Youth Affairs (MCEETYA). (2008). *Melbourne Declaration on Educational Goals for Young Australians*. Available: www.mceecdya.edu.au/mceecdya/melbourne_declaration,25979.html. Accessed 1 May 2022.

Mishler, E. G. (1986). *Research Interviewing: Context and Narrative*. Cambridge, MA: Harvard University Press.

Newbolt, H. (Chair), The Departmental Committee appointed by the President of the Board of Education to inquire into the position of English in the educational system of England (1921). *The Teaching of English in England*. London: His Majesty's Stationery Office.

Reid, I. (1984). *The Making of Literature: Texts, Contexts and Classroom Practices*. Adelaide: Australian Association for the Teaching of English.

Rosenblatt, L. (1978). *The Reader, the Text, the Poem: The Transactional Theory of the Literary Work*. Carbondale, IL: Southern Illinois University Press.

Smith, D. E. (2005). *Institutional Ethnography: A Sociology for People*. Lanham, MD: AltaMira Press.

Teese, R., & Polesel, J. (2003). *Undemocratic Schooling: Equity and Quality in Mass Secondary Education in Australia*. Carlton: Melbourne University Press.

13

NARRATIVES, INSIGHTS AND NEXT STEPS FOR QUESTIONS OF LITERARY KNOWLEDGE AND ENGLISH TEACHING

Larissa McLean Davies, Brenton Doecke, Philip Mead, Wayne Sawyer and Lyn Yates

> 'What will this study do? And what is the aim of it? Where is my knowledge going?'
> *(Angela, third year interview)*

The substantive chapters of the book have shown that, as the researchers, we have approached the project's key questions about literature in English with different emphases, reflecting our own backgrounds, knowledges and experiences, our literary and teacher education, and our professional experiences and standpoints (Smith, 2005). As we indicated in Chapter 2, it is through these personal and professional narratives that we, like the participants in our project, have perceived the intersecting fields of English education, literature teaching, curriculum studies, and literary studies research. The interdisciplinary nature of the project and our conversations – in person and in the pandemic world of 'Zoom', and with colleagues in Australia and internationally, who have generously offered feedback on our thinking – have produced many possibilities for considerations of literature, knowledge and the making of English teachers. This complex work has made us attuned to the value of our different perspectives, and the importance of a multivocal conversation when drawing out insights and key findings.

This is not to say, though, that no conclusions can be arrived at, or to avoid our responsibility for doing so. As Angela reminds us, at the end of her final interview, research into English teaching has the obligation to 'do' something and 'go' somewhere. In this spirit, in this final chapter, we each reflect on what we are taking away from this project, and how our thinking about the project's key questions has changed and developed over the six years we have been working together. In this way, our 'conclusion' is not so much a confirmation of key themes and directions for policy, but an opening up of possibilities and considerations for the present and future of literature in school English in and beyond Australia.

DOI: 10.4324/9781003106890-13

Larissa McLean Davies

In 2018, Wayne and I were asked to give a keynote address at the International Federation of Teachers of English (IFTE) conference in Birmingham, England. This conference drew international participants from the United States, Australia and New Zealand, in addition to strong representation from the United Kingdom. The theme of the conference was 'So many voices, so many worlds' and drawing on the project that has underpinned this book, we titled the keynote 'Making English: Voicing the relationships between literature and knowledge'. The talk was publicised and arranged for the last day of the conference. As I checked the slide presentation and room technology 15 minutes before the scheduled commencement, a British colleague approached me, agitated. 'You can't talk about knowledge', she began, almost breathless, looking at our title slide, 'At least, if you do talk about it, you can't use that word'. We had collaborated previously, and it was clear she wanted to save me from a hostile audience, and professional embarrassment.

I watched the ticking clock and the room beginning to fill. In the Australian context, our project was attempting to open up, rather than close down, debate about texts and language. As a project team, we had not started with a fixed position on either knowledge or literature but were interested in the work teachers do with texts in classrooms, and the kinds of understanding they were bringing to the teaching of school English in the context of diverse, contemporary Australian society. Politically, we were conscious of contributing to a public conversation that had oriented discussion of knowledge in English, manifest in Australia's first national curriculum, towards grammatical, instrumental knowledge of language fundamentally constituted, and away from the literary (McLean Davies & Sawyer, 2018). In the UK context, however, the situation was different. In 2018, the mobilisation of the knowledge curriculum by the previous British Education Minister, Michael Gove, appropriating the argument of Michael Young and colleagues regarding powerful knowledge (Young, 2013), had returned the English curriculum to its canonical, imperial roots (Goodwyn, 2003), and was continuing to have a deeply divisive impact on the English teaching profession (Goodwyn, 2003), with scholars speaking back to instrumental, hierarchical notions of knowledge in this curriculum area. While propositional concepts of knowledge, as we have noted through this book (Chapters 3, 6 and 7), do not sit easily with school English (see also McLean Davies, et al., 2022; Yates et al., 2019) as it is manifest in Anglophone contexts, in the context of hyper-neoliberalism, to talk of knowledge in English seemed synonymous, for many attending the IFTE conference, with a disregard for teacher judgement and the imposition of conservative, canonical approaches to texts (Yandell, 2017; Goodwyn, 2003).

Throughout our project, this professional literary event has become a touchstone for me, a moment to which I have returned when reflecting on the development of my thinking, over time and space, regarding key questions that have concerned us over the course of this research. While I understood, as much as one can as an outsider, the strong desire to orient conversation in the UK away from knowledge, this experience left me with the conviction that, as a profession, we couldn't afford to allow those perpetuating a neoliberal agenda to monopolise and dictate knowledge paradigms. This seemed (then and now) particularly crucial in the context of standards-based cultures, where accountability measures, in Australia, dominate English teachers' work and lives (Doecke, 2019; Manuel et al., 2018), and internationally (O'Sullivan & Goodwyn, 2020; Yandell, 2017), and where the humanities are under threat in tertiary institutions.

Although, as has been discussed in this book (Chapters 4, 6 and 7) and elsewhere (Doecke & Mead, 2018; McLean Davies et al., 2022, Yates et al., 2019), Young's formulations of powerful knowledge fail to capture the complexity of knowledge in English, his provocation that curriculum theorists should be able to answer the question 'What is the important knowledge pupils should acquire at school?' (Young, 2013, p.103) resonated with me, an admission I shared with colleagues at the IFTE conference. Having been responsible for our pre-service English program for several years before this project commenced, I was conscious of the number of times, evoking Medway, Durrant, Dixon and Bullock, that I had introduced a new cohort of English teachers to the subject by framing its changeability, its slipperiness, its fluid centre, and permeable boundaries. I was struck by a participant in a previous study of Lyn's, who had compared her English and physics method classes, reporting that in physics pre-service teachers were able to get down to the business of pedagogy, while in English, considerable time was spent trying to work out what the subject was about (Yates et al., 2016; Yates & Millar, 2016). I could have been the lecturer in charge of this method class, and in the first year of our interviews with early career English teachers, I wondered about the usefulness of this approach.

Many of our teachers conceived literary knowledges, if they chose to think about their work in those terms, in the context of canonical texts, defaulting to conceptions of literature and cultural capital that were not part of their own experiences of reading or of their secondary or tertiary literary educations. As discussed in Chapter 9 and previously (McLean Davies et al., 2022), this conceptualisation evoked a range of responses from our participants. Some rejected the idea of literary knowledge, refusing, to draw on Bourdieu's terms (1979, 1990), to be part of legitimising and consecrating certain practices they felt perpetuated social injustices. For others, this resulted in identifying a body of texts they felt needed to be 'known' and doubting, in some cases, the breadth of textual resources they were bringing to the classroom. These responses articulated with our earlier pilot project data, which showed teachers in both England and Australia negotiating the concept of what it is to be 'well-read' as 21st-century teachers of English (McLean Davies & Sawyer, 2020). Common among the positions offered by our teachers in the first years of interviews was a general unease with the term knowledge itself, and an overriding sense that it could not capture the meaning-making work that was done in English. This concern though was not mirrored by the more experienced teachers we interviewed over the course of the project. Often responsible for senior classes and English coordination, these teachers evoked the language of high-stakes curriculum, identifying specific areas of technical knowledge of language that students needed to demonstrate in order to be rewarded in end-of-year examinations. The reticence to talk about knowledge seemed to belong more to the early career stage, where lack of experience, somewhat paradoxically, resulted in a more expansive sense of literary possibilities.

As a research team, we began to talk more of literature as a way of knowing (Medway, 2010; Walsh, 1969), in part to find a shared language that enabled us to describe the relationship between literature that we were seeing emerge in our conversations with early career teachers. Literary knowing emerged as a concept in the 1960s. For key proponents Walsh (1969) and Cochran (2007), literary knowing takes place on two levels: when the reader engages with the text and then as they imagine and create the text. Like historically similar theoretical approaches to literature, such as reader response (Rosenblatt, 1978) and Growth (Dixon, 1975), literary knowing prioritises the relationship between the reader and the text, rather than the textual object itself. Delehanty, writing later from a literary-critical/historical perspective, suggests that literary knowing enables us to think with the tension between literature as 'being' – an entity itself – or 'doing' to understand the ontological and epistemological interplay between the work, its creator and the reader (Delehanty, 2012, p.10).

As we have discussed in Chapters 7, 9 and 11, the teachers in our study often expressed the desire for students to make a personal and social meaning beyond the text, to elicit an effective response that would enable them to have access to worlds and perspectives that extended and contested those that they had brought with them into the classroom. Similarly, our interviews with literary studies academics (Chapter 6) also articulated the concept of literature as a way of knowing. While, like our teachers, the academics in our study acknowledged the relevance of having certain technical knowledge that enabled the reader to engage with and make meaning with the text, this knowledge of language and form was in the service of a more substantive literary experience beyond the text and the institution. Part of our project has been to trace connections between the tertiary discipline and school subject English and to consider the interface between English teachers' disciplinary training, teaching practice and professional commitments and identity. On the one hand, the project showed that there is often no clear through-line from English teachers' university study to their approaches to teaching. On the other hand, though, the synergy between the views of the early career teachers and literary studies academics, in terms of the broader purposes and relevance of literature beyond classroom encounters, suggests a level of coherence regarding the espoused and desired purposes of a literary education, despite, and in the face of, the decline of the humanities and the neoliberal pressures faced by schools.

If this project has shown that literary knowing and the companion concept of literary sociability (see Chapter 8) offer alternative and productive ways of understanding knowledge in literature, it has, at the same time, drawn attention to the key role teachers play in mediating and brokering literary knowing in classrooms: in focusing on the 'what', and on 'how' meaning is made with and through literature in classrooms, it is important not to underplay the 'who'. This may seem an obvious point to make, in the context of a project which has investigated the relationship between knowledge of and through literature and the making of English teachers, yet what I am arguing here is distinct from, but a result of, the focus of our inquiry. For me, this project has shown as much about what *English teachers make*, as it has shown how and under what circumstances they are made. While the project has drawn to attention, in different ways, the institutional, familiar and textual practices that 'form' 21st-century English teachers, it has also shown teachers' role in shaping literary knowing, and English itself, and alongside this, the challenges they face in ethically enacting this responsibility in the context of decolonising imperatives (Chapter 7).

All of the accounts of practice offered by the early career teachers reveal, at different points, how they are constrained by assessment and accountability agendas. In this context, literary knowing, which as Kasprisin (1987) observes, is always and inevitably mediated by institutions, seems additionally constrained (see Chapters 6, 7 and 8). At the same time, we also observe through the vignettes in this volume the powerful ways in which, amid these challenges, the sociable relationships that teachers have with texts and their reading communities in the past and present can also determine the limits and scope of students access to literary meaning-making (Chapter 9). This is not to say that texts should stand as a proxy for literary knowing (Chapter 4), but rather, as Haraway reminds us, that 'It matters what stories tell stories; it matters whose stories tell stories' (2019, p.1).

What does this mean for English teacher education and professional learning? Books about English teaching often claim that English is at a crossroads, or a crisis – it needs to be understood for 'today and tomorrow' (Watson & Eagleson, 1977); 'rewritten' (Batsleer et al., 1985); 'brought to order' (Goodson & Medway, 1990) and 'reviewed' (Sawyer & Gold, 2004). In some ways, I concur with this sentiment: as the major institutional and educational apparatus for colonisation, in 2022, English in Australia and other settler and Anglophone nations must be recast and reimagined (Phillips et al., 2022). As some early career teachers in our study have shown, students' encounters with literature play a key part in this justice work. While this is often difficult (see Chapter 9; also McLean Davies & Buzacott, 2021), it seems that articulating the personal and collective possibilities of literary knowing, and the role teachers play in mediating textual experiences, is vital. Rather than avoiding or deflecting debates about knowledge or presenting beginning teachers with a vision of English as uncentred and amorphous, this project has shown me, among many other insights, the future value of introducing teachers' literary ways of knowing as a key ontological and epistemological practice in English, so that they might have agency in shaping the subject justly, for their students and themselves.

Brenton Doecke

The stories the early career teachers have shared about their experiences of reading literary texts when they were younger show the salience of their autobiographies for understanding the value a literary education has had for them. This is the key lesson that I have taken from this project. By saying this, however, I am doing more than highlighting the role that anyone's upbringing might play in forming a disposition to engage with literary texts, important though such a focus might be for recognising how subject English has historically acted as a vehicle for discriminating between students with respect to the cultural capital they bring to school and their location in the class structure. As it happens, hardly any of our interviewees experienced a disjunction between the values of their families or communities and the values and expectations associated with formal schooling, though it is noteworthy that very few of them are the products of the wealthy private schools that cater for social elites in Australia and that provide sites for students with the right dispositions and cultural baggage to enjoy educational success (Teese, [2000] 2013, pp.44–49; Teese, 2011, pp.14–15). Several of the stories the early career teachers tell reflect their experiences of being 'first in the family' to make the transition from secondary school to a university education, including moments when they were puzzled and even intimidated by the game of literary interpretation that their English teachers were encouraging them to play. Yet here is the paradox: the literary events they recount as being significant in their literary socialisation were moments when they became aware of possibilities that took them beyond the values and beliefs of the communities where they grew up, while at the same time giving rise to a recognition that it was their education and upbringing that provided the conditions for them to imagine those larger possibilities in the first place.

Janet's story about reading *Jane Eyre* and discovering it 'was all about feminism', Rebecca's recognition of the unsettling effect when she heard Peter Skrzynecki talk about his poetry, Katya's story about becoming aware of the multivalent character of Wilfred Owen's poems – Philip and I have observed how such literary events disrupt any notion of a literary continuum that charts the progress that students make from one level of development to the next as they engage with literary texts judged to be of increasing complexity (see Chapter 11; see also Mead & Doecke, 2020). Those literary events might be said to transcend the moments in which they occurred, constituting the teachers' identities as human beings without giving rise to any definitive answers to questions about who they are and who they might become. The early career teachers continually pose these questions by returning to these events to grapple with their meaning. Their iterative character shows the hold those memories have on them, something that becomes apparent from the importance several of them place on revisiting texts they have read at a particular moment in their lives in order to gauge their significance for them now.

The experience of returning to a particular text some years after you first read it obviously prompts a comparison between your initial response and the meanings you take from it now, but this does not necessarily mean judging one reading to be naïve and the other somehow more sophisticated. Brittney recalls how her responses to particular texts changed after she left university and travelled a bit:

> …I travelled a bit more and sort of met a larger and greater variety of people, I think I brought that experience to the novels that I was reading, and I do remember that being said in one of the university courses and it really

resonated in that the person that you are today is not the person that you were five years ago and is not the person that you're going to be in five years' time, so the way that you approach each of those texts... sorry the way that you approach that same text in each of those different time periods is going to be different.

Brittney is gesturing towards dimensions of reading that elude a dominant educational discourse that reifies the steady acquisition of a set of skills that supposedly culminates in what might be deemed to be an accomplished reader. Similarly, Laura relates how after initially studying *The Great Gatsby* and *The Catcher in the Rye* when she was a senior secondary school student, she returns to those novels 'every year, I read it once every year', even though she has since read more widely and has a richer array of literary resources on which to draw. By contrast, Morgan recalls thinking that *Catch 22* was 'a brilliant book, just a fantastic book' when she read it in secondary school, but she has never read it again 'because I don't ever want to be disappointed by going back and finding that it wasn't as amazing as I thought it was at the time' – an admission that still illustrates how such literary events are constitutive of one's sense of self or identity. Morgan knows that the meaning she was able to make from reading *Catch 22* arose out of her subjective investment in the text at that time, but the 'self' that she has since become would be likely to experience a very different type of encounter if she were to read the book again.

These various reflections by the early career teachers on what it means to re-read a text may hardly appear to be saying anything startlingly new about the complexities of a 'literary' reading. Yet the very commonality of this experience has prompted me to pause and consider why this practice isn't sufficiently acknowledged as a vital dimension of a literary education when it comes to teaching literature in schools (or for that matter universities). One of the abiding impressions that I've taken away from the corpus of interviews we conducted with these early career teachers is the way that so many facets of their autobiographical accounts of their experiences as readers, most notably their emphasis on reading as a sociable activity and all that follows from a recognition of the way that interpersonal relationships mediate the reading of literary texts, seem to be systematically excluded from the official curriculum and the assessment practices that underpin it. Those dimensions are reduced to something incidental to an individual's growth as a reader, or at best to conditions that might support an individual's development as educational systems construct it, when, for example, a teacher gives students opportunities to talk about a novel before requiring them to write about the same text under exam conditions when absolute silence is imposed.

The early career teachers we interviewed have no choice but to live with the paradox of continuing to try to enhance a sensitivity towards literary language on the part of their students while attempting to meet the demands of a system that is geared towards privileging functional literacy and the understanding of language that underpins standardised testing and competitive examinations as an individual cognitive achievement. Language is something you are taught 'about', something external to you requiring you to learn its rules to function effectively within a larger public sphere, not something that you experience subjectively, which is inextricably bound up with the very pulse of your being and your awareness of others. Yet I have found the stories the early career teachers have told heartening for the way they continually register dimensions of their own literary socialisation that exceed the way policy and curriculum documents attempt to classify and hierarchise students' capacities to engage with literary texts. This is so, even though they are working within institutional settings where everything that teachers do is directed towards producing outcomes that conflict with the tentativeness and open-endedness of meaning-making as it unfolds as you engage with a literary text. When I revisit their interviews, I continually find myself speculating on the kind of curriculum development that might be possible were they given an opportunity to build on what they have learned through their autobiographies as readers. This process might, in the first instance, take the form of further reflective conversations with colleagues of the kind they enjoyed through participating in this project. Such conversations might eventually lead to a re-envisioning of the English curriculum and specifically the place of literature within it.

Brittney, for one, immediately teases out the significance of her experience of revisiting literary texts not only for her professional practice but with respect to the larger project of a literary education:

> So, I think I was aware of that sense, and I was also aware that if I was teaching, especially a younger class in Year 7 or Year 8, that they're going to view the text in a very different way than I would view it. And you can't necessarily… I don't think you can necessarily assume how they're going to view it because they've got experiences that you don't know about really.

Brittney is talking about much more than the difference between her knowledge and skills as an English graduate and the more limited interpretive strategies that her students might bring to their reading of the texts chosen for study as these might be set out on a continuum of learning. The challenge as she characterises it is more complex than devising strategies that give her students the same access to the text that is available to her as a 'mature' or 'sophisticated' reader. The difference she is pinpointing between herself and her students isn't primarily one between her knowledge as a teacher and their lack of knowledge, as though it is her job to render her literary theoretical knowledge in a concrete and accessible form for them (as with the valorisation of propositional knowledge underpinning Shulman's concept of pedagogical content knowledge). To conceive of a literary pedagogy in these terms would be to lose sight of the richly complex nature of reading as she is conceptualising it. She gestures towards that complexity through her reference to 'experiences that you don't know about really', paradoxically reversing the hier-archical relationship between herself as a teacher and her students by positioning herself as the one who does not 'know'. She is acknowledging that her students are appropriating the text selected for study based on their own experiences, their own beliefs and values and that it is only thus that it might constitute a personally significant moment in their lives.

For Brittney, the activity of re-reading texts is a vehicle for becoming reflexively aware of her own beliefs and values and how these might mediate her interactions with her students. Such reflexivity is fundamental to her pedagogy as an English teacher. This is a radically different conception of her experience as a reader from the understanding of an individual's growth embedded in the continua of learning that have proliferated since the advent of the outcomes-based curriculum. And it seems reasonable to assume that she is conceptualising the intersection between her students' experiences and the world of the text in the same terms, as an opportunity to engage with questions of who they are and how they relate to the people around them.

Again, I'm hardly pretending that such insights are startlingly new. Yet that is partly the point I am trying to make. A rich historical literature exists that affirms the role that a literary education might play in the lives of people that has been systematically excluded by standards-based reforms and the knowledge those reforms privilege. In the course of my participation in this project, I have found it enriching to revisit this literature to understand the insights the early career teachers have offered us (see Doecke, 2017, 2019; Doecke & Mead, 2018; Mead & Doecke, 2020; Mead et al., 2020). When, for example, Louise Rosenblatt remarks that each reader brings to a literary transaction 'not only a specific past life and literary history, not only a repertory of internalised "codes", but also a very active present, with all its preoccupations, anxieties, questions and aspirations' (Rosenblatt, 1978, p.144), she seems to me to be conceptualising the reading of literary texts in a way that is akin to the insights that many of the early career teachers are attempting to express. Rosenblatt gestures towards the 'powerful educational implications' that flow from a recognition of the need 'to consider texts always in relation to specific readers and specific cultural situations and to honour the role of literary experience in the context of individual lives' (Rosenblatt, 1978, p.161). She insists that the literary transaction is irreducibly 'personal', even when – as is the case with literary scholars and critics who are active within the field of literary studies – you draw on wider fields of knowledge to justify your response to a text (Rosenblatt, 1978, p.174).

I am aware of the dangers of ascribing views to the early career teachers that they do not share, and yet I also feel that they know more than they know, that their insights resonate within a larger history of English curriculum and pedagogy whether they are fully aware of this or not, that the understandings they achieve as they reflect on their experiences as teachers of literature provide a counterpoint to the functional model of language underpinning standards-based reforms. The challenge is for all of us to try to think outside the mental cage that those reforms impose on us.

Lyn Yates

This study began with a focus on literary studies and subject English from a context of current debates and accountabilities about 'knowledge'. We were interested in how new teachers today understand their subject and their purposes, what knowledge and experiences they bring to their work, and what develops or changes over their first three years of teaching. I had recently studied teachers of two other subjects, history and science, and brought some comparative interest in these questions to this study. In Chapter 2, I concluded my own 'biography of the question' by asking whether this study would allow me to 'crack the codes' of what literary studies is about. What I have begun to see from the project is the extent to which that 'cracking the codes' perspective is both helpful and not helpful as an approach to seeing the specificity of literary studies. And even more, I have been struck by the inevitable and irreconcilable tensions between what the teachers understand as the educational project of literary studies and the system-level concerns with 'quality' and 'fairness' and comparability across schools and teachers and students.

It was not a surprise to me that the term 'knowledge' was not readily acceptable to the teachers. They largely interpreted the term in its everyday sense of propositional truths and resisted claims that 'literary knowledge' constituted acquaintance with a specific range of texts or that the point of the textual studies was to convey a set of designated truths, or even that the technical tools or concepts that are part of the subject are the core of what it is. Even more striking to me from our first-year interviews was a comparative insight. Where the history and science teachers I had studied earlier located their subject explicitly in relation to their cognate disciplines (Yates et al., 2016), the teachers in this study seemed to identify more with a concept of English as a *school subject*, and of being an English *school teacher*. In relation to arguments about 'powerful knowledge' or 'pedagogical content knowledge' and the like, these teachers did not see themselves primarily as 'translators' of a discipline they had themselves acquired in their tertiary studies. They had a sense of what they were trying to achieve, but it was more open-ended and multi-faceted than many of the sociological arguments about curriculum discussed in Chapter 4 adequately recognised. In any case (see Chapter 5), the changing forms and contested nature of literary studies in the 'disciplinary' world also limit the appropriateness of any simple ideas of the subject as a translation of knowledge or ways of knowing from that domain.

The sense that there was not one single reference point for this subject of the 'pedagogical content knowledge' or 'disciplinary translator' kind is also there if we consider what we learnt from the teachers over these three years of their school experience. In a number of cases, they were put into positions of leadership over more experienced colleagues. In other cases, their initial awareness of 'holes' in their knowledge, or their initial sense of why they wanted to be an English teacher, did not disappear but were resolved by trying new practices or accepting the inevitability of never perfectly fulfilling the competing tensions they saw as the external expectations for their subject. Almost all of them heightened their sense of different school populations and cultures and the difference this made not only to what they had to do but what it made sense to do. And this wasn't just about adopting a form of student-centred progressivism, it was about their changing, expanding, conflicted sense of literary studies and literature.

Our decision to begin with a question about 'literary knowledge' was prompted by some features of the current context and arguments about schooling, but it was also one way of asking the teachers (over each of the three years) to talk about what is the point or intention of this subject, what are they trying to do with it, what do they want their students to get from it? Here what was striking was the extent to which they were interested in the diversity and specificity of their students and the engagement and exchanges (with texts, with discussions) in the classroom itself. Our teachers certainly kept an eye on how the mechanics of language or literary analysis were understood by their students or needed development and provided strategies and tools to develop these. And they were very alert to the specific criteria at work in standards testing and in their respective State-based high-stakes examination and tried to ensure that students knew enough of the rules of the game and the hidden curriculum to not be disadvantaged. But there was a strong sense too that narrowly adopting a backward-mapping exam-based approach, or simply focusing on technical concepts or tools, was to miss the point of literary studies, which was to draw students into *engaging* with literature, culture, language, meanings and the students' own lives.

From a school system perspective, the knowledge issue touches on some additional agendas, and these too impact on the teachers. Official curriculum frameworks and tests set up an official perspective on which content, concepts and abilities matter for students to be exposed to (and these selections are almost always contested or at least debated by the teachers). And the knowledge issue is linked also to system-level and political approaches to teacher quality (Is teachers' knowledge base sound enough? What needs to be covered in teacher education?), and to national or State approaches to driving what should be developed for students over time (the Australian Curriculum framework to ensure different 'standards' at different year levels). Of course, these system 'interests' have not always been interpreted or enacted with the kinds of micro-management and measurement tools that have become characteristic of recent developments. But what I want to draw attention to here is that the thrust of these orientations to subject English as part of a school system is currently embedded in a 'pinning down' accountability orientation. It seeks evidence and measurements showing that the regulations, constraints and accountabilities are in place and being achieved. What the teachers in the study often talked about as their overall purpose or successes was more like an 'opening up' orientation, a view of school purposes described in earlier times as an 'education' mission as distinct from today's favoured public concept of a 'learning' mission (some of this was discussed earlier in Chapter 9).

Going back to the issue of 'cracking the codes'. Throughout this project, I engaged in an ongoing dialogue with my colleagues from English education and literary studies about 'sociability': what was meant by this term, why they found it helpful, how it differs from other sociological readings of classroom messages and interactions, where were the literary texts in the concept, whether they were sliding from using it as an analytic or methodological tool to a normative one. I did not find this a powerful new idea in the way that they seemed to do. However, what I did begin to see better (as Biesta has also argued, see Chapter 4) were the limits of critical sociological readings of classrooms (of Bourdiuean or Foucauldian types) as distinct from also thinking about educational *purposes* and what of value might be initiated for young people. One of our starting points, Michael Young's case about 'powerful knowledge', was also an attempt to redirect curriculum sociologists to say more about purposes and what is of value in education, not just about the harm schooling does. But as many others have noted, the model of knowledge in those arguments does not translate to a subject or field like literary studies where language, meanings, re-assessments and disputed value judgements are intrinsic. As I understand it, the arguments about sociability in earlier chapters are wanting to emphasise the social world of the classroom as one that not only mediates reading practices and interpretations, but is a specific creator of these, a 'condition of possibility' that has not been given enough weight in relation to broader academic work about literature. That does not mean that critical perspectives on values and meanings and who is excluded or advantaged are not also relevant to the classroom exchange. The tension between teaching creatively and effectively and reflecting critically on its inevitable limitations and harms is very self-conscious in many of these teachers.

When first discussing this chapter, Larissa and Wayne suggested some questions we might return to, in particular 'What is literary knowing?' and 'What is the education project of literary studies?' I think these are interesting and important questions. I did not initially agree with the value of changing 'knowledge' to 'knowing' as the descriptor for this book because I think it gives up the idea that there are different forms of knowledge, and risks undermining the role of the humanities in education (even more than is already happening, at least in Australia). But also, because I find it even harder to answer the question 'What is literary knowing?' than I do the question about knowledge and forms of knowledge. In some ways, as an outsider to literary studies, I could answer it more in terms of what it is not.

I also think about some of the limitations of this project. It was not designed to examine better and worse teaching, or the demands on systems (or individual schools) to decide who can be employed as English teachers, what supports they need, what limits (if any) should be placed on their freedoms to teach whatever they want and however they want. The project was designed to see how these teachers understood their subject, how they negotiated their first years of experiences in particular schools, what they were trying to put together. The teachers in our study were based in different States and had undertaken different kinds of degrees and degree structures. While they shared to some extent the kinds of concerns I discussed above, in putting together awareness of language, understanding exam criteria, engaging with texts and with their students and other teachers about culture, meaning and experiences via textual encounters, they do not all emphasise the same things. Some are concerned most with reading as a tool; or wanting to see noticeable improvements in writing; others with generating critical alertness and sensitivities; others with doing everything they can to have students experience the pleasures of reading. This scope for teachers to have different interests is a challenge in contemporary times, where the emphasis is on visible and uniform criteria for what is being achieved by different teachers and subjects. Yet the experience of school (and of particular schools for different individuals), not just the exam results, matters to students and who they become in the world beyond school (McLeod & Yates, 2006). Murray's recent memoir of one year of his work as a schoolteacher is a vivid and moving literary illustration of this point (Murray, 2021).

When systems of schooling were set up it was in part to draw young people to be part of the nation, to give them skills, particularly literacy and numeracy, that would take them beyond the local. Engaging with selections of literature with civic and colonial purposes was always part of that agenda. I know that my co-authors on this project largely object to the idea of a canon, and particularly one that sidelines Australian literature, and are dismissive of Margaret Mathieson's earlier concept of English teachers in the UK as 'preachers of culture'. And yet I am not so sure that this is an inappropriate phrase (though 'carriers' or 'facilitators' might be more apt than 'preachers') for what I saw in this project as 'the education project of literary studies'. The culture teachers convey or facilitate is not just about author and text selection. When these teachers act as a kind of generalist teacher whose concern is to have students engage with a range of texts and different meanings and readings and the experiences they and others bring to the discussion, or when they explore with students the situated nature of authors and texts, learning to understand more about language and meanings through differently located literatures, they are valuing and attempting to build an engagement with the broader culture, both in the past and present and going forward. Critical and aesthetic judgements are part of this, though the latter are only briefly touched on in this study. Culture is not a monolith, and the kinds of tensions the teachers are aware of and try to work with and open up, in relation to their specific students and the particular texts and institutional settings they work in, reflect this.

Wayne Sawyer

Our early career teachers reflected something of that historical opaqueness that subject English has had with regard to 'knowledge' and which we discussed in Chapter 3 – an opaqueness that especially relates to the teaching of literature. This has been paradoxical because English has usually been positioned to assert knowledge claims through, for example, the role that examinations have in assessment, including in literature. This ongoing institutional imperative around literature's contribution to the knowledge-related functions of schooling may be in tension with those arguments which recognise the very basis of the discipline as 'elusive, problematic and ambiguous' (Parr, 2011, p.82). Central to this paradox is that English holds, and has held throughout the 20th century, a privileged position at the centre of curriculum configurations in the English-speaking world, its status firmly embedded and unproblematic. In fact, English is so central that it is routinely 'more than part of larger changes in education and society; it has been the focus of those changes, a battleground on which fundamental educational issues have been fought' (Goodwyn, 2001, p.149).

The project reported in this book stands at the intersection of literature, knowledge and education. Its central question for me is 'What is the *educational* project of literature?' (with a key related question about the role, and nature, of knowledge in that project). We are accustomed to talking about the nature of literature teaching, as Frow suggests, as 'less the imparting of systematic information than the teaching of a practice – of "reading"' (Frow, 2002, pp.152–153). But what it means to 'teach reading', and what the point of 'teaching reading' is at the secondary school level, are also the central issues here. Considering the educational project of literature in this way means necessarily, I think, beginning with thinking about readers, and all literary theories carry with them an implied position about readers – or, from an educational standpoint, an implied *pedagogy*. As Louise Rosenblatt has argued, 'a theory of literature implies a theory of literary education' (Rosenblatt, 1978, p.146). Critical literacy, for example – which held some prominence in Australia in the 1980s and 1990s – usually rooted in post-structuralist theory, was often consciously 'didactic' (Boomer, 1989) and 'authoritarian' (Ball et al., 1990) in its classroom pedagogy (see also Patterson, 1992). Reader response theories – aligned by John Dixon himself with the Growth Model in *Growth Through English* [1] – have held a prominent position in discussions of literary *education* in schools since the Growth movement precisely because theories that place so prominent an emphasis on the role of the reader also implicitly put the *student* at the centre of such discussion (see Mason & Giovanelli, 2021; Thomson, 1987).[2] Our teachers highly value the experience of literature for their students in their classrooms. They see literature as carrying the key conceptual – indeed, the key intellectual – work of the subject, even though they do not see this as being advanced at the cost of more fundamental literacies.

What does this say about these teachers' understanding of the role that the literary imagination and literary language play in our lives? Our teachers did have an interestingly consistent (though not universal) set of views about the value that literature had for their students: exposing those students to contexts of experience and worldviews; a broadening of perspectives on the world or presenting the world in conceptually new ways. I have referred to forms of knowledge such as 're-cognition' or 'understanding' in these contexts in Chapters 10 and 11 above (Gibson, 2009; Simpson, 2013; Yandell, 2017). None of this is unproblematic in literary-theoretical terms, of course, but neither is it naïve and may be a singularly important aspect of the role of the literary in secondary classrooms with adolescent readers. Along with this is the focus on language. Elsewhere in this chapter strong arguments are presented about literature as a 'way of knowing'. Just as a painting of boots by van Gogh may suggest 'the toilsome tread of the worker' through representing the 'dark opening of the worn insides of the shoes' (Heidegger in Pike, 2003, p.98), so too does literature 'offer ideas and symbols that can serve as foci for things students think and feel about the human condition or the state of the world' (Medway, 2010, p.10). Literature as a way of knowing, then, occurs through the way that language *represents* experience – through its very textuality. Felski speaks in the following terms about 'knowledge' in literature:

...one motive for reading is the hope of gaining a deeper sense of everyday experiences and the shape of social life. Literature's relationship to worldly knowledge is not only negative or adversarial; it can also expand, enlarge, or reorder our sense of how things are.

This repertoire of sense-making devices is firmly anchored in the formal and generic properties of literary texts.

(Felski, 2008, p.83)

Felski's 'motive for reading' here reflects many of the views and pedagogical aspirations of our early career teachers. This is not only a question of the role of experiences that students individually and collectively bring to bear to make meaning of a text but the strong sense that the nature of 'experience' itself is at the centre of the subject. Experience *is* brought to bear to understand texts, but the understanding of the experience that texts and readers enact is itself the focus of literary study.

'Making connections' was a phrase we heard often – in the context of making meaning, in the context of engagement and as the intellectual project of the subject. '[C]onnections... into their own worlds' (Laura) seemed not to be just about students' route to understanding, but to be the point of the subject itself – literature as a field for issues that touch on social/historical/philosophical/psychological worlds (many of which might otherwise exist only outside the formal curriculum). It raises an interesting question in general terms about the kind of disciplined enquiry entailed in a subject in which 'experience' plays such a central part. These teachers convey a sense that 'knowing' relates strongly to personal engagement. Felski's second point that these knowledges are rooted in 'the formal and generic properties of literary texts' highlights textuality, the sense of 'literature as a way of knowing' through representation, through the place of language in meaning-making.

It is interesting – and central to our project – to ask what knowledges are brought to bear by the teacher in this classroom work? What is entailed in a teacher's ability to exploit the 'connections' discussed here, and to see that 'textuality as a form of knowing' goes beyond their students simply knowing *about*, say, literary techniques? For me, the ability to exploit such connections is linked to that teacher's own literary education, as well as being tied to the pedagogies of English education.

In Chapters 10 and 11 above, the prominence of classroom discussion as a central pedagogy in English is an unproblematic given. Enabling students to talk with one another, when they are able to draw on their own experiences to make meaning from texts, or seizing opportunities for them to share their reading – these ideas seem to reflect a similar logic, prompting one to ask: Can the full potential of the literary imagination only begin to be realised when the teaching of literature is reconceptualised around talk and the other forms of sociolinguistic interaction? Turvey and Yandell argue that classroom conversations and pedagogies like role-play mean that:

> Over time, signs – loneliness, 'prejudice', 'power' – are remade, filled with increasingly dense, rich meanings… the everyday knowledge that students bring with them has the capacity to transform and reorganise the curricularised, canonical knowledge of schooling.
>
> *(Turvey & Yandell, 2011, p.165)*

We have discussed in this book the role of the classroom itself as a community in creating knowledge around literature and literary texts. Talk around literature can be where 'funds of knowledge' meet 'powerful knowledge' (Moll et al., 1992; Young & Muller, 2013) – a notion, indeed, that is also thrown up by the conceptualisation of the reading process itself as 'transaction'. Issues such as the place of talk and reading-as-transaction also raise larger questions about the relationship between *knowledge* and *practice* being opened up by this project. This is a different issue from Shulman's (1987) pedagogical content knowledge. It is the case that we are concerned here with how secondary English teaching, the teaching of literature, is shaped in terms of subject-disciplinary focus, but also as situated professional practice (see Doecke et al., 2007). Importantly, as Green argues, in a context in which knowledge is 'made' – in action – then curriculum and pedagogy become effectively inseparable, 'as two sides of the one coin' and with 'knowledge conceived in these terms… understood as a dynamic category' (Green, 2018, p.246).

In any project of this kind, a tension between being simply descriptive of practice and views of normative practice is perhaps inevitable. Are there ways of teaching literature that we see as desirable that were not discussed by our early career teachers? My discussion of imaginative recreation in Chapter 11, for example, opened this issue as just one instance of what I personally see as mainstream pedagogy for literature that can speak back to, say, the 'lit. crit.' essay as the default expression of literary knowledge. Yet the point of the work reported in this book is partly to understand literature teaching and the complexities of teachers' work as framed by this moment. It looks at the kinds of sociability, for example, that are operating under the institutional constraints that separate the current era of schooling from the kinds of sociability originally discussed by Kirkpatrick and Dixon (2012). The relationship between literacy and literature discussed in Chapter 10 is a good example of the need for descriptive research of the sort reported in this book. We did not begin the project with any focus on how 'basic' or 'fundamental' or 'instrumentalist' literacy might especially be an issue for our teachers in relation to questions of literary *knowledge*. In the current global education environment, it is not difficult to find evidence for a dichotomy between the demands of literacy and literature in the larger project of English, as is often done.[3] Documenting what teachers report of their classrooms, however, reveals more complex, nuanced social *practice* to bring into curricular, pedagogical and epistemological discussions. It addresses some ways in which classrooms and systems with a concern for the literary work within a highly instrumentalist and functionalist literacy landscape.

Philip Mead

Part of the context we were aware of throughout this project was the contentious, even troubled, centrality of English. English remains a mandated subject in many countries, as it does in Australia, where it is one of the core subjects or learning areas of the Australian Curriculum across all the years of schooling. Even where the *Australian Curriculum: English* hasn't been fully adopted from F-12, English is usually a core subject of study. English is a privileged subject in this sense, but at the same time its curricular components, teaching modes and assessment regimes differ across jurisdictions; these are also constantly changing, and constantly responding to shifting educational imperatives. Larissa and Wayne's analysis of the AC: E is a relevant case in point (McLean Davies & Sawyer, 2018). There is very little that is settled or agreed about compulsory English's structure.

My perspective is also informed by the very different fate of English, or literary studies, at the tertiary level where its national profile and resourcing reflects the global decline in the humanities, as well as specific governmental disincentives in the humanities in Australia. In 2020, for instance, the Coalition Government in Australia increased the cost of studying some university humanities subjects by more than 100%. It seems like the aim is to discourage young people from studying English in conjunction with media, communications, visual arts, journalism, film studies and, in some cases, creative writing, which they have done for decades now. This is part of a broad higher education policy framework that is focused primarily on STEM fields and the commercialisation of research. The evidence so far, though, is that this attempt at governmental control of educational choices is having little effect. Nevertheless, the dichotomy between English as an assured compulsory secondary subject and its struggles at the tertiary level is stark. The ongoing effects of this difference on the education and experience of early career English teachers are hard to predict. But it reflects a set of contradictions within Australian society about the centrality or privilege of English as an area of study and learning.

Our early career teachers were sensitive gauges of this complex educational terrain. They had been students of earlier versions of English at school, had studied some form of English or related disciplines at the tertiary level, and found themselves in classrooms and teaching roles where English was something they needed to negotiate for themselves. Sidebar: they might also have experienced the diffusion or lack of centrality of English or literary studies in the tertiary curriculum and the precariousness of their teachers' working lives (see Chapter 5). For them, compulsory secondary English wasn't a stable, settled curricular progression they could just walk into the classroom and deliver according to some handed-down pedagogical practice. In the process of encountering the school and the classroom these teachers were creating, in collaboration with their students and colleagues, their professional and personal subjectivities and practices as English teachers. This often involved sometimes stressful degrees of adaptation, significant learning efforts, and often self-doubt. But what carried them through were their very individual ideas of becoming English teachers.

We wanted to address the problems in current thinking about the value of English, or of a literary education – by no means the same thing. An important question here was about the idea of literary knowledge, a seemingly innocent formulation, but one with controversial theoretical, educational and political valencies as Larissa's anecdote here about the UK IFTE conference illustrates. What constitutes literary knowledge and what is its value? What is the relation of knowledge about literature to knowledge about language? Because of their immersion in the intense, everyday work of English teaching these questions tended to remain abstract ones for our teachers. For some, the word 'knowledge' itself had a less than positive connotation; they shied away from it. They could sense that it was a word caught up in an ideological contention that was somehow at odds with their own commitments to and understandings of, English and literature teaching. Often the word was associated in their minds with a conservative notion of a timeless or unquestioned literary canon. Experience was to be privileged over knowledge. Nevertheless, they were able to discuss these perspectives with us.

My thinking about those key questions of literary knowledge, teacher education and pedagogical practice has developed from both the extended dialogue within our research group, including critical reflection and our engagement with our early career teacher interviewees. As an antidote to the idea of literary knowledge as restricted to a prescribed list of iconic texts, it seemed to be important to acknowledge the multiplicity and diversity of literary knowledge, of the many ways of knowing that English encompasses. Anyway, it's easy to rethink our knowledge of texts that have been constructed as canonical simply by asking the question, 'What is a classic?' The multiple modes of literary knowing were evident in the many facets of the English education system that we considered: models of English teaching (cultural preaching, growth, social mission), curricular discourse, instrumentalist pressures (standardised testing), upper secondary external assessment, the sociability of the classroom (and seminar room, lectures, etc), the distinctiveness of linguistic and literary knowledge, theory, national comparisons, the secondary/tertiary nexus, the role of literary production and creative writing. The lines of connection and intersection between these facets comprised a formidably tangled diagram on the whiteboard. But the system of English education is not an aggregate of closely linked elements, despite the appearance of some curriculum documents. Nor, as we know, is the experience of English neatly staged, based on agreed foundations, socially equitable, or politically neutral. English teachers are formed by and work within the loose and shifting constellation of institutions and practices designed to provide formal understandings of, or ways of knowing about, language and literature, usually linked to assessment regimes. And because we all live within the social being of language and language organises the way we see and understand the world, knowledge about language is also knowledge about ourselves and our communal contexts and histories (family, community, society, etc.). We have all made our way through this constellation, just as our interviewees have, but none of our paths through has been the same.

Learning about speaking, reading and writing English can involve a vast array of multi-levelled inquiries, theories, skills, disciplines, practices and histories. Ways of knowing about English can be linguistic, literary, political, digital, historical, performative, national. The word 'knowledge' may sound unchanging and solidified as if it's an object or an edifice, but in reality, it is not that. Knowledge is only ever the result of learning – an activity driven by ways of knowing – and that is an unresolved and open-ended process. Literary knowing, to use the present participle, has a privileged status within this context because it's not just an add-on; it is one of the primary ways in which we understand language. I'm thinking of literary knowing here in the broadest sense – reading, writing, verbal, creative – not in terms of some narrow shelf of heritage texts.

The engagements of this project have also developed my understanding of the realities of literary knowledge, teacher education and pedagogical practice. These realities are always worth recalling because they are part of the everyday professional lives of English teachers, which our interviewees constantly reminded us of, as well as of crucial theoretical import for the discourse of English. Our reading is always partial and incomplete, literary texts can sometimes resist our understanding almost entirely, language is often riddled with ambiguities, meaning-making in the classroom is often unpredictable or formed by sociable contingencies, writing is a process of continual redrafting, verbal communication is a constant battle against misunderstanding, literary knowledge is endlessly evolving. These are not deficits of the system of English that need to be corrected or compensated for, but realities of the engagement with language and literary texts – personal, critical, pedagogical and creative – that underlie the everyday praxis of English teaching.

Talking to early career English teachers about their many struggles in the classroom allowed me to reflect on what's central to English, what is the value of literary knowledge. Some of the pedagogical scenes I could remember seemed to epitomise the value of literary ways of knowing but in contingent, context-specific, interpersonal ways. I thought of a classic site of literary interpretation, a text that I had sometimes taught, a fragmentary story by Franz Kafka called 'Wedding Preparations in the Country'. Kafka didn't finish this story, even though he wrote at least three versions of it, and it was only published posthumously. It is an early piece of writing of his, and he probably just abandoned it. It is a story about a man, full of unease about the future, travelling into the countryside to meet his future bride. The story feels doubly unfinished because the protagonist, Raban, never gets to meet his proposed bride. Although he does meet a friend on his train journey. It is full of close-up descriptive detail and subtle shifts in perception. It presents a mysterious but compelling world of observation and feeling, but one that is also full of enigmas. In my teaching of this story, I would draw attention to the opening sentences that announce so simply, but also almost shockingly, the enigmatic effects of the narrative. It begins:

When Eduard Raban, coming along the passage, walked into the open doorway, he saw that it was raining. It was not raining much.

The uncanny feeling of duality that this opening creates persists throughout the story. Raban's perception differs from the narrator's, at least that is what we are led to believe. Raban might also have observed that it was 'not raining much' but we don't know; it is the narrator's correction that we notice. It's like a glitch in the Matrix moment where we momentarily think Raban may be living in a simulated world, without realising it. Something about Raban's perception is overruled or disallowed. And it is a simulated world, of course, a fictional one. The narrator immediately asserts 'his' third-person authority – it's hard not to think of this narrator as a 'him'. That initial narrative move signals the narrator's proprietary role throughout, where he assumes the control of describing Raban's perceptions, including his inner self, even though the narrative also alternates between Raban's first-person interior monologue, which also alternates between the first person 'I' and a slightly displaced 'one'. Students would be puzzled by the relation of the narrator to Raban and his different voices, but also mindful of the story's fragmentariness, its lack of authorial closure. But that didn't mean that we couldn't discuss the complexities of narrative structure, or Modernism, or early 20th-century European gender relations, or modes of perception (including cinematic effects), or possible creative writing responses to the story. In fact, it was precisely the story's facets of perception and its fragmentariness that stimulated our sense of its meanings – about states of perception, relationships and travelling, ownership of one's life, unfinishedness, the weather and people's moods. Making meaning is a spacious exercise.

We know some things about Kafka and his writing – biographical studies, scholarly and interpretative articles, archival and bibliographical work – but there is also a lot we don't know about Kafka. And his stories and parables embody, in vivid, visual detail, an imaginary version of the early 20th-century European world he inhabited as well as the human enigmas that were at the core of that world. My story about Kafka in the classroom is a personal one, of course, and its lesson is that knowledge is not given; it's collaborative and interpersonal, provisional, and generative, partly because it's produced, in this instance, in relation to a text that is enigmatic and fragmentary. Each time I go back to Kafka's story I think about it in a different way, and I'm sure students and other teachers would do the same. Another part of the lesson here is the way in which the capacity for meaning-making in the classroom remains dynamic. That's what I mean by the spaciousness of literary knowing, the sense that literary and linguistic meaning is always capable of enlarging as it changes.

As we have explored our early career teachers, there are a host of social, educational and political issues and questions that have shaped their backgrounds and that continue to influence their professional practice as English teachers. Literary knowledge is not immune to or separate from any of those factors, primarily because it means ways of knowing about language.

Coda

As our various reflective accounts convey, considerations of literary knowledge in English cannot be constrained to a single voice or one story. Interdisciplinary and expansive dialogue – in our project, and in English classrooms – is core to making textual meanings. At the most fundamental level, in an outcomes and standards-based global context, our work together and with the teachers in our study affirms the value of multivocality when asking questions of English as these are manifest in diverse contexts. Our study has shown that questions of literature and knowledge can't be answered singularly, or according to perceived hierarchies of experience. Angela's request, cited at the start of this chapter, for the research team to make clear where her knowledge 'was going to' is underpinned by the understanding that, as an early career teacher, she has unique insights into literary knowing that will contribute to a greater narrative about the purpose and nature of teaching literature in 21st-century classrooms. English teachers' experiences, beliefs and perspectives are important to scholarship not only because, like teachers of any school subject, they are charged with enacting the curriculum, but also because the nature of literary knowing depends on sociable reading experiences that have, and are, 'making' teachers and their reading of texts and students in classroom contexts (Doecke & Mead, 2018; Mead & Doecke, 2020). As Toril Moi writes, 'Literature isn't one thing, but a loosely defined network of texts and practices. What a work of literature does to a reader will depend on the text, on the reader, on the circumstances of the reading' (Moi, 2017, p.5). Literary knowing is dynamic, then, and multi-faceted; it is being made, by teachers and students and reading communities, beyond the time and space of classroom encounters.

This is not to suggest, though, that literary knowing is somehow not epistemological, but rather that it is also inherently ontological and, because of this, can be 'difficult' (McLean Davies & Buzacott, 2021) for teachers and students in ways that are not so apparent in other school subjects. This perhaps explains why there is value, when pre-service teachers enter university preparation programs, to spend time considering fundamental questions about the nature and purpose of English, not to suggest that English is a subject without a knowledge base but, conversely, to interrogate the ways the 'base' is always being reconceived and rewritten in any social context, which is made up of readers and reading, of texts, conversations, standpoints and interactions (Phillips & Archer-Lean, 2019) that produce understandings with and through texts.

In order to speak productively about the purposes and value of a literary education and the nature of knowing in English, it will be useful, going forward, to consider frameworks and understandings that will enable English teachers, and the profession more broadly, to speak back to neoliberal, standards-based reforms that are directing the work of teachers and students towards instrumental, rather than expansive and generative, notions of texts and knowledge. Throughout this book, we have often returned to literary theories that focus on the reader (Dixon, 1975; Felski, 2008; Rosenblatt, 1978) and the connections between texts and readers (Dymock, 1993), as these seem to us to usefully redirect attention to teachers and students as readers and meaning-makers, rather than archaeologists engaged in more utilitarian activities of excavating texts to reproduce the information in examinations. Activating these theories reminds us that literary knowing is fundamentally relational. Writing about Aboriginal notions of relationality, Mary Graham argues that within the context of an integrated, mutually responsible system, Aboriginal 'relationality embraced uncertainty and imprecision, consented to be driven by feeling, accepted and made room for conflict [and]… provided coherence about the notion of a life' (Graham, 2014, p.2). This perspective on relationality, understood in the context of textual pedagogical practices, offers a generative way of approaching conversations about literary knowing in contemporary renderings of school English, as it has been productively and variously discussed with and by the teachers in our study (McLean Davies & Buzacott, 2021), and is worth further consideration, particularly when, as Moi has argued, the scepticism of literary theory has served to distance readers from the affective and relational impacts of texts, and the kinds of knowing made possible through literary experiences (Moi, 2017).

In a wider sense, to investigate the complex nature of literary knowing, as we have had the privilege of doing through this project, is to also consider questions that are at the heart of education – what is it for, and who is it serving, and what should be the contribution of schooling to a young person's life? As many have noted (Di Leo, 2013; Moi, 2017) literature, and the humanities more broadly, are rendered without social power and immediate relevance and value in the dominant neoliberal paradigms captivating governments and education systems. Arguing that literary knowing, in all its diversity and contextual specificity, has enduring social value, and to provide examples and accounts of this, is part of the ongoing political, interdisciplinary and scholarly work of English education research. This book seeks to contribute to this broader project, and those who will read and use it, contributing their own stories and accounts to those offered here, continue this essential work, rendering this final chapter not so much a conclusion, but a catalyst for further professional and scholarly dialogue.

Notes

1   'What is vital is the interplay between (the pupil's) personal world and the world of the writer' (Dixon, 1975, p. 3).
2   It is no accident that a prominent reader response literary theorist such as Rosenblatt has acknowledged her connections to the work of reading researchers coming out of education such as Goodman (Rosenblatt, 1978, pp. 63, 183), with both describing the reader's relationship with the text as a 'transaction' (Rosenblatt, 1978; Goodman et al, 2016, p. 39 and passim). John Dixon's statement in *Growth through English* that

> 'If an interest in literature is to inform and modify our encounter with life itself, the teacher must bring into vivid relationship life as it is enacted and life as it is represented… a readiness to help pupils explore aspects of their immediate lives'

(1975, p. 54) is almost exactly echoed by Rosenblatt's statement that 'Each reader brings to the transaction not only a specific past life and literary history… but also a very active present' (1978: , p.144).
3   See, for example Muller (1967, pp.4–5), Kitzhaber (1966) and Goodwyn (2003) for how this dichotomy has been expressed in the past – as reported in Chapter 10 here.

References

Ball, S., Kenny, A., & Gardiner, D. (1990). Literacy, politics and the teaching of English. In I. F. Goodson & P. Medway (Eds.), *Bringing English to Order*. London, New York and Philadelphia: The Falmer Press: 47–86.

Batsleer, J., Davies, T., O'Rourke, R., & Weedon, C. (1985). *Rewriting English: Cultural Politics of Gender and Class*. London and New York: Methuen.

Biesta, G. (2017). *The Rediscovery of Teaching*. New York: Routledge.

Boomer, G. (1989). Literacy: The epic challenge beyond progressivism. *English in Australia*, 89, 4–17. https://search.informit.org/doi/10.3316/informit.542851428861996.

Bourdieu, P. (1979). *Distinction: A Social Critique of the Judgement of Taste*. Trans. R. Nice. Cambridge, MA: Harvard University Press.

Bourdieu, P. (1990). *In Other Words: Essays Towards a Reflexive Sociology*. Stanford, CA: Stanford University Press.

Cochran, T. (2007). The knowing of literature. *New Literary History*, 38(1), 127–143.

Delehanty, A. (2012). *Literary Knowing in Neoclassical France: From Poetics to Aesthetics*. Lanham, MD: Bucknell University Press.

Di Leo, J. (2013). *Corporate Humanities in Higher Education*. New York: Palgrave Macmillan US. https://doi.org/10.1057/9781137361530.

Dixon, J. (1975). *Growth through English: Set in the Perspective of the Seventies*. 3rd ed.. London: Oxford University Press.

Doecke, B. (2017). What kind of 'knowledge' is English? (Re-reading the Newbolt Report). *Changing English*, 24(3), 230–245. https://doi.org/10.1080/1358684X.2017.1351228.

Doecke, B. (2019). Rewriting the history of subject English through the lens of 'literary sociability'. *Changing English*, 26(4), 339–356. https://doi.org/10.1080/1358684X.2019.1649116.

Doecke, B., Green, B., Kostogriz, A., Reid, J., & Sawyer, W. (2007). Knowing practice in English teaching? Research challenges in representing the professional practice of English teachers. *English Teaching: Practice and Critique*, 6(3), 4–21.

Doecke, B., & Mead, P. (2018). English and the knowledge question. *Pedagogy, Culture & Society*, 26(2), 249–264. https://doi.org/10.1080/14681366.2017.1380691.

Dymock, S. (1993). Reading but not understanding. *Journal of Reading*, 37(2), 86–91.

Felski, R. (2008). *Uses of Literature*. Malden, MA and Oxford: Blackwell Publishing.

Frow, J. (2002). Literature as regime (Meditations on an emergence). In E. B. Bissell (Ed.), *The Question of Literature: The Place of the Literary in Contemporary Theory*. Manchester: Manchester University Press: 142–155.

Gibson, J. (2009). Literature and knowledge. In R. Eldridge (Ed.), *The Oxford Handbook of Philosophy and Literature*. Oxford: Oxford University Press: 467–485.

Goodman, K., Fries, P. H., & Strauss, S. L. (2016). *Reading – The Grand Illusion: How and Why People Make Sense of Print*. New York and London: Routledge.

Goodson, I., & Medway, P. (Eds.). (1990). *Bringing English to Order: The History and Politics of a School Subject*. London: Falmer Press.

Goodwyn, A. (2001). Second tier professionals: English teachers in England. *L1: Educational Studies in Language and Literature*, 1(2), 148–161.

Goodwyn, A. (2003). We teach English not literacy: 'Growth' pedagogy under siege in England. In B. Doecke, D. Homer, & H. Nixon (Eds.), *English Teachers at Work: Narratives, Counter Narratives and Arguments*. Kent Town: AATE & Wakefield Press: 123–134.

Graham, M. (2014). Aboriginal notions of relationality and positionalism: A reply to Weber. *Global Discourse*, 4(1), 17–22.

Green, B. (2018). *Engaging Curriculum: Bridging the Curriculum Theory and English Education Divide*. New York and London: Routledge.

Haraway, D. (2019). It matters what stories tell stories; it matters whose stories tell stories. *a/b: Auto/Biography Studies*, 34(3), 565–575.

Kasprisin, L. (1987). Literature as a way of knowing: An epistemological justification for literary studies. *Journal of Aesthetic Education*, 21(3), 17–27. https://doi.org/10.2307/3332867.

Kirkpatrick, P., & Dixon, R. (Eds.) (2012). *Republic of Letters: Literary Communities in Australia*. Sydney: Sydney University Press.

Kitzhaber, A. R. (1966). What is English? In A. R. Kitzhaber et al., *Working Party Paper No. 1; Response, Report to the Seminar, and Supporting Papers One through Six*, ERIC document number ED082201. Available: http://files.eric.ed.gov/fulltext/ED082201.pdf. Accessed 16 August 2021.

Manuel, J., Carter, D., & Dutton, J. (2018). As much as I love being in the classroom…: Understanding secondary English teachers' workload. *English in Australia*, 53(3), 5–22.

Mason, J., & Giovanelli, M. (2021). *Studying Fiction: A Guide for Teachers and Researchers*. London and New York: Routledge.

McLean Davies, L., & Buzacott, L. (2021). Rethinking literature, knowledge and justice: Selecting 'difficult' stories for study in school English. *Pedagogy, Culture & Society*, 1–15. https://doi.org/10.1080/14681366.2021.1977981.

McLean Davies, L., & Sawyer, W. (2018). (K)now you see it, (k)now you don't: Literary knowledge in the 'Australian Curriculum: English'. *Journal of Curriculum Studies*, 50(6), 836–849.

McLean Davies, L., & Sawyer, W. (2020). On being 'well read'. In B. Marshall, J. Manuel, D. L. Pasternak, & J. Rowsell (Eds.), *The Bloomsbury Handbook of Reading Perspectives and Practices*. London: Bloomsbury: 145–166.

McLean Davies, L., Yates, L. & Sawyer, W. (2022) Investigating literature as knowledge in school English. In B. Hudson, N. Gericke, C. Olin-Scheller & M. Stolare (Eds) International Perspectives on Knowledge and Quality: Implications for Innovation in Teacher Education Policy and Practice London: Bloomsbury: 109–126.

McLeod, J., & Yates, L. (2006). *Making Modern Lives: Subjectivity, Schooling and Social Change*. Albany, NY:State University of New York Press.

Mead, P., & Doecke, B. (2020). Pedagogy. In *Oxford Research Encyclopedia of Literature*. Oxford: Oxford University Press. http://dx.doi.org/10.1093/acrefore/9780190201098.013.1032.

Mead, P., Doecke, B., & McLean Davies, L. (2020). Contingencies of meaning-making: English teaching and literary sociability. *Australian Literary Studies*, 35(2). https://doi.org/10.20314/als.00225a9681.

Medway, P. (2010). English and Enlightenment, *Changing English: Studies in Culture and Education*, 17(1), 3–12. https://doi.org/10.1080/13586840903556987.

Moi, T. (2017). *Revolution of the Ordinary: Literary Studies after Wittgenstein, Austin, and Cavell*. Chicago and London: University of Chicago Press.

Moll, L., Amanti, C., Neff, D., & Gonzalez, N. (1992). Funds of knowledge for teaching: Using a qualitative approach to connect homes and classrooms. *Theory into Practice*, 31(2), 132–141.

Muller, H. J. (1967). *The Uses of English: Guidelines for the Teaching of English from the Anglo-American Conference at Dartmouth College*. New York: Holt, Rinehart, Winston.

Murray, A. (2021). Love and death: How Huizinga came to write his masterpiece. *TLS. Times Literary Supplement*, 6161, 11–13.

O'Sullivan, K. A., & Goodwyn, A. (2020). Contested territories: English teachers in Australia and England remaining resilient and creative in constraining times. *English in Education*, 54(3), 224–238. https://doi.org/10.1080/04250494.2020.1793667.

Parr, G. (2011). Literature teaching in Australia. In B. Doecke & P-H. van de Ven (Eds.), *Literary Praxis: A Conversational Inquiry into the Teaching of Literature*. Rotterdam: Sense, 69–87.

Patterson, A. (1992). Individualism in English: From personal growth to discursive construction. *English Education*, 24(3), 131–146. https://www.jstor.org/stable/40172828.

Phillips, S., & Archer-Lean, C. (2019). Decolonising the reading of Aboriginal and Torres Strait Islander writing: Reflection as transformative practice. *Higher Education Research & Development*, 38(1), 24–37. https://doi.org/10.1080/07294360.2018.1539956.

Phillips, S., McLean Davies, L., & Truman, S. (2022). Power of country: Indigenous relationality and reading Indigenous climate fiction in Australia. *Curriculum Inquiry*, 52(1), 171–186. https://doi.org/10.1080/03626784.2022.2041978.

Pike, M. A. (2003). On being in English teaching: A time for Heidegger? *Changing English: Studies in Culture and Education*, 10(1), 91–99. https://doi.org/10.1080/1358684032000055154.

Rosenblatt, L. (1978). *The Reader, the Text, the Poem: The Transactional Theory of the Literary Work*. Carbondale, IL: Southern Illinois University Press.

Sawyer, W., & Gold, E. (Eds.) (2004). *Reviewing English in the 21st Century*. Melbourne: Phoenix Education.

Shulman, L. (1987). Knowledge and teaching: Foundations of the new reform. *Harvard Educational Review*, 57(1), 1–23.

Simpson, J. (2013). Cognition is recognition: Literary knowledge and textual 'face', *New Literary History*, 44(1), 25–44. http://nrs.harvard.edu/urn-3:HUL.InstRepos:12872088.

Smith, D. E. (2005). *Institutional Ethnography: A Sociology for People*. Lanham, MD: AltaMira Press.

Teese, R. ([2000] 2013). *Academic Success and Social Power: Examinations and Inequality*. North Melbourne: Australian Scholarly Publishing.

Teese, R. (2011). The new curriculum for English in Australia and student achievement under the old curriculum: Understanding inequality and addressing it. In B. Doecke, G. Parr, & W. Sawyer (Eds.), *Creating an Australian Curriculum for English: National Agendas Local Contexts*. Putney: Phoenix Education: 5–20.

Thomson, J. (1987). *Understanding Teenagers' Reading: Reading Processes and the Teaching of Literature*. North Ryde: Methuen.

Turvey, A., & Yandell, J. (2011). Difference in the classroom. In B. Doecke & P-H. van de Ven (Eds.), *Literary Praxis: A Conversational Inquiry into the Teaching of Literature*. Rotterdam: Sense: 151–167.

Walsh, D. (1969). *Literature and Knowledge*. Middletown, CT: University of Connecticut Press.

Watson, K. D., & Eagleson, R. D. (Eds.) (1977). *English in Secondary Schools: Today and Tomorrow*. Ashfield: English Teachers' Association of New South Wales.

Yandell, J. (2017). Knowledge, English and the formation of teachers, *Pedagogy, Culture & Society*, 25(4), 583–599. https://doi.org/10.1080/14681366.2017.1312494.

Yates, L., McLean Davies, L., Buzacott, L., Doecke, B., Mead, P., & Sawyer, W. (2019). School English, literature and the knowledge-base question. *The Curriculum Journal*, 30(1), 51–68. https://doi.org/10.1080/09585176.2018.1543603.

Yates, L., & Millar, V. (2016). 'Powerful knowledge' curriculum theories and the case of physics. *The Curriculum Journal*, 27(3), 298–312. https://doi.org/10.1080/09585176.2016.1174141.

Yates, L., Woelert, P., Millar, V., & O'Connor, K. (2016). *Knowledge at the Crossroads? Physics and History in the Changing World of Schools and Universities*. Singapore: Springer.

Young, M. (2013). Overcoming the crisis in curriculum theory: A knowledge-based approach. *Journal of Curriculum Studies*, 45(2), 101–118. https://doi.org/10.1080/00220272.2013.764505.

Young, M., & Muller, J. (2013). On the powers of powerful knowledge. *Review of Education*, 1(3), 229–250. https://doi.org/10.1002/rev3.3017.

INDEX

Printed in Great Britain
by Amazon

18342642R00147